REJECTED OR SUSPENDED APPLICATIONS FOR REVOLUTIONARY WAR PENSIONS

With an Added
Index To States

CLEARFIELD

Originally Published
Washington, D. C., 1852

Reprinted with an added Index to States
Genealogical Publishing Company
Baltimore, 1969

Reprinted for
Clearfield Company, Inc. by
Genealogical Publishing Co., Inc.
Baltimore, Maryland
1991, 1992, 1998, 1999, 2003

Library of Congress Catalogue Card Number 69-17127
International Standard Book Number: 0-8063-0348-4

Made in the United States of America

Copyright 1969
Genealogical Publishing Company
Baltimore, Maryland

Made in the United States of America

Index To States

	Pages
Alabama	318-329
Arkansas	439-442
Connecticut	73- 92
Delaware	227-228
District of Columbia	459-462
Florida	449-452
Georgia	302-317
Illinois	421-431
Indiana	406-420
Iowa	454-456
Kentucky	360-380
Louisiana	335-336
Maine	2- 15
Maryland	229-237
Massachusetts	49- 67
Michigan	443-448
Mississippi	330-334
Missouri	432-438
New Hampshire	16- 29
New Jersey	186-198
New York	93-185
North Carolina	263-286
Ohio	337-359
Pennsylvania	199-226
Rhode Island	68- 72
South Carolina	287-301
Tennessee	381-405
Texas	453-
Vermont	30- 48
Virginia	238-262
Wisconsin	457-458

32d Congress, [SENATE.] Ex. Doc.
1st Session. No. 37.

REPORT

OF

THE SECRETARY OF THE INTERIOR,

WITH

A statement of rejected or suspended applications for pensions.

February 16, 1852.
Referred to the Committee on Pensions, and ordered to be printed.

Department of the Interior,
Washington, February 23, 1852.

Sir: In obedience to a resolution of the Senate of September 16, 1850, I have the honor to transmit, herewith, a statement showing the names of all the applicants for pensions under the acts of June 7, 1832, July 4, 1836, and July 7, 1838, respectively, and the acts amendatory thereof, whose claims have been rejected or suspended, the grounds of such suspension or rejection, and the places of residence of such applicants, so far as the same can be given.

I am, sir, very respectfully, your obedient servant,
ALEX. H. H. STUART,
Secretary.

Hon. William R. King,
President of the Senate.

A list of persons residing in Maine, who have applied for pensions under the act of June 7, 1832, whose claims have been rejected, prepared in conformity with the resolution of the Senate of the United States of September 16, 1850.

Names.	Residence.	Reasons for rejection.
Allen, William	Lubec, Lubec	He did not serve six months.
Ayer, Elijah	Wallington, Kent, N. B.	He did not serve in a military capacity.
Allen, Jeremiah	Brunswick, Cumberland	He did not serve six months.
Bean, Phineas	Montville, Waldo	He did not serve six months.
Bartlett, James	Eliot, York	He did not serve six months in person.
Bingham, Abner	Lubec, Washington	He was a deserter.
Barker, Robert	Hope, Waldo	He did not serve six months.
Brewster, Morgan	Leeds, Kennebec	Deserted.
Cobb, Isaac	———, Piscataquis	He did not serve six months.
Chapman, Peter	Roxbury, Norfolk	Deserted.
Crosby, Joseph	Swanville, Waldo	He did not serve six months.
Chase, Ephraim	East Machias, Washington	Privateer service.
Carlton, Moses	Blue Hill, Hancock	He did not serve six months.
Clark, William	Wiscasset, Lincoln	Deserted.
Crawford, John	Bath, Lincoln	He did not serve six months.
Cram, Samuel	Mount Vernon, Kennebec	He did not serve six months.
Coffin, Edmund	Acton, York	Under age.
Coombs, Anthony	Vinal's Haven, Hancock	He did not serve six months.
Cram, Smith	Montville, Waldo	He did not serve six months.
Divinal, Aaron	Lisbon, Lincoln	He did not serve six months.
Doten, Silas	Hartford, Oxford	He did not serve six months.
Dunham, James	Hebron, Oxford	He did not serve six months.
Doughty, Stephen	Topsham, Lincoln	He did not serve six months.
Davis, John	Buxton, York	He did not serve six months.
Dearborn	Scarborough, Cumberland	Deserted.
Dean, James	Frankfort, Waldo	Privateer service.
Dodge, Abraham	Sedgwick, Hancock	Deserted.
Fenderson, William	Parsonfield, York	Privateer service.

Frost, Charles	Westbrook, Cumberland	He did not serve six months.
Graffam, Uriah	Parsonfield, York	Deserted.
Garnett, Laban	Township 1800, Washington	He did not serve six months.
Guptail, John	Washington	He did not serve six months.
Harding, Nathaniel	Newsharon, Kennebec	He did not serve in a military capacity.
Holt, Valentine	Mercer, Somerset	He did not serve six months.
Hunt, Benoni	Owne, Penobscot	He did not serve in a military capacity.
Hubbard, John	Radfield, Kennebec	He did not serve in a military capacity.
Heald, Amos	Anson, Somerset	He did not serve six months.
Harriman, Levi	Litchfield, Lincoln	He did not serve six months.
Holt, Nicholas	Blue Hill, Hancock	He did not serve six months.
Jenkins, Joseph	Skowhegan, Somerset	He did not serve six months in person.
Jordan, Elisha	Cape Elizabeth, Cumberland	He did not serve in a military capacity.
Johnson, James	Hollis, York	He did not serve six months.
Kellock, Findley		He did not serve six months.
Lyford, Nathaniel	Livermore, Oxford	He did not serve six months.
Maddocks, Caleb	Ellsworth, Hancock	Privateer service.
Mansfield, Henry	Portland, Cumberland	He did not serve in a military capacity.
Mitchell, John	Chesterville, Kennebec	He did not serve six months.
Mitchell, Joseph	Unity, Waldo	Deserted.
Mitchell, Benjamin	Cumberland, Cumberland	He did not serve in a military capacity.
Martin, Moses	Pittsfield, Somerset	He did not serve six months.
Moore, Josiah	Phillips, Somerset	He did not serve six months.
Nutt, William	Harmony, Somerset	He did not serve six months.
Nutt, John	Camden, Waldo	He did not serve six months.
Norton, Hannah	Limington, York	Husband died before the passage of the act.
Patch, Samuel	Shapleigh, York	Deserted.
Reed, Andrew	Boothbay, Lincoln	He did not serve six months.
Rose, John	Waterville, Kennebec	Under age.
Smith, Thomas	Cornville, Somerset	He did not serve in a military capacity.

STATEMENT—Continued.

Names.	Residence.	Reasons for rejection.
Snell, Robert	Poland, Cumberland	He did not serve six months.
Staples, Richard	Dearborn, Kennebec	Waggon service in a navy-yard 24th of May, 38, R. Nuss.
Sibley, John	Passadumkey, Penobscot	He was a deserter.
Savage, Edward	Planation, No. 9, Somerset	He did not serve six months.
Small, Nehemiah	Lubec, Washington	He did not serve six months.
Stevens, Elijah	Livermore, Oxford	He did not serve six months.
Shaw, Polly	Portland, Cumberland	Died before the passage of the act.
Tibbetts, Abner	Exeter, Penobscot	He did not serve six months.
Usher, Robert	Baldwin, Cumberland	He did not serve six months.
Ward, Benjamin	Mount Desert, Hancock	He did not serve six months.

A list of persons residing in Maine who have applied for pensions under the act of June 7, 1842—whose claims have been suspended; prepared in conformity with the resolution of the Senate of the United States of September 16, 1850.

Names.	Residence.	Reasons for suspension.
Alden, Benjamin	Turner, Oxford	Suspended for further proof—not on the rolls.
Bartlett, Samuel	Orrington, Penobscot	Suspended for further proof of the public character of the vessel called the Active.
Bagley, Enoch	Belfast, Waldo	Suspended for further proof.
Brown, John	Montville, Waldo	Suspended for further proof—not on the rolls.
Brown, David	Frankfort, Waldo	Suspended for further proof and specification from the Massachusetts rolls.
Beckford, Joseph	Gouldsboro, Hancock	Suspended for reference to eight month's rolls of 1775.
Bishop, Squier	Mount Vernon, Kennebec	Suspended for further proof and explanation.
Boulter, Benjamin	Biddeford, York	Suspended for further proof.
Clever, James	Kennebunkport, York	Not on the returns in this office—he is referred to the Secretary of State at Boston.
Cooper, William	Litchfield, Lincoln	Not on the rolls—suspended for further proof.
Covel, David	Bristol, Lincoln	Suspended for further proof, whether the brig Cabot was a public or private armed vessel.
Coombs, Benjamin	Brewer, Penobscot	Suspended for proof of service from the records at Boston.
Clark, Elisha	Gouldsboro, Hancock	Proof required of the service on board the United States frigate America, and that there was such a frigate.
Crowell, Thomas	Brunswick, Cumberland	Suspended for further proof and explanation.
Coffin, Daniel	Gilead, Oxford	Suspended until reference is made to the records at Boston.
Craige, John (deceased)	Brewer, Penobscot	Suspended for proof of identity with the soldier from Dracut, on the Massachusetts certificate, and his age, and neighborhood reputation —Hon. H. Hamlin, September 28, 1850.
Doyer, Samuel	Levant, Penobscot	Suspended for further proof, and more definite and specific details of service.
Davis, James	Standish, Cumberland	Suspended for further proof and specification.
Doar, Henry	Penobscot, Hancock	Suspended for further proof and specification.
Forole, Samuel	Whitefield, Lincoln	He did not serve six months.

STATEMENT—Continued.

Names.	Residence.	Reasons for suspension.
Foster, John	Bristol, Lincoln	Not on the rolls—no such corps as he alleges was maintained in 1777—he did not serve six months.
Fuller, Job	Wayne, Kennebec	He did not serve six months.
Godfrey, Daniel	Steuben, Washington	Suspended for further proof.
Goodwin, Nehemiah (deceased)	Berwick, York	Suspended for proof of identity with the person whose service is exhibited, and for a new declaration by his son.
Green, Asa (deceased)	Deer Isle, Hancock	He did not serve six months.
Grover, Benjamin (deceased)	Woolwich, Lincoln	Application to be made by the widow or children, or the next heirs, or representatives—papers awaiting this requisition.
Hall, Stephen	East Machias, Washington	He did not serve six months.
Hasey, John	Bristol, Lincoln	Not on the rolls—service not established.
Heath, Samuel	Jefferson, Lincoln	Proof of identity and description do not agree with the service of individuals of himname on the New Hampshire records.
Hobba, Josiah	Newfield, York	Suspended for proof of service from New Hampshire, which has failed to come.
Jordan, Samuel	Augusta, Kennebec	Suspended for a more particular description of his service, discriminating whether State troops or militia.
Jordan, Domonicus	Cape Elizabeth, Cumberland	Suspended for further proof from the Massachusetts Rolls.
Kent, Benjamin	Mount Desert, Hancock	Suspended for further proof.
Kneeland, Abraham	Lincoln, Penobscot	Suspended for further proof, and the return of his original declaration.
McFarland, Ephraim	Belfast, Waldo	Suspended for further proof.
McKillip, Alexander	Steuben, Washington	Suspended for further proof and explanation.
Moody, Samuel	Portland, Cumberland	Under age—served as a waiter—the rolls are silent.
Montgomery, John	Warren, Lincoln	He did not serve six months.
Moore, John	Addison, Washington	He did not serve six months.
Moore, Robert	Steuben, Washington	Suspended for a further search of the Secretary's office records.
Milliken, Samuel	Mount Desert, Hancock	Served in local militia and in the patrol duty.

Norton, Elihu	Jonesport, Washington	He did not serve six months.
Page, Amos	Belgrade, Kennebec	Suspended for further proof and explanation.
Palmer, Samuel	Bristol, Lincoln	Suspended for further proof and specification.
Patch, Jonathan	Shapleigh, York	He died before the passage of the act.
Perry, Eli	Phipsburgh, Lincoln	Suspended for further proof.
Ross, John	Windsor, Hants, province Nova Scotia	Suspended for further proof and explanation.
Sanderson, Stephen	Waterford, Oxford	Suspended for the arrival and inspection of the Massachusetts rolls.
Shackford, John	Eastport, Washington	He did not serve six months.
Sherman, Thomas	Lebanon, York	He did not serve six months.
Sidenberger, John	Warren, Lincoln	Not on the rolls, and the witness incompetent.
Stinson, William	Wiscasset, Lincoln	Suspended for further proof of identity with soldier of Lamont and Walker's company.
Stinson, Jeremiah	Limerick, York	Suspended for further proof and specification.
Talman, Peter	Bath, Lincoln	He did not serve six months.
Tolmon, Curtis	Camden, Waldo	Not on the rolls—witnesses incompetent.
Thomas, Samuel	Pittsfield, Somerset	He did not serve six months.
Tibbetts, Daniel	Gardiner, Kennebec	He has not established as much as six months service.
Tozier, Lemuel	Waterville, Kennebec	Suspended for further proof and specification.
True, Ezekiel	Montville, Waldo	Not on the rolls—further proof awaited.
Tibbetts, Abner	Exeter, Penobscot	Not on the rolls—no proof of service.
Upton, David	—, Cumberland	He did not serve six months.
Ward, John	Harrington, Washington	Not on the rolls—no proof of service.
Wormwood, Joseph	Perry, Hancock	No proof of service—neither his real nor alleged assumed name is on the records.
Wiswall, David	Orrington, Penobscot	Suspended for a further inspection of the rolls of the guard at Springfield, in the office of the Secretary of State at Boston.
Wyllie, James	Bristol, Lincoln	He did not serve six months.
Veazie, Joseph	Portland, Cumberland	He did not serve in any regularly organized corps.

A list of persons residing in Maine who have applied for pensions under the act of July 4, 1836, whose claims have been rejected; prepared in conformity with the resolution of the Senate of the United States, September 16, 1850.

Names.	Residence.	Reasons for rejection.
Collins, Mary, widow of Richard	Harrington, Washington	Deserted.
Collins, Betsey, widow of Abner	York	Not revolutionary service.
Elliott, Anna, widow of Samuel	Buxton, York	A soldier of the regular army.
Fitz, Abigail, widow of John Morgan	Litchfield, Kennedy	He did not serve six months.
Hill, Mary, widow of William	Porter, Oxford	A soldier of the regular army.
Ray, Rachel, widow of William	Harrington, Washington	Privateer service.
Trask, Agnes (deceased), widow of Moses	Edgecomb, Lincoln	Married after service—died before August, 1842.
Towle, Jane, widow of Josiah	Frankfort, Waldo	Married after service.
Wallace, Dorcas, widow of Samuel	Phipsburgh, Lincoln	He did not serve six months.

A list of persons who have applied for pensions under the act of July 4, 1836, residing in Maine, whose claims have been suspended; prepared in conformity with the resolution of the Senate of the United States, September 16, 1850.

Names.	Residence.	Reasons for suspension.
Allen, Polly, widow of James	Turner, Oxford	Suspended for further proof of service from the Massachusetts rolls.
Averill, Sarah, widow of Joseph	Machias, Washington	Not on the rolls of the coast guards, except for twenty-seven days only.
Butler, Love, widow of Ephraim	Farmington, Franklin	He did not serve six months.
Colson, Mary, widow of David	Bath, Lincoln	Married after service.
Evans, Thankful, widow of Benjamin	Exeter, Penobscot	Suspended for better details of service, officers' names, &c., in order to a more perfect inspection of the rolls.
Hatch, Jemima, widow of Simon	Dresden, Lincoln	Proof of identity not satisfactory of her husband with the soldier of the same name, who enlisted on the last three years service in the Massachusetts line.
Haythorn, Lucy, widow of Silas	Brownville, Piscataquis	Suspended for proof of marriage as prior to, or concurrent with the service.
Hood, Martha, widow of Ebenezer Preble	Lincoln, Lincoln	Not on the rolls for service in 1775—suspended for further proof.
Howe, Susannah, widow of Tilly	Marion, Washington	His three years enlistment in Keen, New Hampshire, should be found on the records of New Hampshire.
Hubbard, Abigail, widow of Benjamin	North Brunswick, York	Not on the rolls of Capt. Phil Hubbard, for Roxbury, in 1775.
Johnson, Mary, widow of Adam	Richmond, Lincoln	Suspended for proof of identity with the soldier of the Massachusetts rolls of the same name, and proof of marriage.
Johnson, James, children of	Windham, Cumberland	Service reduced by the rolls from fifteen to nine months, and barred by the act of April 30, 1844.
Jose, Abigail, widow of Jose	Buxton, York	No proof of service in the line—not on any rolls—if he served under militia officers the names must be given.
Lock, Lydia, widow of Simon	Hollis, York	Suspended for an inspection of Poor's regimental rolls in 1775.
Leighton, Deborah, widow of George	Gardiner, Kennebec	No proof of service after marriage.
Newbury, Lucy, widow of John	Venal Haven, Waldo	Suspended for proof of service from the Boston records of State.

STATEMENT—Continued.

Names.	Residence.	Reasons for suspension.
Phillips, Lattice, widow of Andrew	Kittery, York	No rolls of the name—no proof of service—militia service, it is over-rated.
Pollock, Elizabeth, widow of Thomas	———, Kennebunk	Suspended for evidence of identity with the soldier of Colonel Poor's regiment of 1775, and proof of marriage.
Sprague, Miriam, widow of William	Plipsburgh, Lincoln	Suspended for further proof.
Stevens, Mary, widow of Jonathan	Portland, Cumberland	Not on any rolls—no proof of service.
Walker, Abigail, widow of Gideon	Waterboro, York	Suspended for proof of service from the Massachusetts records.
Walker, Rachel (deceased), widow of Supply	Denmark, Oxford	Proof of marriage, and of widow's identity, and of her decease required.
Wilson, Abigail, widow of Gowen	Steuben, Washington	Service not fully specified—the amount is wanting.
Wooster, Eleanor, formerly widow of Mark Honscomb	Shapleigh, York	Suspended for further proof of service.

A list of persons residing in Maine who have applied for pensions under the act of July 7, 1838, whose claims have been rejected; prepared in conformity with the resolution of the Senate of the United States, September 16, 1850.

Names.	Residence.	Reasons for rejection.
Brooks, Susanna (deceased), widow of Daniel	Buxton, York	Not a widow June 7, 1832—died before August 16, 1842.
Allen, Abigail, widow of Seth	Sumner, Oxford	Did not serve six months.
Baker, Lydia, widow of Josiah	Falmouth, Cumberland	Married in 1806.
Bragdon, Sarah, widow of William	Limington, York	Desertion.
Clewly, Abiah (deceased), widow of Isaac	Brewer, Penobscot	Not a widow at the date of the act—died before August 16, 1842.
Cunningham, Eunice, widow of Samuel	Jefferson, Lincoln	Did not serve six months.
Crosby, Lucy, formerly widow of Amos Need	Norridgewock, Somerset	Husband died in 1779, and she was married again.
Dunlap, Elizabeth, widow of James	Litchfield, Kennebec	Desertion.
Fowler, Sarah (deceased), widow of Matthew	Unity, Waldo	Was not a widow at the date of the act, and died before Aug. 16, 1842.
Graves, Mary, widow of Samuel	Alna, Lincoln	Was not a widow at the date of the act.
Greenleaf, Mary (deceased), widow of Daniel	Rumford, Oxford	Was not a widow at the date of the act.
Hagar, Esther, widow of Ezekiel	Union, Lincoln	Did not serve six months.
Lathrop, Martha, widow of Joseph	Hebron, Oxford	Did not serve six months.
Irish, Anna (deceased), widow of Isaac	Gorham, Cumberland	Did not serve six months.
Ingraham, Lucy, widow of Job	Thomaston, Lincoln	Did not serve six months.
Murray, Lucy, widow of James	Portland, Cumberland	Waggon service.

STATEMENT—Continued.

Names.	Residence.	Reasons for rejection.
Mehuren, Mary, widow of Isaac.	Jay, Franklin.	Did not serve six months.
Oaks, Abigail, widow of John.	Exeter, Penobscot.	Was not a widow at the date of the act.
Perkins, Abigail, widow of Abner.	New Castle, Lincoln.	Did not serve six months.
Robins, Mehitabel (dec'd), widow of Daniel.	Green, Kennebec.	Not a widow at the date of the act—died February 27, 1842.
Rounds, Susanna (deceased), widow of Joseph.	Alfred, York.	Died previous to August 16, 1842.
Taylor, Comfort (deceased), widow of John.	Mexico, Oxford.	Died previous to August 16, 1842.
Smith, Hanna, formerly widow of Isaac Thayer.	Buckfield, Oxford.	Not a widow at the date of the act—died before August 16, 1842.
Trash, Anna, widow of Moses.	Edgecomb, Lincoln.	Not a widow at the date of the act.
Warner, Sarah (deceased), widow of Pelatiah.	Monmouth, Kennebec.	Not a widow at the date of the act.

A list of persons residing in Maine who have applied for pensions under the act of July 7, 1838, whose claims have been suspended; prepared in conformity with the resolution of the Senate of the United States of September 16, 1850.

Names.	Residence.	Reasons for suspension.
Barnhock, Sarah, widow of John	Newcastle, Lincoln	Suspended for further proof of service, of marriage, and of the court of probate if a court of record.
Barnett, Susanna, widow of John	Dover, Piscataquis	Service not set forth—marriage not proved.
Benson, Dorothy, widow of Robert	Biddeford, York	Suspended for further proof of service—pensioned without adequate proof.
Blake, Mary, widow of James	Portland, Cumberland	Suspended for proof of residence at the time of entering service in order to identify his service on board the Protector.
Bowe, Hannah, formerly widow of Jacob Merrill	Topsham, Lincoln	Suspended for proof of age, and identity distinct from two of the same name.
Buck, Mary, widow of Ebenezer	Bucksport, Hancock	Not six months service established.
Butterfield, Ruth, widow of Isaac	Wilton, Franklin	Suspended for further examination of the returns of eight month's men of 1775.
Blake, Hannah, widow of Joseph	Portland, Cumberland	Not a widow at the date of the act—died before August 28, 1842.
Cammett, Nabby, widow of Thomas	Portland, Cumberland	Suspended for further proof and specification.
Campbell, Prudence, widow of James	Jefferson, Lincoln	Suspended for proof of marriage.
Card, Sarah, formerly widow of John Frieze	Bowdoin, Lincoln	Proof of identity adverse of claimant's husband with the soldier of the same name, from Wells, York county.
Chapman, Lydia, widow of Shadrach	Westbrook, Cumberland	He did not serve six months.
Clark, Sarah, formerly widow of Thomas Moore	Lewiston, Lincoln	He did not serve six months.
Clark, Phebe, widow of Jonathan D.	South Berwick, York	Suspended for an inspection of the New Hampshire rolls.
Davis, Margaret, widow of Simon	Phipsburgh, Lincoln	Suspended for proof of identity with the soldier of the same name, from the same town (Ringe), and same company (Captain Thomas').
Davis, Sarah, widow of Jesse	———, Hancock	Suspended for a new declaration under the acts July 1, and February 2, 1848, and further proof of marriage, and the children's births.
Donnet, Rebecca, formerly widow of John Holland	Lewiston, Lincoln	Suspended for further proof of the character of the vessels, whether public or private, on board which he served.
Drake, Tamson, widow of Simon	Union, Lincoln	Suspended for more definite proof of marriage.

STATEMENT—Continued.

Names.	Residence.	Reasons for suspension.
Drew, Comfort, formerly widow of Noah Smith	Hollis, York	Suspended for proof of marriage, and the credibility of witnesses.
Dugans, Elizabeth, widow of William	Kilmarnock, Piscataquis	Suspended for further proof and specification, and proof of marriage.
Drinkwater, widow of Daniel	Cumberland, Cumberland	He did not serve six months.
Durrill, Mary, widow of Thomas	Kennebunkport, York	He has not fully proved over five months and twenty-five days service.
Getchell, Elizabeth, widow of Nathaniel	Northport, Waldo	Suspended for further proof of marriage.
Gilman, Anna, widow of William	Norridgewock, Somerset	Proof of identity required that her husband was the soldier on the Massachusetts records of the eight months' service of 1776.
Gould, Rahannas, widow of Lazarus	Bethel, Oxford	No proof of service for over two months and sixteen days.
Hammond, Olive, widow of Rogers	Kennebunkport, York	No proof of identity with the Roger Hammond of the Massachusetts rolls.
Hastings, Betsey, widow of Amos	Bethel, Oxford	Not on the rolls.—no proof of service.
Holland, Polly, widow of Joseph	Canton, Oxford	Service not fully proved—far short of six months.
Hovey, Mercy, widow of Samuel	—, Hancock	No rolls of the ship Alliance, and none of Captains Isaac and Frederick Pope, and no evidence of service.
Kneeland, Hannah, widow of Aaron	Harrison, Cumberland	Pensioned without proof—the rolls since discovered discredit the claim in toto.
Knight, Phebe, widow of William	Poland, Cumberland	Proof of identity required with the soldier of the same name credited on the New Hampshire records, and proof of marriage.
Newbit, Jane, widow of Christopher	Appleton, Waldo	Suspended for proof of service from the Massachusetts records.
Nevins, Joanna, widow of James	Poland, Cumberland	Service not duly supported—proof must be gathered from the Massachusetts rolls.
Newbury, Lucy, widow of John	Venal Haven, Waldo	Name not on the rolls—no proof of service.
Parker, Elizabeth, formerly widow of William Haney	Hartland, Somerset	Six months service not established.
Parkhurst, Sally, widow of Nathan	Unity, Waldo	Not on the New Hampshire rolls—no proof of service.
Patterson, Mary, widow of William	Edgecomb, Lincoln	No satisfactory proof that the vessels were public ones on board of which service was performed.

Poor, Lucy, widow of Samuel	Portland, Cumberland	Suspended for proof of identity of claimant's husband with the soldier of Captain Bell's company, Colonel Symm's regiment.
Potter, Elizabeth, widow of George	Bowdoin, Lincoln	Suspended for proof of identity of Mrs. Potter's husband with the soldier of Captain Reed's company of Colonel Hunter's regiment.
Preble, Isabella, widow of Jedediah	Whitefield, Lincoln	Name not on the rolls of 1775—the records at Boston may furnish proof, as he was, it seems, in the battle of Bunker Hill.
Quimby, Mary, widow of Benjamin	Green, Kennebec	Not a widow under the act, and she died before August 16, 1842.
Sanborn, Betsey, widow of Joseph	Waterborough, York	Suspended for proof of identity that her husband was the three years' soldier of Colonel Scammell's regiment.
Segar, Mary, widow of Nathaniel	Dresden, Lincoln	Suspended for proof of residence at the time of enlistment, in order to his identity with service in 1776.
Severance, Hannah, formerly widow of Daniel Boynton	Buxton, York	Suspended for further proof from the Massachusetts records.
Skolfield, Sarah, widow of William	Bowdoin, Lincoln	Suspended for further proof and specification.
Snow, Elizabeth, widow of Benjamin	Atkinson, Piscataquis	Suspended for further proof.
Smith, Mary, formerly widow of Josiah Long	Portland, Cumberland	Six month's service not fully proved—the identity is not apparent of the present claimant with Joshua Long, who is credited with thirty-three months and three days.
Shaw, Patience, widow of Samuel	Sanford, York	Not a widow at the date of the act—died before August 28, 1842.
Thurley, Betty, widow of Jonathan	South Berwick, York	Not on the rolls of the eight months' men of 1775—no proof of service.
Townsend, Hannah, widow of J. Bela	Wilton, Franklin	Not on the rolls but for very short periods.
Trask, Hannah, widow of Ebenezer	Belgrade, Kennebec	Pensioned before the discovery of the rolls, without adequate proof, which is now not sufficient for six months' service.
Travis, Milly, widow of Oliver	Brownfield, Oxford	Not a widow within the act—died before August 28, 1842.
Trowbridge, Sarah, widow of John	Waldoboro, Lincoln	Suspended for proof of the dates of marriage and decease of her husband.
Twitchell, Sarah, widow of Jacob	Paris, Oxford	Suspended for a further inspection of the Massachusetts rolls for 1775.
Wallace, Rhoda, widow of William	Phipsburgh, Lincoln	Name not on the Massachusetts rolls for the period designated.
Welch, Sarah, widow of James	Woolwich, Lincoln	The soldier of Colonel Tupper's regiment of the same name, with claimant's husband, was from a different town.
Weld, Nabby, widow of Benjamin	Brunswick, Cumberland	Not a widow within the act—died before August 28, 1842.
Weston, Sarah, widow of Joseph	Bloomfield, Somerset	Suspended for further proof of service and marriage.
Whitmore, Lucy, widow of Andrew	Georgetown, Lincoln	Pensioned before the discovery of the rolls, and if his name is not found on them a further prosecution were useless.
Williams, Isami, widow of Jacob	Emden, Somerset	Suspended for further proof and specification.

[37]

A list of the names of persons residing in New Hampshire who have applied for pensions under the act of June 7, 1832, whose claims have been rejected; prepared in conformity with the resolution of the Senate of the United States, September 16, 1850.

Names.	Residence.	Reasons for rejection.
Bascom, Uriel	Hanover, Grafton	Not on the rolls—no proof of service.
Bartlett, Jeremiah	Gilford, Strafford	He did not serve six months.
Batchelder, Jonathan	Raymond, Rockingham	He did not serve six months.
Berry, Levi	Rye, Rockingham	He did not serve six months.
Blake, John	Wakefield, Strafford	He did not serve six months.
Bootman, Thomas	Enfield, Grafton	He did not serve six months, except as a drummer in the recruiting service.
Clark, Josiah	Epping, Rockingham	He did not serve six months.
Chase, Abner	Wendell, Sullivan	He did not serve six months.
Carlton, Benjamin	Plaistow, Rockingham	Deserted.
Caswell, John	Grafton, Grafton	He did not serve six months.
Clement, Jesse	Unity, Sullivan	He did not serve six months.
Currier, Richard	Enfield, Grafton	He did not serve six months.
Dearborn, James	Effingham, Strafford	He did not serve six months.
Dow, John	Gilmanton, Strafford	He did not serve six months.
Doe, John	Alton, Strafford	He did not serve six months.
Doolittle, Thomas	Moultonborough, Strafford	Waggon service not entitled.
Davis, Elisha	Alton, Strafford	He did not serve six months.
Drown, Thomas	New Market, Rockingham	He did not serve six months.
Danford, Joseph	Meredith, Strafford	He did not serve six months.
Dow, Jonathan	New Hampton, Grafton	He did not serve six months.
Emerson, Jonathan	Pelham, Hillsborough	He did not serve six months.
Farmer, Oliver	Bethlehem, Grafton	He was a deserter.
Fisk, Nathan	Dunstable, Hillsborough	He did not serve six months.

Name	Town	Remark
Franklin, Abel	Lyman, Grafton	He did not serve six months.
Gilson, David	Brookline, Hillsborough	He did not serve six months.
Glines, Robert	Plymouth, Grafton	He did not serve six months.
Hamlet, Hezekiah	Dunstable, Hillsborough	He did not serve six months.
Hunt, Ephruim	Boscawen, Merrimack	He did not serve six months.
Harreld, alias Harrod, James (deceased)	Portsmouth, Rockingham	Not on the rolls—no proof of service.
Hill, Willey	Lee, Strafford	He did not serve six months.
Hastings, Thaddeus	Marlborough, Cheshire	He did not serve six months.
Hill, Henry	Strafford, Strafford	He was a deserter.
Hildreth, Ephraim	Haverhill, Grafton	He did not serve six months.
Ham, Ichabod	Dover, Strafford	He did not serve six months.
Kelly, Dudley	Northampton, Strafford	He did not serve six months.
Lovejoy, Jacob	Hebron, Grafton	He did not serve in a military capacity.
Langmaid, John	Lee, Strafford	He did not serve six months.
Lake, James	Canterbury, Merrimack	Privateer service.
Morey, Thomas	Bradford, Orange	Not on the rolls—no proof of service.
Mills, Thomas	Dunbarton, Merrimack	He did not serve six months.
Mallet, Michael	Bath, Grafton	Privateer service.
Morrill, Joseph	Gilmanton, Belknap	He did not serve six months.
Noyes, Samuel	Canaan, Grafton	He did not serve six months.
Putney, David	Dunbarton, Merrimack	He did not serve six months.
Potter, Israel	Guilford, Strafford	He did not serve six months.
Philbrick, Benjamin	Warner, Merrimack	He did not serve six months.
Ramsay, Samuel	Greenfield, Hillsborough	He did not serve six months.
Randel, Gideon	Concsay, Strafford	He did not serve six months.
Randall, John	Lee, Strafford	He did not serve six months.
Rider, James	Jefferson, Coos	He was a deserter.
Swasey, Edward	Exeter, Rockingham	Not on the rolls—no proof of service.
Smith, Simeon	Campton, Grafton	He did not serve six months.
Shaw, Abraham	Kensington, Rockingham	He did not serve six months.
Stiles, Samuel	Strafford, Strafford	He was a deserter.

Ex.—2

STATEMENT—Continued.

Names.	Residence.	Reasons for rejection.
Stickney, Moses	Jaffrey, Cheshire	He did not serve six months.
Thurston, Stephen	Oxford, Grafton	He did not serve six months.
Worthley, Jonathan	Weare, Hillsborough	He did not serve six months.
Weeks, Josiah (deceased)	Bartlett, Coos	Died before the passage of the act.
Wiggin, Andrew	Moultonborough, Strafford	He was a deserter.
Woodman, Abner	Warner, Merrimack	He did not serve six months.

A list of the names of persons residing in New Hampshire who have applied for pensions under the act of June 7, 1832, whose claims have been suspended; prepared in conformity with the resolution of the Senate of the United States, September 16, 1850.

Names.	Residence.	Reasons for suspension.
Babcock, Robert	Tuftonborough, Carroll	Not on any Rhode Island rolls from 1777 to 1779—married after 1800—no claim for the widow.
Bailey, David	Nashua, Hillsborough	No period, length, or grade of service—no officers named—no proof.
Brown, Edward (deceased)	Rindge, Cheshire	He did not serve six months.
Blake, Eleazer	Rindge, Cheshire	Application for an increase from sergeant to quartermaster—rejected for deficient proof.
Burbank, Henry	Haverhill, Grafton	Not on the Massachusetts rolls—no proof of service.
Clough, Simon	Lancaster, Coos	Not on the rolls of Wingate's regiment—witnesses conflict in their statements—no satisfactory proof.
Corel, Isaac	Colebrook, Coos	Suspended for want of proof.
Dearborn, Sherburn	Chester, Rockingham	Suspended for proof of identity with the service credited on the New Hampshire certificate, which bears date before his declaration.
Dolan, Daniel	New Durham, Strafford	He was a deserter.
Dow, Levi	New Hampton, Belknap	Driver of a six ox cart, at twelve dollars per month—not military service.
Downes, Joseph	Lebanon, Grafton	Suspended for further proof—six month's service not established.
Everett, Nathaniel	Lyme, Grafton	A caveat is on file against this claim from his own neighborhood.
Fuller, Luther	Colebrook, Coos	Discredited by the rolls except for two months.
Fernald, Randall	Portsmouth, Rockingham	Not six month's service established of a military capacity.
Harris, James	Guysborough, Sydney co., Nova Scotia	Suspended for authentication before a court of record in one of the States, and for reasons for delay and expatriation.
Hall, Levins (deceased)	Stewartstown, Coos	Suspended for proof of identity between two soldiers of the same name, but differing circumstances—which of these was the claimant.
Huntington, Ziba	Hanover, Grafton	Suspended for further proof of the service and the nature of it.

STATEMENT—Continued.

Names.	Residence.	Reasons for suspension.
Kimball, Samuel	Lisbon, Grafton	Not on the rolls—no proof of service either by claimant or his officers.
Kimball, Jonathan	Lisbon, Grafton	Under age—no proof of service.
Labere, Peter	Brentwood, Rockingham	He did not serve six months.
Leavitt, John	Tuftonborough, Carroll	Suspended for proof of age and of identity with the soldier of the same name, whose services are credited by the Secretary of New Hampshire.
Marsh, Zebulon	Exeter, Rockingham	Not any proof of any kind of service.
Mills, Reuben	Dunbarton, Merrimack	He did not serve six months.
Morrison, Robert	Londonderry, Rockland	He did not serve six months.
Perry, Benjamin (deceased)	Pittsburg, Coos	Suspended for further proof.
Pike, John	Newport, Sullivan	He did not serve six months.
Richardson, William	Londonderry, Rockingham	Suspended for further proof from the rolls at Boston.
Robinson, Robert	Claremont, Sullivan	Suspended for further proof, of which there is now none, either oral or of record.
Rosebrook, Eleazer	Lancaster, Coos	Died before the passage of the act.
Saunders, Samuel	Jaffrey, Cheshire	Suspended for proof of service from the State records at Boston.
Sawyer, Reuben	Manchester, Hillsborough	He did not serve six months.
Seaward, John H. (deceased)	Portsmouth, Rockingham	He did not serve six months.
Sellars, David	Guysborough, Interval co., Nova Scotia	Suspended for want of proof in 1886, and papers withdrawn and not replaced by Hon. J. Cushman in June, 1887.
Smith, Adam	Bedford, Hillsborough	He did not serve six months.
Tenney, Joseph	Lempster, Sullivan	He did not serve six months.
Tilton, William	London, Merrimack	He did not serve six months in a military capacity.
Town, Benjamin	Hinsdale, Cheshire	Suspended for certificate from the Secretary of State of pay and service, and of identity by cotemporary soldiers.
Tucker, William	Andover, Merrimack	There is evidence that he received six pounds, State bounty, but not that he ever rendered any revolutionary service.

A list of the names of persons residing in New Hampshire who have applied for pensions under the act of July 29, 1848, whose claims have been suspended; prepared in conformity with the resolution of the Senate of the United States, September 16, 1850.

Names.	Residence.	Reasons for suspension.
Jackson, Miriam, widow of David	Bath, Grafton	Suspended for proof of marriage, and of her husband's identity with the soldier from Newton, of the Massachusetts line.
Lane, Molly, widow of Jonathan	Piermont, Grafton	Suspended for proof of identity of claimant's husband with the service credited to soldiers of the same name on the rolls.
Marble, Mehitable, widow of Samuel	Deerfield, Rockingham	Suspended for proof of the marriage, and applicant's identity with the late pensioner from Maine.
Morrison, Esther, widow of Jonathan	Sanbornton, Belknap	Suspended for further proof of marriage.
Rich, Leuriah, widow of John	Bath, Grafton	Suspended for proof of marriage, and of claimant's husband's identity with one of the two soldiers of the same name in the certificate of the Secretary of State of New Hampshire.
Wingate, Mary, by Simon Chase, guardian	Rochester, Strafford	In 1820, Wingate stated that he had no family. Now, there are two applicants—one named Mary, who is insane, and is represented by Simon Chase, of Rochester, guardian; while J. D. Chase applies as agent for Sarah Wingate, as widow of the same soldier.

A list of the names of persons residing in New Hampshire who have applied for pensions under the act of July 4, 1836, whose claims have been rejected; prepared in conformity with the resolution of the Senate of the United States, September 16, 1850.

Names.	Residence.	Reasons for rejection.
Abbott, Dorcas	Ossipee, Strafford	A soldier of the regular army, and died in 1814.
Ballard, Maria C.	Herkimer, Merrimack	A soldier of the regular army.
Bartlett, Sarah, widow of Thomas, heirs of	Nottingham, Rockingham	Died before the passage of the act.
Curtis, Hannah (deceased), by Sarah White, her child	New Castle, Rockingham	Died before the passage of the act.
Eastman, John (deceased)	Enfield, Grafton	He did not serve six months.
Eaton, Ebenezer, son of Nathaniel	Bethlehem, Grafton	Died before the passage of the act.
Fassett, Anna, widow of Adonijah	Winchester, Cheshire	He did not serve six months.
Glover, Anna, widow of Stephen	Ossipee, Strafford	A soldier of the regular army.
Hough, Abigail, widow of David	Lebanon, Grafton	Service not under military obligation.
Leonard, Betsey, widow of John	Keene, Cheshire	He did not serve six months.
Smith, Hannah, widow of Israel	Claremont, Sullivan	He did not serve six months.
Salter, Catharine (deceased) widow of Samuel	Keene, Cheshire	Married after service—not a widow under act of 1888—died before August 23, 1848.
Sawyer, Ann, widow of Ichabod	Oxford, Grafton	He did not serve six months.
Tibbatts, Sarah, widow of Henry	Gilmanton, Strafford	He did not serve six months—see same case suspended, act 1888.

A list of the names of persons residing in New Hampshire who have applied for pensions under the act of July 4, 1836, whose claims have been suspended; prepared in conformity with the resolution of the Senate of the United States, September 16, 1850.

Names.	Residence.	Reasons for suspension.
Adams, Sarah, widow of Samuel............	Nelson, Cheshire............	Service admitted—marriage in suspense—requires more definite proof, February 23, 1837—Hon. H. Hubbard.
Bailey, Mary, widow of Joseph............	Boscawen, Merrimack......	He did not serve six months in person.
Barrett, Mercy, widow of Nathaniel.......	Stoddard, Cheshire..........	Suspended for further proof of marriage and service.
Barton, Miriam, widow of William........	Kensington, Rockingham...	Suspended for proof of marriage and identity with the soldier on the lists of depreciation, April 16, 1847—David Murray, New Market.
Brown, Susannah, widow of Edward.......	Rindge, Cheshire.............	He did not serve six months.
Bradley, Bathsheba, widow of David......	Stratford, Coos...............	Application for an increase—not entertained.
Cummings, Mary (deceased), widow of Benjamin...	Cornish, Sullivan............	He did not serve six months.
Chase, Sarah, widow of Solomon...........	Cornish, Sullivan............	Not of the military staff—a private doctor of medicine who received regular pay for his services to the wounded.
Crane, Experience, widow of Samuel......	Bradford, Merrimack.......	Married after service.
Eaton, Betsey, widow of William...........	Sanbornton, Strafford......	He did not serve six months.
Eaton, Betsey, formerly widow of Ichabod Swain...	Gilmanton, Strafford........	Suspended for further proof of the eight months' service in 1775, on record at Concord.
Farmer, Sarah, formerly widow of Benjamin Bower...	Boscawen, Merrimack......	He did not serve six months.
Freeman, Sarah, widow of Jonathan.......	Hanover, Grafton............	Suspended for further proof, February 19, 1840—Hon. J. Wilson.
Flanders, Mary, widow of Nathaniel.......	Wilmot, Merrimack.........	He did not serve six months.
Hall, Lydia, widow of David.................	Walpole, Cheshire...........	He did not serve six months.
Lavitt, Mary, widow of Thomas............	Northampton, Rockingham.	Suspended for further proof of service.
Mason, Sarah, widow of Benjamin.........	Stratham, Rockingham.....	A soldier of the regular army.
Morrison, Rebecca, widow of Alexander...	Canaan, Essex county, Vermont	He did not serve six months.

STATEMENT—Continued.

Names.	Residence.	Reasons for suspension.
Moulton, Mary, widow of Daniel	Sandwich, Strafford	Suspended for proof of marriage.
Paine, Sarah, widow of Zebediah	Westmoreland, Cheshire	Suspended for further proof of service and marriage, March 22, 1841—N. G. Babbett.
Robbins, Hannah, widow of Ephraim	Bethlehem, Grafton	Suspended for further proof, June 12, 1887—Goodall & Wood.
Robbins, Susannah	Strafford, Strafford	A soldier of the regulars in the late war with Great Britain.
Sargent, Mary (deceased), formerly widow of Samuel Emerson	Plainfield, Sullivan	Suspended for further proof.
Smith, Amos, children of	Sutton, Merrimack	She died before the passage of the act.
Taylor, Rachel, widow of Abraham	Landaff, Grafton	Suspended for further proof.
Tuttle, Lucy, widow of Charles	New Boston, Hillsborough	Suspended for further proof.
Whitelock, Mary, widow of John	Portsmouth, Rockingham	Suspended for further proof from the Massachusetts rolls.
Waters, Deborah, widow of Thomas	Chester, Rockingham	Married after service.
Worcesters, Isabel, widow of Samuel	Windsor, Windsor co., Vermont	Suspended for further proof and specification.

A list of the names of persons residing in New Hampshire who have applied for pensions under the act of July 7, 1838, whose claims have been rejected; prepared in conformity with the resolution of the Senate of the United States, September 16, 1850.

Names.	Residence.	Reasons for rejection.
Avery, Betsey, widow of Moses	Ellsworth, Grafton	He did not serve six months.
Babbitt, Ruth, widow of Asa	Hanover, Grafton	He did not serve six months.
Britton, Jerusha, widow of John	Westmoreland, Cheshire	He did not serve six months.
Butler, Sarah, widow of John	Campton, Grafton	He did not serve six months.
Cram, Mary Ann (deceased), widow of Theophilus	Wilmot, Merrimack	Not a widow at the date of the act—died before August 23, 1812.
Glines, Sary, widow of John	Moultonborough, Strafford	Not a widow at the date of the act—died before August 23, 1842.
Heard, Mary, widow of Amos	Piermont, Grafton	Not a widow at the date of the act.
Hadley, Abigail, widow of Abijah	Hancock, Hillsborough	He did not serve six months.
Holman, Martha, widow of Edward	Fitzwilliam, Cheshire	Under age.
Learned, Theodity, widow of James	Eaton, Lower Canada	He did not serve six months.
Morrison, Margaret, widow of David	Peterborough, Hillsborough	He did not serve six months.
Robb, Abigail, widow of Samuel	Stoddard, Cheshire	He did not serve six months.
Tilton, Mehitable, widow of Jeremiah	Sandbornton, Strafford	He did not serve six months.
Towle, Parna, widow of Levi	Epping, Rockingham	He did not serve six months.
Witham, Lydia, widow of Andrew	Somersworth, Strafford	Not a widow at the date of the act—died before August 28, 1842.
Woodbury, Abigail, widow of Jesse	Weare, Hillsborough	He did not serve six months.
Webster, Catharine (deceased), widow of Stephen	Bartlett, Coos	She died the before passage of the act.

A list of the names of persons residing in New Hampshire who have applied for pensions under the act of July 7, 1838, whose claims have been suspended; prepared in conformity with the resolution of the Senate of the United States, September 16, 1850.

Names.	Residence.	Reasons for suspension.
Banks, Betsey, widow of William	Gilsum, Cheshire	Suspended for proof of commission as ensign, and of identity with the records of service to the same name and different grades on the Massachusetts rolls, and records of Oakham.
Benton, Sarah, widow of Elijah	Colebrook, Coos	Suspended for proof of marriage, and of identity with the dragoon of Sheldon's regiment bearing his name.
Blake, Judith (deceased), heirs of, by Baruch Chase, administrator	Salisbury, Merrimack	Suspended during the return of the New Hampshire rolls, July 29, 1841.—Israel W. Kelly.
Brown, Anna, widow of James	Henniker, Merrimack	Not a widow at the date of the act.
Brown, Anna, widow of Aaron	Marlow, Cheshire	Suspended for proof of identity with the soldier credited with service in the New Hampshire militia, and also the length of the term under Captain Humphreys.
Bryant, Tabitha, widow of John	Lempster, Sullivan	Suspended for further proof and specification, November 22, 1843—J. J. Gilchrist.
Calman, Sarah, widow of Thomas	Meredith, Strafford	Fraudulent—her husband obtained a pension in 1828, on forged papers.
Carter, Sarah, widow of Nathan	Canterbury, Merrimack	He did not serve six months.
Chamberlain, Susannah, widow of Elisha	Swanzey, Cheshire	He did not serve six months.
Chase, Louisa, widow of John	Cornish, Sullivan	Not a widow at the date of the act.
Clark, Jane, widow of John	Gilmanton, Strafford	Not on the rolls—no proof of service.
Colcord, Lydia, widow of John	Exeter, Rockingham	He did not serve six months.
Cole, Keziah, widow of John	Somersworth, Strafford	He did not serve six months.
Comstock, Elizabeth, widow of John	Corkville, Coos	Suspended for further proof and explanation.
Crosby, Elizabeth, widow of John	Thornton, Grafton	No specification of service, and not on any rolls of the continental line.
Day, Judith, widow of Timothy	Enfield, Grafton	Eight months five days service, and pension offered for that amount, May 14, 1850.—H. Hubbard.

Name	Residence	Remarks
Dimond, Mary, widow of Reuben	Concord, Merrimack	Suspended action on this case, March 17, 1841, in consequence of the return of the New Hampshire rolls to the Secretary of that State—Philip Carnegant, agent.
Erskine, Freelove, widow of Christopher	Claremont, Sullivan	He did not serve six months.
Falls, Flora, widow of John	Claremont, Sullivan	Service alleged but not proved on board the Tyrannecede, August 31, 1850—John Tall.
Farmer, Lydia, widow of John	Amherst, Hillsborough	Suspended for further proof and specification.
Fifield, Lucy, widow of Moses	Unity, Sullivan	He did not serve six months.
French, Mary, widow of Benjamin	New Market, Rockingham	Barred by act April 30, 1844.
Fullington, Mary (dec'd), widow of Jonathan	Franklin, Merrimack	Not a widow at the date of the act—died before August 28, 1842.
Glines, Lovey, formerly widow of Benjamin	Concord, Merrimack	He did not serve six months.
Gordon, Anna, widow of Zebulon	New Hampton, Strafford	He did not serve six months.
Griffin, Elizabeth, widow of James	Hillsborough	
Hemson, Hannah, widow of Uriah	New Market, Rockingham	Not on the rolls—no proof of service.
Horton, Judith (deceased), widow of Samuel	Ossipee, Strafford	Not a widow at the date of the act—died before August 28, 1842.
Jacquith, Lois, widow of Samuel	Jaffrey, Cheshire	Not on the rolls—no proof of service.
Jewett, Polly, widow of ——	Hollis, Hillsborough	Suspended for further proof from the Massachusetts rolls.
Kenyon, Hezediah, widow of Joseph	Plainfield, Sullivan	Seven months' service admitted, provided widow was alive, July 1, 1848.
Lear, Mercy, widow of Joseph	Lempster, Sullivan	Suspended for further proof.
Long, Sukey, widow of Samuel	Bath, Grafton	Not on the rolls—proof insufficient.
Lyon, Lucy, widow of Jonathan	Pelham, Hillsborough	Not on the rolls—no proof of service.
McDaniel, Hannah, widow of William	Nottingham, Rockingham	Not on the rolls—no proof of service.
Morrison, Susan, widow of William	Petersborough, Hillsborough	Suspended for proof of marriage.
Morse, Anna, widow of John	Cornish, Sullivan	Suspended for proof of identity that he was John Morse, from Dublin, New Hampshire.
Moore, Elisabeth, widow of William	Exeter, Rockingham	He did not serve six months.
Morse, Mehitabel, widow of Daniel, formerly widow of John Clark	Campton, Grafton	Suspended for proof of identity of the husband with one of the same name found on the New Hampshire records, September 21, 1850—H. Hibbard, H. R.
Nay, Mercy, widow of Samuel	Raymond, Rockingham	Suspended for further proof—J. Kelly, September 9, 1889.

STATEMENT—Continued.

Names.	Residence.	Reasons for suspension.
Osgood, Anna (deceased), widow of Ebenezer.	London, Merrimack	Suspended for proof of identity with the soldier of the New Hampshire certificate.
Perkins, Abigail (deceased)	Jefferson, Coos	Died before the passage of the act—but with proof of service prior to, or concurrent with her marriage, she can claim under act July 4, 1836.
Philbrick, Olive, widow of Richard	Weare, Hillsborough	He did not serve six months.
Pitman, Mary, widow of Mark	Portsmouth, Rockingham	Suspended for further proof.
Pratt, Jane, widow of Alvin	Piermont, Grafton	Suspended for further proof.
Rand, Mary, widow of William	Deerfield, Rockingham	Barred by act April 30, 1844.
Randall, Elizabeth, widow of George	Rye, Rockingham	He did not serve six months.
Roberts, Tamson, widow of Joseph	Dover, Strafford	He did not serve six months.
Roberts, Sally, widow of Ephraim	Alton, Strafford	He did not serve six months.
Robinson, Lydia, widow of John	Meredith, Belknap	Suspended for further proof of claimant's identity as the veritable widow of the deceased, February 16, 1850—Nicholas M. Taylor.
Rollins, Betty, widow of Reuben	Bridgewater, Grafton	Not on the rolls—no proof of service.
Straw, Betty (deceased), widow of Jacob	Henniker, Merrimack	Not a widow at the date of the act—died before August 28, 1842.
Shaw, Abigail, widow of David	Chester, Rockingham	Proof of identity required of claimant's husband with either of the soldiers bearing his name, credited with service on the records of New Hampshire.
Shortridge, Lois, widow of Richard	Portsmouth, Rockingham	Under age.
Sinkler, Anna, widow of Zebulon	Holderness, Grafton	Not a widow at the date of the act.
Smith, Sarah (deceased), formerly widow of Benjamin Grant	Lyme, Grafton	Suspended for further proof and papers withdrawn, April 22, 1845—H. & J. E. Kendall.
Sprague, Kata, widow of Jonathan	Peterborough, Hillsborough	Suspended for proof of her identity, and a new declaration under act February 2, 1848—marriage service admitted April 26, 1849—Luke Woodbury.

Thompson, Lydia, widow of Joseph, jr.	Farmington, Strafford.	Not on any rolls—no proof of service.
Thurston, Else, widow of John.	Stratham, Rockingham.	Suspended for further proof.
Turner, Rhoda, widow of David.	Lyme, Grafton.	Suspended for further proof and explanation.
Upton, Sarah, widow of Enos.	Mount Vernon, Hillsborough.	Suspended for proof of identity with the soldier of the rolls.
Watson, Anna, widow of Dudley.	Dudley, New Market.	Suspended for further proof from the New Hampshire records.
Welch, Mary, widow of John.	Barnstead, Strafford.	Suspended for further proof.
Witham, Mehitabel, widow of Elijah.	Rochester, Strafford.	Suspended for further proof.
Whittier, Judith, widow of Abner.	Canaan, Grafton.	Suspended for further proof and specification.
Wood, Esther, widow of Joshua.	Keene, Cheshire.	Not on the rolls—no proof of service.
Young, Mary, widow of Abiathar.	Wendell, Sullivan.	Suspended for further proof.

[37]

A list of persons residing in Vermont who have applied for pensions under the act of June 7, 1832, whose claims have been rejected; prepared in conformity with the resolution of the Senate of the United States, September 18, 1850.

Names.	Residence.	Reasons for rejection.
Adams, John	Burlington, Chittenden	Deserted.
Ashley, William S.	Hartland, Windsor	He did not serve six months.
Allen, Jacob	New Fane, Windham	He did not serve six months.
Avery, Stephen	Brandon, Rutland	Deserted.
Burbank, Elijah	Sharon, Windsor	He did not serve six months.
Boardman, Aaron	Londonderry, Windham	He did not serve six months.
Boyley, John	Newbury, Orange	He did not serve in any regularly organized corps.
Brown, Joseph (deceased)	Hinesburgh, Chittenden	He did not serve six months.
Babcock, Robert	Dover, Windham	Patrol service—not regularly organized corps.
Beckwith, Rufus	Williamstown, Orange	Under age—a waiter.
Birchard, Levi	Moreham, Addison	Team service.
Butterfield, Samuel	Topham, Orange	Did not serve in any regularly organized corps.
Belknap, Simeon	Randolph, Orange	Team service.
Brattle, Dick	Weathersfield, Windsor	He did not serve six months.
Bragg, William	Warren, Washington	No proof of service.
Berry, Elisha	Westminster, Windham	He did not serve six months.
Beebee, Allen	Rutland, Rutland	No proof of service.
Billings, Gideon	Barnard, Windsor	Deserted.
Carpenter, Nathan	Middleburg, Addison	He did not serve six months.
Church, Parley	Waterford, Caledonia	He did not serve six months.
Clark, John	Isle Lamotte, Grand Isle	Patrol service—not in a regularly organized corps.
Clark, Eleazar	Northfield, Washington	He did not serve six months.
Cox, Benjamin	Barnard, Windsor	He did not serve six months.
Cram, Ebenezer	Chesterley, Windsor	He did not serve six months.
Currier, David	Pearham, Caledonia	Deserted.
Cox, William	Vershire, Orange	Team service.
Doubleday, Jacob	Sharon, Windsor	He did not serve six months.
Dimick, Shubal	Sutton, Lower Canada	Deserted.
Dyer, Ebenezer	Sharon, Windsor	Not military service.

Name	Place	Remark
Ellis, John, 2d	Weldon, Caledonia	Deserted.
Eaton, Joseph	Ludlow, Windsor	He did not serve six months.
Eastman, Peter	Compton, Three Rivers, Lower Canada	No proof of service.
Eaton, Samuel	Reading, Windsor	He did not serve six months.
Eesterbrooks, Benjamin	Lyndon, Caledonia	Boat service in the commissary department, October, 1, 1883—J. Bridgeman.
Flint, James	Barre, Washington	He did not serve six months in person.
Fish, Elisha	Danby, Rutland	No proof of service.
Field, Pardon	Chester, Windsor	He did not serve six months.
Freeman, Ezra	Saint Armands, Lower Canada	Fraudulent.
Goodhue, Joseph	Putney, Windham	He did not serve six months.
Griggs, Simeon	Alburgh, Grand Isle	He did not serve six months.
Greenleaf, Stephen	Brattleboro', Windham	He did not serve six months.
Green, Nathan	Whitingham, Windham	He did not serve six months.
Havens, Daniel	Chester, Windsor	He did not serve six months.
Harrington, Sampson	Alburgh, Grand Isle	He did not serve six months.
Henderson, Andrew	Stanstead, Lower Canada	He did not serve six months.
Huckins, Jonathan	Topham, Orange	Deserted.
Hackett, Charles	Holland, Orleans	Deserted.
Hurlbut, Daniel	Williston, Chittenden	Team service.
Hews, William	Milton, Chittenden	He did not serve six months.
Hantoon, Amos T.	Brownington, Orleans	Under age.
Lathrop, Elias	Waterbury, Washington	He did not serve six months, except in the team service.
Lovegrove, Hampton	Fairfax, Franklin	Team service.
Lucas, Elisha	Chester, Windsor	He did not serve six months.
Littlefield, Asa	Beadeborough, Bennington	No proof of service.
Moorehouse, Samuel	Georgia, Franklin	Team service.
Mason, Nathaniel	Ira, Rutland	He did not serve six months.
Mason, David	Starsboro', Addison	He did not serve six months.
Houlton, Phinehas	Randolph, Orange	He did not serve six months.
Mandigo, Judah	Noyan Roveal, Lower Canada	He did not serve six months in person.
Mackintier, Eli	Wallingford, Rutland	Under age—a waiter. Deserted.

STATEMENT—Continued.

Names.	Residence.	Reasons for rejection.
Munsell, Benjamin	Sharon, Windsor	He did not serve six months.
Needham, Jeremiah	Finsburgh, Addison	He did not serve six months.
Nye, Elijah	Montpelier, Washington	Teamster in the quartermaster's department, December 26, 1838.—Hon. B. F. Deming.
Phelps, William	Manchester, Bennington	He did not serve six months.
Pope, John	Eaton, Lower Canada	He did not serve six months.
Power, Abner	Eaton, Lower Canada	Deserted.
Parkhurst, Benjamin	Chester, Windsor	He did not serve in any regularly organized corps.
Pottie, John	Stanstead, Lower Canada	He did not serve six months.
Pool, William W	Hartland, Windsor	Fraudulent.
Rice, Josiah	Guilford, Windham	He did not serve six months.
Ripley, Epaphras	Rockingham, Windham	No proof of service.
Royce, Stephen	Berkshire, Franklin	Under age.
Smith, Jacob	Bridport, Addison	Under age.
Stratton, Jabez	Hartford, Windsor	A waiter for the whole period of his service.
Stanley, Joseph	Greensborough, Orleans	Charcoal burner, and tailor for the soldiers.
Shirts, Hendrick	Swanton, Franklin	Deserted.
Smith, Johnson	Chalham, Lake of the two mountains, Lower Canada	
Sargeant, Edward	Hancock, Addison	No such service—no proof of service.
Starr, George	Highgate, Franklin	Left the service without leave.
Taylor, Edward	Ludlow, Windsor	He did not serve six months.
White, Samuel	Newbury, Orange	He did not serve in any regularly organized corps.
White, Abel	Hyde Park, Lamoille	He did not serve six months.

Whiteman, Benjamin	Duxbury, Washington	Did not serve in the revolution.
Welch, Archelaus (deceased)	Hanstead, Lower Canada	He did not serve six months.
Walker, Elijah	Vershire, Orange	He was a deserter.
Wilder, Joshua	Dunnerston, Windham	His services were not in a military capacity.
Williams, Silas	Royalton, Windsor	He did not serve six months.

Ex.—3

A list of persons residing in Vermont who have applied for pensions under the act of June 7, 1832, whose claims have been suspended; prepared in conformity with the resolution of the Senate of the United States, September 16, 1850.

Names.	Residence.	Reasons for suspension.
Allen, James	Barnard, Windsor	Suspended for further proof.
Austin, Elijah	Arlington, Bennington	Suspended for further proof and specification.
Austin, John	Dorset, Bennington	Suspended for a more correct narrative of service.
Burritt, Andrew	Hinesburgh, Chittenden	Team service previous to March, 1779.
Barlow, Nathan	Shipton, Lower Canada	Suspended for further proof.
Bartlett, Benjamin (deceased)	Jericho, Chittenden	He did not serve six months.
Blossom, David	Richmond, Chittenden	He did not serve six months.
Baker, Elisha	Charlotte, Chittenden	Suspended for proof of his commission as surgeon, and service rendered.
Bennett, Aaron	Pawlet, Rutland	Suspended for further proof and specification.
Bishop, Joel (deceased)	Stanstead, Lower Canada	Proof of identity required with a namesake of the Connecticut rolls.
Blush, Joseph	Williston, Chittenden	Suspended for a more perfect and less contradictory narrative of his services.
Bennett, Ebenezer	Warren, Washington	The rolls of Massachusetts bear his name, but the service is not identical.
Bloss, Zadock	Irasburg, Orleans	Suspended for further proof.
Bradley, Joseph (deceased)	Williston, Chittenden	Suspended for further proof.
Brown, Elijah	Pawlet, Rutland	Suspended for further proof and specification.
Buckman, Asa	Barnard, Windsor	Suspended for further proof.
Briggs, Delius	Derby, Orleans	Not on the rolls—no such officers—no proof of service.
Bliss, Samuel	Strafford, Orange	He did not serve six months.
Clark, Caleb	Rutland, Rutland	He did not serve six months.
Cummings, Ebenezer	Pomfret, Windsor	He did not serve six months.
Crary, Elias	Wallingford, Rutland	He did not serve six months.
Carman, John	Highgate, Franklin	Suspended for further proof.
Cumming, Rummington	Pownal, Bennington	He did not serve six months.
Crooks, Henry	Bainston, Stansford L. Canada.	He did not serve six months.
Campbell, Samuel	Saint Albans, Franklin	He did not serve six months.
Chapman, Benjamin	Grafton, Windsor	No proof of service.
Chase, Simeon	Cornish, Windsor	He did not serve six months.
Cook, Joshua	Chester, Windsor	He did not serve six months.
Cuthbert, Benjamin	Hinesborough, Chittenden	Service in a corps of artificers.

Name	Location	Remarks
Comings, Jonas	Calais, Washington	He did not serve six months.
Davis, David	Wallingford, Rutland	Under age—served as a waiter.
De Line, Uriah	Stanbridge, Mississkoui, Lower Canada	Not on the rolls—no proof of service.
Dake, Benjamin	Windsor, Windsor	No proof of service.
Dunham, Jesse	Royalton, Windsor	The certificate of the Secretary of State of Rhode Island of a namesake in 1775, cannot be used for service alleged in 1776.
Dyer, Charles (deceased)	Shaftsbury, Bennington	Suspended for evidence of identity with the service of a namesake, listed in the certificate of the Secretary of State of Rhode Island.
Evans, Seth	Chittenden, Rutland	Name not on the rolls, but his artillery service is sworn to by Brown, a witness, who is on the rolls—Massachusetts service.
Farron, Seth	Townsend, Windham	Five months twenty-four days service admitted—he alleges further service at the capture of Burgoyne, but fails of proof.
Fenton, Jonathan	Dorset, Bennington	In a corps which was merely always ready for service, but never called out.
Foster, Joseph (deceased), by John L. Wilson, administrator	West Fairlee, Orange	Entitled to a full pension as a sergeant of Infantry upon the return of his certificate, under the act of 1818.
French, Charles	Barnard, Windsor	Not on the rolls—no proof of service.
Field, Elisha	Cornwall, Addison	No intelligible or consistent narrative of service.
Field, David	Jericho, Chittenden	Suspended for further proof and specification.
Fuller, Johnson	Chester, Windsor	He did not serve six months.
Gage, George	Ferrisburgh, Addison	Suspended for further proof.
Gibson, John S.	Sutters, Lower Canada	Not on any rolls—no proof of service.
Gates, Jonas	Chelsea, Orange	Suspended for want of proof by the rolls.
Gouyd, William	Enosburg, Franklin	Suspended for further proof.
Guile, Joseph	Orwell, Rutland	Suspended for further proof.
Hawkins, Abraham	Wallingford, Rutland	The service from the rolls and claimants description of it differs.
Heading, Marcus	Ferrisburgh, Addison	A tissue of mistakes as to dates and facts—no proof or specification of service.
Hewlett, Thomas	Dorset, Bennington	Suspended for further proof and specification.
Herrick, Abel	Royalton, Windsor	He did not serve six months.
Holcomb, Noah	Bristol, Addison	Suspended for explanation of his course under enlistment in the continental line, in leaving the regiment before his term had expired.
Holt, Moses	Shipton, Lower Canada	He did not serve six months.

STATEMENT—Continued.

Names.	Residence.	Reasons for suspension.
Holt, Asa	Barton, Orleans	Suspended for further proof.
Hoyt, Abraham	Royalton, Windsor	No proof of service, either oral or of record.
Hurlbut, Bartholomew	Sheldon, Franklin	Suspended for further proof and explanation.
Huntington, Wightman	Middlebury, Addison	He did not serve six months.
Herrick, James	East Sheldon, Franklin	He did not serve in any regularly organized corps.
Heaton, Orange	Thetford, Orange	He did not serve six months.
Jones, Philip	Brandon, Rutland	He has not established six months service.
Kellam, Nathaniel	Irasburgh, Orleans	He did not serve six months.
Langdon, Seth	New Haven, Addison	Suspended for proof from the Massachusetts rolls.
Locking, Jonathan	Lyndon, Caledonia	Suspended for further proof.
Little, Samuel	Sheldon, Franklin	Suspended for further proof.
Linley (or Linnet), John	Ferrisburgh, Addison	No proof of service—not on any rolls.
Morton, John	Salisbury, Addison	He did not serve six months.
Magoon, John	Pownal, Bennington	Three months and ten days service as a soldier, and twelve months as a teamster in the quartermaster general's department, January 24, 1842—Wm. Smith.
Manchester, James	Pownal, Bennington	Proof not satisfactory—not by witnesses who served with him.
Morse, Jeremiah	Sutton, Lower Canada	The name is on the Massachusetts rolls, and claimant must furnish a witness who served with him to prove his identity.
Morton, John	Salisbury, Addison	A discrepancy of a year in the date of the service between the declaration of claimant and the Secretary of the Massachusetts records.
McMaster, Isaac	Pownal, Bennington	Claimant and his witnesses do not agree—are not consistent.
May, Benjamin	Concord, Essex	Suspended for a more particular account of his grade and service.
Meigs, Abner	Lyndon, Caledonia	Suspended for additional evidence.
Newton, David	Hartford, Windsor	Claims for service in Colonel Sheldon's dragoons, but he left the service before that corps was raised, by his own showing.
Phelps, Elijah	Grafton, Windham	He did not serve six months.

Name	Place	Remarks
Pinnock, Aaron	Craftsbury, Orleans	Suspended for proof and specification of actual service.
Pond, Adam	Weathersfield, Windsor	Service as a waiter seven weeks in 1779, and four months and a half in 1781.
Prentiss, Jonathan	Saint Albans, Franklin	He did not serve six months.
Pratt, Silas	Rutland, Rutland	He did not serve six months in a military capacity.
Pratt, Samuel	Pawlet, Rutland	Not on the rolls—no proof of service.
Putnam, Edward	Grafton, Windham	Suspended for further proof.
Parker, Sarah, widow of Joseph	Westford, Chittenden	The Joseph Parker of the rolls was in the infantry, and is the only one of the name—the widow's husband was a dragoon, and there was no man of the name in the dragoons.
Ripley, John A.	Berkshire, Franklin	Team service, July 11, 1845—T. L. & A. S. Smith.
Runnolds, Silas	Fairhaven, Rutland	Seven months ten days credited on the rolls for service in 1782, but claimant alleges he served previous to 1782—proof of identity with the namesake so credited is necessary.
Rood, Briggs	Fletcher, Franklin	Team service, December 2, 1844—H. H. Sylvester.
Rozer, Charles	Enosburg, Franklin	No proof of service—papers sent to B. Swift, April 24, 1884.
Richardson, Joseph	Weston, Windsor	Suspended for further proof.
Shearman, James	Lyndon, Caledonia	Suspended for a more precise specification, and proof of his minute man's service.
Spofford, John	Ludlow, Windsor	Case remanded for an inspection of the Massachusetts rolls.
Stevens, Henry	Windsor, Windsor	He was a deserter.
Sawyer, Cornelius	Reading, Windsor	He did not serve in a military capacity—service in the commissary and quartermaster's department, March 26, 1835—C. Coolidge.
Spafford, John	Cambridge, Franklin	He did not serve six months.
Sparhawk, Noah	Shrewsbury, Rutland	He did not serve six months.
Stilphen, Cornelius	Saint Albans, Franklin	No proof of service.
Snow, Jesse (deceased)	Brandon, Rutland	Suspended for more positive and direct proof of service.
Stevens, Jacob	Warren, Washington	The New Hampshire rolls credit the name of Jacob Stevens, but claimant has not specified his service, so as to identify him with the soldier of the rolls.
Stearns, Samuel	Stanstead, Lower Canada	He did not serve six months.
Seamans, John	Clarendon, Rutland	Suspended for further proof and specification.
Temple, Jonas	Lunenburg, Essex	Neither claimant's name nor that of his witness is on the rolls.
Trains, John	Tinmouth, Rutland	The proof of identity of claimant with his namesake of the New Hampshire rolls, lacks identity of service.
Tuttle, Thaddeus	Burlington, Chittenden	Suspended for further proof and specification.

STATEMENT—Continued.

Names.	Residence.	Reasons for suspension.
Vails, Nathaniel	Sharon, Windsor	Suspended for further proof.
Vosburgh, Abraham	Pownal, Bennington	Suspended for further proof and explanation.
West, Thomas	Dunham, Lower Canada	Suspended for further proof and specification.
Whitman, Noah (deceased)	Londonderry, Windham	Proof of the soldier's decease, and the names of the children by the court, and if there be no widow, the administrator, if one has qualified.
Wright, Samuel	Stanstead, Lower Canada	Suspended for further proof.
Wilson, Jeremiah	Norwich, Windsor	Wagon service, March 18, 1884—Hon. H. Everett.
Willey, Paul	Cabot, Caledonia	Suspended for further proof.
Williams, William R	Pownal, Bennington	No proof of service—not on any rolls.
Wicker, Samuel	Orwell, Rutland	Suspended for proof from the Massachusetts rolls.
Webster, Israel	Derby, Orleans	Suspended for further proof.
Willis, John	Saint Albans, Franklin	No proof of service—not on the rolls.

A list of persons residing in Vermont who have applied for pensions under the act of July 4, 1836, whose claims have been rejected; prepared in conformity with the resolution of the Senate of the United States, September 16, 1850.

Names.	Residence.	Reasons for rejection.
Durham, Hannah, formerly widow of J. Lawrence 2d	Enosburg, Franklin	He was a deserter.
Hall, Phebe, widow of Recompence	Westminster, Windham	He was a deserter.
Lucas, Abagail, (deceased), widow of Samuel	Sandgate, Bennington	He was a deserter.
Mann, Mary, widow of William	Ira, Rutland	Not military service.
Morrison, Rebecca, widow of Alexander	Cannan, Essex	He did not serve six months.
Pierce, Keziah, (deceased), widow of David	Rutland, Windsor	She died before the passage of the act.
Turner, Elizabeth, (deceased), widow of Samuel	Craftsbury, Orleans	Married after service; died before August 28, 1842.
Waldbridge, Chloe	New Haven, Addison	Soldier of the regular army; wounded prior to act of April 20, 1818.
Willard, Emily, widow of George S.	Rockingham, Windham	Soldier of the regular army.
Worcester, Isabel, widow of Samuel	Windsor, Windsor	Not any proof of service or marriage.

A list of persons who have applied for pensions under the act of July 4, 1836, residing in Vermont, whose claims have been suspended; prepared in conformity with the resolution of the Senate of the United States, September 16, 1850.

Names.	Residence.	Reasons for suspension.
Austin, Ruth, widow of Thomas	Richmond, Chittenden	Suspended for further proof and specification.
Adams, Abigail, formerly widow of Samuel Wyman	Cornwall, Addison	No proof of service; no specification.
Andrews, Sophia, widow of Eldad	Tunbridge, Orange	Suspended for further proof.
Austin, Hannah, widow of Seth	Newbury, Orange	He did not serve six months.
Bailey, Abigail, widow of John G.	Leicester, Addison	Suspended for want of proof and specification.
Barker, Prudence, widow of John	Royalton, Windsor	Proof of service unsatisfactory.
Barnes, Margaret, widow of Elijah	Shoreham, Addison	Died before the passage of the act.
Barnum, Anna, widow of Thomas	Derby, Orleans	To be admitted upon the production of the original of the family record.
Bingham, Elizabeth, widow of Ripley Brown, Abagail, widow of Jeremiah	Castleton, Rutland	Suspended for insufficient proof. Suspended for further proof.
Brownson, Mercy, formerly widow of Lemuel Bradley	Burlington, Chittenden	Suspended for further proof and explanation.
Briggs, Rhoda, widow of Ephraim	Barnard Windham	Suspended for proof of identity.
Clark, Jane, widow of Smith Clark	Sudbury, Rutland	Suspended for proof of marriage, and of her husband's identity with the Connecticut record.
Cleveland, Lydia, formerly widow of Nathan Kinner	Braintree, Orange	No proof of service.
Cole, Mary (deceased), widow of Gale	Monkton, Addison	He was a deserter.
Corless, Jane (deceased), widow of Samuel	Newbury, Orange	Twelve months' service admitted; date of marriage not proved.
Cree, Jane, widow of Joseph	Canaan, Essex	Suspended for further proof and specification.
Delano, Lois, formerly widow of Thomas Coots	Morristown, Lamoille	Suspended for proof of marriage.
Ferguson, Amy, formerly widow of Moses Haight	Starksboro, Addison	Suspended for further proof and specification.
Garvin, Mary, widow of Ephraim	Hydepark, Lamoille	Suspended for proof of the marriage and death of Garvin, and the names of the surviving children.
Gaylord, Lucy, widow of Hezekiah	Stanstead, Lower Canada	Suspended for further proof, and claim withdrawn.
Green, Esther, widow of John	Guilford, Windham	Proof required of marriage and of claimant's identity with one of the namesakes of the Connecticut records.
Green, Olive, widow of Samuel	Waterford, Caledonia	Suspended for further proof and specification to identity with a namesake on the Massachusetts rolls.

Name	Place	Remark
Hall, Sally, widow of Daniel	Burke, Caledonia	Suspended for further proof and specification.
Hawks, Silence, widow of Reuben	Moretown, Washington	No proof of service; name not on the rolls.
Hendricks, Sarah, widow of Joseph	Lunenburg, Essex	Suspended for proof of service from the Massachusetts rolls.
Hickock, Rebecca, widow of Benjamin	Fairhaven, Rutland	Service not proved for six months.
Hill, Jane, widow of Robert	Fort Ann, Washington	Suspended for proof of identity with the Robert Hill of the rolls, and of the marriage concurrent with the service.
Howe, Phebe, widow of David	Wells, Rutland	Six month's service not proved.
Hudson, Elizabeth, widow of Elijah	Minden, Rutland	Suspended for further proof.
Hunt, Hannah, widow of Moses	Troy, Orleans	Suspended for proof of marriage.
Jacobs, Sarah, widow of Lewis	New Haven, Addison	Suspended for more perfect proof of service.
Lewis, Elizabeth, widow of William	St. Armand, Lower Canada	Suspended for further proof from the Massachusetts rolls.
Lindsay, Mary (deceased), widow of David	Peacham, Caledonia	Married after the war.
Livingston, Margaret, (deceased), widow of Benjamin	Peacham, Caledonia	Suspended for further proof of identity with his namesake of the Massachusetts rolls.
Low, Abigail, widow of Obadiah	Bradford, Orange	The bible leaf of the family record is not genuine.
Lucas, Abigail, widow of Samuel	Jackson, Washington	He was a deserter.
Mack, Caroline, widow of Nehemiah	Plainfield, Washington	Plainfield, Washington; papers withdrawn.
Marble, Susan, widow of Joseph	Fayston, Washington	Suspended for further proof.
Messenger, Amy, widow of William S	Jericho, Chittenden	A soldier of the regular army.
Merrifield, Bethia, widow of Abraham	Richmond, Chittenden	Suspended for deficient proof.
Orne, Elizabeth, widow of Joseph	Corinth, Orange	Suspended for deficient proof.
Ovaitt, Sarah, widow of William	Pownal, Bennington	Proof required of the widow's identity with the soldier of the Connecticut rolls.
Parr, Mary, widow of Moses	Alburg, Grand Isle	Suspended for better proof.
Porter, Sarah, widow of Moses	Pawlet, Rutland	Suspended for a specification of the names of the officers and service under them.
Pratt, Sarah, widow of Benjamin	Burlington, Chittenden	No proof of service.
Prentiss, Lucretia, widow of Samuel	Montpelier, Washington	Under age—no satisfactory proof of service.
Richardson, Anna, widow of Stanton	Southfield, Washington	Suspended for further proof and specification.
Robinson, Ruth, widow of Benjamin	Bennington, Orleans	Suspended for further proof.
Smith, Sarah, widow of Frederick	Eaton, Orange	Suspended for proof of service from the records of Vermont.
Rogers, Mehitable, widow of Samuel	Eaton, Lower Canada	Service on board a letter-of-marque.
Smith, Mary (deceased), widow of Millard	Royalton, Windsor	He did not serve six months.
Southworth, Patience, widow of Uriah	Fairfax, Franklin	He did not serve six months.
Spafford, Mary, widow of John	Richford, Franklin	He did not served six months as captain.
Stedman, Hannah, widow of David	Hydepark, Lamoille	Suspended for further proof and specification.
Stebbins, Desdema, widow of Ebenezer	Cornwall, Addison	Suspended for further proof and specification.
Stewart, Huldah, widow of John	Middlebery, Addison	Suspended for further proof.
Stoddard, Elizabeth, widow of David	North Hero, Grand Isle	Suspended for further proof and specification.

STATEMENT—Continued.

Names.	Residence.	Reasons for suspension.
Smith, Sarah (deceased), formerly widow of Benjamin Grant	Strafford, Orange	Suspended for proof of marriage and the names of the surviving children and widow's decease.
Taylor, Lydia, widow of Elnathan	Royalton, Windsor	Suspended for further proof and specification.
Taylor, Sabra, widow of Absalom	Williston, Chittenden	Not properly set forth—no adequate proof of service.
Thatcher, Adocia, widow of Levi	Williston, Chittenden	Suspended for further proof and specification.
Thayer, Hannah, widow of Levi	Braintree, Randolph	He did not serve six month.
Warren, Mary, widow of Jonas	New Fane, Windham	He did not serve six months.
Witherell, Hannah (deceased), widow of Simeon	Reading, Windsor	Suspended for further proof and explanation.
Willeys, Bertha, widow of Ephraim	Middlesex, Washington	Suspended for proof of service.

A list of persons residing in Vermont who have applied for pensions under the act of July 7, 1838, whose claims have been rejected; prepared in conformity with the resolution of the Senate of the United States, September 16, 1850.

Names.	Residence.	Reasons for rejection.
Ball, Abigail, widow of James	Newark, Caledonia	Deserted.
Burton, Abigail, widow of Josiah	Norwich, Windsor	Deserted.
Colby, Lydia, widow of Thomas	Danville, Caledonia	Not a widow at the date of the act.
Capon, Hannah, widow of Ephraim	Williamston, Orange	Married in 1806—not within the act.
Delano, Lois, formerly widow of Thos. Coots	Morristown, Lamoille	Not a widow at the date of the act.
Dickey, Jennett, widow of Adam	Popham, Orange	Not a widow at the date of the act.
Douglass, Sarah, formerly widow of Lebrus Harris	Middlebury, Addison	Team service not provided for.
Fowler, Mary (deceased), widow of Elisha A.	Bethel, Hartford	Not a widow at the date of the act—died before August 28, 1842.
Freeman, Rebecca, widow of Pearson	Rutland, Rutland	A waiter—case not provided for.
Gibson, Abigail, widow of William	Woodstock, Windsor	Not a widow at the date of the act—died before August 28, 1842.
Haney, Martha, widow of Roger	Berlin, Washington	Not a widow at the date of the act—died before August 28, 1842.
Holden, Jemimah, widow of Joseph	Chester, Windsor	She drew a pension as the widow of Samuel Marsh, her former husband, and she cannot draw another as the widow of Joseph Holden.
Justin, Susanna (deceased), widow of Gershom	Whitney, Addison	No claim—married in 1818.
Knox, Anna (deceased), widow of William	Peacham, Caledonia	Not a widow at the date of the act.
Lovewell, Polly, widow of Robert	Saint Albans, Franklin	Not a widow at the date of the act.
Merrill, Mary (deceased), formerly widow of Daniel Clapp	Royalton, Windsor	Not a widow at the date of the act—died before August 28, 1842.

STATEMENT—Continued.

Names.	Residence.	Reasons for rejection.
Moorehouse, Rebecca, widow of David	Sharon, Windsor	Not a widow at the date of the act.
Morgan, Rosanna, widow of Caleb	Rochester, Windsor	Not a widow at the date of the act.
Nutt, Mary (deceased), widow of William	Topsham, Bradford	Died before the passage of the act.
Read, Lavina, widow of Frederick	Westminster, Windham	Married in 1808—no claim.
Rockwood, Sarah, widow of Samuel	Bennington	Not a widow at the date of the act.
Stone, Alice, widow of Nathan	Newtown, Windham	He did not serve six months.
Sturtevant, Priscilla (deceased), widow of Lemuel	Barton, Orleans	Not a widow at the date of the act—died before August 23, 1842.

A list of persons residing in Vermont who have applied for pensions under the act of July 7, 1838, whose claims have been suspended; prepared in conformity with the resolution of the Senate of the United States of September 16, 1850.

Names.	Residence.	Reasons for suspension.
Adams, Betsey, widow of Philemon	Shrewsbury, Rutland	Suspended for further proof.
Ainsworth, Polly, widow of Edward	Marshfield, Washington	Discredited by the rolls.
Barney, Fila, widow of Jeffrey A.	Shrewsbury, Rutland	He did not serve six months.
Batchelder, Susanna, widow of David	Groton, Caledonia	Eight months admitted—required to declare under January 23, 1845.
Bearwort, Barbara, widow of John	Grand Isle	Suspended for further proof.
Boardman, Betsey (deceased), widow of William Alburgh.		
Briggs, Olive, widow of Asa	Vershire, Orange	Married after 1794—died in 1842—no claim.
Bromley, Anna, widow of Joshua	Sherburn, Rutland	Not a widow at the date of the act.
Bugbee, Jemima, widow of Sylvester	Danby, Rutland	Suspended for further proof.
Burgess, Lucretia, widow of Nathaniel	Newbury, Orange	Suspended for further proof.
	Springfield, Windsor	Suspended for further proof of identity with the service of the Massachusetts rolls for six months twenty-one days.
Butler, Tryphena (deceased), widow of Ezra.	Waterbury, Washington	He did not serve six months.
Carver, Lydia, widow of Nathaniel	Pawlet, Rutland	Service not fully proved.
Clark, Martha (deceased), widow of Jonathan.	Sheffield, Midland District, Canada West.	Proof of identity required, and of marriage.
Cobb, Mary, widow of John	Shelburn, Chittenden	Suspended for proof of identity with the soldier of the same name in Colonel Swift's regiment, calling for four years ten months twenty-one days service.
Cook, Mary, widow of Uriah	Shrewsbury, Rutland	Insufficient testimony.
Cramer, Jemima, widow of Henry	West Haven, Rutland	Not on any rolls.
Crocker, Mary, widow of James	Thetford, Orange	Not on any rolls—team service.
Dodge, Lucy, widow of John	Cavendish, Windsor	Suspended for proof of identity with namesake on the rolls.
Dunning, Triphena, widow of Abraham	Weybridge, Addison	He did not serve six months.
Eddy, Hannah, widow of Josiah	Pittsford, Rutland	Suspended for further proof.

STATEMENT—Continued.

Names.	Residence.	Reasons for suspension.
Evans, Nancy, formerly widow of Jos. Bacon.	Randolph, Orange	He did not serve six months.
Fassett, Hetty, formerly widow of John Durham.	Alvey, Bennington	Not military service.
Fairbanks, Tabetha, widow of Pearly	Wardsboro', Windham	Not a widow at the date of the act—barred by act April 30, 1844.
Fay, Mary, widow of Nathan	Essex, Chittenden	Suspended for further proof.
Fellows, Anna, widow of Varney	Weathersfield, Windsor	Admitted upon a relinquishment of all further claim.
Freeman, Mary, formerly widow of John Blys	Bradford, Orange	Suspended for proof of identity with the John Bliss of the rolls, and for proof of marriage.
Freeman, Priscilla, widow of Alden	Orange, Orange	Suspended for further proof.
Frost, Hannah, widow of Daniel	Glover, Orleans	He did not serve six months.
Fuller, Deborah, widow of Witt.	Norwich, Windsor	Suspended for proof of service.
George, Abigail (dec'd), widow of Benjamin	Strafford, Orange	She died in 1839, and survived her husband a pensioner, under act June 7, 1832.
Gibbs, Mehitable, widow of Stephen	Pomfret, Windsor	Suspended for proof of marriage—service admitted.
Godfrey, Elizabeth, widow of James	Waterbury, Washington	He did not serve six months.
Gould, Submit, widow of Seth	Westminster, Windham	This widow has made two claims for the same service, superfluous.
Grant, Eunice, widow of John	Fairfield, Franklin	Artificers not regarded as military service.
Hurd, Abigail, widow of Aaron	Morristown, Lamoille	Suspended for proof of marriage.
Kelly, Naomi D., widow of Theodore	Calas, Washington	No proof of service as surgeon's mate.
Kelsey, Sarah, widow of Seymour	Marlboro', Windham	Suspended for further proof.
Kellog, Mabel, widow of Phineas	Randolph, Orange	No evidence of service yet presented.
King, Azubah, widow of Stephen	Shoreham, Addison	Suspended for further proof, and of identity with namesake of the rolls.
Ladd, Hannah, widow of Thaddeus	Thetford, Orange	No proof of service.
Long, Abigail, widow of Samuel	Peru, Bennington	Suspended for proof from the Boston records.
McAlister, Eleanor, widow of William	Alburgh, Grand Isle	Suspended for further proof.
McCoy, Comfort, widow of John	Rochester, Windsor	Suspended for further proof.

McNeil, Martha, widow of William	Sutton, Caledonia	Six months' service not fully proved.
Noyes, Eunice (deceased), widow of Oliver	Hyde Park, Lamoille	Suspended for further proof.
Palmer, Catharine, widow of Amos	Shoreham, Addison	Suspended for further proof and specification.
Parker, Bertha, widow of Alexander	Montpelier, Washington	Service not proved for as much as six months.
Parkhurst, Rachel, widow of Samuel	Townsend, Windham	No proof of service.
Pease, Rhoda, widow of Edwin	Brookfield, Orange	Married after the limits of the act.
Peck, Hannah, widow of Levi	Westminster, Windham	He did not serve six months.
Phillips, Mary, widow of Ezekiel	Townsend, Windham	Marriage admitted—service not proved.
Pike, Mary, widow of Ezra	Isle La Motte	Objections obviated by act of July 1, 1848—papers sent Hon. G. P. Marsh, February 12, 1846.
Pope, Ruth, widow of Samuel	Shrewsbury, Rutland	Suspended for further proof.
Pratt, Mary (deceased), widow of Josiah Brown	Spofford, District of Montreal, Canada	Strong suspicions of fraud.
Priest, Eunice, widow of Elijah	Mount Holly, Rutland	No marriage between the parties.
Putnam, Susanna, widow of Thomas	Cambridge, Lamoille	Suspended for further proof and specification.
Ritchey, Abigail, widow of James	Maidstone, Essex	Suspended for further proof.
Roberts, Sarah, widow of Joel	St. Johnsbury, Caledonia	Not a widow at the date of the act.
Sanborn, Rhoda, widow of Benjamin	Orange, Orange	Suspended for further proof.
Sanborn, Abigail, widow of Peter	Lowell, Orleans	Suspended for proof of marriage.
Small, Patience, widow of William	Morristown, Lamoille	Served as a waiter—not on the rolls.
Smith, Mary (deceased), widow of David	Braintree, Orange	Not a widow at the date of the act.
Smith, Patience, widow of Zadock	Shelburn, Chittenden	No records of formal application.
Smith, Sarah, widow of Daniel	Clarendon, Rutland	Suspended for further proof and specification.
Smith, Judith, widow of Abijah	Randolph, Orange	Suspended for proof of identity with a namesake of the Connecticut lines.
Spaulding, Lucy, widow of Isaac	Mount Holly, Rutland	Suspended for proof of marriage.
Spear, Polly (deceased), widow of Richard	Burlington, Chittenden	Admission upon proof of the dates of her death and marriage.
Stearns, Phebe (deceased), widow of Samuel	Woltham, Addison	Service admitted, but proof of identity and marriage deficient.
Stone, Rebecca, widow of Ephraim	Warren, Washington	He did not serve six months.
Stowell, Joanna, widow of John	Rockingham, Windham	Suspended for further proof.
Thayer, Mary (deceased), widow of Joseph	Morristown, Lamoille	Suspended for further proof.
Thurber, Bechiah, formerly widow of Samuel Shorey	Stanstead, Canada East	Claim admitted—clerk's certificate required of all the living children by both husbands.

STATEMENT—Continued.

Names.	Residence.	Reasons for suspension.
Walker, Patty, widow of Freeman	Hull, Ottawa, District Montreal, Canada	Not a widow at the date of the act.
Wells, Patty, widow of William	Hinesburgh, Chittenden	Suspended for further proof.
Whitney, Hannah (deceased), widow of Oliver	Cavendish, Windsor	Suspended for proof of identity, and that he was the only man of his name in the town of Natick capable of bearing arms in the revolutionary war.
Wheox, Prudence, widow of Joseph	Halifax, Windham	Suspended for further proof.
Woodworth, Lucy, widow of Ziba	Montpelier, Washington	Suspended for further proof.
Wright, Susanna, widow of Jeriah	Pownal, Bennington	The certificate of service from the Massachusetts records does not apply to claimant's case.

A list of persons residing in Massachusetts who have applied for pensions under the act of June 7, 1832, whose claims have been rejected; prepared in conformity with the resolution of the Senate of the United States of September 16, 1850.

Names.	Residence.	Reasons for rejection.
Adams, Jacob	Hancock, Berkshire	He did not serve six months.
Allen, William	Chilmark, Dukes	He did not serve actually six months; he was merely ready to serve.
Brooks, Edward	Marblehead, Essex	He did not serve six months.
Bates, Eleazar (deceased)	West Springfield, Hampden	He died before the passage of the act.
Blake, Philip	Franklin, Norfolk	He did not serve six months.
Bailey Joseph	Gloucester, Essex	He did not serve six months.
Blatchford, Uriah	Barnstable, Barnstable	He did not serve six months.
Boynton, John	Greenfield, Franklin	He did not serve six months.
Brett, William	North Bridgewater, Plymouth	Team service.
Butler, Rufus	Falmouth, Barnstable	He did not serve six months.
Bradley, David	Boston city	He was a deserter.
Brown, Elisha	Dighton, Bristol	Not military service.
Cook, John	Bellingham, Norfolk	He did not serve six months.
Cobb, Joseph	Fall River, Bristol	He was a deserter.
Callender, Stephen	Sheffield, Berkshire	He did not serve six months.
Campbell, Andrew	Boston	Recruiting service.
Collins, Moses	Shirley, Middlesex	Deserted.
Clark, Jonathan	Tolland, Hampden	He did not serve six months.
Daggatt, Samuel	Tisbury, Dukes	He did not serve six months.
Fowler, Mead	Westfield, Hampden	He did not serve six months.
Fish, Levi	Sandwich, Barnstable	He did not serve six months.
Graves, Samuel	Marblehead, Essex	He did not serve six months.
Grafton, Joseph	Newtown, Middlesex	He did not serve in a military capacity.
Geer, Ebenezer	Worcester, Worcester	Under age.
Greenleaf, Ebenezer	Newbury, Essex	Service aboard vessels sailing under letters of marque.
Hathaway, Joel	Bane, Bristol	No proof of service—no such service at the period designated.

Ex.—4

STATEMENT—Continued.

Names.	Residence.	Reasons for rejection.
Huxford, Cornelius	Edgartown, Dukes	Not on the rolls—no proof of service.
Hunting, Amos	Shutesbury, Franklin	He did not serve six months.
Ingram, Jedediah	Chester, Hampden	He did not serve six months.
James, Richard	Marblehead, Essex	Privateer service.
Loveridge, William	Deerfield, Franklin	He did not serve six months.
Mitchell, Bradford	Bridgewater, Plymouth	He did not serve six months.
Macomber, Rufus	Taunton, Prescott	He did not serve six months.
Monroe, Shubail	Hanover, Plymouth	He did not serve six months.
Miller, Thomas	Charlestown, Middlesex	He appears on the rolls of Massachusetts as an ensign, but there is no length of service stated on them. He also exhibits an ensign's commission, but no evidence of any pay is apparent.
Mason, Ebenezer	Spencer, Worcester	He did not serve six months.
Monroe, Andrew	Danvers, Essex	He did not serve six months.
Merrick, Stephen W.	Concord, Middlesex	Privateer service.
Mallet, Francis	Plymouth, Plymouth	Belonged to the French army.
Pearson, Silas	Newbury, Essex	He did not serve six months.
Pidge, Benjamin	Dighton, Bristol	He did not serve six months.
Pearce, Mial	Swansey, Bristol	He did not serve six months.
Phelps, George	Westfield, Hampden	He did not serve six months.
Porter, Isaac	Westfield, Hampden	He did not serve six months in person.
Pomeroy, Phoebus	Northampton, Hampshire	He was a deserter.
Parker, Elisha	Ashfield, Franklin	He did not serve six months in any regularly organized corps.
Richardson, Reuben	Dracut, Middlesex	He did not serve six months.
Smith, Jonas	Littleton, Middlesex	He did not serve six months.
Sargent, Ebenezer	Newburyport, Essex	Privateer service.
Shaw, Abraham	Abington, Plymouth	He did not serve six months previous to September 8, 1788.

Stacy, Benjamin	New Salem, Franklin	He did not serve six months.
Sibley, Samuel	Barre, Worcester	He did not serve six months.
Smith, Joseph	Deerfield, Franklin	He did not serve six months.
Shearer, David	Palmer, Hampden	Team service in the quartermaster's employ.
Simoms, Paul G.	Springfield, Hampden	He did not serve six months.
Smith, John	Newburyport, Essex	Privateer service.
Tourtelet, Jesse	Mendon, Worcester	He did not serve six months.
Thomas, Jeremiah	Middleboro', Plymouth	He did not serve six months.
Tilton, Salathiel	Goshen, Hampshire	Privateer service.
Tyng, Primus	Petersham, Worcester	No proof of service—no such colonel as he names.
Tupper, Peleg	Kingston, Plymouth	Privateer service.
Toby, Lemuel	Boston	Service in the French fleet.
Walker, Daniel	Rutland, Worcester	He did not serve six months.
Whitman, John	East Bridgewater, Plymouth	He did not serve six months.
Wadsworth, Wait	Duxbury, Plymouth	He did not serve six months.
W.tham, Thomas B.	Newburyport, Essex	Privateer service.
Wilson, John G.	Blandfield, Hampden	He did not serve six months.
Yendell, Samuel	Boston	He did not serve six months.

A list of the names of persons residing in Massachusetts who have applied for pensions under the act of June 7, 1832, whose claims have been suspended: prepared in conformity with the resolution of the Senate of the United States, September 16, 1850.

Names.	Residence.	Reasons for suspension.
Anthony, David	Somerset, Bristol	He did not serve six months.
Blossom, Rufus	Fall River, Bristol	He did not serve six months.
Bcarce, Joseph	Worcester, Worcester	This was an application for pension under act March, 1818, and rejected for want of proof.
Baker, Jeremiah	Dennis, Barnstable	He did not serve six months.
Baker, Ziba	Walpole, Norfolk	He did not serve six months.
Bacon, Norman	Watertown, Middlesex	Suspended for further specification and proof from the Massachusetts rolls.
Bacon, Joseph	Barre, Worcester	Not on the rolls.—no proof of service.
Briggs, John	Berkley, Bristol	He did not serve six months.
Brooks, Joel	Petersham, Worcester	He did not serve six months.
Brown, Ebenezer	Newton, Middlesex	Discredited by the rolls—no proof of service.
Brown, Joseph	Sterling, Worcester	There being more than one Joseph Brown on the rolls, some further proof of identity is requisite.
Brown, David	Attleborough, Bristol	Admitted as sergeant and lieutenant at $260 per annum, on the return of the certificate, under act March 18, 1818, December 9, 1833—J. L. Hodges.
Bates, Reuben	Scituate, Plymouth	Suspended for further proof and explanation.
Bates, Simeon	Scituate, Plymouth	Suspended for further proof and explanation.
Burbank, Henry	Milbury, Worcester	Name not on the rolls—no proof of service. Original application sent to N. Rix, Haverhill, May 30, 1834.
Butler, Eleazer	Boston city	Not on the rolls.—no proof of service.
Bradley, Eli	Lee, Berkshire	Suspended for proof of the public authority of the corps in which he alleges he served, as there does not appear any record of such corps.
Brant, John	Montgomery, Hampden	Suspended for further proof and specification.
Corbin, Moses B. (deceased)	Dracut, Middlesex	Not on the rolls—no proof of service.
Child, Jesse	Webster, Windham	He did not serve six months.
Clough, Jonathan	Belchertown, Hampshire	No proof of service.

53   [37]

Name	Residence	Remarks
Cook, Pitman	Egremont, Berkshire	It appears by a letter of November 20, 1849, to L. D. Alexander, that the papers in this case have not been examined.
Dennison, Thomas	Ware, Hampshire	Suspended for proof from the records at Hartford.
Easton, Ashley	Southwick, Hampden	Application for an increase—not allowed, September 4, 1850—Hon. R. L. Rose.
Fisher, James	Salem, Essex	No records of service known—name of colonel of regiment not given.
Frye, John	Andover, Essex	Suspended for further proof.
Folt, Samuel	West Springfield, Hampden	Papers informal, and there has been no correspondence since letter of July 17, 1832, to J. E. Bates—a copy of which cannot be found in the Pension office.
Grant, Samuel	Boston, Suffolk	Papers informal—blank form sent him, and there his case stands.
Grant, Amos	Marblehead, Essex	He did not serve six months.
Hudson, James	Wareham, Plymouth	Not on the rolls—no proof of service—names of officers not given.
Haskell, Ebenezer	Essex, Essex	He did not serve six months.
Hall, Primus (alias Trask)	Boston city	A waiter and a slave.
Hedges, Henry	Dalton, Berkshire	Suspended for further proof.
Hiller, Edward (deceased)	Roxbury, Norfolk	Suspended for further proof.
Howe, Francis	Barre, Worcester	Suspended for proof of identity with the soldier of the same name in the certificate of the Secretary of State of Massachusetts.
Hobart, Joshua	Leverett, Franklin	He did not serve six months.
Hud on, Obadiah	Huntington, Suffolk	He did not serve six months.
Hunting, Converse	Hubbardstown, Worcester	Suspended for proof of identity with the soldier of the same name in the certificate of the Secretary of State of Massachusetts.
Hurlbut, Asahel	Williamstown, Berkshire	Suspended for further proof and specification.
Huston, Samuel	Gloucester, Essex	Suspended for a certificate from the records at Boston.
Ingals, Daniel	Boston city	A storekeeper in the commissary's department—not military.
Keen, Jesse (deceased)	Fairhaven, Bristol	Suspended until the day of his decease shall be proven.
Kneeland, Abraham	Lincoln, Middlesex	Papers informal—discredited by the Massachusetts rolls.
Little, Nathaniel (deceased)	Newbury, Essex	Service to the same name credited as lieutenant on the Massachusetts rolls—some proof of identity required.
Laird, Joseph	Great Barrington, Berkshire	Team service.

STATEMENT—Continued.

Names.	Residence.	Reasons for suspension.
Mann, Nathaniel	Scituate, Plymouth	Not on the rolls for six months service.
Mann, Samuel	Antigonish, Nova Scotia	Declaration required before a court of record in one of the United States. No such officer belonged to the Maryland line as he names.
Mahew, John	Hopkinton, Middlesex	He did not serve six months.
Miller, Shadrach	Westborough, Worcester	Suspended for proof of identity with the soldier named in the certificate of the Secretary of State of Massachusetts.
Morse, Obadiah	Haverhill, Grafton	Suspended for proof from the Massachusetts rolls.
Morse, Jeremiah	Midfield, Norfolk	Proof of identity required that he was the Jeremiah Morse whose service is certified by the Secretary of State of Massachusetts.
Newhall, James	Boston city	He did not serve six months.
Nicherson, Ebenezer	Warwick, Barnstable	Discredited by the Massachusetts rolls—no proof of service.
Peckham, William		Papers enclosed in letter to Hon. Geo. Grennel, December 26, 1837, to place before Congress.
Pike, Elias	Salisbury, Essex	Not on the rolls—no proof of service.
Pardee, Aaron	Newburyport, Essex	Service in the staff required to be set forth before an increase can be granted.
Pease, Zachariah	Edgartown, Dukes	He did not serve six months.
Pierce, Robert	Marblehead, Essex	He did not serve six months.
Perkins, Elijah	Salem, Essex	He did not serve six months.
Pearce, Thomas	Yarmouth, Nova Scotia	Not on the rolls—no proof of service—under age.
Penn, John	Chelsea, Suffolk	He did not serve in a military capacity.
Potter, Jacob	Cambridge, Middlesex	Suspended for proof from the Massachusetts rolls.
Pratt, William	Freetown, Bristol	Application for increase disallowed.
Reed, Thomas	Williamstown, Berkshire	Suspended for further proof.
Rose Justus	Granville, Hampden	He did not serve six months.
Sanford	Berkley, Bristol	He did not serve six months.
Seymour, Stephen	Ludlow, Hampden	Suspicion of fraud and no explanation given.
Smith, Elijah	Waltham, Middlesex	Proof of service from the rolls offered is defective—name not alike.
Smith, James A	West Stowbridge, Berkshire	Not on the rolls—no proof of service.

Smith, Oliver	Oxford, Worcester	Not on the rolls—no proof of service.
Stafford, Stulley	Coleraine, Franklin	Suspended for proof of service.
Thomas, Peleg	Marshfield, Plymouth	He did not serve six months.
Thompson, Abner	Wales, Hampden	No actual military service.
Terrel, Amos	Plainfield, Hampshire	He did not serve six months.
Titus, Ishmael	Williamstown, Berkshire	Not on the rolls—no proof of service.
Tucker, George	Marblehood, Essex	He was a deserter.
Walden, Robert	Williamstown, Berkshire	Rejected for want of proof.
Ward, James	Boston city	Length of service not perceptible nor definite.
Wells, Ashbel (deceased)		Died before the passage of the act—married after 1794—no claim.
Wilmarth, Stephen	Attleborough, Bristol	He did not serve six months.
Willard, Daniel	Worcester, Worcester	He did not serve six months.
Winchester, Benjamin	Roxbury, Norfolk	Suspended for proof of identity with the service on the rolls.
Woodward, Nathaniel	Dana, Worcester	No proof of service, either oral or of record.
Wheeler, Benjamin	Boston city	Suspended for further proof—served in the commissary department.
Willoughby, Ebenezer	Boston	Under age—not on the rolls—no proof of service.
Woodward, Aaron	Wilbraham, Hampden	Suspended for further proof from the Hartford records.

[37]

A list of the names of persons residing in Massachusetts who have applied for pensions under the act of July 4, 1832, whose claims have been rejected; prepared in conformity with the resolution of the Senate of the United States, September 16, 1850.

Names.	Residence.	Reasons for rejection.
Alton, Susannah	Sturbridge, Worcester	He did not serve six months.
Black, Bethia, widow of George	Oakham, Worcester	Died before the passage of the act.
Bullard, Rachel, widow of Elisha	Franklin, Norfolk	Married after service.
Coffin, Mary, widow of William	Gloucester, Essex	He did not serve six months.
Cole, Anna, widow of Henry	Hamilton, Essex	He did not serve six months.
Chase, Mehitable, formerly widow of Jacob Rowe	Newburyport, Essex	He was a deserter.
Cory, Ann, widow of Benjamin	Westport, Bristol	Married after service.
Chapman, Asenath, widow of Peter	Boston city	Marriage day disputed.
Dunham, Lydia, widow of Cornelius	Abington, Plymouth	Privateer service.
Eaton, Susannah, widow of Nathaniel	West Springfield, Hampden	Married in 1805—not within the act.
Forbes, Elizabeth, widow of John	Rutland, Worcester	He did not serve six months.
Fessenden, Sarah, widow of Samuel	Westminster, Worcester	He did not serve six months.
Gouffram, Sarah, widow of James	Boston city	A soldier of the regular army.
Glover, Mary, formerly widow of Moses Metcalf	Wrentham, Norfolk	He did not serve six months.
Homan, Tabitha, widow of Thomas	Salem, Essex	Married after service.
Higgins, Susannah, widow of Thomas	Wrentham, Essex	Married after service.
Hazletine, Hannah, widow of James	Haverhill, Essex	Married after service.
Hathaway, Sarah, widow of Samuel	Gill, Franklin	He was a deserter.
Hovey, Deborah, widow of Amos	Salem, Essex	Not a widow at the date of the act.
Josselyn, Mary, widow of Francis	Hanson, Plymouth	Married after service.
Liswell, Susanna	West Springfield, Hampden	A soldier of the regular army.

Nichols, Phebe, widow of John	Malden, Middlesex	He did not serve six months.
Newhall, Israel, heirs of	Lynn, Essex	A soldier of the regular army.
Palmer, J. A.	West Springfield, Hampden	Rejected for want of proof.
Phelps, Prudence, widow of Jacob	Lancaster, Worcester	Married after service—died before July 7, 1838.
Perry, Mercy, widow of Noah	Wareham, Plymouth	Not a widow at the date of the act.
Pratt, Jemimah, widow of Benjamin	Middleborough, Plymouth	Married after service.
Pratt, Ruth, widow of Whitcom	Plainfield, Hampshire	Married after the war—died before August 10, 1842.
Rider, Hannah, widow of David	Rochester, Plymouth	He did not serve six months.
Robinson, Hannah, widow of Moses	Greenwich, Hampshire	Married after service.
Sawyer, Molly, widow of Samuel	Newburyport, Essex	Married after service.
Shepherd, Margaret, widow of Stephen	West Springfield, Hampden	A soldier of the regular army.
Vailing, Louisa, widow of John	Boston city	A soldier of the regular army.
Wood, Sarah	Middleborough, Plymouth	He did not serve six months.
Wheeler, Hannah, widow of David	Lanesborough, Berkshire	He did not serve six months.
Weed, Benjamin, heirs of	Marblehead, Essex	A soldier of the regular army.

A list of the names of persons residing in Massachusetts who have applied for pensions under the act of July 4, 1836, whose claims have been suspended; prepared in conformity with the resolution of the Senate of the United States, September 16, 1850.

Names.	Residence.	Reasons for suspension.
Ansart, Catharine, widow of Lewis	Dracut, Middlesex	Her first husband's service were not in a military capacity.
Appleton, Molly, widow of Benjamin	Hamilton, Essex	He did not serve six months.
Alford, Dorothy, widow of Jehiel	Northampton, Hampshire	Not on the rolls—no proof of service.
Alger, Sarah, widow of Daniel	Abington, Plymouth	Six months nine days admitted, but the marriage was too late—service in 1775 if proved, would protect the claim under this act.
Antel, Elizabeth, heir of Ephraim, minor	Windsor, Berkshire	No claim—married in 1829.
Bailey, Hagar, widow of Cæsar	Pittsfield, Berkshire	No proof of service—contradictory statements.
Baxter, Rhoda, widow of Malachi	Fisbury, Dukes	Suspended for further proof of service.
Boomer, Sarah, widow of Martin	Fall River, Bristol	Suspended for further proof and specification.
Bumpas, Abiah, widow of Joseph	Middleboro', Plymouth	Three several soldiers of the same name makes it difficult to identify claimant's service without more perfect details.
Butters, Elizabeth, widow of Benjamin	Medford, Middlesex	One credit for three months and one for five months to two Benjamin Butters's, who were in service at the same period.
Bent, Abigail, widow of William	Wayland, Middlesex	Suspended for further proof and specification.
Bangs, Desire, widow of Joseph	Springfield, Hampden	Suspended for further proof.
Barden, Olive, formerly widow of Benjamin Allen	Taunton, Bristol	Suspended for further proof.
Capen, Theodosia, widow of Purchase	Belchertown, Hampshire	He did not serve six months in a regularly organized corps.
Chandler, May (deceased), widow of Samuel	Duxbury, Plymouth	Marriage and service admitted—children must prove the day of her decease.
Coolidge, Molly, widow of Thomas	Natick, Middlesex	Not on the rolls—no proof of service.
Dana, Eleanor, widow of Stephen	Cambridge, Middlesex	He did not serve six months.
Death, Patience, formerly widow of Robert Potter	Wendel, Franklin	Suspended for further proof.
Davidson, Polly, widow of Benjamin	Charlton, Worcester	Six months' service admitted—marriage incomplete.
Dickman, Phebe, widow of John	Hopkinson, Middlesex	Suspended for further proof from the Boston records.

Douglass, Lydia, widow of John	Plymouth	Suspended for further proof.
Drown, Martha, widow of Frederick	North Dighton, Bristol	Commission as adjutant admitted—proof of service deficient.
French, Elizabeth, widow of Jonathan	Hingham, Plymouth	Not on the rolls—no proof of service.
Gragg, Rachel, widow of Samuel	Groton, Middlesex	Suspended for further proof of service.
Hamilton, Abigail, widow of Nathan	Brookfield, Worcester	Suspicion of fraud—see letter J. Hathaway, May 30, 1851.
Hodges, Mary, widow of James	Norton, Bristol	Suspended for further proof.
Hutchinson, Jane, formerly widow of Daniel Benjamin		Married after service.
Jewett, Ruth, widow of David	Sterling, Worcester	Suspended for proof of identity that her husband was the lieutenant and captain designated in the certificate of the Massachusetts Secretary of State.
Joy, Sarah, widow of Samuel	Great Barrington, Berkshire	No claim—she died without children.
Kirkland, Eunice, widow of Jabez	West Springfield, Hampden	Suspended for further proof.
King, Elizabeth, widow of John	Middleboro', Plymouth	Suspended for further proof.
McFarland, widow of Ebenezer	Hopkinton, Middlesex	No evidence presented in this case.
Marchant, Hannah, widow of William	Gloucester, Essex	Not on the rolls—no proof of service.
March, Elizabeth, widow of Nathaniel	Ipswich, Essex	Name not on the rolls—no proof of service.
Magown, Mary, widow of ——	Pembroke, Plymouth	Suspended for further proof.
Melross, Cynthia, widow of William	Ludlow, Hampden	Not on the rolls—no proof of service.
Merrifield, Rebecca, widow of Robert	Coleraine, Franklin	Suspended for further proof.
Morrell, Ruth, widow of Richard	Amesbury, Essex	Period, length and grade of service, and names of company and field officers required.
Moulton, Mary, widow of Joshua	Lynn, Essex	Not on the rolls—no proof of service.
Myner, Elizabeth, widow of Ephraim	Windsor, Berkshire	Served as a wagoner on the Hudson in 1781.
Nickerson, Isabel, formerly widow of Solomon Dyer	St. John's, Province of New Brunswick	Not on the rolls—no proof of service.
Owen, Elizabeth, widow of James	Boston	Awaiting inquiry about the case—no action yet had.
Pownall, Susannah, widow of John King	Boston	Not on the rolls—no proof of service.
Proctor, Hannah, widow of Daniel	Chelmsford, Middlesex	Not on the rolls—no proof of service.
Pinkham, Bridget, widow of Thomas	Chelsea, Suffolk	Not on any rolls—no proof of service.
Poland, Holland, widow of Joseph	Beverly, Essex	Not on the rolls—no proof of service.

STATEMENT—Continued.

Names.	Residence.	Reasons for suspension.
Pitsley, Mary, widow of Robert	Freetown, Bristol	Suspended for further proof.
Reed, Sarah, widow of Thomas	Swansea, Bristol	Suspended for further proof.
Reynolds, Sarah, formerly widow of Philip Tollett	Marblehead, Essex	A midshipman in 1778—married January 11, 1778—died February 25, 1778—the question is, whether he died in the service, or had resigned in order to get married.
Shaw, Hannah, widow of John	Monson, Hampden	Married after service.
Smith, Perses, widow of Elisha	Worcester, Massachusetts	He did not serve six months.
Smith, Mary, formerly widow of Zachariah Hall	Boston	Suspended for further proof—a master carpenter on board the Alfred.
Snelling, Rachel, widow of Joseph	Boston	Suspended for further proof.
Starkweather, Mercy, widow of Prince	Pittsfield, Berkshire	He did not serve six months.
Stanly, Jane, widow of William	Marblehead, Essex	Privateer service.
Standly, William	Marblehead, Essex	Suspended for proof that the service was on board a public ship.
Seaver, Abigail, widow of Joseph	Sterling, Worcester	Suspended for proof of identity that claimant's husband was the Joseph Seaver named in the certificate of the Secretary of Massachusetts.
Taylor, Eunice, widow of Benjamin	Orleans, Barnstable	Suspended for further proof and specification.
Taylor, Mary, widow of Joseph	Barnstable	Suspended for further proof and specification.
Williams, Elizabeth, widow of Isaac	Stoughton, Norfolk	The question is of marriage whether before or after service ended.
Wilson, Mary, widow of Nathaniel	Dover, Norfolk	Suspended for further proof.
Wetherbee, Ann, formerly widow of Solomon Taylor	Boston	Suspended for proof of identity that her husband was the soldier of May 8, 1777, under Captain Childs, Colonel Wells.
Wood, Mehitable, widow of Jonathan	Seekonk, Bristol	Suspended for proof of identity that he was the Jonathan Wood of the Rhode Island troops, or the soldier of the same name on the books of the Secretary of Massachusetts.
Washburn, Betsey, widow of Holton B.	Lynn, Essex	A soldier of the regular army.
Weed, Elizabeth, widow of Daniel	Great Barrington, Berkshire	He did not serve six months.
Winslow, Anne, widow of John	Boston	Married after service.

A list of the names of persons residing in Massachusetts who have applied for pensions under the act of July 7, 1838, whose claims have been rejected; prepared in conformity with the resolution of the Senate of the United States, September 16, 1850.

Names.	Residence.	Reasons for rejection.
Alden, Rebecca, widow of Elijah	West Bridgewater, Plymouth	Not a widow at the date of the act.
Ammidon, Rhoda, widow of Philip	Harwick, Worcester	He did not serve six months.
Bisbee, Elizabeth, widow of Gideon	Chesterfield, Hampshire	He did not serve six months.
Bliss, Mary, widow of Jacob	Springfield, Hampshire	He did not serve six months.
Briggs, Betty, widow of Jesse	Wareham, Plymouth	Not a widow at the date of the act.
Clark, Esther, widow of Comfort	Otis, Berkshire	Not a widow at the date of the act.
Clapp, Abigail, formerly widow of Benjamin Barnes	Northampton, Hampshire	He did not serve six months.
Cole, Elizabeth, formerly widow of Abraham Bumpas	Middleboro', Plymouth	Not a widow at the date of the act.
Coleman, Betty, formerly widow of Daniel Emery	Nowbury, Essex	Not a widow at the date of the act—died before August 28, 1842.
Cook, Cynthia, widow of Elihu	Hadley, Hampshire	He did not serve six months.
Fiske, Abigail, widow of Nathan	Sturbridge, Worcester	He did not serve six months.
Ford, Abigail, widow of Noah	Boston city	He did not serve six months, in a military capacity.
Fullerton, Persis, widow of Samuel	Worcester	He did not serve six months.
Gilbert, Kate, formerly widow of Scipio Bartlett	Salem, Essex	Not a widow at the date of the act.
Hardin, Rebecca, widow of Reuben	Bridgewater, Plymouth	Not on the rolls—no proof of service.
Harris, Mehitable, widow of Oliver	Windell, Franklin	Not a widow at the date of the act.
Hastings, Rebecca, widow of Moses	Brookfield, Worcester	He did not serve six months.
Hovey, Deborah, widow of Amos	Salem, Essex	Not a widow at the date of the act.
Homan, Tabitha, widow of Thomas	Salem, Essex	Married after service, November 28, 1782.
Holsey, Mary, widow of Dr. Samuel	Townsend, Middlesex	Not on the rolls—no proof of commission—none of service.
Hull, Ruth, formerly widow of Wm. Surrey	Newburyport, Essex	Twice married—first husband died in 1802, second in 1816.

[37]

STATEMENT—Continued.

Names.	Residence.	Reasons for rejection.
Kitfield, Sally, widow of William	Manchester, Essex	Not a widow at the date of the act.
Marshall, Hannah, widow of Moses	Essex, Essex	He did not serve six months.
Mathews, Mercy, widow of Nathaniel	Yarmouth, Barnstable	He did not serve six months.
Marsh, Elizabeth, formerly widow of Bartholomew Houston		
Maynard, Martha, widow of Benjamin	Salem, Essex	Not a widow at the date of the act.
Morton, Hannah, widow of Ebenezer	Shrewsbury, Worcester	He did not serve six months.
Morse, Ann (deceased), widow of Obadiah	Litchfield, Hampshire	He did not serve six months.
Morton, Priscilla, widow of Seth, Jr	Walpole, Norfolk	Not a widow at the date of the act.
	Middleboro', Plymouth	He did not serve six months.
Pratt, Ruth, widow of Whitcom	Plainfield, Hampshire	Not a widow at the date of the act.
Paine, Azubah, widow of Joel	Mansfield, Bristol	He did not serve six months.
Parker, Elizabeth, widow of Benjamin	Dunstable, Middlesex	He was a deserter.
Pease, Desire, widow of Peter	Hadley, Hampshire	Not a widow at the date of the act.
Pickard, Tabitha, widow of Jacob	Rowley, Essex	He did not serve six months.
Swain, Rebecca, widow of James	Nantucket, Nantucket	Not a widow at the date of the act.
Snell, Lydia, widow of Isaiah	Ware, Hampshire	He did not serve six months.
Sargent, Grace Denny, widow of Isaac Denny	Leicester, Worcester	He did not serve six months.
Leaver, Susannah, widow of William	Boston city	He was a deserter.
Smith, Sarah, widow of Amos	Holden, Worcester	He did not serve six months.
Stillowray, Ann, widow of Daniel	Newburyport, Essex	He did not serve six months.
Stimpson, Esther, widow of Ebenezer	Charlestown, Middlesex	He did not serve six months.
Snows, Mehitable, widow of Nathaniel	Chatham, Barnstable	Not a widow at the date of the act.
Thayer, Abigail, widow of Samuel	Windsor, Berkshire	He did not serve six months.
Warriner, Elizabeth, widow of Abner	Wilbraham, Hampden	He was a deserter.
White, Polly Devenport, widow of Thomas	Bridgewater, Plymouth	Not a widow at the date of the act.
Whitney, Susanna, widow of James	Sherburn, Middlesex	He did not serve six months.
Wilson, Nancy, widow of John O.	Natick, Middlesex	He did not serve six months.

A list of the names of persons residing in Massachusetts who have applied for pensions under the act of July 7, 1838, whose claims have been suspended; prepared in conformity with the resolution of the Senate of the United States, September 16, 1850.

Names.	Residence.	Reasons for suspension.
Amsden, Louisa, widow of John,	Southboro', Worcester	Suspended for further proof of service.
Atwood, Hannah, formerly widow of Francis A. Drew.	—, Suffolk	Suspended for proof of marriage.
Atherton, Myriam, widow of Joseph Gill	Gill, Franklin	Awaiting the production of the original family record.
Avery, Eunice, widow of Amos	Claremont, Franklin	Suspended for proof of identity with the soldier from Corentry, as evidenced by the comptroller's certificate.
Bartlett, Elizabeth, widow of Wyman	North Brookfield, Worcester	Not on the rolls of the three years' men from Brookfield.
Bird, Abigail, widow of Ralph Pope	Stoughton, Norfolk	Suspended for proof of identity with the eight months' soldiers of 1776.
Battle, Keziah, widow of Ithiel	Lee, Berkshire	Proof inadequate—not on the rolls.
Bishop, Susanna, widow of Joseph	Ashfield, Franklin	Proof of identity required that he was the soldier of Topham's regiment.
Bliss, Ruth, widow of Reuben	Monson, Hampden	Not on the rolls of Nixon's regiment.
Bowman, Susanna, widow of Francis	Lexington, Middlesex	He did not serve six months.
Boynton, Lucy, widow of Moses	Georgetown, Essex	Suspended for further proof and specification.
Bragg, Jenny, widow of Thomas	Yarmouth, Barnstable	He did not serve six months.
Brooks, Sarah, widow of Joshua	Lincoln, Middlesex	He did not serve six months.
Brown, Martha, widow of William	Royalton, Worcester	Served as waiter to his father—not on the rolls.
Burnham, Mary, widow of Nathan	Essex, Essex	He did not serve six months.
Chandler, Joanna, widow of William	Westford, Middlesex	Suspended for proof that the police court is a court of record, and for a certificate of the credibility of the witnesses.
Cheeseman, Mehitable, widow of Ziba	Braintree, Norfolk	An unsuccessful inspection of the rolls, under Captains Benniman, Wild, Thayer, Belcher and Hollis.
Cheeseman, Mary, widow of Abel	Hinsdale, Berkshire	Suspended for further proof and specification.
Chute, Ruth, widow of David	Georgetown, Essex	He did not serve six months.
Clark, Hannah, widow of Samuel	Lenox, Berkshire	Proof of identity by a recital of the officers under which he served to distinguish him among the six Samuel Clarks of the Connecticut line.
Claflin, Hannah, widow of Phineas	Attleboro', Bristol	Not on the rolls—witness mistaken—no proof of service.

STATEMENT—Continued.

Names.	Residence.	Reasons for suspension.
Clark, Ursula, widow of Amos	Medway, Norfolk	Suspended for proof of identity with the soldier on the roll of the same name, whose service must be specified.
Cobb, Margaret, widow of Samuel	Medway, West Parish	Suspended for further proof of marriage and decease.
Cole, Elizabeth, widow of Justice	Dalton, Berkshire	Evidence of identity compromised—claimant's husband was from Dalton, the soldier of the Massachusetts rolls from Hatfield.
Cole, Asenath, widow of Elisha	Sheffield, Berkshire	Suspended for proof of identity with the warsman of the rolls.
Curtis, Sally, widow of Daniel	Stoughton, Norfolk	Suspended for proof of identity with soldier of the same name credited with service on the Massachusetts rolls.
Dewey, Sally, widow of Silas	Deerfield, Franklin	Discredited by the records, both here and at Boston.
Dickinson, Elizabeth, widow of Aaron	Ludlow, Hampden	Suspended for further proof and specification.
Davis, Ruth, widow of Daniel	Haverhill, Essex	Suspended for further proof and a change of agent.
Ellmes, Elizabeth, widow of Benjamin	Scituate, Plymouth	Suspended for further proof and specification.
Edson, Lydia, widow of David	Northbridge, Plymouth	Suspended for further proof and specification.
Farran, Mary, widow of Joseph	Petersham, Worcester	No evidence of service—not on any rolls.
Flagg, Azubah, formerly widow of Rouland Lawrence	Groton, Middlesex	Suspended for proof of service from Boston, and of marriage.
Forestoll, Lydia, widow of John	Orange, Franklin	Service not fully proved—service in 1777 requires specification.
Gibbs, Chloe, widow of Benjamin	Plymouth, Plymouth	Suspended for further proof.
Gibbs, Hannah, widow of Joshua	Wareham, Plymouth	Further proof required from the Boston records.
Goodwill, Sally, widow of John	Chester, Hampden	Suspended for period, length and grade of service, and names of company and field officers.
Goddard, Sophia, widow of Gardner	Shrewsbury, Worcester	He did not serve six months.
Gould, Phebe, formerly widow of Silas Rose	Abingdon, Plymouth	Not a widow at the date of the act.
Griggs, Beulah, widow of Samuel	Boston, Suffolk	No service proved in this case.
Green, Mary, widow of Thomas	Auburn, Worcester	He did not serve in a military capacity.
Green, Waitstill, widow of John	Roxbury, Norfolk	Suspended for proof from the Harrisburg records.
Green, Sally, widow of Andrew	Gloucester, Essex	Service not proved—name not on the register rolls.

Name	Residence	Remarks
Hammond, Isabel, formerly widow of E. Whittemore.	Pelham, Hampshire	Married twice—not the widow of the soldier for whose service she claims.
Harman, Rebecca (deceased), widow of Elijah.	Charlemont, Franklin	Proof of identity required with the soldier of the same name of the Massachusetts rolls.
Haskell, Sarah, widow of Noah	Sandwich, Barnstable	He did not serve six months.
Hathaway, Elizabeth, widow of Isaac	Dighton, Bristol	The soldier of the same name on the rolls was from the same town where claimant says her husband resided during the war.
Heald, Elizabeth, widow of Eleazer	Lincoln, Middlesex	Not on the rolls—no proof of service.
Heely, Sarah, widow of Timothy	Boston, Suffolk	He did not serve six months.
Henshaw, Mary, widow of William	New Bedford, Bristol	Suspended for further proof.
Hitchings, Ruth, widow of Thomas	Saugus, Essex	Not a widow at the date of the act.
Holbrook, Judith, widow of David	Holden, Worcester	Suspended for proof of identity with the soldier of the same name on the records.
Hopkins, Thankful, widow of Giles	Barnstable	He did not serve six months.
Hunt, Elizabeth, widow of Joseph	Quincy, Norfolk	Proof of identity required with the soldier credited in Colonel Craft's regiment of the same name.
Jarvis, Abigail, widow of Joseph	Lanesborough, Berkshire	Suspended for proof of service.
Johnson, Martha, widow of Joshua	Andover, Essex	Five months seventeen days admitted—service in 1775 must be verified by the Boston record.
Johnson, Rebecca, widow of James	Medway, Norfolk	Suspended for further proof and specification.
Kimball, Mary, widow of Samuel	Lunenburg, Worcester	Proof of service inadequate.
Knight, Lillis, widow of Richard	Adams, Berkshire	Suspended for further explanation and identity with the soldier of the same name in Craig's regiment.
Knowlton, Abigail, widow of Malachi	Hamilton, Essex	He did not serve six months.
Knowlton, Betsey, widow of Joshua	Ashfield, Franklin	Not on the rolls—no proof of service.
Loomis, Zilpha, widow of Abner	Williamsburg, Hampshire	Records of the commissary department not in this department.
Lacy, Melitable, widow of Ephraim	Andover, Essex	Not a widow at the date of the act.
Lane, Alice, formerly widow of Moses Abbott.	Charlestown, Middlesex	Suspended for further proof of service.
Lapham, Sarah, widow of Caleb	Pembroke, Plymouth	A case for the joint resolution of January 23, 1845—If she be alive and will make a short deposition availing herself of its provisions.
Lamson, Miriam, widow of Samuel	Whately, Franklin	Suspended for further proof of more service.
Lawrence, Azubah, widow of Roland	North Bridge, Worcester	Not on the rolls—no proof of service.
Maker, Chloe, widow of Seth	Brewster, Barnstable	Not on the rolls for sufficient service—further proof awaited.
McKinstry, Bernice, formerly widow of Elijah Egleston.	Great Barrington, Berkshire	He did not serve six months.

[37]

STATEMENT—Continued.

Names.	Residence.	Reasons for suspension.
Miller, Sarah, widow of Leonard	Ludlow, Hampden	A difference in the term of enlistment, duration and grade between the service of claimant's husband, as stated by herself, and the soldier of the same name on the rolls whose service she claims.
Morse, Tabitha, widow of Joseph	Amesbury, Essex	No identity apparent, except in name, between claimant's husband and several soldiers of the various rolls of Massachusetts.
Nickerson, Deborah, widow of Enos	Harwich, Barnstable	Eleven months twenty-four days service admitted—date of the marriage required.
Nichols, Sarah, widow of Ambrose	Hingham, Plymouth	He did not serve six months.
Noble, Molly, widow of Eager	Westfield, Hampden	No evidence of six months' service.
Parker, Priscilla, widow of Elijah	Tyngsboro', Middlesex	Not on the rolls—service not proved—no such officer as Captain Wm. Abbott.
Parmenter, Zilpah, widow of Joel	Northborough, Worcester	He did not serve six months.
Payne, Keziah, widow of Ebenezer L.	Lenox, Berkshire	Suspended for further proof and specification.
Pierce, Elizabeth, widow of John	Newbury, Essex	Suspended for proof of further service.
Pratt, Lucy, widow of Alderton	Granville, Hampden	No proof of service can be discovered from the rolls from the statement given.
Randall, Amy, widow of Zilba	Easton, Bristol	He did not serve six months.
Rhodes, Relief, widow of Zebulon	Belchertown, Hampshire	Suspended for further proof and specification.
Rich, Sarah, widow of John	New Salem, Franklin	Not on the rolls—no proof of service.
Rice, Rebecca, widow of Samuel	Orange, Franklin	Married a second husband—not the widow of the soldier whose service she claims for.
Ryder, Mercy, widow of Edward	Yarmouth, Barnstable	Suspended for a more correct naming of officers and events.
Robbins, Hannah, formerly widow of George Runey	Charlestown, Middlesex	He did not serve six months.
Sampson, Betsey (deceased), widow of Isaiah, by Thomas H. Sampson, administrator	Pembroke, Plymouth	Barred by act April 80, 1844—not entitled under acts 1843 and 1844, as she died before their passage.
Simmons, Abigail, widow of Seth	Somerset, Bristol	No satisfactory proof of service.
Smith, Anna, widow of Calvin	Middlefield, Hampshire	Suspended for proof of service from the comptroller at Hartford.

Name	Place	Remarks
Snow, Sarah, widow of Amaziah	Stockbridge, Berkshire	No satisfactory evidence has been furnished in support of this claim.
Snow, Hannah, widow of Abner	Leicester, Worcester	Proof of service for six months insufficient.
Sprague, Deborah (deceased), widow of Saml, heirs of	Boston, Suffolk	Proof of identity of the widow with the pensioner of the Massachusetts roll required, and the day of her decease, and surviving children's names.
Steer, Lois, widow of Elisha	Southwick, Hampden	Not six months' service established.
Stone, Bridget, widow of Josiah	Shrewsbury, Worcester	He did not serve six months.
Sweetser, Dorothy, widow of Benjamin	Saugus, Essex	He did not serve six months.
Thomas, Polly, widow of Winslow	East Bridgewater, Plymouth	Service not proved by the rolls.
Thayer, Elizabeth (dec'd), widow of Benjamin	Minden, Worcester	He did not serve six months.
Tillson, Polly, widow of Elisha	North Bridgewater, Plymouth	No traces of the alleged three years' enlistment in the continental army.
Toppan, Ednah, widow of Stephen	Newbury, Essex	Suspended for further proof and specification.
Treat, Keturah, widow of Jonathan	Tyringham, Berkshire	Team service not regarded as military service.
Waldron, Mary, widow of Nathan	Dudley, Worcester	He did not serve six months.
Webb, Betsey (deceased), widow of Samuel, heirs of	Pembroke, Plymouth	Suspended for proof of service from the Secretary of Massachusetts.
Wheeler, Anna, widow of William	Middlefield, Hampshire	Proof of identity required, that the service credited to a soldier of the same name of fifth regiment, continental line, with claimant's husband.
White, Mary, widow of Luther	Sheffield, Berkshire	Proof of service and marriage not satisfactory.
Wilder, Relief, widow of William	Lancaster, Worcester	No captain's name for the eight months' service in 1775, and the rolls cannot be tested without it.
Williams, Dinah, widow of Nathaniel	Brownfield, Oxford	Suspended and returned for further proof, which has not appeared.
Williams, Elizabeth, widow of Thomas	Dorchester, Norfolk	Suspended for proof of identity and residence when he enlisted, to induce a credit for service by a soldier of the same name on the Massachusetts rolls.
Woodruff, Ruth, widow of Asaph	West Stockbridge, Berkshire	No service proved by the rolls.
Wright, Roxana, widow of Jude	Montgomery, Hampden	He did not serve six months.
Wyeth, Elizabeth, widow of Jonas	Cambridge, Middlesex	Suspended for proof of identity that he was the very Jonas Wyeth, a sailor, who served on board Captain Manly's vessel, the Hague.
Wade, Asenath, widow of Isaac	Hanson, Plymouth	He did not serve six months.

A list of the names of persons residing in Rhode Island who have applied for pensions under the act of June 7, 1832, whose claims have been rejected; prepared in conformity with the resolution of the Senate of the United States, September 16, 1850.

Names.	Residence.	Reasons for rejection.
Cornell, Benjamin	Newport, Newport	He was an armorer or artificer.
Frost, Gideon	Smithfield, Providence	He did not serve six months.
Green, Mary, widow of Thomas	Charlestown, Washington	Soldier died before the passage of the act, and rejected December 19, 1833, before widows' laws of 1836 and 1838 were passed.
Gould, Joseph	North Kingston, Washington	He did not serve six months.
Helme, Samuel	South Kingston, Washington	He did not serve six months.
Hopkins, Daniel	Foster, Providence	He did not serve six months.
Jones, Uriah	Cumberland, Providence	He was a deserter.
Kaull, John	Providence, Providence	He did not serve six months.
Perkins, Sands	South Kingston, Washington	He did not serve six months.
Potter, Olney	Gloucester, Providence	He held no commission as surgeon or surgeon's mate—did not belong to the army—never left his home.
Smith, Benjamin	North Kingston, Washington	Under age previous to September 27, 1781, subsequently, he did not serve six months.

A list of the names of persons residing in Rhode Island who have applied for pensions under the act of June 7, 1832, whose claims have been suspended; prepared in conformity with the resolution of the Senate of the United States of September 16, 1850.

Names.	Residence.	Reasons for suspension.
Arnold, Joseph	Hopkinton, Washington	Specification and proof of service required.
Arnold, William	Scituate, Providence	He does not appear to have served actually over one month.
Babcock, Cæsar	Newport, Newport	He did not serve in any regularly organized corps.
Bates, John	West Greenwich, Kent	Specification and proof of service required.
Bates, Mowry	Exeter, Washington	Specification and proof of service required.
Baxter, Thomas	North Providence, Providence	Service not verified by the rolls—minute men (except when in actual service) not under the act.
Brownall, Thomas	Portsmouth, Newport	He did not serve in a military capacity.
Brumley, Jesse	Hopkinton, Washington	Specification and proof of service required.
Chapin, Seth	Providence, Providence	Suspended for want of satisfactory proof—sent papers to Hon. Jos. Johnson, December 23, 1845.
Cole, Ebenezer	Gloucester, Providence	Not on the rolls—no proof of service.
Cornell, Thurston	Tiverton, Newport	Proof of six months' service deficient—claim disallowed.
Fish, Elihu	Providence city	Privateer service not allowed, otherwise he did not serve six months.
Gardiner, Stephen C.	Exeter, Washington	Suspended for further proof and specification.
Gorton, Hezekiah	West Greenwich, Kent	Suspended for specification and proof of service.
Hicks, Gabriel	Tiverton, Newport	He did not serve six months.
Hill, Jacob	Smithfield, Providence	Suspended for further proof of service, and of his age.
Lamb, William	Cumberland, Providence	Not on the rolls—no proof of service.
Lewis, Simeon	West Greenwich, Kent	Suspended for further proof and specification.
Proud, Samuel	Providence city	Readiness to serve is not service—he did not serve six months.
Richmond, William (deceased)	Little Compton, Newport	Suspended proof of. his death, and the widow if any, and children's names—see letter July 31, 1888.—A. B. Brownal.

A list of persons residing in Rhode Island who have applied for pensions under the act of July 4, 1836, whose claims have been rejected; prepared in conformity with the resolution of the Senate of the United States of September 16, 1850.

Names.	Residence.	Reasons for rejection.
Salisbury, Mehitable, widow of Charles	Gloucester, Providence	Not a widow at the date of the act.
Sims, Anna, widow of Samuel	Westerly, Washington	Married after January 1, 1794.
Tewgood, Mary, widow of Jonathan	Foster, Providence	Not a widow at the date of the act.

A list of persons residing in Rhode Island who have applied for pensions under the act of July 4, 1836, whose claims have been suspended; prepared in conformity with the resolution of the Senate of the United States of September 16, 1850.

Names.	Residence.	Reasons for suspension.
Burlingame, Content, formerly widow of Elisha Alrich	Foster, Providence	Suspended for further proof of service and of marriage, March 10, 1838—J. L. Tillinghast.
Deavenport, Comfort, widow of Pardon (late of Woodstock, Windham, Connecticut)	Providence	Period, length and grade of service, and names of company and field officers, September 9, 1839—J. L. Tillinghast.
Eddy, Sarah, widow of Oliver	Warren, Bristol	Eight months' service in 1775, and one month in 1778 admitted—proof of marriage required—Levi Haile, November 9, 1836.
Freeborn, Mary (deceased), widow of Henry	Newport	Not a widow at the date of the act—died before August 16, 1842.
Green, Anna, widow of Jonathan	Hopkinton, Washington	Suspended for further proof and specification of service, April 21, 1840 —sent to Mr. Wilcox.
Hopkins, Mary, formerly widow of Gale Burden (deceased)	Gloucester, Providence	Suspended for further proof, July 21, 1838—S. A. Atwell.
Luther, Charity (deceased), widow of Eddy	Warren, Bristol	Evidence yet insufficient to bring this claim within the act.—B. Cowell, November 8, 1841.
Phillips, Susannah, widow of Joseph	Richmond, Washington	Suspended for further proof, August 3, 1840—Wilkins Updyke.
Place, Mary, widow of Philip	East Greenwich, Kent	Suspended for proof of service—N. Whiting, September 8, 1836.
Sprague, Amey, widow of Samuel	North Providence, Providence	Not on the rolls—no proof of service, July 28, 1888—B. Cowell.
Thurber, Elizabeth	Providence city	He did not serve in a military capacity, April 28, 1845—B. Cowell.
Waterman, Elizabeth, widow of Elisha	Cumberland, Providence	The evidence predominates against admitting service for six months in this case, January 11, 1845—B. Cowell.

[37]

A list of the names of persons residing in Rhode Island who have applied for pensions under the act of July 7, 1838, whose claims have been suspended; prepared in conformity with the resolution of the Senate of the United States, September 16, 1850.

Names.	Residence.	Reasons for suspension.
Abel, Lucy, widow of Preserved	Bristol, Bristol	Service admitted—marriage in suspense.
Allen, Sarah, widow of Jeffroy	North Kingston, Washington	Service admitted—marriage in suspense.
Brown, Elizabeth (deceased), formerly widow of William Allen	Providence	Suspended for further proof of service, and decease, and names of children.
Butler, Betsey, widow of William	Providence, Washington	Awaiting a formal declaration and the necessary proof.
Burdick, Mary (deceased), widow of Ichabod	Charlestown, Washington	Suspended for further proof of service.
Clark, Ruth, widow of William	Newport	Suspended for further proof of service.
Cornell, Martha, widow of Benjamin	Newport	Period, length and grade of service, and names of company and field officers required.
Dexter, Lucy, widow of N. B. Dexter	Providence	Suspended for further proof.
Guild, Molly, widow of Ebenezer	North Providence	Suspended for further proof.
Macomber, Rebecca, widow of Jonathan	Charlestown, Washington	Suspended for further proof and specification.
Miller, Martha, widow of Nathan H	Providence	Not on the rolls—no adequate proof of service.
Potter, Miriam (deceased), formerly widow of Abel Slocumb	Providence	He did not serve six months.
Rathbun, Mary, widow of Ebenezer	Westerly, Washington	Suspended for further proof and specification.
Tiffany, Mary Ann, widow of Ebenezer	Barrington, Bristol	Period, length and grade of service, and names of company and field officers required.
Wilcox, Patience, widow of Robert	Newport	No definite proof of service, or that he was in public service when taken prisoner.

A list of persons residing in Connecticut who have applied for pensions under the act of June 7, 1832, whose claims have been rejected; prepared in conformity with the resolution of the Senate of the United States, September 16, 1850.

Names.	Residence.	Reasons for rejection.
Ackley, Nathaniel	Chatham, Middlesex	He did not serve in any regularly organized corps.
Armstrong, Jabez	Norwich, New London	He did not serve six months.
Asahel, Allen	Columbia, Tolland	He did not serve in a military capacity.
Anderson, Samuel	Sterling, Windham	He did not serve six months.
Barnard, Cyprian	Hartford, Hartford	Records of the commissary service of the revolution are in Washington, but they afford no proof of service in this case.
Beecher, Moses	New Haven	He did not serve in any regularly organized corps.
Bunnell, Daniel	Burlington, Hartford	He was a deserter.
Baxter, Simeon	Tolland, Tolland	He did not serve six months.
Barker, Jonas	Thompson, Windham	He did not serve six months.
Betts, Silas	Norwalk, Fairfield	Discredited by the rolls—no such officers nor service.
Bixby, Moses	Webster, Worcester, Mass.	No proof of service.
Buck, Josiah (deceased), children of	New Milford, Litchfield	Both parents died before the passage of the act.
Coit, Benjamin	(Papers withdrawn by A. F. Hudson, December 9, 1835)	
Cable, Nathaniel	Colebrook, Litchfield	He did not serve six months.
Clark, Jonathan	East Hartford, Hartford	Not six months military service.
Case, Reuben	Simsbury, Hartford	He was a deserter.
Cogswell, William	Tolland, Tolland	He died the first month of the service.
Cole, Nathan	Plainfield, Windham	Under age.
Converse, Damon R.	Kent, Litchfield	He did not serve six months.
Churchill, Samuel	Withersfield, Hartford	He did not serve six months.
Cowles, Samuel	Berlin, Hartford	He did not serve six months.
Curtis, David	Sharon, Litchfield	He did not serve in a military capacity.
Dutton, Thomas	Watertown, Litchfield	He did not serve six months.
Downer, Avery	Preston, New London	He did not serve in a military capacity.
Edgecomb, Samuel	Groton, New London	He did not serve six months.
Eggleston, Samuel	Windsor, Hartford	He did not serve six months.

STATEMENT—Continued.

Names.	Residence.	Reasons for rejection.
Ellsworth, Job	East Windsor, Hartford	Team service.
Fox, Amon	Waterford, New London	He did not serve six months.
Fox, Appleton	Chatham, Middlesex	He did not serve six months.
Godard, Tilly	Granby, Hartford	He did not serve six months.
Goodrich, Crafts	Bolton, Tolland	He did not serve in a military capacity.
Gillet, Adna	Granby, Hartford	He did not serve six months.
Griswold, John	Litchfield, Litchfield	He did not serve six months.
Gordon, Alexander	Bradford, New Haven	He did not serve six months.
Goodrich, Simeon	Wethersfield, Hartford	He did not serve in a military capacity.
Griswold, Samuel	Colebrook, Litchfield	He did not serve six months.
Grover, Daniel	Tolland, Tolland	He did not serve six months.
Hoyt, Nathan	New Milford, Litchfield	He either deserted or was expelled without pay.
Harrison, Lemuel	Waterbury, New Haven	He did not serve six months.
Hough, Asahel	Bozrah, New London	He did not serve six months.
Hyatt, Isaac	Norwalk, Fairfield	He did not serve six months.
Hall, George	Salisbury, Litchfield	He was a deserter.
Hart, Ard	Burlington, Hartford	He did not serve six months.
Harger, Elijah	Oxford, New Haven	He did not serve six months.
Huntley, Martin	Lyme, New London	He did not serve six months.
Humphrey, Noah	New Hartford, Litchfield	He did not serve six months.
Jones, Henry	Montville, New London	He was a deserter.
Johnson, Joseph, alias Thomas Rosencratz	Bethlehem, Litchfield	He was a deserter.
Judd, Reuben	Weston, Fairfax	He did not serve six months.
Kingsley, Asahel	Columbia, Tolland	He did not serve in a military capacity.
Kingsley, Warham	New Milford, Litchfield	He was a waiter.
Kingsley, Alpheus	Columbia, Tolland	He did not serve in any regularly organized corps.
Ladd, Elisha	Bolton, Tolland	He did not serve six months.

Lane, Joseph	Killingworth, Middlesex	He did not serve six months.
Leavenworth, Edmund	Bridgeport, Fairfield	Under age—a waiter boy.
Lilly, Jonathan	Sturbridge, Worcester, Mass.	He did not serve six months.
Lindsley, Obed	Branford, New Haven	Privateer service.
Lockwood, Reuben	Weston, Fairfield	Team service.
Lovell, Joshua	Sharon, Litchfield	He did not serve in a military capacity.
Le Barron, Solomon	Killingworth, Middlesex	He did not serve six months.
Lounsbury, Jacob	Stamford, Fairfield	He did not serve six months.
Marshall, Preserved	Avon, Hartford	Team service.
Mallory, David	Waterford, New London	He was a deserter.
Marcy, Alfred	Woodstock, Windham	Team service.
Mason, Robert	Simsbury, Hartford	Not on the rolls—no proof of service.
Norton, Eber	Guilford, New Haven	He did not serve six months.
Osborne, Abijah	Watertown, Litchfield	Not on the rolls—no proof of service.
Prindle, Samuel	South Lyme, New Haven	He did not serve six months.
Pierce, Benjamin	Brooklyn, Windham	He did not serve six months.
Porter, John	Columbia, Tolland	He did not serve six months.
Powell, John	Huntington, Fairfield	He did not serve six months.
Penfield, Abel	Portland, Middlesex	He did not serve six months.
Rogers, Abel	Lyme, New London	He did not serve in a military capacity.
Reed, Bejamin	Granby, Hartford	He did not serve six months.
Raymond, Moses	Bethlehem, Litchfield	He did not serve six months.
Strong, Eben	Warren, Litchfield	He did not serve six months.
Savage, Luther	Hartford, Hartford	He did not serve six months in person.
Sanger, Pearly	Woodstock, Windham	He did not serve six months.
Smith, Robert	Bethany, New Haven	Not on the rolls of artificers, to which he claimed to have belonged.
Sellick, Jesse	Darien, Fairfield	He did not serve in a military capacity.
Spicer, Abel	Preston, New London	He did not serve six months.
Sherwood, Jonathan	Ridgefield, Fairfield	He was a deserter.
Shailer, Hezekiah	Haddam, Middlesex	He did not serve in a military capacity.
Sherman, Jesse	Sherman, Fairfield	He was a deserter.
Simonds, Jeduthan	Windham, Windham	Team service.
Siely, David	Stratford, Fairfield	He did not serve six months.
St. John, Samuel	Ridgefield, Fairfield	He did not serve in a military capacity.

STATEMENT—Continued.

Names.	Residence.	Reasons for rejection.
Sipon, Jonathan	Lyme, New London	He did not serve six months.
Starr, Eli	New Milford, Litchfield	He did not serve six months.
Strickland, Stephen	Gastenburg, Hartford	He did not serve six months.
Strickland, Jonah	Bolton, Tolland	He did not serve six months.
Snow, John	Ashford, Windham	He did not serve six months.
Squie, Abiathar	Roxbury, Litchfield	Under age—served as a waiter.
Thompson, Amos	Mansfield, Tolland	He did not serve six months.
Townsend, John	New Haven, New Haven	He did not serve six months.
Tucker, Reuben	Derby, New Haven	He did not serve in a military capacity.
Thrasher, Seth	Ashford, Windham	He did not serve six months.
Webb, John	Windham, Windham	He did not serve six months.
Wilkinson, Joseph	New Fairfield, Fairfield	He did not serve six months.
White, Peregrine	Woodstock, Windham	He did not serve in a military capacity.
Waters, Theodore	Hebron, Tolland	He did not serve in a military capacity.
Wheeler, John T	Huntington, Fairfield	He did not serve six months.
Wolcott, Abiel	East Windsor, Hartford	He did not serve six months.
Walden, David	Windham, Windham	He did not serve in a military capacity.
Welsh, William	Chatham, Middlesex	Not on the rolls—no proof of service.
Whiting, Joseph	Hartford, Hartford	He did not serve six months in person.
Webb, William	Saybrook, Middlesex	He did not serve six months.
White, Elisha	Haddam, Middlesex	He did not serve six months.

A list of the names of persons residing in Connecticut who have applied for pensions under the act of June 7, 1832, whose claims have been suspended; prepared in conformity with the resolution of the Senate of the United States, September 16, 1850.

Names.	Residence.	Reasons for suspension.
Allen, David (deceased), heirs of	Somers, Tolland	Application for increase not allowed—full pension $480 per annum already granted.
Appell, Peter	North Branford, New Haven	Privateer service.
Adams, Titus	Simsbury, Hartford	Suspended for a more correct description of service.
Avery, Griswold	Waterford, New London	Under age—served as a waiter.
Bailey, Stephen	Miriam, New Haven	He did not serve six months.
Baldwin, John	Litchfield, Litchfield	The guard in which he served does not appear to have been raised and maintained by public authority.
Barber, Reuben	Windsor, Hartford	He did not serve six months.
Bartlett, Samuel	Guilford, New Haven	He did not serve six months.
Bennett, Benjamin	Lebanon, New London	Service of the rolls by a soldier of the same, not identified as claimant.
Bibbins, Benjamin	Windham, Windham	Wagon service.
Bishop, Jared	Guilford, New Haven	Service as substitute not sanctioned by the rolls.
Burchurd, Joseph	Wilton, Fairfield	The claimant being dead, the agent can no longer assert the claim.
Blakeslee, Ambrose	Plymouth, Litchfield	He did not serve six months.
Brooks, James	Haddam, Middlesex	He did not serve six months.
Button, Newbury	North Haven, New Haven	The artillery corps for two years permanent service under Captain Gallup, should be verified by the State records.
Burroughs, Isaac (deceased), heirs of	Mansfield, Tolland	Requisitions for proof of service not met during his life, nor did he make any application under act March, 1818.
Camp, Chauncey	Washington, Litchfield	Service of the corps in which he alleges service, must be verified by the records at Hartford.
Carpenter, Simeon	Tolland, Tolland	Militia service overrated—the duration wholly unprecedented and incredible.
Caswell, Julius	Kent, Litchfield	Commissary service if under commission will cover a pension, but if merely hired, it will not.
Catlin, Lewis	Harwinton, Litchfield	Not on the rolls of artificers in the department, nor at Hartland, and if there are none at Boston, the claim is null.
Couch, William (or Freeman, colored)	Fairfield	He was in the wagon service at the age of eleven.

STATEMENT—Continued.

Names.	Residence.	Reasons for suspension.
Cook, Submit, widow of Uriah	Barkhampstead, Litchfield	No proof of service—no specification—mere heresy service in the militia.
Cory, Sheffield	Voluntown, Windham	Militia service of Rhode Island overrated—claim rejected.
Crandall, Amariah	Willington, Tolland	He did not serve six months.
Clark, Gideon	Columbia, Tolland	Not on the rolls—no proof of service.
Davidson, Zachariah	Wallingford, New Haven	Not on the rolls—no proof of service.
Davis, Solomon	New Haven, New Haven	No admissible evidence of service.
Dart, Jonathan	Bolton, Tolland	Suspended for further proof.
Dickins, Martha, widow of Iristrene	Stonington, New London	Not on the rolls—no proof of service.
Dibble, Abraham	Granby, Hartford	Under age.
Downs, Elijah	New Milford, Litchfield	Suspended for proof from the State records, that the militia forces alleged in 1781, were draughted and paid for six months.
Dudley, Medad	Guilford, New London	Evidence of age and character, and proof of the authority, and length of service by the comptroller of Hartford required.
Dummer, Stephen	New Haven, New Haven	Suspended for further proof and specification.
Eno, Isaac	Simsbury, Hartford	He did not serve six months.
Fenn, David	Roxbury, Litchfield	Suspended for proof of service from the records and pay rolls at Hartford.
Fowler, Eli	Branford, New Haven	Under age.
Frothingham, Samuel	Middletown, Middletown	Claim for an increase disallowed—not entitled as an artificer, he worked at his trade as a tailor for his mess, under enlistment.
Fuller, John (deceased)	Burlington, Hartford	No action since his death—his case was suspended for want of proof.
Gage, Moses	Woodstock, Wyndham	Proof of service deficient.
Galphin, Amos	Litchfield, Litchfield	The paper in this case is copy of a petition to Congress to have his name restored to the pension roll, under act 1818, whence it was discontinued, because of the schedule of his estate being above the limit of the law.
Gardiner, Jonathan	Colchester, New London	Suspended for further proof of service from the Hartford records.
Gates, Caleb	Voluntown, Windham	Militia service in Rhode Island overrated.

Gregory, Nathaniel	Danbury, Fairfield	Suspended for further proof—the archives of the committee of safety should be consulted.
Griswold, Abel	Windsor, Hartford	Service not proved.
Goodwin, Nathaniel	Litchfield, Litchfield	Not on the rolls—no proof of service.
Hall, Timothy	East Hartford, Hartford	Claims for an increase as surgeon, instead of surgeon's mate required to be sustained in his grade by the certificate of the Secretary of State of Massachusetts—if he received more pay than is allowed by the computation of his certificate, he will of course be entitled to the increase.
Hartwell, Samuel	Washington, Litchfield	Suspended for proof of service from the comptroller at Hartford.
Hart, Hosea (deceased)	Avon, Hartford	He did not serve six months.
Hayward, William	Ashford, Windham	Proof of identity required of three years' service by a soldier of the same name in Colonel Bedford's regiment, continental line, from July 1777 to 1780.
Hazard, Thomas S.	East Windsor, Hartford	Suspended for further proof and the return of the original papers.
Hill, Reuben	Madison, New Haven	He did not serve six months.
House, Abner	Glastenbury, Hartford	No satisfactory proof of service.
Hyde, Joseph	Oxford, New Haven	Proof of six months' service falls short for want of the record evidence of the comptroller of Connecticut.
Jerome, Thomas	Bristol, Hartford	Not military service—a wagoner.
Johnson, Eliphalet	Kent, Litchfield	He did not serve six months.
Jones, Reuben	Wallingford, New Haven	Five months five days admitted—service in 1776 not specified by officers or particulars, and service at New Haven has neither date nor officers.
Johnson, Edward	Middletown, Middlesex	Not proved to the extent of six months' service.
Johnson, Reynolds	Lyme, New London	Coast guard service was not a continuous service, but were paid by the day—therefore, claimant must give the exact time he served.
Johnson, Ebenezer	Bristol, Hartford	Teamster's service claimed in the continental service under the special act of April 17, 1779, not proved.
Keeney, Ethel	Derby, New Haven	Suspended for the regimental officers' names, that the pay tables at Hartford may be inspected.
Kimberly, Ezra	Bethany, New Haven	Service not verified by the rolls, nor other proof—he was under age.
King, Joshua	Ridgefield, Fairfield	Petition for an increase not allowed—it does not appear from his papers that he was entitled to any greater pension than was allowed already.
Lyon, Hezekiah	Lewisboro', West Chester, New York	Suspended for further proof from the Hartford records, and some proof of identity, and causes of delay.

STATEMENT—Continued.

Names.	Residence.	Reasons for suspension.
Lamphear, Daniel	Bozrah, New London	Suspended for further proof and specification.
Lester, Joshua	New London, New London	The records discredited his original description, and the supplemental one corresponds with the records, and cannot be received.
Lucas, Israel	Glastenbury, Hartford	Not on the rolls—no proof of service.
Manville, David	Watertown, Litchfield	Suspended for further proof of service.
Marsh, Ashbel	Litchfield, Litchfield	He did not serve in a military capacity.
Mansfield, Joseph	Canaan, Litchfield	No actual service in this case—mere readiness to serve is not service.
Morey, Robert	Lisbon, New London	He has not established six months' service.
Morgan, Jonathan	North Stonington, New London	He did not serve six months.
Morse, Jedediah	Canterbury, Windham	Not any period of service stated, but those engaged in Sullivan's expedition were not in service six months.
Munson, Walt	Barkhampsted, Litchfield	Not recognized as actual service—no such corps is known to the department as that he claims to have acted as a sergeant for, for a year, in 1777.
Myers, Henry	Windsor, Hartford	Not entitled—no proof of service—there were no men received into the line of either of the States named for eight months, nor had they any militia under engagement for that length of time.
Mead, Thomas	Ridgefield, Fairfield	The regiment of Colonel Beebe was raised by act of assembly in November, 1780, which was not known until Mr. Mead's papers were returned to him—some explanation must be given of claimant's service in that regiment for nine months from April 1, 1780.
Neff, Oliver	Chaplin, Windham	He did not serve six months.
Northam, Jonathan	Marlborough, Hartford	Team service not provided for.
Oscar, Anthony F. (deceased)	Milford, New Haven	He was a deserter.
Olmsted, John	East Haddam, Middlesex	He will be allowed for two months' service in 1776, and for such term as the records of the secretary or comptroller of Connecticut may show that Colonel Tyler served in 1777.
Overton, Seth	Chatham, Middlesex	Privateer service.
Palmiter, Paul	Burlington, Hartford	Not on the Rhode Island rolls—no proof of service.

Name	Location	Remarks
Parker, Stephen	Cheshire, New Haven	Suspended for more satisfactory proof of service.
Pennoyer, William	Stamford, Fairfield	Not on the rolls—no proof of service.
Penny, Butler	Simsbury, Hartford	Not on the rolls of Colonel Webb's regiment in which it is said he served.
Perry, William	Lebanon, New London	There were no troops raised in Rhode Island in 1775 for twelve months.
Phillips, Ayer	Plainfield, Windham	He did not serve six months.
Platt, Nathan	Waterbury, New Haven	He did not serve six months.
Porter, Elias C	Hartford, Hartford	He did not serve six months.
Prior, Gideon	Waterbury, New Haven	Served as a wagon driver of the French army.
Reed, David (deceased)	Hebron, Tolland	No evidence of service whatever.
Robbins, Joshua	Wethersfield, Hartford	Suspended for proof of identity that he was the soldier of the same name on the rolls of the Connecticut continental line for 1781.
Robinson (or Robbins), Samuel	Central Village, Windham	Service whether sergeant or clerk in dispute.
Root, Nathan	Tolland, Tolland	Petition for increase not allowed—no more service proved to call for it.
Rees, Asa	Ashford, Windham	Remanded for the regimental and field officers, and a more specific description of service.
Savage, Luther (deceased), by Thomas his brother	Middletown, Middlesex	Administrator not entitled, except for the benefit of children—claim rejected for arrears of pension.
Scranton, Timothy	Madison, New Haven	He was once stricken from the pension rolls and afterwards restored, and he now petitions for the money withheld *ad interim*—not allowed.
Seymour, Henry	Hartford, Hartford	A commissary clerk—served the contractor for supplies for West Point in 1782—no claim.
Sherman, Elijah (dec'd), by Betty his widow	Woodbury, Litchfield	Not on the rolls of the continental line, and if the case is the same with the pay tables at Hartford, the conclusion is, he employed a substitute, and is not entitled.
Smith, Benjamin (deceased)	Windham, Windham	Fraudulent—attempt at imposition—see letter June 26, 1846—Hon. J. Dixon.
Starr, Thomas	Reading, Fairfield	He did not serve six months.
Stoddard, William	Chatham, Middlesex	Name not on any rolls—no proof of service.
Terry, James, senior	Stafford Springs, Tolland	Eight months' service alleged in 1775—not on the rolls of Captain Jos. Stebben—perhaps he has made a mistake in the captain's name.
Thompson, Abraham	New Haven	Not six months' service fully proved in this case.
Thompson, Jedediah	Griswold, New London	No such service—no such officer—destitute of the shadow of proof.
Todd, Eli	Litchfield, Litchfield	Not on the rolls—no proof of service.
Tomlinson, Henry	Oxford, New Haven	Only three months' service sufficiently proved.

STATEMENT—Continued.

Names.	Residence.	Reasons for suspension.
Turner, Stephen	Coventry, Tolland	A certificate of service in this case is presented, which bears evident marks of alteration.
Turner, Enoch	Sherman, Fairfield	Suspended for further proof.
Tyler, Daniel	Lebanon, New London	Suspended for further proof.
Wolcott, Oliver (deceased)	Litchfield, Litchfield	Laura W. Gibbs, the only surviving child, is the only person authorised to make application in this case.
Woodruff, Jason	Farmington, Hartford	Service extremely doubtful—see letter to L. Whitman, September 28, 1886.
Wells, Ashbel	Hartford, Hartford	He died before the passage of the act.

A list of the names of persons residing in Connecticut who have applied for pensions under the act of July 4, 1836, whose claims have been rejected; prepared in conformity with the resolution of the Senate of the United States, September 16, 1850.

Names.	Residence.	Reasons for rejection.
Avery, Rebecca, widow of Nathan	Lyme, New London	He did not serve six months.
Andrews, Anne, widow of Abraham	Hartford, Hartford	A soldier of the regular army.
Barnum, Abigail, widow of Josiah	Cornwall, Litchfield	Not on the rolls—no proof of service.
Clark, Sarah, widow of David	Granby, Hartford	Not the wife of the person whose services were certified—proof of identity not satisfactory.
Crandall, Katharine, widow of Simeon	Groton, New London	Married after service.
French, Elizabeth, widow of Cromwell	Stratford, Fairfield	He did not serve six months.
Frances, Mary, widow of James	Middletown, Middlesex	He was a deserter.
Foot, Lucy, widow of Jacob	Burlington, Hartford	He did not serve six months.
Fairchild, Assiah, formerly widow of Noadiah Holcomb	Granby, Hartford	Not a widow at the passage of the act of July 7, 1838—was married also after service, and died before August 23, 1842.
Hillyer, Jane, widow of Pliny	Granby, Hartford	He did not serve six months.
Hillyer, Penelope, formerly widow of David Goodrich	Granby, Hartford	He did not serve six months.
Jones, Lucretia, widow of George	Harwinton, Litchfield	Married after service—not a widow at the date of the act July 7, 1838.
Jessup, Rebecca, widow of Ebenezer	Greenwich, Fairfield	Married after service, viz. in 1784.
Olmsted, James (deceased)	East Hartford, Hartford	Both parties died before the passage of the act.
Potter, Martha, widow of Timothy	New Haven, New Haven	Married after service.
Pardee, Sarah, widow of Joseph	East Haven, New Haven	Not a widow at the date of the act.
Ripley, Mary, widow of Jabez	Coventry, Tolland	He did not serve six months.

STATEMENT—Continued.

Names.	Residence.	Reasons for rejection.
Sampson, Tamar, widow of Zephaniah	Lisbon, New London	Married after service—died before July 7, 1888.
Sargent, Sarah, widow of Elijah	Thompson, Windham	Married after service.
Tucker, Huldah, widow of Zephaniah	Woodstock, Windham	He was a deserter.
Thorp, Naomi, widow of Amos	New London, New London	Married after service.
Watson, Ann, widow of Timothy	East Windsor, Hartford	He did not serve six months.

A list of the names of persons residing in Connecticut who have applied for pensions under the act of July 4, 1836, whose claims have been suspended; prepared in conformity with the resolution of the Senate of the United States, September 16, 1850.

Names.	Residence.	Reasons for suspension.
Adams, Hetty (deceased), formerly widow of Asa Hoskins.	Bloomfield, Hartford.	His service as a wagon driver was not considered military service.
Brockway, Sarah, formerly widow of Isaac Sill.	Hebron, Tolland.	Suspended for proof of service by the Hartford comptroller—seven months in 1775—marriage also in suspense.
Booth, Sarah, widow of John.	Hartford, Hartford.	Married after service—service in 1777—marriage in 1778.
Brooks, Hannah, widow of Lemuel.	Norwalk, Fairfield.	Evidence of service in a military capacity not sufficient.
Carrier, Rebecca, widow of David.	Conway, Franklin.	Suspended for proof of service from the Secretary of State and Comptroller of Connecticut, also proof of marriage required.
Champlin, Thankful, widow of Oliver.	Montville, New London.	Evidence not complete that he served in any regularly organized corps.
Clark, Olivia, widow of Jesse.	Granby, Hartford.	The date of the wedding, and the period, length and grade of service, and names of company and field officers required.
Cole, Lois, widow of Jonathan.	Kent, Litchfield.	A more specific description required of the last three months' term, compared with the comptroller's records for verification.
Davis, Betsey, widow of Micajah.	Norwich, New London.	Proof required of the three months' service under Captain Deshon, by the comptroller, and some further proof of marriage.
Doolittle, Sarah, widow of Ezra.	Cheshire, New Haven.	Suspended for the officer's names and for reference to the comptroller.
Elderkin, Mary, widow of Elisha.	Kellingworth, Middlesex.	Married in September, 1781—it will be necessary to prove that Captain Elderkin was paid for service after September 29, 1781, or no allowance can be made under this act.
Foster, Pruilla, widow of John.	Reading, Hartford.	Suspended for further proof of the date of the marriage—proof of service admitted.
Foster, Lucretia, widow of Wareham.	Ellington, Tolland.	A definite statement of the soldier's services, grade officers, and duration is required, in order to an inspection of the rolls.
Foote, Hannah, formerly widow of Robert Kimberly.	Guilford, New Haven.	Married after service—service in 1777—marriage in 1781.

STATEMENT—Continued.

Names.	Residence.	Reasons for suspension.
Gibbs, Ruth (deceased), widow of Steven, heirs of.	Hartford.	Married after service.
Goddard, Rosanna, widow of Isaac.	Granby, Hartford.	Suspended for further proof of marriage and service.
Hopson, Sarah, widow of Rew.	Branford, New Haven.	Names of officers wanted for the service of 1776, and proof of service.
Howard, Sarah, widow of James.	Hampton, Windham.	He did not serve in a military capacity.
Lyman, Sarah, widow of Jonathan.	Derby, New Haven.	Married June 26, 1788, after her husband had left the service.
Loomis, Hannah, formerly widow of Charles Webster.	Torrington, Litchfield.	No evidence that her husband was the person named in the comptroller's certificate as having served in the short levies of 1780, for five months thirteen days—proof of marriage not satisfactory.
Leonard, Abigail, widow of Ebenezer.	Ledyard, New London.	Her husband died in 1776, and his name is not on the rolls—the probability is he was taken sick before he had served six months.
Miller, Sarah, formerly widow of Wm. Blake	Greenwich, Fairfield.	Proof of marriage not precise, and service must be more particularly set forth.
Mix, Lucy, formerly widow of Sharp. Liberty.	Cheshire, New Haven.	The time he served is doubtful, and the marriage day is not proved with requisite certainty.
Mills, Sarah, widow of Jedediah.	Hartford, Hartford.	Proof of service for six months not sufficient—her husband was an invalid pensioner, and died in 1832.
Moss, Lucy, widow of Thomas.	Cheshire, New Haven.	Explicit statement of service, officer's names, grade, and duration of the claimant's husband's military duty required.
Pease, Elizabeth, widow of Joseph.	Derby, New Haven.	Suspended for further proof and specification.
Peck, Isabel, widow of David.	Brookfield, Fairfield.	Proof of service doubtful.
Root, Phebe (deceased), by Marvin Curtis, administrator.	Hebron, Tolland.	Widow died in 1833, and was not a widow at the date of the act.
Rood, Lucretia, widow of David.	Canaan, Litchfield.	Evidence wanting to identify her husband with the soldier of the Connecticut line bearing his name.
Sawyer, Mary, widow of Samuel.	Cornwall, Litchfield.	He died in 1812, and there are no records of his revolutionary service to be found.

Sherwood, Jane, widow of David	Fairfield, Fairfield	Suspended for further proof.
Simons, Prudence (deceased), widow of Abner	Wethersfield, Hartford	Married after service, and died before the passage of the act July 7, 1888.
Simons, Julia, widow of Lycus	Haddam, Middlesex	Testimony of witness wholly discredited—seven years' proof of service in no way satisfactory—he was pensioned for one year's service in 1776, and never pretended to any other.
Spencer, Anna P., widow of Jehiel	Derby, New Haven	The original proceedings in this case are wholly inadmissible, and not to be countenanced by the department.
Spencer, Mary, widow of John	Hartford, Hartford	Not six months' service established.
Stedman, Lucy (deceased), formerly widow of Abriel Huntley	Salem, New London	Proof of marriage required, and of identity of claimant's husband with the soldier bearing his name, whose services are certified by the Comptroller of Connecticut.
Thompson, Lucy, widow of Thomas	Tolland, Tolland	It will be assumed until proved otherwise by the Hartford records, that Hosford's regiment was, like the other militia of that State, in service but two months' in the fall of 1776.
Young, Abigail, widow of Robert	Stamford, Fairfield	Married after service—admitted under act July 7, 1888.

A list of the names of persons residing in Connecticut who have applied for pensions under the act of July 7, 1838, whose claims have been rejected; prepared in conformity with the resolution of the Senate of the United States, September 16, 1850.

Names.	Residence.	Reasons for rejection.
Bixby, Mary (deceased), widow of Aaron.	Thompson, Windham.	Was not a widow at the date of the act.
Curtice, Eunice, widow of Andrew.	Trumbull, Fairfield.	Not a widow June 7, 1832—died before August 16, 1842.
Cressy, Eunice, widow of Gould.	Southington, Hartford.	Not a widow at the date of the act.
Darrow, Sally, widow of William.	Waterford, New London.	Married in 1808.
Dorman, Mabel, widow of David.	New Haven, New Haven.	He was a deserter.
Dennis, Anna, widow of Captain S. Billings.	Bozrah, New London.	Not a widow at the date of the act.
Dalton, Elizabeth, widow of Josiah Buck.	New Fairfield, Fairfield.	Both parties died before the passage of the act.
Fowler, Ruth, widow of Nathaniel.	Guilford, New Haven.	Not a widow at the date of the act.
Hayward, Nancy, widow of William.	Ashford, Windham.	He did not serve six months.
Hibbard, Rebecca, widow of Bushnell.	Pomfret, Windham.	Not a widow at the date of the act.
Lord, Mercy, formerly widow of Jona. Whaley	Pomfret, Windham.	Not a widow at the date of the act.
Maynard, Anna (deceased), widow of Francis	Norwich, New London.	He was a deserter.
Rowe, Mary, widow of Isaiah.	Farmington, Hartford.	He did not serve six months.
Safford, Mary, widow of Rufus.	Canterbury, Windham.	He did not serve six months.
Seymour, Mabel (deceased), widow of George	East Hartford, Hartford.	Died before the passage of the act.
Stent, Rhoda, widow of Eleazer.	Bransford, New Haven.	He did not serve six months.
Smith, Lydia, widow of Benjamin Cox.	East Haven, New Haven.	He was a deserter.
Stoddard, Lucretia (dec'd), widow of Daniel.	Ledyard, New London.	Not a widow at the date of the act— died before August 28, 1842.
Tucker, Elizabeth, widow of Elisha.	Voluntown, Windham.	Not a widow at the date of the act.
Wallis, Eleanor, widow of Zebulon.	Granby, Hartford.	He was a deserter.

A list of the names of persons residing in Connecticut who have applied for pensions under the act of July 7, 1838, whose claims have been suspended; prepared in conformity with the resolution of the Senate of the United States, September 16, 1850.

Names.	Residence.	Reasons for suspension.
Allen, Lucy, widow of Benjamin	Ellington, Tolland	No proof of service—name not on any roll in the companies and regiments specified.
Andrews, Elizabeth, widow of Samuel	Southington, Hartford	Proof of identity deficient—the soldier of the same name died, by the rolls, in the service, and the department would be certified if he was claimant's husband.
Banks, Molly, widow of Jonathan	Fairfield, Fairfield	They were captured and held as prisoners at the burning of Danbury; but it does not appear that they were soldiers in service.
Barlow, Lucy, widow of David	Bridgeport, Fairfield	He was a deserter.
Bassett, Damarius, widow of Edward	Oxford, New Haven	Suspended for further proof of marriage.
Beach, Sarah (deceased), widow of Miles	Hartford, Hartford	Not six months' service in proof in this case.
Benson, Barsheba, widow of Charles	Colchester, New London	The claimant's name and witnesses' are neither of them borne upon the rolls—proof of marriage also defective.
Blackman, Phebe, formerly widow of Joshua Northup	Watertown, Litchfield	Suspended for proof of marriage and of identity of her husband with the soldier of the rolls.
Brown, Lydia, widow of David	Stonington, New London	The David Brown who was paid for twelve months' service in 1781, enlisted January 1, 1781, for three years. There were several of the same name; but the twelve-months' man is claimed, and the proof of identity is wanting.
Buckland, Lois, widow of Alexander	Ellington, Tolland	Team service not admissible.
Burrit, Elizabeth, widow of Elihu	Berlin, Hartford	Neither principal nor substitute are found on the rolls of the service specified—claim discredited in toto.
Canfield, Betsey, widow of Itharmar	New Milford, Litchfield	Service admitted—marriage requires proof by the production of the original family record they make mention of.
Case, Abigail, widow of Aaron	Simsbury, Hartford	Suspended for want of proof of service and marriage.
Chapman, Mary, widow of Jason	Waterford, New London	The alleged enlistment and service for twelve months in 1781, are discredited by both pay and muster-rolls.

STATEMENT—Continued.

Names.	Residence.	Reasons for suspension.
Chatfield, Dinah, widow of Jonathan	Roxbury, Litchfield	There is no satisfactory proof of service in this case for over three months and twenty-two days.
Clark, Sally, widow of Joseph	Milford, New Haven	If she was living January 28, 1845, (and otherwise entitled under this act), the bar by act April 30, 1844, will now be obviated.
Clark, Olive, widow of Jesse	Granby, Hartford	Suspended for further proof.
Cleveland, Hannah, widow of Solomon	Woodstock, Windham	The six months' service in this case falls short of satisfactory proof.
Colt, Sarah, widow of Benjamin	Norwich, New London	Pensions by special act are not allowed to carry the privileges of the general pension laws, which rejects this widow's claim.
Cook, Mercy, widow of Joseph	Harwinton, Litchfield	Proof of service and wedding day deficient.
Couch, Phebe, widow of Amos	Farmington, Hartford	Service admitted—marriage in suspense.
Crosby, Caroline, widow of Prince	Lyme, New London	Not on the rolls—no proof of service or marriage.
Cunnington, Hannah, widow of Robert	Windham, Windham	Suspended for a more specific description of the service, to be verified by the comptroller's certificate.
Davis, Lois, formerly widow of Elihu Judd	Danbury, Fairfield	Proof of service deficient—witness differs from previous testimony in his own case.
Davis, Matilda, widow of Silas	Granby, Hartford	No evidence of service furnished nor specific detail given so as to enable a search to be had.
Dayton, Naomi, widow of Samuel	Watertown, Litchfield	Six months' service not satisfactorily proved.
Dodd, Ann, widow of John	Danbury, Fairfield	There is no proof of six months' service in a military capacity.
Draper, Hannah, widow of Nathan	Hartford, Hartford	Five months and seventeen days' service admitted. The R. I. term in 1776, should be specified by some surviving comrade, and the full name of the captain given.
Duncan, Dolly, widow of Jarad	Reading, Fairfield	He was an invalid pensioner, but the department is not in possession of any data of any service on which to base a pension to the widow.
Edson, Mehitable, widow of Caleb, heirs of	Norwich, New London	Service in Col. Putnam's regiment by one "Edson," requires some proof of identity that the soldier was the husband of claimant.
Edmonds, Esther, formerly widow of Peter Rose	Bridgeport, Fairfield	Not a widow at the date of the act—died before August 23, 1842.
Elbridge, Bethiah, widow of Zorth	Wellington, Tolland	Seven months' service under Captain Wells disproved by the comptroller's certificate—other terms not sufficient.

Name	Location	Remarks
Foster, Esther, widow of Isaac	Milford, New Haven	No proof that he was a soldier of the revolution.
Gates, Rachel, widow of Thomas	East Haddam, Middlesex	He did not serve six months in a military capacity.
Gardiner, Elizabeth, formerly widow of Ezekiel Tucker	Waterford, New London	Proof of her marriage and husband's decease and of service, by the comptroller required.
Gennings, Mary, widow of Jesse	Stafford, Tolland	He did not serve six months.
Hitchcock, Eunice, widow of John L.	Cheshire, New Haven	No such name as her husband's witnesses on the rolls, except John Cole, who was not in service during the term credited to the two soldiers of the same name with her late husband. Proof of identity with one of these is required.
Hoyt, Sally, widow of James	Stamford, Fairfield	No records of the name of Hoyt exhibited as a soldier of the revolution, and the statements of the witnesses conflict with each other.
Hillard, Lucretia, formerly widow of Charles F. Brown	Voluntown, Windham	Service not set forth—name not on the Connecticut rolls. If he received bounty land, it must be shown what he did with it.
Hayden, Olive, widow of Ezra	Windsor, Hartford	He did not serve six months.
Hall, Rebecca, widow of Moses	Meriden, New Haven	Suspended for proof of marriage.
Hooker, Mary, widow of James	Bloomfield, Hartford	He did not belong to the army as military storekeeper.
Jacobs, Lois, widow of Enoch	New Haven city	Husband an invalid pensioner—died in 1795—papers destroyed in the war office by fire. Service should be set forth and proved, as the act of June 7, 1832, requires.
Johnson, Thankful, widow of Constant	Middletown, Middlesex	He did not serve six months.
Kendall, Rachel, widow of Isaac	Ashford, Windham	He did not serve six months.
Kilbourne, Jemima, widow of Elisha	Colebrook, Litchfield	Suspended for further proof of service.
Lewis, Elizabeth, widow of Samuel	Sterling, Windham	Suspended for proof of marriage.
Lewis, Mary, widow of John	Suffield, Hartford	Period, length and grade of service, and names of company and field officers required.
Luce, Lucy, formerly widow of Dr. Daniel McClune	Somers, Tolland	Service in 1775 for five months admitted—service in 1777 and 1778 not verified by the rolls.
Maguire, Ruth, widow of Peter	Hartford city	Suspended for proof of marriage by some private record, since there are no public ones in her case.
North, Abi, formerly widow of Justus Francis	Berlin, Hartford	Service not in a military capacity.

STATEMENT—Continued.

Names.	Residence.	Reasons for suspension.
Noble, Sally, widow of Timothy	Suffield, Hartford	He did not serve six months.
Phelps, Mary, widow of Darius	Norfolk, Litchfield	He did not serve six months.
Russell, Elizabeth, widow of Timothy	Chatham, Middlesex	Not a widow at the date of the act.
Sheppard, Sarah, widow of Jonathan	New Haven city	Fraudulent.
Simons, Sarah (negro), widow of Simeon	Plainfield, Windham	Suspended for evidence of the day of marriage.
Simmons, Patty, widow of Benjamin Simmons, alias Black	Orange, New Haven	No proof of marriage, and her alleged husband swore in 1820 that he had no family.
Smith, Mary, widow of David	Milford, New Haven	Suspended for further proof of marriage and service from the records at Hartford.
Smith, Naomi, widow of Ebenezer	Fairfield city	Proof of six months service defective.
Smith, Amelia, widow of Benjamin	Windham	His services were not of a military character.
Starkweather, Hannah, widow of John	Preston, New London	He did not serve six months.
Stevens, Rachel, widow of Amos	Madison, New Haven	Suspended for further proof—captain's name might afford an advantageous search of the rolls in Swift's and Sherman's regiment, now silent.
Taylor, Sarah H., widow of William	Osborn, Hartford	Evidence of identity wanted that her husband was the soldier of the comptroller's certificate.
Tracy, Sarah (deceased), widow of Dudley	Franklin, New London	Not a widow at the date of the act—died before August 16, 1842.
Upson, Ruth, widow of Asa	Bristol, Hartford	He did not serve six months.
Upson, Mary, widow of James	Southington, Hartford	Service not specified—no officer named—witness recites service which claimant's husband did not put down when living.
Wakeman, Rachel (deceased), widow of Joseph	Westport, Fairfield	Not a widow at the date of the act—died before August 16, 1842.
Wentworth, Lydia, widow of Amos	Franklin, New London	He did not serve six months.
Weed, Hannah, widow of Joseph Hoyt	Stanford, Fairfield	Service defective in proof.
Williams, Frances, widow of Jacob	New London	An invalid pensioner, and as his papers were burned in 1814, it will be difficult to procure a specification of his services.

A list of persons residing in New York who have applied for pensions under the act of June 7, 1832, whose claims have been rejected; prepared in conformity with the resolution of the Senate of the United States, September 16, 1850.

Names.	Residence.	Reasons for rejection.
Atwater, Jonathan	Coventry, Chenango	He did not serve six months.
Anderson, Andrew	Livonia, Livingston	Service not in a military capacity.
Andrews, Daniel	Nunda, Allegheny	He did not serve six months.
Allen, John	Huntington, Suffolk	He was a deserter.
Andrews, John	Colesville, Broome	He did not serve six months in a military capacity.
Andruss, Ebenezer	Cortlandtville, Cortlandt	He did not serve six months.
Acker, Henry	Cato, Cayuga	He was a deserter.
Allen, Eliphalet	Chautauque, Chautauque	He was a deserter.
Brodick, Bartholomew (deceased)	Rome, Oneida	He died before the passage of the act.
Barber, Zachariah	De Peyster, St. Lawrence	He did not serve six months.
Bartlett, Samuel (deceased)	Urbana, Steuben	He died before the passage of the act.
Barber, Stephen	Manakating, Sullivan	He was a deserter.
Barnum, Eliakim	Manlius, Onondaga	He did not serve in a military capacity.
Barnhart, Peter	Chautauque, Chautauque	He did not serve in a military capacity.
Barso, Adam (deceased)	Vienna, Oneida	He did not serve six months.
Barnet, Simon	Greene, Chenango	He did not serve in a military capacity.
Barnum, Levi	Bloomfield, Ontario	He did not serve six months.
Betsinger, John	Laws, Madison	He was a baker, not a soldier.
Betts, Bartlett	Gaines, Orleans	No proof of service.
Browning, Daniel	Northampton, Fulton	He was a deserter.
Belsinger, John	Clockville, Madison	He was a baker, not a soldier.
Beckwith, Joseph	Buttermuts, Otsego	He was a wagon driver, not a soldier.
Bevier, Elias	Conklin, Broome	He did not serve six months.
Bicknell, Amos	Stockholm, St. Lawrence	He was not of an age to perform military service.
Bishop, John	Canaan, Columbia	He was a deserter.
Blodget, Isaiah	Wales, Erie	Not six months' military service.
Bogardus, Jacob	Greenville, Greene	He did not serve six months.
Board, Cornelius D.	Warsaw, Genesee	He did not serve six months.
Bolls, Amos (deceased)	Manlius, Onondaga	No proof of service.
Borth, Philip	Claverack, Columbia	He did not serve six months.
Booth, Isaiah	Nelson, Madison	An artificer, not a soldier.

STATEMENT—Continued.

Names.	Residence.	Reasons for rejection.
Brown, William (deceased)	Avoca, Steuben	He died before the passage of the act.
Brown, James C.	Elmira, Tioga	He did not serve in any regularly organised corps.
Bradley, Nathaniel	Whitestown, Oneida	He did not serve six months.
Breise, John	Milford, Otsego	His service was a teamster.
Burdick, Peleg	Otsego, Otsego	He was a deserter.
Burt, Aaron	Davenport, Delaware	Not military service—he was a cook and washer.
Butler, Joel	Le Roy, Genesee	He did not perform military service.
Burr, Thomas	Tully, Onondaga	He did not serve in a military capacity.
Burder, Abraham	Manlius, Onondaga	He did not serve six months.
Carr, John	Minisink, Orange	He was a deserter.
Carter, John	Cayuga county	He did not serve six months.
Camp, Joseph	Otsego, Otsego	He was a privateersman.
Camp, John	West Lodi, Cattaraugus	He was a deserter.
Cheeseman, Calvin	New Hudson	He was a teamster.
Chaddeston, Lewis	Aurora, Erie	He was too young for military service.
Cornwell, Amos	Cairo, Greene	He did not serve six months.
Corey, Joseph	Willett, Cortlandt	He did not serve six months.
Christman, Frederick	Columbia, Herkimer	No evidence of service.
Cory, Thomas	Marion, Wayne	No evidence of service.
Crofut, John	Williamson, Wayne	He did not perform military service.
Coons, John A.	Taghanic, Columbia	He did not serve in any regularly organised corps.
Chapin, Samuel	Livonia, Livingston	He was a deserter.
Cook, George	Ticonderoga, Essex	He did not serve six months.
Comstock, Nathan	Galeway, Saratoga	Not military service.
Cornwell, Daniel	Durham, Greene	He did not serve six months.
Cowell, Samuel	Ballston, Saratoga	He was a deserter.
Crandall, John	Ontario, Wayne	He was a deserter.
Crispel, Thomas	Saugerties, Ulster	He was a deserter.
Crosby, Obadiah	Root, Montgomery	He was a wagoner, and his military service was not six months.
Cornell, Jacob	Coxsackie, Greene	He did not serve six months.
Champenoit, William	New York city	He did not perform military service.
Combs, John	Hampden, Delaware	He did not serve six months.

Name	Residence	Reason
Collard, Thomas F	Walkill, Orange	He was of an age too youthful for military service.
Daggett, Thomas	Pittstown, Rensselaer	He did not serve six months in a military capacity.
Davis, Phinehas	Brookhaven, Suffolk	He did not serve six months.
Delamater, John (deceased)	Mooers, Clinton	No proof of service.
Derrick, John	Newfield, Tompkins	No proof of service.
D'Wolf, Daniel	Lenox, Madison	He did not serve six months.
Demarest, John, jr	New York city	He did not serve six months in a military capacity.
Demott, Isaac	Newburgh, Orange	He did not serve six months.
Denison, John	Seneca, Ontario	He did not serve six months.
Depuy, James	Salina, Onondaga	He was a slave, and not amenable to military duty.
Deming, James	Troy, Rensselaer	He did not serve six months.
Dean, Stewart	Lima, Livingston	He did not serve six months as a soldier.
Dimick, Peter	Kirkland, Oneida	He did not serve six months.
Dop, John	Westport, Essex	He was a deserter.
Drew, William	New Baltimore, Greene	He was a blacksmith—name not on the rolls.
Dunkle, Francis	Canajoharie, Montgomery	His service was when under age, and was not of a military character.
Dunbar, Jeremiah	Cazenovia, Madison	He was too young to incur military responsibility.
Dusten, Paley	Stockholm, St. Lawrence	Petition for increase as an adjutant, but can produce no satisfactory proof.
Dimmick, Benjamin	———, Saratoga	
Elghmey, Daniel	Middletown, Delaware	He did not perform six months' military service.
Evans, William	Sidney, Delaware	He was a deserter.
Ellis, Nichols	Queensbury, Warren	He did not serve six months.
Emmerson, Joseph	Truxton, Cortlandt	He did not serve six months.
Evans, Benjamin S	Kirkland, Oneida	No evidence of service.
Fiddes, Hugh E	Tioga, Tioga	Privateer service not provided for by law.
Furman, Benjamin	Ithaca, Tompkins	He did not serve six months.
Flansburgh, David	Bethlehem, Albany	He did not serve six months.
Flansburgh, Richard	Russia, Herkimer	Batteau service not entitled.
Franklin, John	Hanover, Chautauque	Team service not entitled.
Forrest, George	Unadilla, Otsego	He did not serve in the revolutionary war.
Foster, Peter	Riverhead, Suffolk	No proof of service.
Farnsworth, Edmond	Perrysburgh, Cataraugus	He did not serve six months.
Fryer, Isaac W	Guilderland, Albany	He did not serve in a military capacity.
Freeman, Peleg (deceased)	German Flats, Herkimer	Defective proof of service.
French, James	Bath, Steuben	Team service—not entitled.
Fenn, Titus	Royalton, Niagara	He did not serve six months in a military capacity.

STATEMENT—Continued.

Names.	Residence.	Reasons for rejection.
Fink, John	Dunkirk, Chautauque	He was a deserter.
Fisk, Samuel	Otsego, Otsego	He was a deserter.
Fonda, Jacob G.	Schenectady, Schenectady	He did not serve six months in a military capacity.
Ford, Abijah (deceased)	——, Oneida	He died before the passage of the act.
Fowler, John L.	Lyons, Wayne	He did not serve six months in a military capacity.
Fridenburg, Elias	Bainbridge, Chenango	Not six months military duty.
Friar, Anderson	Poughkeepsie, Dutchess	He did not serve six months.
Fitzgibbon, James (deceased)	Mentz, Cayuga	He died before the passage of the act.
Fuller, Ignatius	Peru, Clinton	He did not serve six months.
Gale, Henry	Brighton, Monroe	No proof of service.
Gales, Daniel (deceased)	Adams, Jefferson	No proof of service.
Garrison, John	Victor, Ontario	He was a deserter.
Garlough, Adam	Canajoharie, Montgomery	He did not serve six months, except as teamster.
Gibbs, Zenas	New Hartford, Oneida	He did not serve six months.
Gleason, Moses	Middlebury, Genessee	He did not serve six months, except as teamster.
Goodsell, Isaac	Dover, Dutchess	He did not serve six months.
Goodspeed, Elijah	Hastings, Oswego	His service was on board private armed vessels.
Goodman, John	New York city	He did not serve six months.
Gray, Daniel	Balston, Saratoga	He served as teamster.
Gregory, Ebenezer B.	Owego, Tioga	He did not serve in any regularly organized corps.
Groesbeck, Gerret J.	Bethlehem, Albany	He was an artificer, but not from the ranks.
Gross, Thomas	Lancaster, Erie	He did not serve six months.
Grant, Jehu	Milton, Saratoga	He did not serve except as a waiter and wagon-master.
Grant, Isaac	Gainsville, Genessee	He was a deserter.
Griffing, Joel	Malone, Franklin	He was only 14 years old.
Humaston, Abraham	Rensselaerville, Albany	He was a deserter.
Hartwell, Asahel	Northumberland, Saratoga	He did not serve six months.
Haaver, Andrew	Chenango, Broome	He did not serve in any regularly organized corps.
Haviland, Isaac	Cold Spring, Putnam	He was a teamster, not a soldier.
Halenbake, Ephraim	Union, Broome	He did not serve six months.

Name	Place	Remarks
Hauser, Jacob	Sullivan, Madison	He did not perform military service.
Hatch, Ebenezer	Mexico, Oswego	He was only twelve years of age at the date of his alleged service.
Hawks, William	Otselic, Venango	He was only ten and a half years of age when he entered the service.
Hand David	Southampton, Suffolk	Service on a privateer.
Ex Hathaway, Abial	Hartford, Washington	He served less than six months in a military capacity.
Ex Head, Fobes	Marshall, Oneida	He did not serve in any regularly organized corps.
Heminway, Rufus	Geneva, Ontario	Already pensioned under the act of 1818.
Henderson, Thomas	Manchester, Ontario	Repeated desertion. He ran away thrice.
Henry, John	Glenville, Schenectady	He did not serve six months.
Hermance, Simon	Red Hook, Dutchess	He did not serve six months.
Hewett, John (deceased)	Sand Lake, Rensselaer	He died before the passage of the act.
Hickcox, Amos (deceased)	Harpersfield, Delaware	He died before the passage of the act.
Hilton, Richard	Richland, Oswego	Not military service and no proof of any offered.
Hogeboom, Richard C.	Stuyvesant, Columbia	He did not serve in a military capacity.
Howell, Matthew	Southampton, Suffolk	He did not serve six months in a military capacity.
Hooker, Increase M.	Truxton, Courtland	He did not serve six months.
Hooper, Zalmon	Dryden, Tomkins	He did not serve six months in a military capacity.
Holmes, Axel (deceased)	Rome, Oneida	No proof of service.
Hunt, Davis	New York city	Not military service.
Hurd, Rosewell	Wilton, Saratoga	Service on board a privateer.
Huston, James	Chautauque, Chautauque	Desertion—he ran away April 8, 1779.
Hutchins, William	Westfield, Chautauque	He was only 18 years of age.
Huntley, Reynold	Manlius, Onondaga	He served only three months.
Huntley, Andrew	Mooers, Clinton	He served only four months and eleven days.
Ingham, Joseph	Rome, Oneida	Service on board privateers.
Jarred, Benjamin	Smithtown, Suffolk	Desertion—he ran away July 27, 1782.
Jones, David	Haverstraw, Rockland	Service as a blacksmith—not considered military service.
Johnson, Rufus	Gosham, Ontario	He has made no application under this act. He applied under the act of May, 1828, and his claim was rejected, having served only six months in the Massachusetts line, in Col. Bigelow's regiment. (See letter June 20, 1840—N. H. Earll.
Jacobs, Francis	Watervliet, Albany	He was a domestic in the service of Gen. Washington during the war, but not a soldier.
Jump, Gilbert	Greenville, Green	He did not serve six months.
Joy, Jacob	Ira, Cayuga	He did not serve six months.
Jones, Ezra	Phelps, Ontario	He did not serve six months.
Clump alias Klumpb, Jeremiah	Fredonia, Chautauque	Service as an express rider and teamster, not entitled.

STATEMENT—Continued.

Names.	Residence.	Reasons for rejection.
Keeler, James	Augusta, T. S., county Greenville, District of Johnstown, Upper Canada	He was a deserter.
Kirkland, Joshua	Rome, Oneida	Service on board privateers—not entitled.
Konnicutt, Edward	Mayfield, Montgomery	He did not serve in any regularly organized corps.
Kinney, Jonas	Bridgewater, Oneida	He did not serve six months.
King, Henry	Whitehall, Washington	He did not serve six months.
Keith, John	Brookfield, Madison	He did not serve six months.
Koons, Peter	Half Moon, Saratoga	No proof of service.
Keyser, Michael	New York city	No proof of service.
Keeler, Aaron	Skaneateles, Onondago	Under age—only twelve years old when he entered the service.
Lootborrow, Isaac	New York city	He was a deserter.
Loomis, Daniel (deceased)	Plainfield, Otsego	He did not serve six months in a military capacity.
Leech, Stephen	Cooperstown, Otsego	He died before the passage of the act.
Lull, William	Lawrence, Otsego	He did not serve six months.
Lane, Nathan	Bethany, Genesee	He served in the French army—no claim.
Long, Adam	New Scotland, Albany	He did not serve six months.
Leonard, David	Austerlitz, Columbia	He did not serve six months.
Lewis, Ebenezer	Gosham, Ontario	He deserted on the first muster.
Lent, Isaac	Yonkers, Westchester	He did not serve six months in any regularly organized corps.
Lownsberry, William	Fenner, Madison	He did not serve six months.
Lewis, Abel	Peterburg, Rensselaer	He did not serve six months.
Lemoreaux, Peter	Pittstown, Rensselaer	He did not serve in any regularly organized corps.
Malary, David	Venice, Cayuga	He was a deserter.
Manwaring, Samuel	Mexico, Oswego	He was a teamster, not a soldier.
Manin, David	Northampton, Montgomery	He did not serve six months in a military capacity.
Mason, Jeremiah	Johnstown, Montgomery	He was only thirteen years old in 1780, when he alleges he enlisted.
Mersereau, Joshua	Lindley, Steuben	No proof of service.
McPherson, Daniel	Danby, Tompkins	He did not perform military service.
McConnell, John	Starkey, Yates	No proof of service.
Merrit, Aaron	Otsego, Otsego	He did not serve six months.

Name	Residence	Remarks
McMaster, James (deceased)	Caroline, Tompkins	He did not serve six months.
McGinnis, Jacob	Claverack, Columbia	He did not perform six months' service in a military capacity.
Merritt, Jeremiah	Mount Pleasant, West Chester	He was a deserter.
Mead, Daniel	Cairo, Greene	He did not serve in a military capacity.
Mead, Eli	Chester, Warren	He did not serve six months in a military capacity.
Merrills, Ephah	New Lebanon, Columbia	He did not serve six months.
Mellin, Gilbert	Hounsfield, Jefferson	He did not serve six months.
Merriam, Aaron	Cazenovia, Madison	He did not serve six months.
Miller, William	Martinburgh, Lewis	He was a deserter.
Mighell (alias Miles), Thomas	Peru, Clinton	He did not serve six months.
Michael, Andrew	Canajoharie, Montgomery	His service was in the French army.
Mills, Zebulon	Amsville, Oneida	He did not serve six months.
Mosher, Thomas (deceased)	Schenectady, Schenectady	He died before the passage of the act.
Morgan, James	New York city	He did not perform military service.
Morrison, Hugh	Milton, Saratoga	He was a deserter.
Monroe, Samuel	Lee, Oneida	He did not perform military service.
Munn, Gideon	Augusta, Oneida	Excepting team service, he did not serve six months.
Newkirk, William J	Florida, Montgomery	He did not serve in any regularly organized corps.
Negro, Marlin (colored)	Montgomery, Orange	He was a slave, and not subject to military duty.
Nottingham, William	Urbana, Steuben	He did not serve six months.
Nicholas, John	Frankfort, Herkimer	He was not of an age to be subject to military duty.
Neple, John	Half Moon, Saratoga	He was not of an age to be subject to military duty.
Nichols, James	Lowville, Lewis	The rolls as well as his age discredit his service.
Nevil, John	Sharon, Schoharie	No proof of service either documentary or oral.
Onderdonk, John	Westerloo, Albany	Not six months' service—no proof.
Oznunnd, Abraham	Lansing, Tompkins	He did not perform military service.
Olmsted, Asahel	Triangle, Broome	He was under age, and he did not serve six months.
Oliver, John	Bethlehem, Albany	He did not serve six months.
Patrick, Ralph	Sangerfield, Oneida	Transportation service.
Passage, George	Duaneaburgh, Schenectady	He did not serve six months.
Pease, Ephraim	Lee, Oneida	Service as an impressed teamster.
Peck, Joseph	Milton, Saratoga	He did not serve six months.
Paddock, Peter	Pamela, Jefferson	He did not serve six months.
Palmer, Elijah	Columbus, Chenango	He did not serve six months in a military capacity.
Palmer, Miles	Rome, Oneida	He did not serve six months in a military capacity.
Palmer, Nehemiah	Columbus, Chenango	His service was as a wagoner.
Parker, Benjamin	Ellery, Chautauque	His service was as a wagoner.

STATEMENT—Continued.

Names.	Residence.	Reasons for rejection.
Parker, Elijah	Middletown, Delaware	He was a deserter.
Parr, Thomas	Candor, Tioga	He served as a captain of a privateer.
Peck, Henry	Harrisburgh, Lewis	He did not serve six months.
Peabody, Dudley	Schodack, Rensselaer	He did not serve six months.
Pattengell, Samuel	Rose, Wayne	He did not serve six months.
Pendleton, Nathan	Norwich, Chenango	Service discredited by the rolls.
Peck, Eleazar	Bennington, Wyoming	Team service—not provided for.
Perell, Jacob	Mayfield, Montgomery	Bateaux service or militia tours, not definitely recited—not over three months' service established.
Pearce, Shabel	Hampton, Washington	Not six months' service—no proof.
Phillips, John	Pamela, Jefferson	Service as a boatman—not entitled.
Philo, Adams	Half Moon, Saratoga	He did not serve six months in a military capacity.
Pitman, William	New Hartford, Oneida	His age, only eleven years, precludes his claim for military service.
Pierce, David	Butler, Wayne	He was a deserter.
Phelps, James	Homer, Cortland	Under age—not amenable to military responsibilities.
Plumb, Joseph (deceased)	Bangor, Franklin	He was a deserter.
Plumb, Samuel	Williamstown, Oswego	He did not serve six months.
Post, Isaac	Phillipstown, Putnam	He did not serve six months.
Postle, Francis	Friendship, Allegheny	He did not serve six months in a military capacity.
Pomroy, Heman	North Granville, Washington	He was a deserter.
Porter, Ephraim	Mamakating, Sullivan	He did not serve six months.
Powers, Jacob	Groton, Tompkins	He did not serve six months.
Preston, Moses	Grove, Allegheny	Only four months twelve days' service.
Price, Charles C.	Ellery, Chautauque	He was a deserter.
Prayne, Lewis	Danube, Herkimer	He did not serve six months.
Purdy, Joshua	Yorktown, West Chester	He did not serve six months.
Pettingell, Joseph	Cicero, Onondaga	No proof of service.
Rexford, Dennison	Augusta, Oneida	He did not serve six months.
Robinson, John (deceased)	Pompey, Onondaga	No proof of service.
Rogers, Jonathan	Lowville, Lewis	He was a deserter.
Reed, Daniel	Greenville, Washington	He did not serve six months.
Roberts, Samuel	Cincinnatus, Cortlandt	Pensioned already under act 1818.

Riker, Abraham	New York city, Riker's Island	An artificer—not entitled.
Remington, Josiah	Poundridge, West Chester	He did not serve six months.
Race, Andrus A	Ancram, Columbia	He served as a wagoner.
Rice, Noah	Northumberland, Saratoga	He did not serve six months.
Randall, Joseph	Sanford, Broome	He served as a waiter—did not belong to the ranks.
Russell, Daniel	Vienna, Oneida	He was in the privateer service.
Reid, John	Brooklyn, Kings	He did not serve in any regularly organized corps.
Reed, John	Exeter, Otsego	He served as a waiter—he was too young for the ranks.
Robinson, David	Amity, Allegheny	He did not serve six months.
Runyan, Henry	Manlius, Onondaga	He was a deserter.
Ridgeway, Thomas R.	New York city	No proof of service.
Robinson, Jason	Russell, St. Lawrence	He did not serve six months.
Rust, Zebulon	Salina, Onondaga	He did not serve six months.
Ryan, Rulife	New Baltimore, Greene	He did not serve six months.
Renson, Luke	Newtown, Queens	He did not serve six months.
Rouse, Jonathan	Pittstown, Rensselaer	He did not serve six months.
Sayles, Thomas	Marcellus, Onondaga	He did not serve six months.
Sanborn, Elijah	Stafford, Genesee	He did not serve six months.
Sauquayounk, Cornelius (Oneida chief)		He did not serve in any regularly organized corps, nor by virtue of any competent authority.
Sampson, Daniel	Shelby, Orleans	He did not serve six months.
Schell, Christian	Township Vaughan, U. Canada	He was a deserter.
Seidmore, Zopher	Saratoga Springs, Saratoga	He did not serve six months.
Schram, Henry	Openheim, Fulton	He did not serve six months.
Scott, Alexander	Mamakating, Sullivan	No proof of service.
Scouton, Simon S.	Fishkill, Dutchess	He did not serve six months in a military capacity.
Searle, Jeremiah	New Baltimore, Greene	No proof of service.
Searle, Samuel	Walls, Erie	No proof of service.
Sevart, Tewalt	Starkey, Yates	Team service—not entitled.
Sevart, Baltus	Starkey, Yates	Team service—not entitled.
Sbely, Martin	Alexandria, Jefferson	No proof of service.
Shevill, Abraham	Easthampton, Suffolk	Service as an express rider—not entitled.
Simpson, Matthew	Salem, Washington	No proof of service—not on the rolls.
Simpkins, Isaac	Poundridge, Westchester	Too young for military service, and no proof that he performed any.
Skutt, Stephen	Aurelius, Cayuga	He did not serve six months.
Sly, William	New Windsor, Orange	He did not serve six months.
Smith, Joel	Buttermits, Otsego	Team service—not entitled.
Smith, John	Onondaga, Onondaga	Team service—not entitled.

STATEMENT—Continued.

Names.	Residence.	Reasons for rejection.
Solmes, Nathaniel	Sophiasburg, T. S., Prince Edward district, Province of Upper Canada	No proof of service.
Spencer, Samuel B	New York city	Service on board a privateer.
Spaulding, Phinehas	Danby, Tomkins	He did not serve six months.
Spencer, Zachers	Centreville, Allegheny	He did not serve six months.
Schermerhorn, John L	Bern, Albany	He was taken prisoner by the Indians, and a squaw adopted him as her son, and his constructive service ceased from that time, which reduces his services below six months. See letter October 17, 1884, Erastus Williams.
Sikes, Francis	Springfield, Otsego	He did not serve six months.
Simons, Isaac	Newstead, Erie	He was a deserter.
Sears, Isaac (deceased)	Ramapo, Rockland	Died before the passage of the act—married in 1797.
Stephens, Asa	Lockport, Niagara	He did not serve six months.
Stiles, Silas	Keen, Essex	Team service—not entitled.
Story, Thomas	Lysander, Onondaga	He did not serve six months.
Stark, Aaron	Beekman, Dutchess	He was a deserter.
Store, John	Ellicott, Chautauque	He did not serve six months.
Sturgess, Aquilla	Barre, Orleans	He was a deserter.
Strader, Nicholas	Martinsburg, Lewis	No proof of service—name not on the rolls.
Stevens, Elijah	Stanford, Dutchess	He was a deserter.
Sutphen, James	Lee, Oneida	Team service—not entitled.
Swart, Tanis (deceased)	Rotterdam, Schenectady	He died before the passage of the act.
Swift, William	Westrow, Otsego	He served as a waiter—not entitled.
Taylor, Jonas	Sempronius, Cayuga	He did not serve in a military capacity.
Tall, William	(Oneida tribe)	He did not serve in any regularly organized corps.
Tirboss, Henry	Marbleborough, Ulster	He did not serve six months in a military capacity.
Terry, Isaac	Colesville, Broome	He did not serve in any regularly organized corps.
Torry, John	Southampton, Suffolk	He did not serve six months.
Thurber, Francis	Chateaugay, Clinton	He did not serve six months.
Titus, John	Mariah, Essex	A soldier in the late war with Great Britain—no claim.
Towner, Comfort	Crown Point, Essex	He did not serve six months.

Travis, George	Phillipstown, Putnam	He did not serve six months.
Trickey, William	Lauddowne, Upper Canada	No proof of service.
Tryon, Salmon	Brooklyn, Kings	He did not serve in a military capacity.
Tuemper, Jacob	Lyme, Jefferson	No proof of service.
Travis, James	Rotterdam, Schenectady	No proof of service.
Tuttle, James	Bolton, Warren	He did not serve six months.
Tucker, Benjamin	Chautauque, Chautauque	Too young—not on the roll—no parol proof.
Twist, Elias	West Troy, Albany	No proof of service—not on the rolls.
Van Lieu, Frederick F.	Lodi, Seneca	He did not serve six months.
Vickory, Timothy	Hastings, Oswego	He was a teamster to the French army.
Van Deuzen Mathew	Lansingburg, Columbia	Alleged service by his slave as a substitute, of which service there is no proof.
Vanderwarker, John R.	Northumberland, Saratoga	He did not serve in any regularly organized corps.
Venus, Michael	Canajoharie, Montgomery	He did not serve six months in a military capacity.
Vanorden, Peter	Windham, Greene	Other than patrol duty, he did not serve six months.
Van Etten, Abraham	Glenville, Schenectady	He received no pay, and was, of course, not engaged in real military service.
Vedder, Cornelius	Attica, Wyoming	He was not engaged in military service in any respect.
Vosburgh, Jacob	Albany, Albany	He served only five months.
Van Vleek, Benjamin	Fowler, St. Lawrence	He was a laborer and carpenter, but did not belong to the ranks.
Wells, Obadiah	Southold, Suffolk	He was a deserter.
Woodward, Frederick	Cambridge, Washington	He did not serve six months.
Wilcox, Isaiah	Danube, Herkimer	He did not serve six months.
Wise, Abner	Conewango, Catarangus	He was a deserter.
Walter, Elijah	Newark, Tioga	He did not serve six months.
Waldron, Oliver	Yorkville, New York city	He did not serve six months.
Whitney, Seth	Delhi, Delaware	He was a deserter.
Warner, Jesse	Phelps, Ontario	Team service—not entitled.
Warren, Jonathan	Pesona, Oneida	Privateer service—not entitled.
Wiede, Jared	Troy, Rensselaer	He served on board a privateer.
Whitcomb, Thomas	Frankfort, Herkimer	He did not serve six months—he was only fourteen years of age.
Wilsey, James	Cobleskill, Schoharie	He did not serve six months.
Wilcox, Jeremiah	Warrensburg, Warren	He did not serve in a military capacity.
Wilcox, George	Milford, Otsego	He did not serve six months.
Webber, John	Glenville, Schenectady	He was a deserter.
Wright, Abraham	Buffalo, Erie	He was a deserter.
Winslow, Timothy	Essex, Essex	He did not serve six months—his name is not on any roll, and he was only fifteen years old.

STATEMENT—Continued.

Names.	Residence.	Reasons for rejection.
Wheeler, Joshua	Lisle, Broome	He did not serve six months.
Williams, David	Rome, Oneida	He did not serve six months.
Williams, Daniel	Clymer, Chautauque	No proof of service—name not on any roll.
Whiting, Samuel	Macedon, Wayne	He was a deserter.
Welt, Moses	Salisbury, Herkimer	He did not serve six months.
Wilson, James	Whitestown, Oneida	He did not serve six months.
Wood, John	Greenwich, Palatine	He did not serve six months before the revolutionary war terminated.
Woolf, Valentine	Palatine, Montgomery	No claim—he was captured by the Indians when only eight years of age.
Wood, Amos	Essex, Essex	He was a deserter.
Widrig, Conrad	Columbia, Herkimer	He did not serve six months in a military capacity.
Young, Peter	Canajoharie, Montgomery	He did not serve in any regularly organized corps.
Young, Jacob A.	Starks, Herkimer	Service in a frontier fort for self-defence, without military authority of a public character.
Yeomans, Jonathan	Clarkstown, Rockland	He did not serve six months in a military capacity.
York, Joseph	Cuba, Allegheny	He did not serve six months.
Zeigler, Christopher	New Baltimore, Greene	No proof of service, name not on the rolls.

A list of persons residing in New York who have applied for pensions under the act of July 7, 1832, whose claims have been suspended; prepared in conformity with the resolution of the Senate of the United States, September 16, 1850.

Names.	Residence.	Reasons for suspension.
Abbey, James..............	Sidney, Delaware........	An attempt at fraud—see letter February 19, 1846, to W. L. Dayton.
Adams, Abijah (deceased)...	Milton, Saratoga.........	Suspended for defective proof of service.
Addoms, Jonas (deceased)...	New York city...........	For increase, he has already received the highest pension to which his services entitle him.
Adams, John...............	Sharon, Schoharie........	Suspended for proof of age and identity, and service by the New York records.
Adams, Elisha.............	Rochester, Monroe.......	He does not claim to have served six months.
Adriance, Isaac............	Fishkill, Dutches........	Suspended for proof of service by the certificate of the New York comptroller.
Adner, George.............	Rutland, Jefferson.......	No proof of service, and no evidence of such kind of service.
Allen, Jonathan............	Queensbury, Warren.....	Suspended for further proof of service.
Allen, Elias...............	Oswego, Tioga...........	Suspended for further proof of service.
Allen, Henry..............	Minisink, Orange.........	The New Jersey records repudiate his service, and he must furnish proof otherwise.
Allen, Samuel.............	Charlton, Saratoga.......	Suspended for further proof—there are no New Jersey rolls of the period designated.
Allen, Reuben.............	Thompson, Sullivan......	Alleged service in the Connecticut militia is repudiated by the rolls of that State.
Allen, Salmon.............	Oswegatchie, St. Lawrence	He alleges three years eleven months' service in Craft's regiment, no part of which is supported by the rolls of that regiment in Boston.
Allen, Jedediah............	Georgetown, Madison....	The regimental and company officers of each tour are required.
Allen, Joseph..............	Petersburgh, Rensselaer..	Service in the Massachusetts militia requires proof from the Secretary of State at Boston.
Allison, Jeremiah..........	Haverstraw, Rockland....	Not any evidence of over three and a half months' service.
Aldrich, Aaron (deceased)..	Edmeston, Otsego.......	The service and identity requires proof—claim must be asserted by widow, and if no widow, by the children.
Aldrich, Jacob.............	Southold, Suffolk........	Suspended for specification of tours of service, officers, date, grade and locality.
Aldrich, Robert............	Neversink, Sullivan......	Further proof of service required.
Anderson, John............	New York city...........	He did not perform military service.

STATEMENT—Continued.

Names.	Residence.	Reasons for suspension.
Anson, John	Perrysburgh, Cattaraugus	Suspended for information and proof—name not on the New Jersey continental rolls, and there was no Colonel Frolinghuysen in the revolutionary war from New Jersey.
Appleby, Michael	Cazenovia, Madison	Not six months' service established in this case.
Armstrong, James	Canadice, Ontario	The service alleged in the continental ranks is not sustained by the rolls.
Arnold, Abimelech	Unadilla, Otsego	Suspended for further proof and specification.
Arnold, Levi	Jay, Essex	Service in Connecticut in 1776, under Captain Smith, Colonel Ely, and in 1778, under Captain Baldwin, Colonel Swift, has no evidence to sustain it.
Austin, Benjamin	Albany, Albany	He was a deserter.
Austin, Jonathan	Harrisburgh, Lewis	If he could state the colonel's name of the artillery in which he alleges twelve months' service, it might probably be sustained.
Baker, Samuel	Cameron, Steuben	Suspended for want of proof.
Baker, Edey	Malta, Saratoga	Name not on Colonel Warner's rolls, and proof insufficient for service under Van Vechten.
Baker, Abraham	Haverstraw, Rockland	Suspended for further proof—there were no such tours as are described in claimants' declaration.
Baker, Abraham	New Berlin, Chenango	Claims for twenty-eight months militia service in Rhode Island—proof and explanation fall short.
Barber, Samuel	Johnsburgh, Warren	Suspended for further proof and specification.
Baker, Isaac (alias Jacob Johnson)	Sag Harbor, Suffolk	Claims for three years' service in Lamb's regiment, under Captain Roman—neither claimant's name nor his captain's are on these rolls.
Baker, Jonathan	Shendaker, Ulster	Five months admitted—the alleged three months under the authority of Massachusetts must be certified by Mr Bangs, Secretary of State.
Backus, John	Hoosick, Rensselaer	He was carried into Canada by the enemy, but the proof is deficient that he was in the ranks of the army at the time.
Babcock, Daniel	Elba, Genesee	Suspended for further proof.
Baker, Justus	Lisle, Broome	The rolls are silent, and the present exhibits are inadmissible.
Baker, Paul	Gates, Monroe	The rolls allow four months instead of six as claimed, and as his name is not on Captain Rattebone's rolls in 1777 for three months, that will require two witnesses.

Name	Location	Remarks
Baker, James	Lee, Oneida	Disallowed—has furnished no evidence of his service.
Bakeman, Henry	Granby, Oswego	Suspended for evidence of identity of the service credited to a soldier of the same name in Colonel Willet's regiment, Captain Peter B. Toare's company.
Baldwin, Nathan	Ithaca, Tompkins	The service claimed by him as a substitute for his brother, is credited by the rolls to his brother's name.
Ball, Walt (deceased)	Cortlandt, Cortlandt	His service was as a teamster—not allowable.
Ball, Jonathan (deceased)	Canada East	His claim was suspended for defective proof, and withdrawn July, 1835.
Baley, John	Jerusalem, Yates	Suspended for further proof and reasons for delay.
Barnhart, Cornel		No evidence of twelve months' enlistment at the period designated, and the officer's names not given. [Papers withdrawn Jan. 24, '34.]
Bailey, Joseph	Potsdam, St. Lawrence	Suspended for further proof of service.
Bailey, Jesse (deceased)	Ovid, Seneca	Suspended for want of proof in 1836, and withdrawn to be presented to Congress—papers probably on file at the Capitol.
Barden, Ebenezer L	Neward, Tioga	Claimant's account of his services entirely discredited by the Connecticut records.
Bartman, Joseph	New York city	No proof of service.
Bartiss, John	Windsor, Broome	There is no ascertainable term of actual service in this man's papers.
Barnett, Nathaniel	Hoosick, Rensselaer	Suspended for further proof, either by comrades or the Connecticut records.
Banested, Davis	German, Chenango	In suspense for want of proof of service.
Barstow, Job	Eaton, Madison	The mistakes are apparent in his account throughout, and he is also discredited by the Connecticut records.
Bates, Archibald (deceased)	Cazenovia, Madison	Suspended for details of service to be furnished.
Bates, Hickey	Pleasant Valley, Dutchess	All privateer service, exclusive of two months in the Rhode Island militia.
Bates, Israel	Barre, Orleans	A Massachusetts militia man from Ingham—must find proof in his neighborhood, and also on the records at Boston.
Baxter, Moses	Fort Ann, Washington	Suspended for good proof, of which there is abundance in Massachusetts living, and on the records at Boston.
Barnes, Jared	Salem, Washington	Suspended for defective proof in November, 1888, and the papers withdrawn at that time, and not replaced.
Basset (or Basso), Peter	Schoharie, Schoharie	Discredited both in his own and officer's names by the rolls of both States, viz: Rhode Island and New Hampshire.
Baxter, Nathan	Norfolk, St. Lawrence	Suspended in 1834 for defective proof and papers withdrawn.
Baxter, John	Durham, Lower Canada	A certificate of his service is required from the office of the Secretary of State at Boston.
Becker, Jacob	Walsingham, Lower Canada	Names of officers, date, duration, grade and locality of each tour is required.

STATEMENT—Continued.

Names.	Residence.	Reasons for suspension.
Benedict, Elias	Columbia, Herkimer	He was only fifteen years old, and not subject to draft when he was abducted.
Bennett, Gershom	Tyrone, Steuben	He was only thirteen years old when he entered service, and fifteen when it expired.
Becker, John P.	Brownville, Jefferson	Suspended for further proof.
Berringer, David	Troy, Rensselaer	Service as a ranger not allowed—his other service not distinctly set forth.
Benedict, Aarop	Lisle, Broome	He must detail his service in so specific a style, that the records at Boston can be inspected with precision.
Bebee, John	Austerlitz, Columbia	Claim not sustained by the rolls of Massachusetts for 1775, and his proof otherwise erroneous and defective.
Beardsley, Ichabod	Ithaca, Tompkins	Proof of his age required in order to admit a claim for twelve months' service, which awaits his response.
Beach, Aaron	Cambria, Niagara	The entire service fairly established does not exceed thirty days—the depositions being so vague and uncertain.
Benjamin, Josiah	Johnstown, Fulton	Service as a teamster not admitted—other service not over two months.
Bentley, Elisha	Mayfield, Montgomery	Such an amount of service as he claims, would be surely susceptible of proof by numerous records and numerous comrades, but he has furnished none.
Betts, Nathan	Lysander, Onondaga	Not six months' service established by the rolls and accounts.
Bennet, Cromwell	Rushford, Allegheny	Twelve months' service alleged—no application under the act of 1818, and no proof offered at present.
Betts, Richards	Broadalbin, Montgomery	His five months' tour has no officers' names, and there is no evidence of such nine months' service in Rhode Island, and the minute men organized in 1775, served but short tours.
Beatty, Robert	Olive, Ulster	Name not on the pay rolls of either Captains Hornbrook, Turnpenny, or Westbrook.
Beardsley, Moses	Prattsville, Greene	Name not on any of the Connecticut rolls in this office—two witnesses wanted.
Betts, Robert	North Hempsted, Queens	Suspended for more precise details of service—officers' names, date, duration, grade, locality, &c.
Belknap, Isaac	Newburgh, Orange	Suspended in 1834 for proof and explanations.

Name	Location	Remarks
Bennett, Joseph	Nelson, Madison	Suspended for further proof, viz: the affidavit of Mr. Wm. Borden, the witness mentioned in his own supplemental declaration.
Bellinger, John	Seward, Schoharie	Proof required from the comptroller's office, and of his age, and of his reasons for delay.
Billinger, Peter B	Danube, Herkimer	He did not serve six months.
Bixby, Benjamin	Ridgeway, Orleans	Proof required from the records of Massachusetts.
Biddlecomb, Daniel	Deerfield, Oneida	Names of officers, date, grade, duration and locality of each tour required.
Bicknell, Amos	Stockholm, St. Lawrence	Claims for eight months' service in a fort in 1781—there is no proof of such service.
Blackman, John H	Harmony, Chautauque	Not six months' service—claims for but five months in two terms, and both discredited by the rolls.
Bliven, Arnold	Rensselaerville, Albany	Not military service.
Bloss, Joseph	Rochester, Monroe	Claims for five tours amounting to two and a half years in Connecticut—such a length of service is surely susceptible of proof, and claimant must seek it.
Bonker, Oliver	Mentz, Cayuga	Claimant's name not on any rolls, and evidence wanting of every kind.
Bowman, Nicholas	Schuyler, Herkimer	He did not serve six months.
Bowers, Lewis S	Hoosick, Rensselaer	Suspended for further proof and details of service—service as waiter and wood-cutter not admissible.
Bohannon, John	Mexico, Oswego	Evidence wanting to show a special act for six months' men in New Jersey, as the New Jersey militia were in classes to serve one month at a time alternately.
Bond, Benjamin	Charleston, Montgomery	If he served in the six months' men of New Jersey, some evidence of it may be on the records at Trenton.
Burdan, Nathan	Lysander, Onondaga	Suspended for proof from the Massachusetts rolls at Boston, or from surviving witnesses.
Boylan, James	Batavia, Genesee	Such long militia tours in New Jersey did not exist—no such service as is described could have been performed.
Bouton, Benajah	Huntington, Suffolk	Without further specification—in regard to the service in Captain Delavan's dragoons, no more than two months seven days' service can be allowed therein.
Boon, Francis	Collins, Erie	Two months and twenty days services only established; and if his claim to eight months' service in 1775 be well founded, he may, by stating the officers names correctly find proof in the Secretary's office, Boston.
Borst, John J	Elbridge, Onondaga	He served in a fort as a ranger or patrol; and if he served in any regularly organized corps, he should give the actual tours of service and the officers in command.
Boothwick, George	Middleburg, Schoharie	No service performed under sixteen years of age can be admitted without satisfactory proof.

STATEMENT—Continued.

Names.	Residence.	Reasons for suspension.
Brady, Benjamin	Pavilion, Genessee	Documents not sufficient to establish as much as six months service.
Bradley, Thomas	West Point, Essex	Suspended for some proof of service in the continental line.
Bradley, Sturges	Bradford, Steuben	He was only fourteen years old in 1779, and the department is not aware that there was any such service as he alleges his first tour to have been.
Bradley, Moses	Simnett, Cayuga	He did not serve six months.
Brannock, Levi	Kingsbury, Washington	No claim for service, without direct proof, can be admitted, when the party is only twelve or thirteen years old.
Brandon, Nicholas	Catskill, Greene	Proof required from Lieutenant Salisbury, who served with claimant, and particularly that the service of the second term was under a regularly organized corps.
Brewster, Timothy	Ellisbury, Jefferson	Proof of service by surviving comrades required.
Briggs, Cary	Stephentown, Rensselaer	Testimony of service insufficient.
Briggs, Joshua	Cartwright, Delaware	The certificate of the comptroller and the tours set forth by claimant differ so widely, that they prove no identity whatever.
Briggs, Matthias	Clarkstown, Rockland	Suspended for specific details of service, officers, places, dates, grade and length.
Bristol, John	Troy, Rensselaer	The certificate of the comptroller is against him. The order for his pay does not agree with the names of the officers by him set forth.
Bred, Amos	New Lebanon, Columbia	He did not serve six months.
Brown, Samuel	New York city, 23 McDougal St.	The claim is wholly unsustained by proof, and the term under Col. Lasher was less than six months.
Brown, Jonathan	Bloomingburg, Sullivan	His age precludes a service and the rolls refuse all aid or mention.
Brown, Israel	Fort Ann, Washington	Suspended for proof and specification.
Brown, Ephraim	Buffalo, Erie	He did not serve six months.
Brown, Philip	Warsaw, Genessee	Suspended for proof and specification.
Brown, David	(Papers withdrawn.)	His claim for three years as prisoner in Canada, from 1780 to 1783, is not credited. If he stayed so long it must have been voluntary. There is no evidence to justify this case.
Brown, Isaac	Rochester, Ulster	He did not serve six months in any embodied corps.
Brownson, Asbel	Elizabethtown, Essex	Cannot state the officers' names. Not six months' service established in this case.
Brooks, Joseph R	Lexington, Greene	Seven months and 14 days shown, (see Comptroller's certificate, which

Name	Place	Remarks
Brooks, John	Monroe, Orange	must be identified as applying to claimant in person, as well as by name.
Brooks, Joshua	Hudson, Columbia	Tours in 1776 not recited as to period and length. Twelve months and four days captivity not proved satisfactorily.
Brooks, Caleb E.	Antwerp, Jefferson	Alleges nine months service in 1776, and nine months in 1777. There is no evidence here of any such service as he describes.
Bryant, Fowler	Camden, Oneida	Not on Col. Butler's rolls. Col. Ledyard commanded State troops, and claimant is referred to the Connecticut comptroller for proof.
Bryan, John	Albany, Albany	More satisfactory proof required.
Buckman, Jacob	Lodi, Cattaraugus	All that the claimant has been enabled to establish, is three months' service in the levies of 1780.
Burdick, Perry	Cortlandt village, Cortland	His alleged service of three years and three months in the Massachusetts line is discredited by the rolls of the office. His service in the state troops must be proved in Boston.
Burgess, Isaac	Barrington, Yates	Less than six month's service in this case.
Burgher, Jeremiah	Gallatin, Columbia	Service lacks specification and proof from the records at Trenton.
Burke, Thomas	Bath, Steuben	Suspended for further proof and specification.
Burnham, Joshua	Lansingburg, Rensselaer	Suspended for defective proof.
Bush, Alpheus	Tyrone, Steuben	He is required to furnish some proof from the office of the Connecticut comptroller.
Bush, Henry	Lansing, Tompkins	Not on Captain Seabring's rolls; nor does it appear that he commanded nine months men in 1776.
Butterfield, Jonathan	Dickinson, Franklin	Two first terms not sustained by the rolls; and the department knows of no authority here for seven months' men under Captain Van Ellen. He appears to have served as a minute-man; but it seems impossible to get a specification for each tour.
Burton, John	Herkimer, Herkimer	No claim—he was too young—eleven years is too juvenile to permit the incurring of a soldier's duties and penalties.
Camp, Samuel J.	New York city	Rolls complete—name not on any of them.
Camp, James (deceased)	Alexander, Genessee	No part of the alleged services are verified. There is no proof that the designated officers were ever in service.
Cass, John	Troy, Rensselaer	Not in actual service six months.
Card, Elisha	Corinth, Saratoga	Not being on the designated rolls, he is required to produce living witnesses.
Campbell, Patrick, heirs of	Rome, Oneida	Both parents died before the passage of the act.
Carruth, Isaiah	Clarence, Erie	If he served as he states, proof should be found in the records at Boston.
Caster, Marks	Blacklake, Herkimer	Not in military service—not in any regularly organised corps.
Carey, Seth	Salina, Onondaga	Not stated with any precision, and he declines neighbourhood proof.
Camel, Thomas	Lenox, Madison	Suspended for deficient proof.

STATEMENT—Continued.

Names.	Residence.	Reasons for suspension.
Candu, Nehemiah	Cazenovia, Madison	Suspended for deficient proof.
Capwell, William	Attica, Genessee	Names of officers, dates, tours, grade, locality and length of service required.
Cary, Nathan, (deceased)	Hornelsville, Steuben	The certificate of the comptroller at Harrisburg is required, as claimant furnished no evidence of his service while living.
Corey, Peleg	Otisco, Onondaga	Period, length, grade, names of officers and localities required.
Carman, John J.	Pompey, Onondaga	Period, length, grade, names of officers and localities of each tour called for.
Carpenter, Jeremiah	Wales, Erie	Suspended for proof of service.
Caswell, Samuel	Randolph, Cattaraugus	Suspended for proof of service.
Campbell, Thomas	Sullivan, Madison	Period, duration, grade, locality and names of officers of each tour required.
Cornell, John	Clifton Park, Saratoga	Particulars of grade, date, duration, locality and officers names wanting.
Chase, Isaac	Hopewell, Ontario	Not on Col. Elliott's rolls—and service must be proved otherwise.
Chase, James	Henrietta, Monroe	Soldier died in 1828, and the widow in 1840; still, if the children can prove six months' service and the marriage before 1794, claim may be made.
Chase, Jonathan	Warsaw, Genessee	If the records at Albany afford no evidence of the long service he alleges, it will be useless to urge it further.
Chase, Ebenezer	Galen, Wayne	Claim wholly unfounded.
Christy, Daniel	Thompson, Sullivan	Further information (without which no decision can be had) is indispensible.
Chapman, Jehiel	Watson, Lewis	Name not on Captain Cady's company rolls. His alleged two tours of three months' each, are wholly discredited, and he must make other proof.
Chapman, Zachariah	Stephentown, Rensselaer	No proof of service. By giving the names of the officers, he may find some evidence by application to the comptroller of Connecticut.
Chapman, Ezekiel	Camillus, Onondaga	Service allowed by the rolls in Van Rensselaer's company three months and 26 days; service to White Plains two months and four days—making six months.
Chick, Nathaniel	Mount Hope, Orange	Repeatedly examined and rejected—name not on any rolls—no satisfactory proof of any kind—no intelligible account of any officer or regiment.

Name	Location	Notes
Chism, John T.	Schenectady, Schenectady	The only proof to be expected in this case must be found on the records at Albany.
Cheesebrough, Ass	Elbridge, Onondaga	Discrepancy between comptroller's certificate of Connecticut and claimant's statement.
Cheesbrough, James	Alden, Erie	No one tour is set forth as the rules require.
Church, David	Watervliet, Rensselaer	If he served as he stated, some evidence may be found at the comptroller's office in Albany.
Churchill John	Murray, District of New Castle, Upper Canada	Name not on the roll of Webb's regiment, continental line, 1779—no captain stated—not any lieutenant by the name of Allen—name not found on the final settlements.
Chaffee, Joseph	Melson, Madison	He did not serve six months.
Church, John	Barre, Orleans	He is referred to the state rolls at Boston for proof of service in the Massachusetts militia.
Champlain, Elisha	Beekman, Dutchess	Suspended for ambiguity.
Champlin, Thomas	Cazenovia, Madison	Tours must be specified as to date, length, grade, locality and field and company officers, especially in New Jersey, where they were short and alternate.
Clanson, Jacob	Kent, Putnam	Service not military—not in any embodied corps.
Christie, John G.	Caledonia, Livingston	Name not on the rolls—two witnesses required.
Clark, Elias	Adolphus Town, Prince Edward District, Canada West	Evidence of identity required with the soldier in Captain Earl's company.
Clark, Noah	New Hartford, Oneida	Team service—not entitled.
Clark, John	Smithtown, Suffolk	Alleged boat service for nineteen month's discredited by the well-established history of that service.
Clark, Josiah	Adams, Jefferson	No proof of service.
Clark, Daniel (deceased)	Ticonderoga, Essex	The recital of his service is so vague and imperfect, that no allowance by the regulations could be made of it.
Clinton, Henry	Potsdam, St. Lawrence	No claim—service as a waiter.
Close, Jesse	North Salem, West Chester	Period, tour, grade, officers, localities and length of service all deficient in description.
Clute, Frederick	Perry, Wyoming	Not six months' service.
Clute, Jacob P.	Schenectady, Schenectady	Application for an increase rejected—no claim.
Conce, Peter	Greenbush, Rensselaer	Not six months' service proved by the present exhibits.
Conant, Ebenezer	Lorraine, Jefferson	Name not on any rolls—unsupported by evidence of any kind—a civil contract most probably.
Conklin, James	Deerpark, Orange	Name on neither of the rolls of Graham's regiment—further proof required.
Coons, Jacob	Brutus, Cayuga	If the records at Albany are questioned with the designated officers and periods, his military service may be sustained.

STATEMENT—Continued.

Names.	Residence.	Reasons for suspension.
Cook, Job	Blenheim, Schoharie	Service insufficient. Proof may be found in Providence if he served as he states in 1777.
Cook, Nathan	Dryden, Tompkins	No proof of service.
Cooper, James	Oswego, Oswego	No proof of service.
Conge, Uzziah	Ira, Cayuga	The duration of each tour of actual service, the date, locality, grade and by whom commanded, are all deficient in description.
Conkling, William N	Bethel, Sullivan	Not six months' military service.
Corwin, Jacob	Brookhaven, Suffolk	He did not serve six months.
Court, John	Cato, Cayuga	Service on board privateer.
Coney, John	Portland, Chautauque	Suspended for further proof and explanation.
Coleman, David	Mount Hope, Orange	He must be identified as the soldier named in the certificate of the Secretary of State of New Jersey.
Coleman, Daniel	Calhoun, Orange	Name not on any rolls or final settlement certificates.
Cole, Jacob S	Cobleskill, Schoharie	The duration, locality, date, grade, and by whom commanded, are all deficient in his narrative of service.
Cole, Jacob	Albany, Albany	The discrepancies in his narrative repudiate his claim.
Cole, Joseph, 1st	Greenfield, Saratoga	If he served as lieutenant, the records of the State department at Rhode Island should show it.
Cole, Joseph, 2d	Balston, Saratoga	He is required to produce proof, if there be any, from the Albany records.
Corey, Benedict	Champen, Jefferson	Suspended for further proof.
Cooper, John	New York city and county	The period, locality, grade and length of each tour, and by whom commanded, in field and company, are indispensable.
Collier, Richard	Bath, Steuben	Not military service.
Compton, John	Enfield, Tompkins	He did not serve six months.
Conyne, Abraham	Lowville, Lewis	Not military service—no proof of any.
Covell, Jacob	Plymouth, Chenango	There were no such lengthy militia tours—proof required from living witnesses.
Connelly, Hugh (deceased)	Jefferson, Schoharie	Six months' service allowed, which the widow can be paid for upon presenting her papers.
Conrall, Thomas	Kinderhook, Columbia	No proof of service.
Cartright, David	Owego, Tioga	Some proof of service, or of the amount of pay received, will aid in the adjustment of his claim.

Colegrove, William	Newfield, Tompkins	Team service not admissible.
Covenhoven, Jacob	Glenn, Montgomery	He did not serve six months.
Countryman, Nicholas	Danube, Herkimer	First tour under age, and in no regularly organized corps—and his services after he became of age are not detailed sufficiently.
Cowan, Isaac	Stephentown, Rensselaer	He was a deserter.
Coures, Ebenezer	Litchfield, Herkimer	Proof not sufficient.
Covert, Thomas	Ovid, Seneca	Proof from his neighbors required.
Corey, William	Marion, Wayne	Proof and specification deficient.
Cramer, Conrad	Alexandria, Jefferson	A requisition of some material facts in this case was made January 8, 1884, to P. G. Keyes, which have not been furnished.
Cramer, Henry	Mamakating, Sullivan	This case was placed before Congress, and the papers under this act have never been filed in this office.
Crawford, John	Benton, Yates	To specify each term of service, period, length, grade, names of officers and places, the papers were sent to Martin Gage, Benton, N. Y., April 8, 1884.
Cranlle, George	Smithville, Chenango	Defective in preparing declaration—deficient in substance and form.
Craft, Charles	New York city	Defective in specifying dates, tours, localities, grade and length of service, and names of company and regimental officers.
Crawford, James	Dix, Chemung	Suspended for further proof and identity.
Crego, William	Decatur, Otsego	Contradictory and diverse in his narrative—no proof of service.
Critchett, John P	Depeyster, St. Lawrence	Not on the rolls—no proof of service.
Cron., John	Benton, Yates	Boys of the age of fourteen and fifteen were not admissible into the ranks, according to the regulations of the service.
Crouts, Henry	German Flatts, Herkimer	Not military service, except such as is not specified as to period, length, grade, officers, &c.
Crocker, Peter	Stephentown, Rensselaer	No proof of service.
Cross, Lemuel	Ovid, Seneca	No proof of service.
Cross, William	Osselie, Chenango	No proof of service.
Curtis, Samuel	Kirkland, Oneida	Proof of service defective.
Curtis, Joseph	Maria, Essex	No proof of service.
Culver, Samuel	Elmira, Tioga	No proof of service.
Cuddeback, William, jr	Deerpark, Orange	Claims or service in the levies of 1779, '80, '81 and '82; for 1779, there are no rolls—but for 1780, '81 and '82, there are rolls which discredit his claim throughout.
Cuddeback, William A	Finchville, Orange	Suspended for defective proof—claim withdrawn January 9, 1889, by Hon. H. Jones.
Davidson, Hezekiah	Oswego, Oswego	No evidence in the Connecticut records, and none otherwise.
Davis, Thomas	Mayfield, Montgomery	Proof of service not sufficient.
Davis, Benjamin	Warwick, Orange	Deficient proof and specification.

STATEMENT—Continued.

Names.	Residence.	Reasons for suspension.
Davis, Adaliah	Augusta, Oneida	Deficient proof and specification.
Davis, John	Bolton, Warren	He did not serve six months.
Davenport, Henry	Seward, Schoharie	Part of his service was team service, and the residue wants proof.
Davenport, William	Phelps, Ontario	Suspended for more specific details and further proof.
Darby, Abner	Batavia, Genesee	Suspended for further proof.
Dailey, Nathaniel	Day, Saratoga	Proof of service required.
Dailey, Cornelius	Brockport, Monroe	Proof of his service as a dragoon required, as his militia service is insufficient.
Dana, Joseph	Cobleskill, Schoharie	He served as a waiter, and it remains to be proved if he was detailed from the ranks.
Darling, Samuel	Clarkson, Monroe	No proof of service.
Darby, Squier	Friendship, Allegheny	He is referred to the Secretary of State of Massachusetts for proof of service.
Dart, Thomas	Keene, Essex	He is referred to the Secretary of State of Massachusetts for proof of service.
Dake, John M.	North Almond, Allegheny	He was required to specify the period, duration, grade, and place of each tour, with the names of the regimental and company officers.
Day, Asa	Massena, St. Lawrence	Petition for an increase—no evidence to warrant it.
Dean, John	Pamela, Jefferson	Evidence not satisfactory.
Decker, Evert	Shawangunk, Ulster	New York militia service should be verified by New York records.
Decker, James	Taghkanic, Columbia	Not military service for as much as six months.
Dewry, Elias	Clinton, Oneida	He was a deserter.
De Witt, Francis	Syracuse, Onondaga	Not entitled—probably a slave, who lived in a fort with his master's family black and white, on the frontiers.
Deming, David	Butternuts, Otsego	Too young—not entitled—not six months' service.
Deming, Zebulon	Italy, Yates	Suspended for defective proof of service.
Deming, Chauncey	—, Steuben	Proof of service required March 4, 1884—none furnished.
Denny, Henry (deceased)	Rochester, Monroe	Evidence of identity required with the soldier bearing his name on Captain Outwater's rolls.
Depew, John	N. York city, 48 Greenwich st.	Name not on the rolls—two witnesses required instead.
Depuy, James	Salina, Onondaga	Not entitled—Indian frontier service in a fort without any military authority but neighborhood defence.

Decker, Matthew	Mamakating, Sullivan	Not on the rolls, and two witnesses required.
Lewit, J. C.	Catskill, Green	Suspended for defective proof and claim withdrawn by Jno. Adams, October 18, 1833.
Demary, David	Shelby, Orleans	Suspended for further proof of service.
Decker, Henry	Newburgh, Orange	He served as a baker.
Deronde, John	Ramapo, Rockland	Name not on the rolls nor settlement certificates—other proof wanting.
Dewey, Enos	Norwich, Chenango	Proof from Hartford and from surviving comrades required.
Dewey, David	Plainfield, Otsego	Discredited by the rolls except for four months, and the service in Rhode Island also disproved by various facts.
Dewey, Samuel	Medina, Orleans	Only three months' service proved—he alleges he was taken prisoner after he had served about six months, but his name is not on the complete list of prisoners.
Dodd, John	——, Hamilton	Evidence not sufficient to establish his claim.
Douglass, Peleg	Chateaughy, Franklin	Suspended for details and proof of service.
Doxtater, Peter	——	The period, time, grade, events and localities not furnished, nor officers' names. [Papers delivered to Hon. D. Wardwell.]
Doty, Levi	——	Period, term, grade, events, localities, and officers' names required. [Papers delivered to Congress.]
Dorr, Elisha	Albany, Albany	There is no evidence on the records of Connecticut that he was ever in any military service.
Doty, Gilbert	Bangor, Franklin	None of the New York records as far as heard from claimant, sustain his case.
Doty, Elias	Milan, Dutchess	No satisfactory proof of the service has been received.
Drew, Samuel	Pultney, Steuben	Suspended for further proof.
Dubois, Samuel	Woodstock, Ulster	Alleged militia tours overrated—the tours were rarely over a month—the case requires explanation and proof.
Dun, Henry	Stillwater, Saratoga	Claim enlarged by supplement must be in open court—evidence called for in the department must be described specifically.
Dunning, Luther	Amsterdam, Montgomery	No proof of service—he is referred for some to the Connecticut records.
Dygert, Safrinus	Johnstown, Fulton	The question is, whether at the age of fourteen he could have been a member of his father's military company.
Eastman, Peter	Kirkland, Oneida	Not entitled—evidence not sufficient—there could not have been such tours performed as claimant narrates.
Earl, Watson	Hannibal, Oswego	Suspended for imperfections in form—the claimant received bounty land, and the evidence of his service should be at Albany.
Eckler, Christopher	Warren, Herkimer	Not military service—frontier fort under neighborhood, not military authority, State or federal.
Eckert, Jeremiah	Esophus, Ulster	Suspended to receive better evidence of the facts and nature of the service.

STATEMENT—Continued.

Names.	Residence.	Reasons for suspension.
Eckle, Anthony	Canajoharie, Montgomery	Militia tours of eight days summed up to eighteen months without particularizing names of officers, dates, duration of each, where performed, and in what grade—not entitled.
Ehle, Hermanus	Canajoharie, Montgomery	He did not serve six months.
Eldridge, Edward	Hoosick, Rensselaer	The records at Boston and numerous survivors, afford means of abundant proof of military service performed under the authority of Massachusetts.
Eldridge, Elisha	Lansingburg, Rensselaer	No evidence of six months' service.
Eddy, Esek	Boston, Erie	No evidence of such service in this department. By giving the names of the officers, some proof may possibly be found in the R. I. records.
Eells, Daniel	New Hartford, Oneida	A brief detail of the service should be submitted to the comptroller at Hartford, Connecticut, and compared with his records.
Ellicott, Jonathan	Chili, Monroe	Name not on the rolls of the New York continental line—the alleged service must be referred to the comptroller at Albany.
Ells, John (deceased)	Unadilla, Otsego	There is no satisfactory proof of any particular length of service.
Ellis, Phenix Carpenter		Suspended for defective proof. Papers sent to Hon. L. Woodbury, Secretary of the Treasury, February 2, 1835.
Eckler, Peter	Warren, Herkimer	Not military service—not in any embodied corps.
English, William	Easton, Washington	No evidence of such service as claimant narrates, and further proof and explanation is required.
Evans, William	Princeton, Schenectady	No satisfactory proof of service for six months.
Elliott, Heirg	Summit, Schoharie	No proof offered. So long a service must be susceptible of proof if real.
Earrell, Robert	Skaneateles, Onondaga	Date, duration, locality, rank and by whom commanded are the essential elements to be stated in the militia service.
Evarts, Edward	Green, Chenango	Suspended for further and more specific details and proof of service.
Eddy, Olney	Norwich, Chenango	He was long since, without effect, required to specify each tour of service with its particulars.
Esmond, Isaiah	Copake, Columbia	Suspended in 1833 for defective proof.
Edmonds, Aaron	Durham, Greene	Only twelve and thirteen years of age—no proof of his service as a militia man at twelve years old, or a regular state soldier at thirteen.

Fey, Paul	Cicero, Onondaga	Not on Warner's rolls of Marshall's regiment, and proof is wanting also for his short military tours.
Failing, John D.	Oppenheim, Montgomery	He did not serve six months.
Ferguson, Alexander	Dryden, Tompkins	He did not serve six months.
Ferguson, Isaac	Red Hook, Dutchess	He is referred to the New York records for more satisfactory proof.
Fisher, John	Naples, Ontario	No proof of service in the militia of New Jersey.
Fitch, James	Middlesex, Yates	The essential requirements as to specific narrative and proof must be insisted upon if this case is to be reasserted.
Freymin, John	Middleburg, Schoharie	No specification of tours and no proof of service.
French, John	Saratoga, Saratoga	Service in the New York militia not distinctly set forth.
Fletcher, James (deceased) heirs of	Ithaca, Tompkins	Proof satisfactory for nine months and ten days' service. The day of his death and the names of his children must be given.
Flansbury, David	Cobleskill, Schoharie	Suspended for defective proof.
Felter, Tunis	——, Rockland	Suspended for deficient details and papers withdrawn by L. Condict, November 30, 1836.
Fenton, Benjamin	Collins, Erie	There were no nine months enlistments at the period stated, and of the two terms of three months each there is no evidence.
Ferris, Squire	Chazy, Clinton	No evidence—claim rejected in the department and in Congress.
Ferris, John A	Plattsburg, Clinton	The complete rolls of 1781 discredit his service, and his claim is disallowed.
Fero, Peter	Hornby, Steuben	He does not establish six months' service.
Filkins, Isaac	Nassau, Rensselaer	Disproved by all the rolls in range of his alleged service except for 1776, and the absence of correct and specific details preclude the inspection for 1776.
Foot, John	Vernon, Oneida	Mr. Banks' certificate of service was promised on May 6, 1834, but it has not made its appearance.
Fosgate, Ezekiel	Fishkill, Dutchess	Its has not specified each tour of service. This must be done and submitted for verification or disproof to the New York comptroller.
Fort, John	Hoosick, Rensselaer	Suspended for deficient details and proof.
Flamburgh, John	Harpersfield, Delaware	Service for six months not proved.
Field, Joarab	Batavia, Genessee	Service without pay could not have been under military organization.
Fosdick, William	Angelica, Allegheny	Suspended for defective details.
Fonda, Dowe (deceased)	Hudson, Columbia	He did not serve six months.
Ferris, Gilbert	Windham, Greene	Suspended for defective proof.
Fink, John (deceased)	Lepander, Onondaga	He must detail his service to the comptroller at Albany for proof or disproof.
Fitzsimmons, Thomas	Scio, Allegheny	He was too young for military service.
Finch, Timothy	Newstead, Erie	Defective proof—not sustained by the treasury records of Vermont.
Foster, Jacob	Cobleskill, Schoharie	His service will have to be proved as set forth by the Secretary of State of New York; and his age is also to be proved.

STATEMENT—Continued.

Names.	Residence.	Reasons for suspension.
Foley, John	Rome, Oneida	Suspended for further proof and specification.
Fowler, Samuel	Sherburn, Chenango	His age would exclude his claim, but his services on board a private vessel is conclusive to that effect.
Fosdick, John	Roland, Chautauque	Discredited by the rolls. He was also under age—no claim.
Force, Benjamin	Dover, Dutchess	Not on the requisite rolls, and other proof must supply the deficiency.
Ford, Isaiah	Elliottsville, Cattaraugus	Proof deficient; and the events unfavourable as claimant has detailed them.
Fox, William	Ovid, Seneca	Alike discredited by the silence of the rolls and of any other kind of proof.
Fox, Peter	Palatine, Montgomery	His claim, suspended in 1832 for defective proof, was withdrawn in May, 1833, and not replaced.
Fuller, Shubael	Boston, Eri	The rolls contain proof against his claim as substitute for his brother.
Fuller, Ebenezer	Orleans, Jefferson	No proof of service in the department, and he is referred to the comptroller of the State of New York.
Furman, Nathan	Warwick, Orange	He should produce his sergeant's warrant, and state with precision the time of his escape from imprisonment.
Finch, Ezra	Granville, Greene	Period, grade, duration, locality and commanders in field and company are all indispensible for each tour.
Field, John	Alexandria, Jefferson	Three years service as a drummer not on the rolls appearing, must be sustained by credible witnesses.
Freeman, Alexander	Lockport, Niagara	Period, length, grade, officers commanding battles and localities are all necessary to the examination of a tour.
Frost, Solomon	Windsor, Broome	Discredited by the rolls, and he is referred to the Connecticut comptroller.
Freeman, Israel	Richfield, Otsego	Suspended for proper details of service, officers' names, &c.
Gates, Stephen	Schenectady, Schenectady	Service in 1776, 1777, 1778, and 1779, is referred to the Comptroller's office, New York.
Gansevoort, Leonard	Albany, Albany	He did not serve six months.
Gallup, Nathaniel	Newstead, Erie	The records of the treasury department of Vermont do not confirm his claim.
Gainer, Edward	Jackson, Washington	Names of officers and other details indispensable to be known.
Gardiner, John	Schodack, Rensselaer	He did not serve six months.

Gannon, Joseph	Elmira, Tioga	His claim for four years service in the Pennsylvania militia, is not specified by a single tour. Two monthly tours were the limit for the Pennsylvania militia.
Geesler, John	Canajoharie, Montgomery	Claim, in the absence of the comptroller's certificate, cannot pass.
Genter, Genter	Springfield, Otsego	Proof of service defective.
Gile, Wray	Oneonta, Otsego	Name not on the rolls of those captains he names. He is probably mistaken in the names of his commanders.
Gillis, Alexander	Dryden, Tompkins	A case out of which neither Congress nor the department can make any thing; papers withdrawn.
Gardiner, John	Root, Montgomery	He did not serve in any regularly organized corps.
Ganoung, Moses	Drydeng, Tompkins	Suspended for defective proof.
Gilbert, Joseph	Clifton Park, Saratoga	From his youth he was not able to bear arms until about the close of the war.
Gilbert, Timothy	North East, Dutchess	No intelligible narrative and no proof of the service.
Gilbert, John	Upper Canada, Lansdown, county Leeds	No evidence appearing he is required to furnish a detail of his service, and submit it to the Connecticut comptroller.
Giltner, Francis	Ithaca, Tompkins	Suspended for further proof—see letter Feb. 24, 1847.—Hon. S. Strong.
Goff, William	Burlington, Otsego	Some proof of so much alleged service is surely possible.
Goddard, Louis	Fort Covington, Franklin	No service defined—no officers' names given.
Godhard, David	Ballston, Saratoga	An attempt at fraud. See letter October 5, 1848, to Joshua A. Spencer, U. S. District Attorney, Utica.
Goodenough, Salmon	Oneonta, Otsego	The period, length, grade and locality of each tour, with the respective officers in command, should be submitted to the Secretary of State at Boston.
Grawberger, Henry	Ballston Spa, Saratoga	Suspended for further proof.
Graves, Bela	Scio, Allegheny	Must furnish such evidence as is stated in letter July 29, 1846, to Hon. A. Smith.
Gray, Robert	Guilderland, Albany	Suspended for defective proof.
Griffith, Eli	Gates, Monroe	No proof of service, the rolls being silent.
Gray, Ichabod	Verona, Oneida	Claim not yet asserted. See letter March 23, 1846, to A. J. Graves, Oneida Castle.
Granger, Moses	Greenwich, Washington	Claim unsupported by any evidence except his own declaration.
Graves, Nathaniel	Attica, Genessee	Fourteen years old at his first term. If he were of an age to bear arms, he has not specified his service as he should have done.
Graves, Noadiah	Hartland, Niagara	The details of his service were directed to be submitted to the comptroller at Albany for proof or discredit.
Grannis Robert	Evans, Erie	Suspended for further proof, which was promised but did not come.
Gray, Andrew	Danville, Livingston	Suspended for defective proof, and papers by P. C. Fuller, March 1, 1846.

[37]   122

STATEMENT—Continued.

Names.	Residence.	Reasons for suspension.
Grant, Vincent	Canandaigua, Ontario	Rolls in the office discrediting his claim, and no other proof offering, it was rejected June 6, 1884, in a letter to T. Beales.
Greatsinger, John	Marbletown, Ulster	Suspended for proof of more service.
Green, John G.	Berlin, Rensselaer	No specification as to distinct tours and details, officers, dates, localities, grade or length of service.
Green, Gideon	Bainbridge, Chenango	No evidence of service.
Grey, Ichabod	Verona, Oneida	Very long pretensions of service, but no proof whatever—his claim has no documentary traces as far as discovered, and no oral evidence.
Green, James	Johnstown, Montgomery	Suspended for further proof.
Green, John	Benton, Yates	Specification of the details of service required.
Green, Joseph	Eaton, Madison	Suspended to afford a search into the rolls of Massachusetts at Boston.
Hall, John	Athol, Warren	Defective proof.
Hall, John	Rome, Oneida	Suspended for an inspection of the Massachusetts rolls.
Hall, John	Charlotte, Chautauque	Suspended for lack of evidence.
Hall, Asahel	Salisbury, Herkimer	Evidence in this case may be had from the comptroller of Connecticut. Captains' names and each regiment in which he served must be given, and one witness must identify him with the service he describes.
Hall, Eli	Watertown, Jefferson	
Hallock, John	Minisink, Orange	Twenty-two months' service alleged in 1776, '77 and '78, which must be specified in detail, and submitted to the comptroller at Albany.
Halsey, Zephaniah	Fayette, Seneca	He did not perform military service.
Harris, Richard	Grantham Township, District of Niagara, Upper Canada	It is necessary that he should be identified by a credible witness as the soldier who describes himself to be in the Maryland line.
Hamilton, Charles	Hamilton, Madison	No proof on the rolls of Massachusetts, and his fourth term, under the authority of Vermont, must be authenticated by the rolls in the treasurer's office of that State.
Hall, Isiah	Berlin, Rensselaer	Suspended for further proof.
Hawley, Solomon	Almond, Allegheny	Papers lost or mislaid by claimant's agent, who withdrew them for amendment in 1838.
Hall, James	Murray, Orleans	Proof of service by two witnesses required specifying details.
Harrington, Isaac	Galen, Wayne	Specification of each tour, its date, duration, locality, and officers commanding is required.

Hayden, Samuel	Middlefield, Otsego	Suspended for proof of service from the rolls at Boston.
Harris, David	Guilford, Chenango	He was required to produce proof of his service, but has failed to do so.
Hagaman, William	Hector, Tompkins	He alleges four years' service as a minute man, and cannot find a living witness who recollects his services.
Harford, Peter	New York city	Suspended for proof by living named persons, which it appears has not been procured.
Hammond, Daniel	Brookhaven, Suffolk	Not six months military service.
Halsted, Timothy	Lysander, Onondaga	He was advised October 28, 1823, that his proof was defective.
Hall, Elisha	Camillus, Onondaga	Service in the militia under sixteen years of age—should be established by the records at Boston.
Harrington, Benjamin	Winfield, Herkimer	He was but twelve years old when his alleged service began—an age entirely too juvenile for a soldiers' responsibilities.
Hasbrouck, Benjamin S	Marbletown, Ulster	Claim disallowed—discredited by the comptroller's certificate.
Hartwell, Asahel	Saratoga Springs	Name not on the rolls of Captain John Fuller, in 1775, and his other tour of two months under Captain Pope not sufficient.
Hartshorn, Andrew	Virgil, Cortlandt	Evidence of service required from the Massachusetts rolls at Boston.
Haskin, Isaac H	Willet, Cortlandt	He was too young to bear arms.
Harris, James	New Lisbon, Otsego	Suspended for proof of service—name not on Captain Fleming's pay roll.
Halsey, Job	Binghampton, Suffolk	He was too young to bear arms.
Hatch, Asa	Farmersville, Cattaraugus	His name is not on any roll, and his case, at present, stands on his own declaration.
Havens, Jo	Livonia, Livingston	Suspended for defective proof.
Hatfield, Peter	New York city	The evidence in this case preponderates against the claim.
Hawley, Philo	Centerville, Allegheny	No proof of service adduced.
Hayes, Aaron	Lewis, Essex	His claim is not supported by any evidence in this office, and he is advised to apply to the comptroller at Hartford, Connecticut.
Hays, Conrad	New Haven, Oswego	Suspended for further proof.
Hays, Benjamin	Bolton, Warren	He did not serve six months.
Heath, Simon	Wethersfield, Genesee	He must verify his service by the records of the Secretary of State at Concord, N. H.
Hempsted, Nathaniel	——, Chautauque	Suspended for deficient proof April 12, 1834, and papers sent to Hon. A. Hazeltine, and not replaced.
Helm, Simon	Springport, Cayuga	No specific narrative—no details of service so necessary to enable an adjustment of a pro rata pension.
Helme, James	Schenectady city	He did not serve six months.
Hecox, Samuel	New Hartford, Oneida	Suspended for the production of his authority as a sergeant—and of some proof, perhaps, from the comptroller of Connecticut.
Hendricks, Francis	Blenheim, Schoharie	He should specify the date, duration, locality, and commanders of each tour of actual service.

STATEMENT—Continued.

Names.	Residence.	Reasons for suspension.
Hendricks, Philip	Kingston, Ulster	His tours in the militia of 1777 and 1781 are overrated—there is no evidence of such service at the periods designated.
Hempstead, Nathaniel	Brooklyn, Kings	Suspended for further proof.
Hewitt, Thomas	Charlton, Saratoga	Served on board a private armed vessel.
Herod, Joseph	Groveland, Livingston	Not verified by the Harrisburg records, nor by the recollection of the ensign of the company—further proof required.
Hess, Conrad	German Flats, Herkimer	He was required to specify under what officers he served, when and where, and how long, which have not been done.
Henry, Robert	New York city	Doubtful—see if it be not a forgery.
Hight, John M		Suspended for specification of details of each tour of service. [Claim and papers withdrawn.]
Heacock, Samuel	Otsego, Otsego	Evidence insufficient—see letter September 25, 1884, Chester Jarvis.
Hickey, John	Hempstead, Queens	He did not serve six months.
Hicks, Thomas	Springfield, Otsego	He was a deserter.
Hillsinger, Elias	Cherry Valley, Otsego	Four years claimed in the New York militia—he must state who commanded him, and when, and how long he served each tour—and where he was marched to, or stationed, and verify his service by the records at Albany.
Hurd, Roswell	Northumberland, Saratoga	Time and manner of entering and leaving service—company, regiment and line, and field and regimental officers required.
Hinsdale, Elias	Otsego, Otsego	Suspended for want of proof.
Hocketrasser, Baltus	District of Niagara, U. Canada	He did not serve six months.
Hodskins, Jonas (deceased)	New Lisbon, Otsego	Suspended for further proof.
Hooker, William (deceased)	Truxton, Cortlandt	He did not serve six months in a military capacity.
Hollister, John	Sparta, Livingston	No such named officers served during the war in New Jersey—the records at Trenton must be consulted for proof if this be not so.
Hoolsapple, William	Saint Armand, Lower Canada	Period, length, grade, locality, and company and field officers must be set forth for each tour of actual service.
Hagodorn, Jacob	Otsego, Otsego	Period, length, grade, locality, and company and field officers must be set forth for each tour of actual service, and submitted to the comptroller at Albany.
Hogle, Nicholas	Greenbush, Rensselaer	No evidence to establish as much as six months' service.
House, Eleazar	Lowville, Lewis	Service neither set forth nor proved.

Howard, Elisha..............	Covington, Genesee.......	Service at Springfield as a guard must be shown by the Massachusetts records at Boston.
Holcomb, Luther............	Coventry, Chenango	No evidence in the department of such service, nor of any tour of the duration of that described—some evidence may possibly be had of the Connecticut comptroller.
Holcomb, Roger.............	Lexington, Greene	He asserts service of a kind totally different from any thing the department has on record.
Howard, Hezekiah...........	Veteran, Tioga...........	He did not serve six months.
Howell, Isaac...............	Rochester, Monroe........	He left the service and enlisted with the British—having been a prisoner.
Hodge, Benjamin............	Buffalo, Erie.............	Referred for further proof to the comptroller at Hartford, Connecticut.
Hoffman, Herman............	Bainbridge, Chenango.....	Referred to E. D. Baggs, Secretary of State, Boston, for further proof.
Hoskins, Benoni.............	Truxton, Cortlandt........	Claims to have been an ensign of the militia from May 1, 1782, to the end of the war—a very unusual militia tour, and requires some proof and explanation.
Hoard, Samuel..............	Berlin, Rensselaer........	Specification required of each tour of actual service—its beginning and ending, locality, grade, and officers commanding.
Hoover, John...............	Manheim, Herkimer.......	A certificate required from the New York Secretary of State, of Hoover's appointment as captain in Colonel Billington's regiment, and to specify the duration of each term of actual service.
Hoxie, Benjamin............	Johnstown, Montgomery....	Period, length, grade, locality, and company and regimental officers should be set forth.
Howe, David................	Van Buren, Onondaga.....	He was required to present a certificate of the Massachusetts Secretary of State.
Hollister, Josiah (deceased)...	Mansfield, Cattaraugus....	The original journal in which claimant recorded his service, and on which he bases his claim, should be sent to the department.
Honeywell, Rice.............	Upper Canada............	He did not serve six months.
Horn, Patrick...............	Lewiston, Niagara........	He did not serve six months.
Hornbeck, Matthew..........	Liberty, Sullivan.........	Neither claimant's name nor his witnesses on the New York rolls.
Hudson, Obadiah............	Huntington Commac, Suffolk...	Date, length, grade, station, names of officers in each tour required, and submitted to the comptroller at Albany.
Hull, Eli...................	Murray, Newcastle, U. Canada...	Service seems sufficient to grant him a full pension under this act, but before a certificate can issue it must be proved that he is still living —or if he be dead, the names of his children and the exact day of his death.
Huntington, Jeremiah (deceased)...	Springfield, Otsego.......	No specification of the period, length, grade, localities, or names of officers for each term of service, and no decision can be had without them.
Hutchinson, Samuel.........	Tully, Onondaga..........	He was referred on December 5, 1886, to the records of Connecticut for proof, but it has not made its appearance.
Hulbut, Asahel..............	Le Roy, Genesee.........	He did not serve six months.

STATEMENT—Continued.

Names.	Residence.	Reasons for suspension.
Humphrey, Peter	Florence, Oneida	No proof—name not on any rolls.
Hunter, Daniel	Colchester, Delaware	Service by substitute—present applicant not entitled.
Hempsted, Thomas	Southold, Suffolk	There were no enlistments in 1776 for six months.
Hulet, Asa	Springwater, Livingston	First tour of three months not set forth—and second tour, three months, has no aid from the Massachusetts rolls.
Huskens, Benjamin	Camden, Oneida	Proof insufficient.
Hyatt, Hezekiah	Fenner, Madison	Suspended for further proof.
Hyatt, John	Barton, Tioga	Suspended for more perfect details and specification.
Holmes, John	Pawlings, Dutchess	Claim as deputy commissary not sufficiently set forth and proved.
Jarvis, Henry	Fleming, Cayuga	He did not serve six months in a regularly organized corps.
James, Henry	Hopewell, Ontario	Name not on Colonel Webb's rolls—suspended for further proof.
Jewell, George	Weedsport, Cayuga	Except patrol duty, he did not serve six months.
Jouson, Jacob	Easthampton, Suffolk	No proof of six months' service—claim rejected by Congress and by this department.
Johnson, William	New York city	No part of his alleged service can be allowed upon the proof on file.
Johnson, Abraham	Westfield, Richmond	No evidence of such service as gunboats during the revolutionary war.
Johnson, Joseph	Vernon, Oneida	Name not on the rolls of Colonel Meig's regiment.
Johnson, Samuel	Albion, Orleans	Proof of service not sufficient.
Johnson, Henry	Perinton, Monroe	There were no enlistments in Colonel Home's regiment New Jersey militia for three years—some proof required.
Jones, William (deceased)	Scarborough, Canada West	Before certificate can be issued to the children, their names and places of abode must be stated and certified by the court.
Jones, Jesse	Coshocton, Steuben	He was too young for military service at the age of thirteen or fourteen years—his name is not on the rolls of those officers under whom he alleges service.
Jones, William	Chesterfield, Essex	He is referred to the Massachusetts rolls at Boston for proof of service.
Jordan, Adam	Stark, Herkimer	The original pay roll must be produced, alleged to be in the possession of Peter Young, and referred to as evidence.
Judd, Isaac	Candor, Tioga	Each tour of actual service must be specified, and its details submitted to the Connecticut comptroller.

Name	Location	Notes
Ingersoll, Thomas	Salina, Onondaga	Service not established.
Jeffreys, Henry	Elbridge, Onondaga	There were no three or four months tours in New Jersey—the tours were but for one month, and each must be described separately in its details.
Jones, John	Varick, Seneca	He did not serve six months.
Kennedy, Thomas	Manchester, Ontario	Not on any rolls—no evidence offered oral or of record—no claim.
Kebly, Isaac	Peru, Clinton	Not on any rolls, and statements adverse to well known historical facts—claim very doubtful.
Kelly, David	Middletown, Delaware	He did not serve six months.
Kennedy, John (Indian Oneida tribe)	Vernon, Oneida, Castle Oneida	Claim cannot be investigated without the names of the officers under whom he served.
Keyes, Ebenezer	Linklaen, Chenango	Suspended for proof from Connecticut comptroller and surviving comrades.
Kenyon, David	Hague, Warren	Suspended for further proof.
Kirtland, Eleazar	Greenville, Greene	He did not serve six months in a military capacity.
Keach, James	Westernville, Oneida	Claim exceedingly doubtful—see letters April 28, 1834, August 4, 1835—B. P. Johnson.
Kendall, Ephraim	Sandy Creek, Oswego	Alleges three several tours in 1775, '76 and '77, as drummer, making seven months, which should be found on the records of Massachusetts at Boston.
Kentner, John P.	Turin, Lewis	He is required to apply to the New York comptroller for proof.
King, David	Prattsburgh, Steuben	No proof of service—claim rejected July 19, 1860—letter Secretary of the Interior.
King, Isaac	Paris, Oneida	Suspended for further proof.
King, Joshua (deceased)	Albany, Albany	Claim for increase as lieutenant of dragoons in the staff, act May, 1828, at $400 per annum—rejected on the ground that he was not in the staff.
Kip, James	Rhinebeck, Dutchess	No details of actual service—drilling and holding in readiness must be omitted in his new declaration, and actual service only specified.
Kitts, John	Lowville, Lewis	Details of each tour, duration, period, grade, localities, and officers required.
Knapp, Lemuel	Granville, Washington	Testimony of surviving comrades required, of which there are numbers, October 1, 1834.
Knapp, Libbens	Haverstraw, Rockland	He did not serve six months.
Knapp, William	Warwick, Orange	Specification of dates, officers, and other details required.
Koon, John	Taghkanic, Columbia	Suspended for better proof of actual service.
Koyl, Ephraim	Baylston, Oswego	No satisfactory proof.
Krum, Jacob D	Rochester, Ulster	No evidence of such service, and none in his case.

STATEMENT—Continued.

Names.	Residence.	Reasons for suspension.
Kniffin, Thomas	Rye, West Chester	Boat service at short intervals for occasional use for a few days, and sometimes only for hours—requires more proof than is now filed to sustain a claim for eighteen months.
Knight, Charles	Warsaw, Genesee	He was a hired teamster, and has no claim.
Kronkwhite	Windham, Greene	He did not serve six months.
Kyle, Ephraim (deceased)	Canada West	Suspended for further proof.
Labar, Henry	Lansing, Tompkins	Alleges three years in the line—not on the rolls where it ought to be, and no other proof presented.
Lawson, Isaac	Watervliet, Albany	No such long militia tours are performed—required to specify more particularly each term of service and its material facts.
Lake, David	Paris, Oneida	He was under age at the period of all of his alleged service, and proof is required from the Connecticut records.
Linsley, Solomon	Madrid, St. Lawrence	Claim disallowed—discredited by the rolls.
Lyon, Daniel	North Castle, West Chester	The rolls being silent, his claim requires proof by two witnesses.
Loomis, Gamaliel	Livonia, Livingston	Application must be made with the details of his service to the comptroller's office at Hartford.
Loomis, Thaddeus	Richfield, Otsego	Suspended for specification of officers, dates, places, and all the material facts of the several tours.
Loomis, Martin	Floyd, Oneida	Suspended for further proof.
Lockwood, George	New York city	Suspended for a more perfect exhibit of his service, as mentioned in the certificate of the Connecticut comptroller—also some proof by the survivors of the coast guards.
Lord, William		Suspended for further proof in letter to claimant September 10, 1833, and papers delivered to Hon. S. Beardsley.
Love, John	Schroepple, Oswego	Claim rejected—patrol service and neighborhood vigilance on a frontier not proper military service.
Lovewell, Zacheus (deceased)	Gaines, Orleans	He did not serve six months.
Lovering, Jesse (deceased)	Canaan, Columbia	Suspended for proof of the rightful heir and date of his father's death, and proof of his father's identity with the soldier of the rolls.

Loucks, Jeremiah	Middleburgh, Schoharie	He did not serve six months.
Lowrey, James	Loraine, Jefferson	Past service as a teamster—the residue less than six months—claim rejected.
Loucks, Andrew	Middleburgh, Schoharie	By the rolls he served only one month twenty-three days in 1778 to 1781—his service in 1779 excepted, which is not specified—and for which he must furnish details.
Losley, James	Pleasant Valley, Dutchess	A claim for six years' service as a revolutionary soldier should surely be backed by proof enough to furnish the details as to officers, field and regimental, and dates, without which the rolls cannot be inspected.
Luther, Ezra	Angelica, Alleghany	He did not perform six months military service.
Luther, Hezekiah	Sweden, Monroe	He is advised to frame a detail of his services, and exhibit it to the Secretary of State of Massachusetts, at Boston, where he will doubtless find satisfactory proof.
Lyon, Kimberly	Easton, Washington	Suspended July 19, 1836, for an inspection of the Massachusetts rolls at Boston.
Lyon, Alvin	Yorktown, West Chester	The name of the officer commanding the company required—this service was most probably a domestic patrol service.
Lyon, John	Oswegatchie, St. Lawrence	The declaration was vitiated by an interlineation without the authority of the court, after the papers had been in this office, and remanded for correction.
Lyon, Samuel	Yonkers, West Chester	His claim is directly discredited by the records of the service of Colonel Drake's regiment within the period designated.
Lyle, Jacob	Milan, Dutchess	Service in the New Jersey militia was for one month, and each tour should be specified by itself—suspended for such specification.
Lyon, Joseph	New York city	Suspended for further proof—the name of Joseph Lyon occurs twice on Captain Lyon's roll, and is credited with five months twenty days service.
La Jenessee, Prudent	Champlain, Clinton	He was connected with the army only as a baker.
Lawyer, David	Cobleskill, Schoharie	Suspended for further proof and details of service.
Lavarnway, Tousant	Chazy, Clinton	He did not serve as a soldier—he was a wagoner.
Laucks, Richard (alias Dietrich)	Palatine, Montgomery	He did not serve six months.
Lamont, Archibald	Fulton, Schoharie	Claim cannot be admitted upon the present proof.
Lambert, George	Canajoharie, Montgomery	The militia service which he thinks to prove is not supported by the records at Albany.
Landon, Thomas	York, Livingston	No additional evidence has been adduced since this case was suspended, November 5, 1832, in a letter to G. N. Skinner.
Lape, George	Claverack, Columbia	No such name appears on the rolls of Van Rensselaer's regiment—claimant should cause his service to be specified by a credible witness, who can give the names of the officers.

Ex.—9

STATEMENT—Continued.

Names.	Residence.	Reasons for suspension.
Lawyer, Lawrence		Having been suspended for further proof, letter February 18, 1847, to Hon. Charles Goodyear. [Papers withdrawn.]
Loycraft, Willett	Flushing, Queens	Suspended for the specification of the details of his service.
Leup, Frederick	Oswegatchie, St. Lawrence	Suspended for further proof of service.
Loet, Miles	Malone, Franklin	Suspended for further proof of service.
Lewis, Joseph	Aurelius, Cayuga	No proof of service—discredited by the Massachusetts rolls—claim disallowed.
Lewis, Jacob	Glenn, Montgomery	Claim rejected—he was a waiter.
Leueav, Peter	Elizabethtown, Essex	Rejected—if he had served as alleged, the evidence had appeared on the rolls of his regiment in this office, or on the list of refugees who received bounty lands from the State of New York.
Livingston, Beekman	Johnstown, Montgomery	There is no evidence of a volunteer company from the body of the militia who served three years continuous service—the authority for such organization must be shown.
Linsabaugh, Adam	Montgomery, Orange	No service under age can be admitted without direct proof—his age, fourteen years, precludes his claim, especially as his witness does not specify any service before 1780—when he was only ten years of age, and that was less than six months.
Marenus, John		Proof of service should be established by the certificate of the comptroller of New York. [Papers withdrawn.]
Martine, Daniel	Mamakating, Sullivan	Referred to the office of the New York comptroller for proof of service.
Marble, Isaiah	Greensburgh, Rensselaer	Part of his service was not in a military capacity, and the rest requires further proof and explanation.
Marble, Thomas	Van Buren, Onondaga	Requisite proof of service has never been established in this case.
Martling, Daniel (deceased)	Troy, Rensselaer	No claim—the North Carolina rolls are complete, and neither claimant's name nor the service of his officers are noticed upon them.
Marshall, Joel	Clay, Onondaga	Suspended for adequate evidence which had not been furnished as late as September 7, 1847.
Manrow, Asahel	Hampton, Washington	Suspended for deficiency in the proof.
Martin, Joseph (deceased)	Johnsburgh, Washington	He proved nine months' service under act March 18, 1818, and his widow may claim under the act of July 7, 1838.
Mastin, Ezekiel	Thompson, Sullivan	He did not serve six months.

Name	Place	Notes
Matteson, William	Harmony, Chautauque	If claimant served as alleged, evidence should be found with the Connecticut comptroller.
Maxson, Asa	Petersburgh, Rensselaer	Suspended for further investigation respecting the tours last specified amounting to eight months.
Manly, Nathan (deceased)	Cazenovia, Madison	His case, during his life, failed for the want of specific details, which, now he is dead, cannot be expected to be supplied.
Manly, Daniel	Hounsfield, Jefferson	Such a detail of his services was required as would enable the Secretary of State of Massachusetts to inspect the rolls.
Mandeville, Jacob	Skaneateles, Onondaga	Remanded for a certificate to the witnesses' credibility, and also a more perfect explication, if his company was, or was not in service three months on Constitution Island.
Mays, Abraham	Lexington, Greene	Required to prove somewhat directly, and to state if he served in the militia or State troops of Pennsylvania.
Merselles, John J	Constantia, Oswego	He claims for three years' service in the New York line, but the muster and pay rolls discredit in toto, both himself and his witnesses.
Marsh, David	New York city	He is required to show whether there is evidence for or against his claim in the records of the Connecticut comptroller.
Manrow, Noah	Rutland, Jefferson	For his first term he was under age—for his second, he fails to state the names of his officers—and he might prove his third term by abundant evidence, if he would seek it where it is most likely to be found.
Marsh, Benjamin	Granville, Washington	He was required on April 10, 1834, to produce proof from the records at Boston, but he has failed to do so.
Matthews, Gideon	Broome, Greene	Some evidence of his service may be had by application to the Connecticut comptroller.
Mather, Stephen	Edmiston, Otsego	Each tour, its beginning and ending, where stationed or marched—by whom command in companies and regiments, and his own grade should be stated.
Mattieson, Joshua	Laurens, Otsego	Name of claimant not on the Massachusetts or Rhode Island rolls—additional proof showing the names of the officers and all the material facts of his service is called for.
Mabb, Thomas	Sharon, Scholarie	If claimant has been mistaken in the names of his officers, he should state the fact in a supplemental declaration.
Maze, Abraham	Lexington, Greene	He overrates his service in the Pennsylvania militia, and in his service in New York, he does not name his officers.
Maybee, David	Paris, Oswego	Suspended for more perfect details—he claims four years' service under Captain Dygart, of Colonel Willit's regiment, New York line—and the records at Albany must sustain his service.
Maynard, Elisha B	Harrison, West Chester	He did not serve six months.
Mastice, Lawrence		Suspended for proof and specification, and papers withdrawn March 26, 1846, by Hon. C. Goodyear.

STATEMENT—Continued.

Names.	Residence.	Reasons for suspension.
Mattice, Joseph	Schoharie, Schoharie	He did not serve in any regularly organized corps.
McCarty, Daniel	Rhinebeck, Dutchess	Proof absent of his commission as lieutenant in the State troops of Connecticut, and of his service also—when his rank is established he must furnish the deposition of George Mills, of New York.
McAlpin, John	Schenectady, Schenectady	The papers in this case, which was defective in proof, were enclosed to J. McComike, Troy, December 19, 1832.
McCarty, Moses	Nichols, Tioga	Suspended for lack of proof, October 29, 1838.
McCann, John	Arcadia, Wayne	Evidence from the Secretary of State at Trenton, N. J., and from the comptroller's office, Albany, N. Y., for proof of service in the several States.
McCoy, Daniel	Buffalo, Erie	Claims for six years—name not on the rolls of Captain Moody—two witnesses required.
McIntosh, Alexander	Livingston, Columbia	Service should be proved by certificate of the comptroller of New York, who should be furnished with a copy of the draft of McIntosh's service, in the hands of Mr. Esselstyne.
McKee, William	Seneca, Ontario	No proof of service, and no intelligible narrative of his services—his claim cannot be acted upon without a better account and evidence.
McFarland, William	Arcadia, Wayne	He should produce his sergeant's warrant, and it is believed Lieutenant Nicholas Van Rensselaer, under whom applicant alleges he served, is now living in Greenbush, Albany county.
McFarland, John	Angelica, Allegheny	By giving the name of the town in which he resided when he enlisted, he may procure some proof of his service in the Secretary of State's office, Boston.
McKinney, Daniel	——, Ontario	Suspended for defective proof, and papers withdrawn by Hon. J. Fory, jr, May 21, 1836.
McNeil, Neil	Danube, Montgomery	No records of his commission either as lieutenant or captain—rolls of Schyler's regiment are silent, and the general abstract showing the bills rendered by the militia officers, don't show his name.
Mead, Jasper	Chester, Warren	He did not serve six months.
Mead, Eli	Elmira, Chemung	He did not serve six months.
Mead, Zelek	Harrisburgh, Lewis	Captain Benedict, under whom one tour was performed, being now living in North Salem, West Chester co., his affidavit should be procured—the twelve months' tour in Captain Delavan's company cannot pass without further evidence.

Name	Place	Remarks
Mead, Isaiah	Junius, Seneca	Suspended for further proof.
Merrill, John	Howard, Steuben	He was a deserter.
Merrill, Frederick	Northfield, Richmond	There is no evidence of such service as he allegs in a company called Washington Guides, for two or three years continuously in the field—and if not continuously there, each term should be separately stated.
Mercer, John (deceased)	Lansingburgh, Rensselaer	No claim—he died in 1812.
Messor, Timothy	Day, Saratoga	He did not serve six months.
Messler, John (deceased)	Covert, Seneca	It is not competent for an agent in the absence of the widow or children to revive the claim of the deceased applicant.
Merrifield, William	Ghent, Columbia	He did not serve six months.
Merrill, Thomas (deceased)	Plymouth, Chenango	Name not on the rolls, and there is no other evidence offered.
Miller, Dyonisius (deceased), administrator of	Canjoharie, Montgomery	Supposed fraud—see letter Joshua Spencer, United States district attorney, Albany, January 18, 1843.
Millerd, Abiathur	Hampton, Washington	He must frame a detail of the facts of his service, period, length, grade, officers, &c., and submit it to the Secretary of State of Massachusetts, and announce the result.
Miller, Jeremiah Jacob	Millehide, Loudon District, Upper Canada	He did not serve six months.
Mills, Kanah	Kirkland, Oneida	Suspended for further proof.
Milles, Jacob	Verona, Oneida	The duration, date, locality, grade, and officers of each tour must be specified.
Millet, Jonathan A	Walworth, Wayne	The rolls are silent, and two credible and competent witnesses are required.
Middough, Jasper	Phelps, Ontario	No evidence of service—name not on the rolls of Captain Westfall's company.
Miller, Philip	Elizabethtown, Essex	He was under age and there is no proof of his service—Thomas Boggs, as a lieutenant under Captain Stockwell, is not found.
Miller, Peter	Poughkeepsie, Dutchess	No evidence has been furnished to substantiate this claim—it should be proved that claimant belonged to Colonel Hay's regiment, and that in making coal, he was acting under competent military authority.
Moffatt, Enoch (deceased)	Butternuts, Otsego	Suspended for further proof by inspection of the rolls at Boston.
Moosknug, Henry	Saugerties, Ulster	Claims for three years in the Pennsylvania line—but he is not noticed by pay rolls or muster rolls, and other proof is required.
Morgan, Timothy	Elliottville, Cattaraugus	Suspended for further proof and specification.
Mott, Jacob	Brookhaven, Suffolk	Neither details of service nor evidence.
More, Jacob A.	Schodack, Rensselaer	His name not on the requisite rolls—proof from comrades required.
Morrell, James (deceased)	New York city	Claim suspended for defective proof and papers withdrawn.
Morrill, Abraham	Ogden, Monroe	Not proved sufficiently—two months seven days only by the rolls.
Mosher, William	Port Bay, Wayne	No proof sent on, and he is required to furnish some.

STATEMENT—Continued.

Names.	Residence.	Reasons for suspension.
Mount, Adam D	New York city	He was a baker and not entitled.
Monty, Francis (deceased)	Plattsburgh, Clinton	He died before the passage of the act.
Mowers, John	Lenox, Madison	Suspended for further proof.
Myrick, Joshua		Suspended for further proof.
Monroe, Walter	New York city	Rejected—he did not serve in the revolutionary war.
Murdock, Elisha	Otisco, Onondaga	No proof of service—has not given the name of a single officer for his service in 1779, nor any satisfactory answer to the interrogatories.
Newcomb, Thomas	Onondaga, Onondaga	No additional evidence since his case was suspended in 1882—the alleged service in the Connecticut line is not noticed by the rolls—he should find some comrades who may be able to give him all the aid he seeks.
Newcomb, Azariah	Hector, Tompkins	He did not serve six months.
Nellis, John D	Whitestown, Oneida	He is referred to the New York comptroller for proof of service.
Nellis, George H	Canajoharie, Montgomery	No proof of service unless the comptroller at Albany can aid them.
Newell, Seth	Crown Point, Essex	The comptroller at Hartford, Conn., must be applied to for proof of service.
Newman, Joseph	Manheim, Herkimer	He was not in the army when he was taken prisoner by the Indians, and his other alleged service requires direct proof.
Nichols, Benjamin	Farmington, Ontario	He does not prove six months' service.
Norton, Josiah	Granville, Washington	Suspended for specification of the details of service.
Norton, Isaac	Trenton, Oneida	More claimants than soldiers for the service in the guard at Leet's Island who have applied for pensions—there were but eight men, and the present must prove his identity with one of them.
North, Robert	Walton, Delaware	He did not serve six months in a military capacity.
Nichols, Daniel	Walton, Delaware	Specification required August 16, 1833, not furnished.
Nolter, John	Buffalo, Erie	Suspended for defective proof.
Oakley, Jared	Schuyler, Herkimer	Evidence insufficient.
Ogden, Obadiah	Queensbury, Warren	He did not serve in a military capacity.
Ogden, Gilbert	Queensbury, Warren	If he served as alleged, evidence must be found in the comptroller's office, Albany.

Overhiser, Conrad.....	....	He was employed as a wood-cutter, and if he was detailed from the ranks, he must specify his officers.
Owen, Alvan...........	Hornby, Steuben........	Comptroller of Connecticut may furnish proof in his case.
Owen, Elisha..........	Northampton, Montgomery....	The New York comptroller must furnish proof in this case.
Owen, Ephraim........	....	Claim rejected—he did not serve six months. (Papers withdrawn.)
Olney, William........	Whitestown, Oneida.....	Some mistake in the names of the officers. His service in Vermont, under Captain Enos Parker, of Colonel Simond's regiment, is not sustained by the rolls in point.
Osborn, Roswell.......	Sullivan, Madison.......	If, as appears from the letter of the Secretary of the State of Vermont, the records afford no trace of the service in question, it is doubtful if the application can be sustained.
Osborn, Ephraim.......	Northumberland, Saratoga.....	Suspended for defective proof and specification.
Osborn, Joel..........	——, Montgomery........	In suspense from November 12, 1833, for defective proof and specific details. (Papers withdrawn.)
Out, Matthias.........	Preble, Cortlandt.......	He has not specified each tour as required, and made the necessary distinction between patrolling and readiness to service and actual service.
Olney, Amos...........	Chazy, Clinton..........	No evidence which may be relied upon has been given to sustain any part of this service. It is necessary, therefore, that each term of actual service shall be specified by credible witnesses.
Palmer, Joseph.........	Staten Island, Richmond.	Under age; also privateer boat service—rejected.
Palmer, James.........	Mount Morris, Livingston	Further proof wanted, for which he is advised to refer to the comptroller of Connecticut.
Palmer, William.......	Amity, Allegheny.......	In suspense for want of some proof, and he must resort either to surviving comrades or the Connecticut comptroller.
Palmer, Samuel (deceased)..	Middleburg, Schoharie...	The deceased never alluded to such a service as an artificer in any declaration he ever made, and the probability is that he was not the person of the same name on the records.
Palmer, George........	Candor, Tioga..........	Reference should be had to the Secretary of State or comptroller at Hartford to ascertain if his records sustain or disprove said service.
Palmer, Noah..........	Depeyster, St. Laurence.	Five months' service admitted. His service in 1775, as a minute man, to be admitted must be set forth in proper form.
Parks, Smith..........	Hamilton, Madison......	Suspended for further proof both from his State records and comrades.
Pasco, Ezra...........	Junius, Seneca.........	Suspended for proof from the Massachusetts rolls. The period and term of his tour in Sprout's regiment should be shown with more precision.
Palmakeer, John D.....	New Paltz, Ulster.......	Suspended for a more precise specification of the details of each militia tour, including the rate at which he was to be paid under Captain Simmonds.

STATEMENT—Continued.

Names.	Residence.	Reasons for suspension.
Palmater, John	Marysburg, Upper Canada	Name not on Captain Van Cortlandt's rolls.
Paddock, Henry	Vienna, Oneida	Suspended April 11, 1884, for want of specification, which remains in full force.
Palmer, Nathaniel	Walworth, Wayne	No information with regard to the character of the service. The Secretary of State of New York can probably tell whether the regiments were in the State or militia service.
Parker, William	Haight, Allegheny	Suspended for more perfect details of service.
Pangbourn, Peter	Butternuts, Otsego	Suspended October 26, 1883, for defective proof. The Captain Ten Eyck under whom he served being living, and many of his comrades, should preclude any difficulty in his procuring the best evidence.
Patchin, William	Buffalo, Erie	Suspended for further proof from comrades and the records at Hartford.
Patterson, Robert (deceased)	Erwin, Steuben	He did not establish six months' service before he died.
Page, Joseph	Columbus, Chenango	In suspense since March 25, 1885, for want of proof, at which period he was told, through Isaac Jones, his friend, that the living comrades in his neighbourhood could furnish an abundance of the best evidence.
Pardee, John	Niagara, Niagara	Not any proof on our records for much over two months service.
Parshall, Israel	Palmyra, Wayne	Discredited by the rolls in the whole range of 1780, 1781 and 1782.
Parkinson, Reuben	Carlisle, Schoharie	Suspended for further proof and specification.
Paul, Richard	Johnstown, Fulton	Service in New Jersey not properly set forth, and proof required from surviving comrades.
Paul, Christopher	Palatine, Montgomery	He must specify his officers' names, and when and where, and how long he served under them.
Peck, Isaac	Sandlake, Rensselaer	Period, length, grade, locality, and officers to his service, must be furnished to the Connecticut comptroller.
Pedrick, Abijah	North Salem, West Chester	Specification of details, and names of officers required.
Peckham, Prince (deceased)	Middletown, Delaware	His claim wants support from the records of the Boston Secretary of State's office.
Pendleton, Zebulon	Sempronius, Cayuga	Suspended for proof of service by his comrades.
Perkins, Zopham (deceased)	Auburn, Cayuga	The affidavit of Jonathan Tompkins in support of this claim, was filed with other testimony in the office of the Clerk of the House of Representatives, testifying for upwards of two years' service.
Penny, William	New York city	Suspended for more satisfactory proof.

Name	Place	Remarks
Perry, Jonathan	Reading, Steuben	His tours were too long for Rhode Island militia; and if the service was under a special act it should be shown.
Perry, Isaac	Morristown, St. Lawrence	Suspended for further proof of service.
Pease, Joel	Rome, Oneida	The services on record in the comptroller's office, Connecticut, and that claimed by Mr. Pease, does not agree in any one important particular. The service on record could not have been performed by one man.
Peauyer, Reuben, jr. (deceased)	Nassau, Rensselaer	Name not on any of the full returns of all the persons employed in the quartermaster's department on the Hudson.
Phillips, Jacob	New York city	No claim—he was a teamster.
Phillips, Samuel	——, Oswego	He does not specify his officers' names, and there were no such service or drafts in the Rhode Island militia like he describes—papers sent to House of Representatives.
Phillips, Zebedee	Urbana, Steuben	Suspended for want of proof.
Phelps, John	Prattsburgh, Steuben	Suspended for want of proof.
Pickard, John	Danville, Livingston	No part of his claim can be admitted upon the present proof.
Pierce, Joseph	Brutus, Cayuga	The evidence furnished is not sufficient to establish six months' service.
Pinckney, John E	Schoharie, Schoharie	The evidence is uncertain as to duration and grade of service.
Piper, Thomas	Watertown, Jefferson	Only two months and eight days' service established. Evidence of further service should be found in the Massachusetts rolls at Boston.
Porter, Trueman	Brookhaven, Suffolk	In suspense for an inadmissible mode of stating the minute-man service.
Powers, Abner	Clark, Upper Canada	He deserted on May 15, 1782.
Poucher, James	Germantown, Columbia	This claim was found among Mr. Luci's papers after he had left his desk at the office, and no action has ever been had upon it.
Potter, Nathaniel (deceased)	Easton, Washington	No evidence in support of the alleged service in this case has been introduced. The records at Albany should furnish some.
Powers, Joseph	Ghent, Columbia	He did not serve six months.
Powell, Elisha	Livonia, Livingston	No part of this claim is admissible in the present state of the papers.
Powers, Timothy	Lansingburg, Rensselaer	Suspended for defective proof.
Pratt, Stephen		Suspended for defective proof, and papers sent to Hon. A. Hazletine, April 16, 1834.
Pratt, Russell	Waterloo, Seneca	Suspended for defective proof.
Praul, Nathan	Fayette, Seneca	The proof of six months' service is very far short.
Pressler, Abraham	Prattsburg, Steuben	Unless he can produce something more satisfactory, it is wholly unnecessary for him to attempt to prosecute it further.
Price, John	Fairfield, Herkimer	Discredited by documentary evidence in the department.
Putnam, Jonathan	Greenwich, Washington	No proof in the vicinity of the minimum amount of service has been sent in this case.
Putnam, Jonathan	Easton, Washington	Not on the list of officers in Rhode Island, which is complete, and his setting forth of his service is entirely vague and indefinite.

STATEMENT—Continued.

Names.	Residence.	Reasons for suspension.
Pritchard, Asahel	Tioga, Tioga	Rejected—no claim; not military service.
Quackenboss, Peter J	Glenn, Montgomery	He did not serve six months.
Randolph, Thomas F	Birdsall, Allegheny	His alleged militia service in New Jersey is no doubt overrated. He should specify each tour by itself, no matter how short.
Ralston, John	Manheim, Herkimer	Names of company and regimental officers wanted.
Rayner, William	Warwick, Orange	The character he bore during the revolution precludes any application he may make for a pension.
Redfield, Samuel	Perrysburgh, Cattaraugus	The comptroller's certificate makes no allusion to any pay-tables for guards under the designated officers in 1778, as alleged by claimant. The amount of service claimed extends through four summers, and can doubtless be proved by cotemporary comrades.
Redding, Wright	Reading, Steuben	Suspended for further proof and specification.
Rew, Ephraim	Phelps, Ontario	Suspended for more perfect details and proof by the Connecticut comptroller.
Reid, Thomas	Duanesburgh, Schenectady	Suspended for further proof. Should the Massachusetts rolls prove inauspicious, he must find some of his surviving comrades.
Reynolds, Silas	New York city	The duration of each term of actual service must be specified. The statement is too indefinite at present to form any determination upon.
Reeves, James (deceased)	Mills Corner, Orange	He was an invalid pensioner, and died in 1837, and made no effort to obtain a recognition under this law. He claimed for service in 1779, when he was wounded.
Reynolds, David	Niles, Cayuga	By the pay roll of Captain Bell, it would seem that a private of the same name served three months in 1778, and five months in 1779.
Rhodes, Samuel	Berlin, Rensselaer	Proof unsatisfactory. He brings a witness who specifies eight tours for claimant who could not specify one of his own.
Richardson, Daniel	Delhi, Delaware	Petition for an increase rejected. His present pension under act May 15, 1828, is precisely as it would be under this act.
Rice, Daniel	Howard, Steuben	No service can be admitted without direct proof, which is alleged to have been performed under sixteen years of age.

Richards, Israel	Nichols, Tioga	Suspended for further proof and specification.
Rickey, Israel	Chemung, Tioga	Nine months' service in Col. Hawthorn's regiment requires the Captain's name, if there were such a long term, which is doubtful.
Richards, Luther	Paris, Oneida	The names of officers not given in the narrative of second term. His others are insufficient, and as a waiter is not entitled.
Risley, Moses	Vienna, Oneida	It does not appear that there were any such company officers attached to Col. Eno's regiment as applicant alleges he served under. The Hartford record may possibly afford some evidence of his service.
Rives, Daniel	Lodi, Seneca	Suspended for further proof.
Robinson, Isaac	Marbletown, Ulster	He should submit a brief of his service to the comptroller at Albany for proof or disproof, and announce the result.
Rood, Joseph	Pomfret, Chautauque	The certificate of the comptroller of Connecticut does not sustain his claim to the service set forth in any one particular.
Rook, Amos	New York city	Suspended for further proof and specification.
Rowan, James		No proof of service. Papers withdrawn by H. C. Martindale January 21, 1834.
Rose, Benjamin	Victor, Ontario	No such company under Captain Lee in Col. Arnold's regiment. Babcock was not in service as alleged. If such officers were in service, the Albany records should show it.
Roberts, John	Canada, Tioga	Five months as ensign and nine months as lieutenant in New Jersey, cannot be admitted without proof; such a length of service in those grades must be susceptible of proof by survivors of the service.
Rouse, John	Locke, Cayuga	Suspended for a more perfect detail of the several facts of his service. Papers withdrawn.
Rogers, Lewis	18 Sullivan street, New York	The Secretary of State of New York must furnish evidence of his commission as lieutenant.
Robbins, Solomon	Union, Broome	The New Hampshire rolls are in this office and cannot be examined unless claimant furnishes the names of his officers.
Rice, Moses	Solon, Cortlandt	He did not serve six months.
Rider, Christian	New York city	Suspended for defective proof.
Rose, Samuel	Wheeler, Steuben	Suspended for more satisfactory proof—the evidence that he returned to camp after furlough is not perfect.
Rogers, Michael	Chatham, Columbia	Suspended for officers' names and specific tours.
Rogers, Samuel	Webster, Monroe	Rejected—not on muster or pay rolls, nor final settlement certificates, nor tour records, whence he said he enlisted.
Rolston, John	Little Falls, Herkimer	Rejected—not on the depreciation certificates, nor bounty land applicants for New York or the federal government.
Ruleeson, Harman	Blenheim, Schoharie	Places, dates, officers, grade, and duration of service deficient.
Randall, Joshua	Petersburgh, Rensselaer	Suspended for adequate proof and specification.
Russell, Abraham	Hurley, Ulster	Further and more endurable proof required.

STATEMENT—Continued.

Names.	Residence.	Reasons for suspension.
Russell, Reverius	York, Livingston	Period, length, grade, dates and places, and names of company, and field officers must be stated—and some proof elicited thereby, if possible, from Connecticut comptroller.
Ryfenburgh, Henry (deceased)	Albany city	He did not serve six months.
Stevens, Thomas (deceased)	Dover, Duchess	He did not serve six months.
Sharp, Richard	Wolcott, Wayne	Some proof beyond what is offered must come.
Sage, Zadoc (deceased)	Leyden, Lewis	His claim is neither set forth nor proved—he must specify officers, dates, places, of each term, with length and grade of service—the aggregate fourteen months must be detailed.
Sandors, Luke	Boston, Tioga	Length, period, grade, locality and commanders must be specified before any examination can be had.
Sandford, Robert	Morristown, St. Lawrence	If he served in the Vermont militia, by specifying his service in detail to the Secretary of State of Vermont, it is expected he will be afforded some proof.
Sary, Stephen	Chemung, Tioga	In suspense for more satisfactory proof.
Safford, David	Jackson, Washington	Defective proof—papers sent Hon. H. C. Martindale January 21, 1834, and not replaced.
Safford, Gideon	Salem, Washington	Papers withdrawn January 21, 1831, by Hon. H. C. Martindale, to presented to Congress, and have not been replaced.
Sabin, Timothy	Ontario	Rejected—claimed as a continental teamster three years seven months, November, 1777—continental teamsters were not established before 1779. [Papers withdrawn.]
Schimmel, Valatine	Palatine, Montgomery	Names of officers required.
Schofield, William	Ellery, Chautauque	Suspended for proof from the Albany and Hartford records, and the aid of his comrades to identify him.
Scott, James	Sparta, Livingston	Service as a minute man must be specified with regard to the number of days and times he was actually marched out, or stationed in service in an embodied corps.
Scisim, Peter	Saghtanic, Columbia	Names of company and regimental officers required in order to an examination of his service.
Scribner, Jered	Stanford, Dutchess	Proof from surviving comrades required.

Schermerhorn, Jacob	Maryland, Otsego	There is no evidence that Captain Hart commanded a company of nine months' men in 1782—if such was the fact, evidence should be found in the records of the Secretary of State at Albany.
Scovil, Abijah	Hounsfield, Jefferson	No evidence of as much as six months' service.
Schuyler, Nicholas (deceased)	Danube, Herkimer	Suspected of having been a tory in the revolution.
Schureman, Hercules	New York city	Suspended for defective proof—but he was a slave, and there is no evidence that he was emancipated before his discharge.
Schuyler, Philip S.	Watervliet, Albany	Not specified nor proved.
Schermerhorn, Leonard	Knox, Albany	The principal part of his time he served as a wood-chopper, and there is no evidence of his enlistment.
Scudder, Kenneth A.	Homer, Cortlandt	He did not serve six months.
Sears, Samuel	Montgomery, Orange	In suspense since letter May 28, 1834, to S. W. Eager, requiring details of dates, localities, officers' names, and the length and grade of his service.
Seger, Gerrit J.	Albany city	Suspended for defective proof, and papers withdrawn by G. Y. Lansing, April 7, 1837, and not replaced.
Selden, Benjamin	Mina, Chautauque	Suspended for further proof.
Seely, Gideon (deceased)	Ovid, Seneca	He made no claim during his life, and yet there are records of service of a soldier of the same name upon the New York books—the point is to prove his identity with that soldier.
Seamans, John	Eaton; Madison	He was required to specify his service according to the rules, but had not complied with the request May 17, 1834.
Seymour, Samuel	Walton, Delaware	The duration of each term is wanted, and he is referred to Elisha Phelps, comptroller of Connecticut, for further proof.
Serls, Amos	Middlefield, Otsego	Suspended for further proof and specification.
Shaw, Richard	Ledyard, Cayuga	Proof of his captaincy must come from the records of Pennsylvania, and from the Connecticut comptroller his service—which will require a particular specification of each tour.
Sherlock, Ichabod	Brownville, Jefferson	Alleged service in the Connecticut continental line—the complete rolls of that service do not notice his service.
Sheffield, Paul (deceased)	Macedon, Wayne	Claim wholly unsustained and cannot be admitted.
Shepherd, Edward S.	Canton, St. Lawrence	Claims for nearly four years' service in the Connecticut troops, and there is no evidence thereof adduced either from the rolls or otherwise.
Shepherd, Jonathan 3d	Chateaugay, Franklin	Suspended for further proof and specification.
Sherwood, William	Italy, Yates	Suspended for further proof.
Shearer, William	Homer, Cortlandt	He is referred to the records of the Secretary of State at Boston for proof of service.
Shutter, Henry	Woodstock, Ulster	Referred to the Secretary of State of New York for proof, that such corps and officers served as alleged at the respective dates.

STATEMENT—Continued.

Names.	Residence.	Reasons for suspension.
Shultz, John	Milo, Yates	The officers under whom he alleges to have served in 1779, are not known to the department—his service was surely a mistake.
Shuler, John	Canandaigua, Ontario	No papers on file, and no letters noted, except one to James Rogers, May 12, 1834, of which no copy can be found.
Sharpe, John	Greenbush, Rensselaer	His case is very far from sufficient in proof, and specification of the details.
Shelly, Medad	West Bloomfield, Ontario	He did not serve six months.
Shipperly, Barent	Germantown, Columbia	Not sufficient to establish his claim to six months' service.
Shoemaker, Abraham	Erin, Chemung	Service so out of the usual routine of the militia, must have been under a special law—proof, therefore, is required, of the kind of service, as well as the special employment of claimant.
Shipman, David	Smithfield, Madison	Suspended for deficient proof.
Shultz, John (deceased)	Milo, Yates	Not any evidence whether of parol or of record—suspended for defective proof and specification.
Sibley, Gibbs (deceased)	New York city	Declaration not complete—see instructions in letter May 30, 1845—L. D. Chapin.
Sickles, John (deceased)	Russia, Herkimer	The certificate of the comptroller of New York, of service, to a soldier of the same name in several cases, is not evidence identifying claimant with the service.
Sickler, John (deceased)	Norway, Herkimer	Rejected—name not on the rolls—he claimed full pension as a warsman for the whole period of the war.
Sidman, John	Ramapo, Rockland	Rejected—he served as a waiter.
Sidore, Isaac	Town Richmond, Lenox county, Midland District	Specification of officers' names, date, duration, locality, and grade of service must be set forth.
Sillcock, Joseph	New York city	Suspended for further proof.
Simmons, Aaron	Orleans, Jefferson	Proof and specifications defective.
Simpson, John	Springfield, Otsego	He was required November 6, 1834, to specify the date, duration, grade, locality, and officers of each term of service—which has not been done.
Siscoe, Nicholas	New York city	Rejected—claimant was a slave, and not amenable to draft or enlistment.
Slade, Jacob	Stockport, Columbia	Claim rejected—he was a soldier in the French army.

Slaight, John A.	Fishkill, Dutchess	Six months' men were not in service at the period alleged by claimant—further proof required.
Stout, Philip (deceased)	Lodi, Seneca	Suspended for better proof.
Slater, Robert	Rotterdam, Schenectady	Suspended for proof from the New York records.
Smith, Elijah (deceased), heirs of	Scipio, Cayuga	Not allowed—there is no evidence that their father filed a declaration in this office—there is no proof in this case, and no claim.
Smith, Elijah	Scipio, Cayuga	The certificate of the Hartford comptroller, that a soldier named Elijah Smith is credited with service, does not prove that claimant and he were one and the same person.
Smith, Benjamin	Walworth, Wayne	Suspended in July 1836, and proof required from the New Jersey records, which has not been sent.
Smith, Jonathan	Genoa, Cayuga	Suspended for the return of the original declaration.
Smith, Albertson (deceased)	Fallsburgh, Sullivan	No evidence in this case to justify the admission of a claim—the widow must apply under the act of July 4, 1836, and prove the service.
Smith, Daniel	Parma, Monroe	Suspended for further proof of service.
Smith, Amos	York township, Upper Canada	He served as a teamster.
Smith, Comfort	Wheatland, Monroe	He did not serve six months.
Smith, Thomas G.	Greensburgh, West Chester	Suspended for further proof and specification.
Smith, Joseph	Johnstown, Montgomery	Officers' names, times and places, and the duration and rank of the service are deficient.
Smith, David	Otego, Otsego	He did not serve six months.
Smith, Francis	Attica, Genesee	Proof of service defective.
Smith, Michael	Glenville, Schenectady	Suspended for the production of Colonel Faulkner's rolls, who resides in Walkill, Orange county.
Smith, Isaac S.	White Creek, Washington	He must give the details of his service, and apply to the Secretary of State at Boston, for an inspection of the Massachusetts rolls.
Smith, Enos	Germantown, Columbia	Suspended for proof by the Connecticut comptroller, and by witnesses living at Fairfield, Connecticut.
Smith, John	Rochester, Monroe	Officers' names, date, duration, rank, locality, are wanted for each tour by itself.
Smith, John	Jamaica, Queens	He did not serve six months.
Smith, Joshua	Elba, Genesee	Suspended for proof by the comptroller's record at Hartford, and from surviving comrades, neither of which has been done.
Snyder, Peter	Glenville, Schenectady	If he served as he states, he may find some proof in the comptroller's office at Albany.
Snedaker, William	Onondaga, Onondaga	Not on the rolls of the New York line—no proof of service—his claim as a wariman is rejected.
Snedaker, Isaac	Troy, Rensselaer	He did not serve six months.
Son, Thomas	Chatham, Columbia	No evidence of service—all the calls for proof have failed.
Soper, Timothy	Pitcher, Chenango	Proof not sufficient.

STATEMENT—Continued.

Names.	Residence.	Reasons for suspension.
Soper, Jesse 2d	Plattsburgh, Clinton	His claim is too diffuse and indefinite—he must condense it, and detail the facts, and give more satisfactory proof.
Smith, Zedekiah	Glenn, Montgomery	Specification of officers' names, dates, duration, grade and locality are necessary to any examination.
Spaler, William	Brooklyn, Kings	He is told he will be allowed a pension for thirteen months, provided he relinquish all other claim under this act.
Sperbrock, Martin	Perinton, Monroe	Suspended for further proof.
Sprague, Ebenezer	Phelps, Ontario	Suspended for further proof and specification.
Sprague, Elijah	Perry, Wyoming	Suspended for further proof.
Sprague, Samuel H	Hudson, Columbia	Suspended for further proof.
Spalding, Jeremiah	Spafford, Onondaga	He did not serve six months.
Springer, William M	Randolph, Cattaraugus	Suspended for further proof—name not on the rolls.
Springsteen, Benjamin	Schodack, Rensselaer	No evidence to justify the allowance of this claim.
Starks, Ebenezer	Champlain, Clinton	He did not serve six months in a military capacity—a teamster.
Stanton, John		Suspended for further proof. [Papers sent to O. Kellogg January 30, 1849.]
Stall, Peter	Ephratah, Montgomery	Suspended for additional proof; but what is presented is not yet sufficient.
Stanton, Nathan	Florida, Montgomery	He did not serve six months.
Stockman, Benjamin	Bennett, Cayuga	Suspended for proof and specification of the details of service.
Steele, Rudolph	German Flatts, Herkimer	In suspense for further proof of his commission as quartermaster and service under it.
Steenburg, Simon	New Utrecht, Kings	Not sufficiently proved.
Stone, Samuel	Buffalo, Erie	Not entitled—he was only thirteen years of age and a drummer for a neighborhood fort.
Storrs, Chipman	Plattsburg, Clinton	Service not established.
Starr, Jonathan	Butternuts, Otsego	He did not serve six months.
Stanley, Jesse	Mount Morris, Livingston	He did not serve six months.
Stanley, Salmon	Otisco, Onondaga	Suspended for adequate proof.
Stewart, Samuel	Cazenovia, Madison	Suspended for proof from the records of Connecticut.
Stewart, Joseph	Minnisink, Orange	Suspended for proof and specification.
Strong, Ezekiel	Moriah, Essex	Specification not clear—officers' names, date of service, duration, where performed, and his own rank, all insufficient unless clearly set forth.

Name	Place	Notes
Sutherland, Laurence	Rampo, Rockland	He did not serve six months.
Sutlif, David	Dryden, Tompkins	He has not, as required, exhibited any proof, and yet there are many surviving comrades now applying, for service at the same period alleged, and under the same officers.
Sullivan, Peleg	Mina, Chautauque	He was allowed to have served five months and a half, and his claim was for over seven. He must reinforce his proofs.
Swartout, Ralph	Ovid, Seneca	His service could not have been under military obligation, as his name is not on the muster or pay rolls—rejected.
Swart, Adam	Rochester, Monroe	Rejected—he was seventy-six years of age in 1844, which would make him fifteen at the conclusion of the war. His name is not on the pay rolls, and his claim without foundation.
Sweet, William	Berlin, Rensselaer	Claims about two years and nine months in the Rhode Island militia. In no instance, so far as record evidence goes, did the Rhode Island militia serve over three months in one year in that State after 1776.
Swift, Ambrose	Minden, Montgomery	His name is not on Captain Daniel Williams' rolls, and he must prove his service by two witnesses who can testify to the officers, date, duration, grade and localities of each actual tour.
Swartwood, Peter	Cayuta, Tioga	Five months' service admitted, but he claims eighteen. If the residue of the service in Captain Hoover's company was included as one of the militia, he should specify the duration of each term of actual service; but if in the State troops, it should be sustained by evidence from the records of New Jersey.
Tabor, Earl	Wales, Aurora	Claims as a lieutenant, but can show no commission; and if he persists as a private, he must specify each tour as to grade, period, duration, and names of officers and places.
Talcott, Daniel	Warren, Herkimer	Services for three months not objected to. The term of three months under Captain Clark, Col. Wyllis's regiment, short levies in 1780, should be established by the comptroller's certificate of Connecticut.
Terwilligan, Aaron, (deceased)	——, Ulster	Suspended for proof of service by the New York comptroller and identity by comrades.
Taylor, Noah	Cazenovia, Madison	Two months and eighteen days admitted. Two witnesses are required to prove three months and twelve days' service in Captain Jacob Brown's company in 1776.
Taylor, Harman	Livingston, Columbia	Not entitled—he did not serve under a military organization.
Tennant, John	Ripley, Chautauque	Not entitled—name not on the rolls—no evidence of service.
Terwilliger, Lucas	Elmira, Tioga	Several militia tours as a volunteer—no details and no evidence.
Teed, William	Somers, Westchester	He must submit a narrative of his service in detail to the comptroller at Albany, and announce how far his records verify or discredit his service.

Ex.—10

STATEMENT—Continued.

Names.	Residence.	Reasons for suspension.
Tozer, Richard	Farmersville, Cattaraugus	Not on the rolls of Durkie's and Butler's regiments, and the most satisfactory proof otherwise must obviate that fact.
Thompson, William	Verona, Oneida	Deficient in proof.
Thomas, Joseph P.	Edinburg, Saratoga	Claimant's name is not borne on the depreciation certificates, which were issued to all who served in the Rhode Island brigade.
Thew, Garret	Peru, Clinton	Five and a half months admitted—claims for 19 months. He must reinforce his proofs.
Thompson, John	Springport, Cayuga	He claims to have rendered service as a ranger at under sixteen years of age, and cannot be admitted without some proof.
Thomas, Israel	Luzerne, Warren	He was required to specify his service to the New York comptroller for further proof, which has not been done.
Tubbs, Clement	Ellisburg, Jefferson	The service should be established by the certificate of the comptroller of New York, in whose possession are the rolls of service subsequent to 1778.
Tidd, Jesse	Scipio, Cayuga	The department is not aware that there were militia tours alternate by month in and month out in New York, and some explanation is necessary, by which may be shown if one half of that force was in constant service.
Thompson, Caleb	Norwich, Chenango	Suspended for specification of the several details of service and thereby elicit proof if to be had from the comptroller at Albany.
Trapp, James	Lansing, Tompkins	Deficient, specification, which must be supplied, and proof thereby obtained from the New York records.
Travis, Amos	New York city	Claimant should give the names of the officers, particularly the Colonel of the regiment. If the records at Albany afford no evidence that the officers were in service, it would discredit his statement altogether.
Treat, Theaus	Port Byron, Cayuga	Claim not before the department. Withdrawn December 17, 1845—Hon. H. T. Janes, H. R.
Tripp, Anthony	Barre, Orleans	The evidence by the comptroller's certificate is short of six months, and the other service is not proved.
Thorn, Thomas	New York city	The original declaration was demanded June 22, 1835, but it has not been sent to the department.

Name	Place	Remarks
Thurston, Daniel	Vernon, Oneida	Claims for three years and eight months uninterrupted service in the militia of Rhode Island, commencing in 1779. There is no evidence in the department of any such service. The only officer he can name is Barton; but that officer had not a command of a regiment of militia in 1779.
Turner, Thomas	Lansingburg, Rensselaer	Name of Thomas Turner or Tanner appears on the rolls of Col. Sherman's regiment for six months. See letter of November 25, 1833—Samuel Kendrick.
Turner, Alexander	Homer, Cortlandt	He served only three months and eighteen days.
Tuttle, Benjamin	Seneca, Ontario	He is referred to the Connecticut comptroller for proof of his service in 1775 at Roxbury, near Boston.
Tuttle, James	Bolton, Warren	Name not on the rolls—no proof of service.
Tuttle, Joseph	Royalton, Niagara	Suspended for further proof and specification.
Tuttle, Abijah	Camillus, Onondaga	Suspended for further proof and specification.
Upton, John	Hawsbury, Richmond, Nova Scotia	Claim cannot be sustained. If he was captured at Charleston and taken to Nova Scotia and released, and forever after adhered to the enemy, it was out of the usual destination of the great body of prisoners taken at the same time.
Underhill, Gilbert	Croton, West Chester	If claimant is unable by himself or by witnesses to furnish a statement in detail of his services, he cannot bring his claim before the department.
Uddell, William	Maryland, Otsego	There is no evidence that Col. Barrett had command of a regiment at all, not to say six months, at the period set forth by claimant.
Valentine, Peter	Peeham, West Chester	The declaration of claimant and the certificate of the Secretary of State and comptroller do not agree. He sets forth no officers named in the certificates.
Vandervoort, John	Blenheim, Schoharie	Service four months and twelve days allowed. The tours in the militia require further proof and specification.
Voorhis, Ruliff	Stamford, Delaware	The rolls of all the officers under whom he alleges service are in the comptroller's office, and his certificate is wanting to prove or discredit his service.
Vosburg, Jacob	Rochester, Monroe	A very vague and indistinct account is afforded of the period, length, grade of each term, and the names of the company and field officers. He is required to make a full statement specifying each tour and establish it by the certificate of the comptroller at Albany.
Van Vracken, John J	Root, Montgomery	He did not serve six months.
Vrooman, Lawrence	Schenectady city	Proof insufficient.
Veeder, John B	Providence, Saratoga	He did not serve six months.

STATEMENT—Continued.

Names.	Residence.	Reasons for suspension.
Van Buren, Martin B.	Maryland, Otsego	Alleges tours running through three years, but offers no proof. His service at Fishkill as a kind of guard, is a service not known to the department.
Van Buskirk, Peter	Phelps, Ontario	He did not perform military service.
Van Campen, Moses	Danville, Livingston	Claim for increase rejected. Parol evidence not sufficient to establish the rank of adjutant.
Van Dusor, Adolph	Erin, Chemung	Until 1779 he was incapable of a military contract, and after that the rolls at Albany are complete for the military service, and his statement must embrace the period, length, grade, locality and officers' names, in applying at Albany.
Van Mattor, Isaac	Salisbury, Herkimer	He must set forth each term of service, the length, grade, time and place, beginning and ending and officers commanding, and fortify his claim by a certificate from the Albany comptroller.
Van Vleet, John	Glenville, Schenectady	Name not on the rolls, nor Lieutenant Hamstreel's. He should furnish, by a witness, such proof as shall specify the duration of each term of actual service rendered in 1776 and 1777.
Van Wickel, Evert		Suspended for proof to be procured from the comptroller at Connecticut, and papers withdrawn and not replaced.
Van Walkenburgh, Bartholomew	Johnstown, Montgomery	Proof by the records falls short, and unless he can better specify his services and the names of his officers, his claim may be abandoned.
Van Oram, John	Cattskill, Greene	If he cannot find proof among the numerous living comrades in his neighbourhood, nor from the complete rolls of Massachusetts, his claim may be regarded as desperate.
Van De Bogart, Myndert	Almshouse, Albany	A man of his name deserted, but if this suspicion were waived, the difference between his statements and the certificate of the comptroller would preclude his claim.
Van Pelt, Jacob	Unadilla, Otsego	He alleges two years' service in New York without furnishing any evidence of any part of it.
Van Surdam, Anthony	Hoosick, Rensselaer	After specifying each term of service, with the usual details, he must apply with a copy to the comptroller at Albany, and in case his services should tally with the records, he must find some surviving comrades who can identify him as the soldier who so served.
Verity, Samuel	Jerusalem, South Queens	Suspended for further proof and specification.

Name	Location	Remarks
Van Vorst, Gershom	Schenectady city	His service as a stable boy at fourteen years of age was not soldierly service, and his militia tours in 1779, '80 and '81, must be compared with the records at Albany.
Voorhees, John	Oswego, Oswego	The original papers were sent to Hon. A. P. Grant, June 7, 1888, and have not been replaced—the claim was defective in proof of service.
Voorhees, Isaac	Pultney, Steuben	He must specify the period, length and grade of each term, with the names of the officers, stations, &c., and have his case authenticated by the Secretary of State of New Jersey.
Vose, Henry	Bennington, Genesee	Neither claimant's name nor his witnesses have been found on the rolls of the regiment wherein they alleged service.
Van Fleet, James	Haight, Allegheny	The allegation of a continuous service of three years in the militia cannot be received—the regulations require each tour to be described by itself.
Van Waggenen, Hendricus	Esopus, Ulster	There is no evidence of the service in Pawling's regiment, or that such service was performed by that regiment at that period of the war—if such was the fact, the records in the Secretary of State's office at Albany would show it.
Van Waggenen, Johannes	Harley, Ulster	There is no evidence in the department that Captain Lefcore was at any time in Pawling's regiment—if the claimant belonged to any other, he should so state it in a supplement—no part of service can be allowed which is alleged in gross, and not in detail at the various periods.
Vermilyeo, Benjamin	Otego, Otsego	The twelve months' service in the governor's life guards cannot be allowed without some authority shown under which it was raised and commanded—if by the State of New York the records at Albany should show it.
Van Vranken, Garret	Broadalbine, Montgomery	He must specify by his witnesses the period, duration, grade, locality, and officers' names of the service of each tour.
Waterbury, Thomas	North Castle, West Chester	He must specify each tour of service with the usual details, and submit it to the comptroller at Hartford for verification or disproof.
Waterbury, Samuel	Stockton, Chautauque	Suspended for further proof from the Connecticut records and from surviving comrades.
Waggoner, George (deceased)	Rose, Oneida	He was an invalid pensioner, and claims to have served in 1776, under Captain Henry Duffendorff, Colonel Ebenezer Corey's regiment, until August, 1777, when he received a wound which broke his thigh—if satisfactory proof of the service under these officers can be shown, the claim can be admitted.
Waldron, Benjamin	Fishkill, Dutchess	Suspended for further proof.

STATEMENT—Continued.

Names.	Residence.	Reasons for suspension.
Wabroth, Jacob H.	St. Johnsville, Montgomery	His service has not been detailed as it should be to facilitate an investigation.
Warner, Olive	Athens, Greene	Suspended for defective proof, which must be amended by a statement of the original facts, to be proved by the records at Albany.
Warner, Timothy	Oppenheim, Fulton	Evidence of a witness who cannot sign his name not acceptable—the certificate of the comptroller at Hartford would be received with more respect.
Warner, Jason	Canaan, Columbia	The evidence preponderates that he was ever ready to serve as a grenadier, but that he was never in actual service.
Wait, Peleg	Petersburgh, Rensselaer	Since requisition for further proof was made for his service under Lieutenant Burlingame, in Colonel Christopher Greene's regiment in 1779, nothing has been done.
Warden, James	Danby, Tompkins	Suspended for proof of service in the New York line to be found in the records at Albany.
Watson, Jude	Oppenheim, Fulton	His name is not on either of the rolls of the six months' Massachusetts levies, and his service for six months is far from apparent.
Walker, Jonathan	Allen, Allegheny	Proof from the Massachusetts rolls and of claimant's identity required.
Wainwright, Joseph	——, Saratoga	Suspended for defective proof, and returned to S. Kendrick, November 25, 1833, and papers not replaced.
Warren, Enoch	Chemung, Tioga	His name is not on the rolls of Colonel Webb's regiment, and he is required to adduce evidence by two witnesses, who must specify the details of the service.
Warren, Abijah	Bristol, Ontario	Alleges fourteen and a half months' service in 1775, '76 and '77, which he is required to specify in detail, and establish by the records at Hartford.
Wares, Comfort	Westport, Essex	No proper documents prepared and filed in this case.
Walker, Thomas	Plattsburgh, Clinton	Alleges nine months' service under Captain Brady, Colonel Hannom, in 1777—there is no evidence in the department of such tours of service—there was no militia service in Pennsylvania at that period longer than two months.

Name	Location	Notes
Wallace, Jacob	Manlius, Onondaga	Five months twenty-eight days' service admitted—he claims two years in Captain Delavan's company of dragoons.
Warmsley, James	Brookfield, Madison	He did not serve six months.
Weaver, Jacob		Suspended for defective details of service, and papers withdrawn and not replaced July 30, 1833.
Weaver, Andrus	Van Buren, Onondaga	Not one of the names of the officers he mentions is found on the muster or pay rolls of the regiments and dates designated.
Weaver, Josiah	Elmira, Tioga	He alleges three years' service as a guard and sentry—not military service under a regularly organized corps.
Weaver, George	Watertown, Jefferson	Service as a minute man in Colonel Bellinger's regiment not specified nor details given—the numerous survivors of this service in Herkimer, if applied to, might afford the best evidence of service.
Wescott, Arnold	Berlin, Rensselaer	His service in the Rhode Island militia must be more clearly specified.
Webb, Libbeus	Constantia, Oswego	He did not serve six months.
Welton, Josiah	——, Chautauque	There is no evidence that there were any enlistments in Connecticut in 1777, for the term of eight months—papers withdrawn and not replaced.
Wendall, R. H.	Schenectady city	He is required to sustain his service by application to the comptroller at Albany.
Westgate, James	Smyrna, Chenango	The discrepancies between his statement and the certificate of Mr. Bangs, at Boston, prove that claimant's memory is not to be depended upon.
Weaver, Jabez	Lowville, Lewis	He proved nineteen months' service as a sergeant in his application under act of 1820, but not making ofit a case of indigence his claim was rejected.
Westbrook, John	Chemung, Tioga	Only fifteen years old when he performed his first tour—not admissible.
Wentworth, Gibbens (deceased)	Middlesex, Ontario	Suspended for want of proof.
Wentworth, Ezekiel	Lodi, Seneca	Not being on the roll of artificers in the department, he is required to prove his service by two credible witnesses.
West, Joseph	Minerva, Essex	The period, grade, duration, locality and names of officers should be correctly stated, and application made to the Connecticut records.
Whittaker, Nell (deceased)	Hamburgh, Erie	This claim by letter January 27, 1884, to Bates Cook, was allowed, and the day of his death was required, and name of widow—or if no widow, his children.
Whitmore, John	——, Livingston	Allowed for eleven months ten days upon a relinquishment of any further claim—see letter January 22, 1884, to John Dickson. [Papers withdrawn.
White, Ebenezer	Onondaga, Onondaga	Neither claimant's name, nor that of the man he substituted for, are on Colonel Willy's rolls, and other proof is required.

STATEMENT—Continued.

Names.	Residence.	Reasons for suspension.
Wheeler, Job	Litchfield, Herkimer	The tour under Captain Backus, in Colonel Douglas's regiment of Connecticut militia, was not over two months—and the residue of his service must be specified by period, length, grade, locality and officers commanding.
Whitaker, Ephraim (deceased)	Troy, Rensselaer	The special act of Congress was for a larger pension than the present proof would call for under this act, and the claim for an increase is unnecessary.
Whitman, John R.	——, Sullivan	Proof by the records at Albany required, and by credible witnesses to identify him should the rolls report favorably.
Whitney, David	Walton, Delaware	Suspended for further proof.
Whittenhour, Henry	Ramapo, Rockland	Claims for eighteen months' service in the New Jersey militia under one engagement, an utterly improbable arrangement—the New Jersey militia were only in service by classes, who served month by month in alternate cases as they were wanted.
White, Henry	——, Seneca	His services both in New Jersey and New York are improperly stated, and over estimated—and the discrepancies in his narrative tend to render an adjustment impracticable.
Wood, Benjamin 2d	Sackett's Harbor, Jefferson	Suspended for further proof which has never been furnished, and papers placed before Congress January 14, 1850.
Wood, Benjamin	Bloomingsburgh, Sullivan	Period, length, grade, locality and names of officers of each tour required.
Wood, Amos	Queensbury, Warren	Period, length, grade, locality, names of officers and the corps in which he was enrolled called for.
Wood, Levi	Macedon, Wayne	He is required to submit the details of his service to the Secretary of State, at Boston, to ascertain how his services tally with the rolls.
Wood, Charles	Dayton, Cattaraugus	Proof required of his alleged service in the commissary department.
Wood, David	Root, Montgomery	No data to establish a pension on frontier service without regular military organization or responsibility.
Woodard, Samuel	Bainbridge, Chenango	Under age—born in 1763, and was thirteen, fourteen and fifteen years old only during the years 1776, '77 and '78, when he served some fifteen months—not admitted.
Woodward, Jehiel	Attica, Genesee	He did not serve six months.

Woodworth, Roswell	New Lebanon, Columbia	He did not serve six months.
Woodruff, Lambert	Wolcott, Wayne	Suspended for defective proof.
Wolleber, John	Manheim, Herkimer	He claims two years eight months from 1779 to fall of 1782, but it appears from the rolls of his regiment, that all the service he rendered after 1779 was only two months—his service as a batteau-man must be proved by two witnesses.
Wright, Joseph H.	Fishkill, Dutchess	His age preludes military responsibility.
Wynans, William	Goshen, Orange	Service not distinctly set forth—a brief must be submitted to the comptroller at Albany, and ascertain how far his rolls verify or discredit the service.
Wick, Severenies	Palatine, Montgomery	He did not serve six months.
Widger, Samuel	Hastings, Oswego	He was required to specify the duration of each term of actual service and the names of his officers, and has not complied with the requisition.
Wilkinson, Peter	Bethany, Genesee	Not military service—he was a teamster.
Wilbeck, Abraham	Greenbush, Rensselaer	Suspended for defective proof.
Wibbort, John	Greenfield, Saratoga	Unsupported by any evidence—claimant's name nor his captain's on the rolls of Van Tchaick's regiment—other and better proof required.
Wilcox, John	Corymans, Albany	For his service in 1777, under Captain Hosea Bebee, some evidence maybe found in the office of the secretary or comptroller of New York.
Wilmarth, Ebenezer	Lyons, Wayne	The service in this case is disproved by the silence of the entire records of both officers and service in Massachusetts.
Williamson, Samuel	Richfield, Otsego	His claim for a term of continuous service neither in the militia nor continental line requires the authority and nature of the corps to be set forth.
Wilson, James 1st	Marcy, Oneida	He did not serve six months.
Wilson, James	Whitehall, Washington	If he should be willing to accept a pension for fourteen months as a private, he should make a relinquishment of the other parts of his claim.
Wilson, Lewis	Brooklyn, Kings	He did not serve six months.
Williams, William	Gowans, Kings	He did not serve six months.
Williams, Nathan	Walton, Delaware	Suspended for further proof.
Williams, Robinson	Schuylersville, Saratoga	Period, length, grade, locality, officers and dates required to be furnished to the comptroller at Hartford.
Winegar, Samuel	Fort Ann, Washington	Suspended for a more detailed account, especially as his service was rendered in the militia before he was of an age to be called upon.
Wilford, Joseph	Elba, Genesee	Proof of the source of his commission—the authority under which he served, and names of officers, and where marched or stationed.

STATEMENT—Continued.

Names.	Residence.	Reasons for suspension.
Wilkinson, Amos	Bethany, Greene	He is required to give the details of his service, and consult the records of Vermont or Massachusetts.
Williams, Cornelius	Rome, Oneida	Suspended for defective proof.
Wilber, Benjamin	Elliottville, Cattaraugus	He is referred for proof to the Secretary of State at Boston.
Williams, Ebenezer	Central Bridge, Schoharie	A pensioner under act May 15, 1828, applies for an increase under this act, and his claim is disallowed, for sufficient reasons in his defective proofs.
Williams, Hiram	Candor, Tioga	Suspended for further explanation and proof.
Williamson, William	Caledonia, Genesee	Suspended for further proof from the records of the State department at Harrisburg, which have all the rolls of the Pennsylvania line.
Wilson, Peter	Sawpits, West Chester	No claim—name not on the rolls of Captain Mead's company—he alleges six years' service, and there was none such as is described in in his narrative.
Winn, Joseph (deceased)	Syracuse, Onondaga	A person of the same name is found upon Connally's return of the first New York regiment, as having enlisted in it for three years, and the identity of claimant with that soldier is to be shown.
Winslow, Timothy		Suspended for comptroller's certificate, and papers delivered May 4, 1834, to Hon. R. Whallon.
Wisner, Adam	Genesee, Livingston	No proof of service, and the agent says he cannot furnish any.
Wetherill, David	Granville, Washington	Suspended for further proof.
Witter, William	Gorham, Ontario	Suspended for further proof.
Yorden, John P.	Canajoharie, Montgomery	He did not serve six months.
Young, George	Fultonville, Montgomery	Service of a teamster not military service.
Young, Jeremiah	Seward, Schoharie	There is a discrepancy in his alleged service and the date of his commission which requires explanation.
Young, James	Duanesburgh, Schenectady	The rolls of Colonel Vrooman's regiment for the years 1778, '79, '80 and '81, have been examined, and claimant's name is not found thereon.
Young, John D	Bahan, Middlesex, District London, Upper Canada	No evidence of six months' service—the officers under whom he served have rolls, but they do not credit him.

Yule, James (deceased)	Danube, Herkimer	Papers mislaid, and claim cannot be adjudicated until they are found.
Zee, Nicholas	Williamsburg, Dundas	He did not serve six months.
Zimmerman, George	Phelps, Ontario	Claim for service in the Maryland militia—each term should be specified either by claimant or witnesses, of all the material facts and details of the service.
Zeilly, Thomas	Geneva, Ontario	Service in the militia—suspended for the original memoranda by which the witnesses are guided in describing the short tours.

[37]

A list of persons residing in New York who have applied for pensions under the act of July 4, 1836, whose claims have been rejected; prepared in conformity with the resolution of the Senate of the United States, September 16, 1850.

Names.	Residence.	Reasons for rejection.
Ackerson, Maria Elizabeth, widow of John....	Gaines, Orleans............	He did not serve six months.
Allerton, Bathsheba, widow of Jonathan......	Cairo, Greene..............	No proof of service—not confirmed by the rolls.
Baker, Phebe (deceased), widow of David....	Sackett's Harbor...........	She died before the passage of the act.
Brown, Elizabeth, widow of John............	Brooklyn, Kings............	He was a deserter.
Clark, Rachel, widow of Abraham............	Chatham, Columbia.........	He did not serve six months.
Cole, Martha, widow of Benjamin............	Hebron, Washington........	Married after service—not a widow July 7, 1838.
Cornell, Anna, widow of Joseph..............	Camillus, Onondaga........	He did not serve six months.
Conklin, Ann, widow of Nathan..............	Carmel, Putnam............	Married after the service.
Crane, Eliza, widow of Caleb................	New York city..............	No claim—an officer in the regulars—died in 1814.
Chute, Mary, widow of John F...............	Watervliet, Albany..........	He did not serve six months.
Crawford, Margaret, widow of Joseph........	Tompkins, Delaware........	Married after service.
Dains, Chloe, widow of Jesse................	Milo, Yates.................	He did not serve six months.
Davis, Mehitable, widow of Herms...........	Canton, St. Lawrence.......	He was a deserter.
Decker, Mary, widow of Andrew.............	Warwick, Orange...........	He was a deserter.
De Graff, Jane (deceased), widow of Michael..	Deerfield, Herkimer.........	He did not serve six months.
Dockstader, Dorcas, widow of John Nicholas..	Root, Montgomery..........	He did not serve six months.
Duskill, Elizabeth, widow of William	Greene, Chenango..........	Married after service.
Dygert, Anna, widow of William............	———, Herkimer...........	He did not serve six months.
Fisk, Mehitabel, widow of Jonathan..........	Freedom, Cattaraugus......	Married long after service—not a widow July 7, 1888, and died befor August 16, 1842.
French, Mary, widow of William H..........	Brooklyn, Kings............	He was a soldier of the regular army.
Fling, Sarah, widow of Lemuel..............	Potsdam, St. Lawrence.....	He was a deserter.
Goble, Julian, widow of George..............	Minisink, Orange...........	She died before the passage of the act.
Goodrich, Julia Ann, widow of Levi..........	New York city..............	Married after service.

156

Name	Place	Remarks
Gouge, Hannah, widow of Edward McCollom	New York city	He did not serve six months.
Grandy, Rachel (deceased), widow of John	New York city	Not in service after marriage—married after conclusion of the war.
Green, Caty Ann, widow of Peter A.	Middleburgh, Schoharie	Case not provided for by law—he was a soldier in the regular army.
Grandy, Sarah, widow of Asa	Essex, Essex	Married after the revolution.
Hewett, Susannah, widow of Ephraim	Royalton, Niagara	Not in service after marriage.
Hathaway, Mercy, widow of Peleg	Groton, Tompkins	Married after service.
Harden, Elizabeth, widow of John	Germantown, Hudson	Married after service.
Hughie, Jane, widow of John	Seneca, Ontario	No claim—he was a soldier of the late war.
Hinman, Caty, widow of Jonas	Pitcher, Chenango	He did not serve six months.
Johnson, Huldah, widow of Henry	New York city	Married after service.
Kepley, Ann, heir of James Butler	New York city	He died before the passage of the act.
Lansing, Hannah, widow of Abraham H.	Watervliet, Albany	He did not serve six months.
Lemington, Sarah, widow of Thomas	New York city	Fraudulent—she has already received all she is entitled to.
Lincoln, Relief, widow of Macy	Moriah, Essex	Married after service, and not a widow on July 7, 1838.
Morely, Prudence, widow of Ebenezer	Van Buren, Onondaga	Married long after service.
Odell, Azariah, children of	Ballston Spa, Saratoga	Not provided for—a soldier of the regular army.
Parker, Lydia, widow of Reuben	Granville, Washington	Married after service.
Phelps, Mary, formerly widow of Richard Austin		He was a deserter.
Parmenter, Lydia, widow of Isaac	Alexander, Genesee	Married after service.
	Coshocton, Steuben	
Ripley, Priscilla, widow of David	Scott, Cortlandt	He did serve six months in a military capacity.
Roberts, Everada O. S., widow of Richard B.	New York	She was not living at the passage of the act.
Shay, Hannah, widow of Timothy	North Salem, West Chester	Married after service.
Sexton, Elizabeth, widow of Jonathan	Darlington, Newcastle, Canada	He did not serve six months.
Schofield, Mary F., daughter of William	New York	No claim—a soldier of the regular army.
Scovel, Sarah, widow of Jonah	Albany, Albany	He did not serve six months.
Shoemaker, Margaret, widow of Rudolph	Paris, Kent	A militia officer in the late war of 1812—no claim.
Tier, Margaret, widow of Alexander L. Miller	New York city	A ship carpenter under civil contract.

STATEMENT—Continued.

Names.	Residence.	Reasons for rejection.
Van Duesen, children of Joseph L.	Schenectady city.	No claim—a soldier of the regular army.
Van Buskirk, Maris.	Lansingburg, Rensselaer.	He did not serve six months.
Wilbur, Nancy Ann, formerly widow of John Smith.	Genoa, Cayuga.	She was not a widow July 4, 1836.

A list of persons residing in New York who have applied for pensions under the act of July 4, 1886, whose claims have been suspended; prepared in conformity with the resolution of the Senate of the United States, September 16, 1850.

Names.	Residence.	Reasons for suspension.
Abell, Eunice, widow of Thomas	——, Chautauque	No proof of service—name not on the rolls—claim disallowed.
Abell, Betsey, widow of Simon	Franklin, Delaware	Suspended for further proof.
Adams, Catharine, widow of Oliver	Charlton, Saratoga	Suspended for further proof of identity with the soldier of the rolls.
Addoms, Mary (deceased), widow of John	Plattsburg, Clinton	No proof as to service or to grade—the claim since her death must be reopened only upon additional evidence.
Adkins, Mercia, widow of John	——, Oswego	Imperfect in its details, and deficient in proof.
Allen, Eve, formerly widow of Lambert Sawyer	Middleburg, Schoharie	Proof of marriage defective, and of the identity of her first husband with the three years' soldier of Col. Livingston's regiment.
Alworth, Mary, widow of Thomas	Rensselaerville, Albany	He did not serve six months.
Austin, Grizell, widow of Picus	Bennington, Gennesse	In suspense for further proof.
Averill, Catharine, widow of Josiah	Pierpoint, St. Lawrence	Not six months' service established.
Ayer, Temperance, widow of Peter	Nelson, Madison	Proof of service and of marriage insufficient.
Ayers, Mary, widow of Reuben	New York city	Suspended for specification and proof by the marginal records of New Jersey.
Babcock, Typhena, widow of Daniel	Green, Chenango	Suspended for further proof.
Badcock, Abiah, widow of John	New York city	Suspended for defective proof, and papers withdrawn.
Bellinger, Catherine, formerly widow of Richard M. Petrie.	Danube, Herkimer	Suspended for further proof.
Baker, Polly, widow of Elisha	Eagle, Allegheny	Suspended for further proof.
Baker, Mary, widow of Justice	——, Sullivan	Proof of service defective—married long after the service terminated.
Baily, Jane, widow of ——	Linklaen, Chenango	Suspended for further proof.
Bailey, Sarah, widow of Jacob	Henrietta, Monroe	She died only four days after the passage of the act—proof not sufficiently precise.
Bennett, Catharine, widow of Isaac	Stephentown, Rensselaer	No proof of service—no portion of it established.
Bennett, Harris, widow of Isaac	Weedsport, Cayuga	No claim—a widow of a soldier of the regular army.
Berthoff, Anna, widow of Henry	——, Orange	No proof of as much as six months' service.
Blodget, Lucy, widow of Joseph	Denmark, Lewis	Suspended for proof of identity—there were three of the same name credited with service.
Blue, Amey, widow of Isaac	Ovid, Seneca	Suspended for proof by comrades, as fortified by the records of New Jersey.

STATEMENT—Continued.

Names.	Residence.	Reasons for suspension.
Booge, Tripheua (deceased) widow of Samuel	—, St. Lawrence	Proof of service, of marriage, and of the decease of the parties not satisfactory.
Booth, Mary, widow of Peter	New Haven, Orange	Suspended for proof of marriage, and to identify her husband with the soldier of the same name, who served nine months in Massachusetts and eight months in Connecticut.
Bond, Angelica, widow of Richard	Princeton, Schenectady	Proof of service and of marriage not sufficient.
Borden, Sarah, widow of Benjamin	Cortlandville, Cortlandt	Suspended for proof of service and of marriage prior to or concurrent with service.
Boardman, Nancy, widow of Elijah	—, Erie	Service from April, 1777, to the end of the war. Proof of identity required that the soldier who so served was claimant's husband.
Bortle, Patty, widow of Philip	Stillwater, Saratoga	Nineteen months' service claimed—suspended for further proof thereof and of the marriage.
Bouck, Maria, widow of John	Schoharie, Schoharie	He did not serve six months.
Bowers, Sarah, widow of John	Plymouth, Chenango	Suspended for proof of marriage prior to or concurrent with service.
Brasted, Molly (deceased), widow of Henry	Cuba, Allegheny	Suspended for further proof and specification.
Briggs, Sarah, widow of Michael	Burlington, Otsego	Further proof of service required.
Brink, Diana, widow of John	Phelps, Ontario	Rejected—no proof of service.
Brown, Mary, widow of William	Rotterdam, Schenectady	Suspended for proof of identity.
Brown, Annis, widow of Jabez	Windham, Greene	Deficient in proof of six months' service.
Brown, Mary, widow of Joseph	—, West Chester	He was a pensioner under the act of 1818, and his pension was stopped the first six months for an error in his first name. His widow has not recovered the original pension certificate, nor the name it bore.
Bullard, Rebecca, widow of Nathan	Thompson, Sullivan	Suspended for proof of the marriage.
Burlington, Elizabeth (deceased), widow of Solomon.	Lyons, Wayne	Suspended for further proof of the marriage.
Burrows, Sarah, widow of William	New York city	Suspended for defective proof.
Burt, Susannah, widow of Henry	Louisville, St. Lawrence	Proof of the wedding day deficient.
Byington, Zeba, widow of Joseph Pratt	Mooers, Clinton	No proof of service or of marriage.
Caldwell, Mary, widow of James	Portland, Chantauque	Suspended for further proof of marriage and service.
Campbell, Asenath, widow of Robert	Pike, Allegheny	He did not serve six months.
Christian, Phebe, widow of William	New York city	Suspended for further proof.
Case, Aruhah, widow of Ashbell	Schenectady	Suspended for further proof.

161 [37]

Name	Location	Remarks
Champlin, Hannah, widow of Pitcher	Chenango county	Suspended for further proof.
Casey, Hannah, widow of Albert	Constantia, Oswego	No proof of service.
Case, Lydia, widow of James	——, Wyoming	No proof of service. Details required, and the report thereon of the Connecticut records.
Ex.—11		
Casler, Mary C., widow of Jacob	Herkimer, Herkimer	No claim. Both parties died before the passage of the act.
Chapman, Elizabeth, formerly widow of Joseph Smith	Murray, Orleans	Suspended for further proof.
Coan, Phebe, formerly widow of Joseph Hull	Minden, Monroe	Suspended for further proof.
Cogswell, Mary, formerly widow of Jonathan Turbill	Richmond, Berkshire	Suspended for further proof.
Cock, Hannah, widow of James	New York city	Suspended for further proof.
Coleman, Elizabeth, widow of Timothy	Spring Water, Livingston	Service and marriage both admitted, but rejected under this act. Application should be made under act July 7, 1888.
Collins, Leah, widow of Thomas	Lansing, Tompkins	He did not serve six months.
Coon, Lydia, widow of Peter	New York city	Deficient in proof of marriage and decease.
Conklin, Elizabeth, widow of William	Hackensack, Bergen	Suspended for further proof.
Conklin, Agnes, widow of Jonathan	Onondaga, Onondaga	No proof of service.
Converse, Abigail, widow of Nathaniel	Troy, Rensselaer	Suspended for further proof of service.
Cook, Hannah, widow of Rudolph	Lyme, ——	No proof of service.
Cook, Clarissa M., widow of William R.	Thompson, Sullivan	No claim—her husband was a soldier of the regular army.
Cook, Sylvia, widow of Stephen	Plattsburgh, Clinton	Specification required for each term of actual service, period, length, grade, and names of officers and localities.
Crandall, Anna, widow of Azariah	Virgil, Cortland	Suspended for further proof.
Curtis, Lydia, widow of Joel	Warrensburg, Warren	In suspense for proof of service and wedding day.
Davenport, Henrietta, widow of John	New York city	The witness has not testified to the length of the service.
Dart, Margaret, widow of Caleb	Palermo, Oswego	Proof of service by the records at Hartford required.
Decker, Sarah, widow of Samuel	New York city	Proof of the wedding day not satisfactory.
Deitz, Margaret, widow of Adam	Bern, Albany	No proof of service.
Dreimer, Margaret, formerly widow of Thomas Cromwell, also of Dr. Abraham Teller	——, Columbia	No proof of service.
Doolittle, Grace, widow of George	Utica, Oneida	Proof of wedding day not precise, nor the day of her death.
Dowen, Nelly (deceased) widow of Francis	Wilton, Saratoga	Suspended for proof of marriage, and of identity of widow's husband with the soldier of the rolls.
Doty, Mary, widow of Joseph	Homer, Cortland	Suspended for further proof.
Dumbolton, Ruth, widow of John	Alexandria, Genesee	Suspended for proof from the Albany records.
Davis, Ruth (deceased), widow of Daniel	Haverhill, Essex	No proof of service.
Durgey, Eunice, widow of Moses	Jackson, Washington	Rejected under this act, and claim may be renewed under act July 7, 1888, if the records of Vermont confirm the service.
Dusenbury, Sarah, widow of Moses	——, Rensselaer	Not military service.

STATEMENT—Continued.

Names.	Residence.	Reasons for suspension.
Dubois, Jane, widow of James	——, Orange	No proof of service.
Edwards, Betsey, widow of Jasper	Windsor, Broome	The company he served in when made prisoner, the day he was captured, and the date of his release are required.
Ekker, Anna Elizabeth, widow of Johannes	Starks, Herkimer	Rolls do not corroborate six months' service.
Eaton, Deliverance, widow of Elijah	Willett, Cortlandt	Suspended for further proof and specification of service.
Everhart, Rebecca, widow of Frederick	Newfield, Tompkins	No proof nor specification—name not on the rolls of the Pennsylvania line—proof of marriage not satisfactory.
Earl, Leah, formerly widow of James Vanhorn	New York city	Suspended for further proof, which has not been furnished.
Farmer, Sybil, widow of Henry W	Herkimer, Herkimer	He did not serve six months.
Fellows, Barbara, widow of Jacob	Constantia, Oswego	He did not serve six months.
Fisk, Joanna, widow of John	Brookfield, Madison	Suspended for proof of service from the New Hampshire records.
Fitch, Elizabeth, widow of ——	New York city	Not six months service established, and papers withdrawn.
Foght, Rachel, formerly widow of James English	New York city	Suspended for further proof.
Forbes, Sarah (deceased) widow of Nicholas	Morrisville, Madison	Suspended for further proof of service.
Foster, Anna, formerly widow of John Poppino	Goshen, Orange	He did not serve six months.
Fuller, Mary, widow of Benjamin	Freetown, Cortlandt	Proof of service from the Albany records required; also, proof of the wedding day.
Fuller Martha, widow of Ichabod	Sheldon, Genesee	Discredited by the rolls—no proof of service.
Genung, Jemima, widow of Cornelius	Milo, Yates	He did not serve six months.
Godrich, Sarah (deceased), widow of Isaac	Hampden, Delaware	Rejected under this act, but is open to act July 7, 1838, upon same proof of marriage and service.
Gordon, Anna, widow of Herrick	Ripley, Chautauque	He did not serve six months.
Gould, Betsey, widow of Asa	La Fayette, Onondaga	Suspended for proof of service concurrent with or subsequent to the marriage.
Grinnell, Martha, widow of Jonathan	Rome, Oneida	For period, length and grade of service, and the officers, dates and localities of each tour.
Groat, Sarah, widow of John	Windham, Greene	He did not serve six months.
Groesbeck, Alida, widow of Peter W	Albany city	He did not serve six months.
Haddon, Mary, widow of Thomas	New York city	He did not serve six months.

Name	Place	Remarks
Hall, Rhoda, widow of Joshua	Amboy, Oswego	He did not serve six months.
Halleck, Hannah, formerly widow of John Shutts	Broome, Schoharie	Suspended for proof of identity with the soldier of the rolls. Six months twenty-seven days' service admitted—proof of marriage and of husband's death not established.
Hanyen, Charity, formerly widow of Mordecai Mott	Warwick, Orange	
Harvey, Mary (deceased), formerly widow of Jonathan Joice	Schoharie, Schoharie	He did not serve six months.
Harrington, Waity (dec'd), widow of David	Poestenkill, Rensselaer	He did not serve six months.
Hadley, Catharine, widow of Frederick	New Paltz, Ulster	Suspended for further proof of service.
Hayes, Eunice, widow of Samuel	Plattsburgh, Clinton	The names of the officers and proof of the marriage required.
Haines, Anna, widow of Jacob	Fulton, Schoharie	Suspended for further proof of service and of the wedding day.
Harder, Eve, widow of Peter	Argle, Washington	He did not serve six months.
Hickey, Catharine, widow of George	Canajoharie, Montgomery	Proof of marriage insufficient—service not properly specified.
Henksen, Anna (deceased), widow of John	———, Wyoming	Proof of her marriage and decease required, and to identify her husband as the soldier of the secretary's certificate of New Hampshire —ten months' service under Colonel Bedell, from July 21, 1775, to May 25, 1776.
Hibbard, Abigail, widow of Israel	———, Orleans	Suspended for defective proof.
Hinman, Caty, widow of Jonas	Pitcher, Chenango	He did not serve six months.
Holcomb, Lucretia, widow of Beriah	Stephentown, Rensselaer	Suspended for defective proof—not six months' service.
Haskins, Zipporah, formerly widow of Timothy Howe	New Haven, Allegheny	No proof of service.
Hopkins, Ruth, widow of Caleb	Angelica, Allegheny	Suspended for defective proof.
Hoar, Lydia, widow of Leonard	———, Seneca	He did not serve six months.
Hubbard, Mary, widow of Ezekiel	Chazy, Clinton	Only two months eight days established.
Hudson, Susannah, widow of Elisha	Arcadia, Wayne	Name not on the rolls nor his witness—no proof of service, unless he is mistaken in the officers, in which case the return of the eight months' men in 1775, in the secretary's office at Boston will correct it.
Hurd, Olive, widow of Robert	Warsaw, Wyoming	He was a deserter.
Halburt, Sarah, widow of John	———, Rutland	Suspended for the service to be set forth as required.
Hutchens, Ann W., formerly widow of John Campbell	New York city	Proof of marriage, and of identity with the deputy quartermaster for two years' service required.
Ingalls, Mary, widow of Elisha	———, Columbia	These papers were enclosed to the Secretary of War, March 7, 1844, and a five years' pension under act July 7, 1838, offered and declined, and an appeal had to Mr. Wilkins, date as above.
Jackson, Sally, widow of Reuben	Scribe, Oswego	No proof of service—name on the rolls but for a few days.
Jackson, Sarah, widow of Robert	Fairfield, Herkimer	Suspended for further proof.
Jeffers, Martha (deceased), widow of George	———, Tompkins	Suspended for proof of service.

STATEMENT—Continued.

Names.	Residence.	Reasons for suspension.
Jones, Mercy, widow of Samuel........	Saugerties, Ulster........	No proof of service.
Johnson, Hannah, widow of Isaac......	Plattskill, Ulster........	Suspended for proof of identity of the soldier of the rolls with claimant's husband.
Johnson, Sarah, widow of Jeremiah.....	Albany, Albany........	Suspended for proof from the Albany records.
Johnson, Chloe, widow of Timothy.....	Rochester, Monroe........	Service admitted—proof of marriage before or concurrent with the service not precise.
Johnson, Caty, widow of John.........	Augusta, Oneida.........	For proof of marriage, and of her husband's identity with the soldier of Colonel Willit's regiment in 1782 and '83.
Johnson, Mary, formerly widow of Daniel Brewster.........................	Leroy, Jefferson........	Did not serve six months unless the tour in 1775 should be proved.
Johnson, Ruth.......................		Suspended for defective proof, and papers returned to Hon. B. Bicknell, June 11, 1838.
Johnson, Huldah, widow of Henry......	New York city............	Rejected under this act—and if application is to be made under act July 7, 1838, the marriage must be proved to have occurred before January 1, 1794.
Knouts, Elizabeth, widow of Jacob.....	Starbs, Herkimer.........	Some mistake connected with the date of the marriage—if, as widow alleges, she was married in September 1778, her husband was only twelve years three months old.
Kilham, Mary, widow of Thomas.......	Turin, Lewis.............	No satisfactory proof of service or of marriage.
Kyrk, Jane, widow of William.........	Walkill, Orange..........	Suspended for proof from the Albany records.
Lansing, Jane, formerly widow of Elbert Van Denberg.........................	Watervliet, Albany.......	No proof of service—name not on the rolls.
Lawyer, Anna (deceased), widow of Jacob...	Schoharie, Schoharie.....	Suspended for defective proof, and no application has been made since widow's decease to renew the claim.
Lee, Elizabeth, widow of James.......	Beekmantown, Dutchess...	No evidence of service to cover six months.
Lewis, Margaret, widow of William....	Bath, Steuben............	Petition for increase rejected—neither husband in 1818, nor wife in her application in 1832, said a word about the present service.
Lewis, Sarah, widow of Walker........	Fredonia, Chautauque....	Suspended for further proof.
Lytle, Mary, widow of James.........	Sterling, Cayuga.........	Rejected—no claim—pretensions groundless.
Locke, Persis, widow of Josiah.......	Litchfield, Herkimer.....	Suspended for further proof.

Name	Place	Remarks
Martin, Susannah, widow of Anthony	Greenfield, Saratoga	No claim under this act, nor under act July 7, 1838, for she died before the joint resolution of August 16, 1842, was passed.
Merriam, Desire, widow of Ichabod	Smithville, Chenango	Rejected—but she died before the joint resolution of July 1, 1848, which, had she lived, had reinstated her claim.
Maxon, Nancy, widow of Clark	Bridgewater, Oneida	Proof from the Rhode Island records required in 1839, but have not been furnished—there is no satisfactory proof of service or of marriage.
McCain, Charlotte	——, Orange	Suspended for defective proof, and papers laid before Congress.
Mickle, Catrina, widow of Carl	Sand Lake, Rensselaer	Not any satisfactory proof of more than three months twenty-five days' service—no other term is set forth as to names of officers, &c.
Millington, Anne (deceased), widow of Peter	——, Oneida	Evidence not satisfactory to identify her husband with the soldier of the same name found on the Vermont records, nor the proof of her marriage.
Miller, Freelove, widow of Increase	New Castle, West Chester	Proof of a precise nature required of marriage and of the service, by a certificate from the Albany comptroller.
Miller, Helen		Suspended for defective proof, and papers withdrawn by Hon. J. Wy, jr.
Morrison, Rebecca, widow of Daniel	Duanesburgh, Schenectady	Proof of identity required of claimant with the soldier of the same name on the certificate of the Secretary of State, and proof of marriage prior to or concurrent with the service.
Munson, Mary, widow of John	Hebron, Washington	Not six months' service proved.
Myers, Eleanor, widow of Cornelius	Troy, Rensselaer	Suspended for further proof.
Nash, Sarah (deceased), formerly widow of John Hughan	Ballston, Saratoga	Several soldiers of the same name with claimant on comptroller's books—the difficulty is to identify and appropriate the service where it belongs.
Neal, Silence, formerly widow of John Shaw	Eaton, Madison	Suspended for defective proof.
Nicholson, Mary, widow of Charles	New Windsor, Orange	No proof of service.
Nimix, Zerriah, widow of Richard	Martinsburg, Lewis	Name not on the rolls for the company designated—no proof of service.
Noorstrant, Maria, widow of Johannes	Preble, Cortlandt	No proof of service—name not on the New York rolls.
Nottingham, Ann, widow of Stephen	Marbletown, Ulster	Claim for six months offered to be allowed under act July 7, 1838.
Osborne, Dorcas, widow of William	Barker, Broome	Not six months' service established in this case.
Overbagh, Sarah, widow of Jeremiah	Saugerties, Ulster	Not over four months twenty days' service proved in this case.
Orvis, Asenath, widow of Gershom	Le Roy, Jefferson	No evidence of service—papers sent to Hon. O. Hungerford.
Paddock, Sarah, widow of Nathan	Mount Pleasant, West Chester	Suspended for further proof.
Page, Patience, widow of Jonathan	Tague, Warren	No proof of service—not on the rolls.
Pardee, Elizabeth, widow of James S., jr	——, Ulster	Suspended for proof of service by the Hartford records.
Parkhurst, Mary (deceased), widow of John	Bethany, Genesee	Suspended for proof of her demise and the names of her children.

STATEMENT—Continued.

Names.	Residence.	Reasons for suspension.
Peck, Hannah, widow of John	New York city	Suspended for proof of the marriage.
Perrine, Catharine, widow of Henry	Canajoharie, Montgomery	He did not serve six months.
Perry, Elizabeth, widow of Johanies	——, Greene	Evidence of identity wanted of claimant's husband with the soldier credited on the comptroller's certificate.
Phelps, Mary, formerly widow of Richard Austin	——, Genesee	He was a deserter.
Philleo, Sarah, widow of Enoch	Russia, Herkimer	No proof of service.
Peckard, Kynret, widow of John	Sparta, Livingston	The evidence of the date of the marriage is doubted—if they were married in 1773, her husband born in 1757, was only sixteen years old.
Pierce, Catharine, widow of William	Antwerp, Jefferson	The three years' soldier of the rolls could not have been the husband of claimant.
Platt, Meletian, widow of Abel	Turin, Lewis	The rolls show a warsman of the same name with the *junior* appended, but the claimant in her recent declaration omits the *junior*.
Plunket, Penelope	Belona, Yates	Suspended for further proof and specification.
Pullman, Esther, widow of John	Norway, Herkimer	Period, grade, duration, locality and officers commanding required for each tour of actual service.
Price, Beula, widow of Elijah	Owasco, Cayuga	The warsman of the same regiment was not claimant's husband—one was of the line and the other the militia.
Quackenboss, Caty, widow of Abram J	Glenn, Montgomery	Suspended for further proof of service.
Raymond, Lucy, formerly widow of Daniel Raymond	Coshocton, Steuben	Proof of service and of marriage defective.
Relay, Mary, widow of Robert	Albany city	Suspended for insufficient proof of six months' service.
Remsen, Deborah, widow of Christopher	Amsterdam, Montgomery	Suspended for proof of marriage and of service.
Remsen, Catharine, widow of Garret	Brooklyn, Kings	He did not serve six months in a military capacity.
Reeve, Phebe, formerly widow of Wm. Clark	Brookhaven, Suffolk	Rejected—he did not serve six months.
Reynolds, Sarah, formerly widow of Spencer Campbell	New Hudson, Allegheny	No proof of service—not on the New Jersey rolls—no specification.
Rhinewault, Mary, widow of William	Patterson, Putnam	He died before the passage of the act.
Roberts, Jane, widow of Peter	Plattsburgh, Clinton	He did not serve six months.
Rogers, Sarah (deceased) widow of Jabez	Moriah, Essex	Period, duration, grade, locality and officers must be specified and compared with the State records where the service occurred.

Name	Place	Remarks
Root, Mary, widow of Moses	Pitcher, Chenango	Suspended for further proof of service.
Rosenkrause, Susannah, widow of Henry	Rochester, Monroe	He did not serve six months.
Royce, Lucy (deceased) widow of Abiram	Watson, Lewis	No claim under this act—service in 1776, marriage in 1780.
Russell, Hannah, widow of Ichabod	Fairfield, Herkimer	No service specified or proved—referred to the Hartford records.
Ryan, Mary, widow of Jeremiah	Berne, Albany	Proof of marriage not decisive—service doubtful.
Romans, Elizabeth, widow of Bernard	New York city	Suspended for defective proof.
Saxton, Huldah, widow of James	Pomfret, Chautauque	No proof of service to cover six months—papers withdrawn and laid before Congress.
Seabury, Catharine, widow of Tilman	Poughkeepsie, Dutchess	Name not on the rolls for but a few days—no proof of six months' service.
Seabury, Hannah, widow of John	Poughkeepsie, Dutchess	Suspended for proof from the Albany records.
Sherman, Chloe, widow of George	Brighton, Monroe	Suspended for proof from the Vermont records.
Shepard, Hannah, widow of Israel	——, Madison	Marriage too late for the service—no claim under any act, for she died in 1842, before the joint resolution of that year and of July 1, 1848.
Short, Olive, widow of Asa	——, Cayuga	Service to be set forth, and full proof of identity required.
Shell, Elizabeth, formerly widow of Abraham Van Dewzen	Albany city	Attempt at fraud by a forged certificate of marriage.
Smalling, Mary, widow of Jacob	Windham, Greene	He did not serve six months.
Smith, Dimeous, widow of Edward	Freetown, Cortlandt	Rejected—no proof of any specific service.
Smith, Sarah, widow of Caleb	Bethany, Genessee	He did not serve six months.
Shaffer, Gitty, widow of George	Blenheim, Schoharie	Suspended for proof of marriage.
Smith, Joanna, widow of Shadrach	New Hartford, Oneida	Supended for specification of period, grade, duration, locality and officers, commanding each tour of actual service.
Smith, Sophia, widow of John	Walkill, Orange	Suspended for further proof and explanation.
Smith, Hannah (deceased), widow of Elijah	Rushford, Allegheny	The service on the records credited to Elijah Smith would be sufficient to place this case on the pension roll; but there is no certainty.
Smith, Hannah, widow of George	Steuben, Oneida	No proof of service.
Smith, Mary, widow of William	Gosham, Ontario	Not six months' service nor wedding day proved satisfactorily.
Snell, Susannah, widow of Peter	Manheim, Herkimer	Evidence required from the Albany records—no satisfactory proof of the marriage.
Snider, Maria (deceased), widow of Hendricks	Gosham, Ontario	Not six months' service established.
Sortore, Charity, widow of Henry	Friendship, Allegheny	No satisfactory proof of service.
Sparling, Heyltze, formerly widow of Jeremiah Fleming	Tioga, Tioga	Required to identify her husband as the soldier of the New Jersey line, who served to the end of the war and received bounty land.
Spencer, Anna, formerly widow of Hosea Hamilton	Fairfield, Herkimer	Rejected—no proof of any definite term of service.
Starke, Phebe, widow of Joseph	Hume, Allegheny	Proof of the wedding not precise.
St. John, Lois, widow of Samuel	Fabius, Onondaga	No evidence of as much as six months' service.
Stevens, Abelinah, widow of Solomon	Greenville, Greene	Suspended for further proof of service and marriage.
Stevens, Love, widow of Israel	Western, Oneida	Suspended for further proof.

STATEMENT—Continued.

Names.	Residence.	Reasons for suspension.
Steever, Mary, widow of George	Ballston, Saratoga	Service not set forth nor proved, nor the date of the wedding.
Stewart, Mary (deceased), widow of John	Albany city	Proof of service and of marriage defective.
Strong, Hannah, widow of Joseph	New York city	Proof of identity required of claimant's husband with the soldier whose services are specified by the comptroller's certificate.
Swartwout, Sarah, widow of Cornelius	Brunswick, Rensselaer	Suspended for proof to identify her husband as the soldier of the New York line bearing his name.
Sweet, Mary, widow of John	Stockbridge, Madison	Suspended for further proof of service and of marriage.
Strong, Martha	Albany city	Suspended for deficient proof, and papers withdrawn by A. J. Parker, December 22, 1887.
Tambling Mary, otherwise called Mary Cogswell, widow of Nathan.	Stockholm, St. Laurence	Period, grade, duration, localities and commanders of companies and regiments required, and family records of marriage.
Tenbrook, Gertrude, widow of Leonard	Livingston, Columbia	Her husband was improperly pensioned and did not serve six months.
Terwilliger, Sorchy, widow of Simon	Greene, Chenango	Not six months' service proved.
Thomas, Eunice, widow of Daniel	Milton, Saratoga	Defective in proof of service—name not on the rolls.
Thorn, Sarah, widow of Richard	North Hempstead, Queens	He did not serve six months.
Tillotson Phebe, widow of Nathan	Pittsford, Monroe	Period, grade, duration, officers' names, places, &c., required, and the usual proof of the wedding day.
Tilton, Mariam, widow of John	Covert, Seneca	No part of the service in this case has been proved or admitted.
Tolon, Peggy, formerly widow of Aaron Yerks	—, Orange	Suspended for further proof.
Tonubs, Lucina, widow of James	Castile, Genessee	No proof of service—name not on the rolls.
Tucker, Turner, widow of Jedediah	Evans, Erie	Not sufficient proof of service.
Tucker, Abigail, widow of Ephraim	Athol, Warren	No proof of service—discredited by the rolls.
Tzor, Margaret (deceased), widow of Gabriel	Chazy, Clinton	Suspended for deficient proof, and papers withdrawn March 17, 1837, by Hon. A. Gallup.
Truax, Elizabeth, widow of Abraham	Schenectady city	Suspended for deficient proof, and papers withdrawn March 18, 1838, by Hon. A. Gallup.
Valkenburg, Catharine, widow of Christian	Clermont, Columbia	Suspended for further proof from the Albany records.
Viele, Rachel (deceased), widow of Philip	Glenville, Schenectady	He did not serve six months.

Vischer, Lydia, widow of Matthew	Albany city	He did not serve six months.
Vorce, Zeniah, formerly widow of Barah Jordan	Chautauque, Chautauque	Names of company and field officers and other details of service required.
Vanderwerker, Mary, widow of Martin	Northumberland, Saratoga	Not six months' service shown in this case.
Vandorn, Nuel, widow of Christian	Charlestown, Montgomery	Each tour of actual service required to be specified.
Van Deusen, Catharine, widow of Peter	Bethlehem, Albany	Suspended for more satisfactory proof.
Van Deusin, Rachel, widow of William	Albany city	If this claim is well founded, the names of the officers are not correctly stated. There is no proof from the rolls as it stands.
Van Eps, Engetty, widow of James	Glenville, Schenectady	No part of this claim can be allowed from the proof on file. A brief of the details of service must be submitted to the comptroller at Albany for verification or disproof, as the case may be.
Van Nooy, Mary, widow of Peter	Wawarsing, Ulster	
Van Nostrand, Polly, widow of Isaac	Boonville, Oneida	Evidence of the marriage not satisfactory.
Van Slyck, Maracha, widow of Martin	——, Cattaraugus	Because husband and wife died without making any claim, the soldiers' service for the whole war from 1777 cannot be appropriated by the children, without direct proof of identity apart from the naked records.
Van Vanken, Sarah, widow of Maus	Schenectady city	Suspended for further proof, and details of grade, date, duration, locality and names of officers.
Van Vranken, Getty, widow of John G.	Clifton, Park, Saratoga	He did not serve six months.
Van Vleak, Margaret, widow of Abraham	La Grange, Dutchess	Proof of marriage not satisfactory. If she was married in 1788 as her declaration states, she is not entitled under this act.
Ward, Mary, widow of Charles	New Port, Herkimer	Rejected for want of evidence, both as to service and to marriage.
Wakefield, Relief, widow of Joseph	Watertown, Jefferson	Not on the rolls of Captain House in 1776. Service under Captain Crosby was before the marriage, and she has no claim under the act July 7, 1838, for she died before it was passed.
Walmsley, Mary E., widow of Robert McGinnis Walmsley	St. Johns District, Montreal	No claim—he was a soldier of the war of 1812.
Ward, Susannah, widow of Daniel	Pleasant Valley, Dutchess	No such named officers were in service at the period and place and in the regiments designated.
Worden, Margaret, widow of Ichabod	Brighton, Monroe	Suspended for proof of marriage.
Waters, Phebe, formerly widow of Samuel Judd	Russell, St. Laurence	He did not serve six months.
Waters, Catharine, widow of Michael V. D.	Russia, Herkimer	Suspended for proof of service and of marriage.
Wells, Eleanor (deceased), widow of William	Eagle, Allegheny	For a long time no proof of service, oral or documentary, was produced in this case until recently the records were searched and service discovered, which was performed by another soldier. Letter April 25, 1851—A. J. Lyon.
Weller, Mary, widow of Thomas	New York city	Date, duration, grade, localities and officers wanted in the New Jersey militia for each tour of actual service.
Wentworth, Sophia, formerly widow of Jacob Wheeler	Syracuse, Onondaga	Suspended for proof from the records of New York and Vermont.

STATEMENT—Continued.

Names.	Residence.	Reasons for suspension.
Westcot, Mercy, widow of Daniel	Rushford, Allegheny	Period, grade, duration, places, names of officers—all requisite for each tour of actual service, however short.
Westervelt, Sarah, formerly widow of David Doremus	Penfield, Monroe	No proof of service oral or documentary.
Whaley, Olive, widow of Samuel	Verona, Oneida	Proof of marriage and of service defective.
Wheaton, Avis, widow of Andrew	Auburn, Cayuga	Suspended for proof of service and of marriage.
Wheeler, Louisa, widow of Zadock	Ellington, Chautauque	Only five months and ten days service performed.
Whitcomb, Abigail, widow of Simon	Westerlo, Albany	Part team service—balance less than six months.
White, Sarah, widow of John	Penfield, Monroe	Defective proof and specification. Informal declaration.
White, Eunice, widow of Laurence	Cincinnatus, Cortlandt	Marriage in 1782 and service in 1781 excludes this claim under this act. But application under the act of July 7, 1838, modified by joint resolution of August 16, 1842, and positive proof of the marriage, may be successfully prosecuted.
Wilson, Elizabeth, widow of William	Amsterdam, Montgomery	Claims for service credited to the name of Wm. Wilson as a private and lieutenant on the comptroller's books at Albany. Although her husband lived until 1841, he made no claim. Direct proof of identity will be required before this service by the records can be apportioned.
Williams, Margaret, widow of Cornelius	New York city	Suspended for further proof and explanation.
Winfield, Anna, widow of Benjamin	Esopus, Ulster	Her husband was pensioned in 1833 before the rolls were inspected, and his claim was subsequently discredited. He did not serve six months.
Wiles, Elizabeth, widow of Henry	Freetown, Cortlandt	Suspended for further proof and specification.
Wies, Elizabeth (deceased), widow of Daniel	Volney, Oswego	Daniel Wies was a soldier of nine months' service in 1778, in New York, as appears by the certificate of the Secretary of State; but it does not appear that this soldier was claimant's husband.
Wood, Abigail, widow of John	Pike, Allegheny	Contradictory evidence in the date of the marriage. Service defective in proof.

A list of persons residing in New York who have applied for pensions under the act of July 7, 1838, whose claims have been rejected; prepared in conformity with the resolution of the Senate of the United States, September 16, 1850.

Names.	Residence.	Reasons for rejection.
Archer, Sarah, widow of Albert.	Groveland, Livingston.	Deserted.
Barce, Freelove, widow of Josiah.	——, Monroe.	Not a widow at the date of the act.
Brown, Sally, widow of Solomon.	Castile, Genesee.	No proof of service—name not on the proper rolls.
Burhouse, Abigail, widow of John.	Whitestown, Oneida.	Married after January 1, 1794, to wit: February 24, 1794.
Burlingame, Mary, widow of Nathan.	Canton, St. Lawrence.	Not a widow at the date of the act.
Crippin, Mary, widow of Elisha.	Oxford, Granville, U. Canada.	He did not leave the service creditably.
Clark, Lucy, widow of Elijah.	Naples, Ontario.	Service in 1776—marriage fifteen months after.
Crawford, Katharine (deceased), widow of Isaac.	Ovid, Seneca.	Not a widow June 7, 1882—died before August 16, 1842.
Chesley, Hannah, widow of Nathaniel.	Stafford, Genesee.	No proof of service.
Close, Hannah (deceased), widow of Charles.	Webster, Monroe.	Not a widow June 7, 1882—died before August 16, 1842.
Comfort, Maria, formerly widow of Adam Zair	——, Orange.	No proof of service.
Cox, Huldah, widow of William.	Canandaigua, Ontario.	Not a widow at the date of the act.
Doubleday, Lois, widow of Ammi.	New Hartford, Oneida.	Not a widow at the date of the act.
Edgarton, Sarah (deceased), widow of Jediah.	Richford, Tioga.	Not a widow at the date of the act.
Emory, Mary, widow of Peter.	King township, York county, Home district, U. Canada.	Not a widow June 7, 1882—died before August 16, 1842.
Farmer, Tamar (deceased), widow of Samuel	Redfield, Oswego.	Not a widow June 7, 1832—died before August 16, 1842.
Foster, Susannah, widow of William.	Albany, Albany.	Not a widow at the date of the act.
French, Lucretia, formerly widow of William Day.	——, Cattaraugus.	He did not serve six months.
Foster, Sarah, formerly widow of James Follingsby.	Carlton, Orleans.	He did not serve six months.
Glazier, Rachel, widow of Eliphalet.	Evans, Erie.	He did not serve six months.
Hopkins, Catharine, widow of Robert.	Fort Ann, Washington.	Was not a widow at the date of the act.

[37]

STATEMENT—Continued.

Names.	Residence.	Reasons for rejection.
Hardin, Martha (deceased), widow of George	Sandy Creek, Oswego	Not a widow at the passage of the act.
Hosier, Phebe, widow of John	New York city	No claim—married in 1818.
Havens, Theolesia (dec'd), widow of William	Prattsburgh, Steuben	Died before August 16 and 23, 1842.
Humphrey, Charity, widow of Charles	Phelps, Ontario	No proof of service or of marriage.
Ingalls, Mary, widow of Caleb	Keene, Essex	He did not serve six months.
Kingsbury, Esther (dec'd), widow of Thomas	Canton, St. Lawrence	Not a widow July 7, 1888, and died before August 28, 1842.
Koenig, Maria, widow of Johannes	Summit, Schoharie	No proof of marriage.
Lynch, Mary, widow of John	New York city	Married after January 1, 1794.
Michael, Anna, widow of Andrew	Oppenheim, Fulton	A musician in the French army.
Morey, Rachel, widow of James	Moira, Franklin	Divorced—no claim—not a widow.
Morgan, Lucy, widow of William	Scipio, Cayuga	Not a widow at the date of the act.
Morrill, Hester, widow of Jesse	New Town, Queens	Married in 1808.
Noble, Sarah (deceased), widow of Goodman	New York city	Died before August 23, 1842.
Potter, Rebecca, widow of David	Sanford, Broome	Died before August 23, 1842.
Richardson, Lois, widow of Lysander	Riga, Monroe	He did not serve six months.
Raymond, Esther (deceased), widow of John	Nelson, Madison	Died before August 23, 1842.
Robbins, Rebecca (deceased), widow of Evans	Summer Hill, Tompkins	Died before August 23, 1842.
Scott, Susanna, widow of William	Farmington, Ontario	Desertion.
Squier, Priscilla (deceased), widow of Ephraim	Knowlesville, Orleans	Died before August 28, 1842.
Smith, Miriam, widow of Reuben	Bolton, Warren	He did not serve six months.
Shurtliff, Mary, widow of Amasa	New York city	Not his lawful widow.
Sheely, Elizabeth, widow of Conrad	Neversink, Sullivan	Not a widow June 7, 1882—husband died December 8, 1886.
Thornton, Olive, widow of Thomas	Unadilla, Otsego	Married after service.
Turner, Anna (deceased), widow of Simeon	Cairo, Greene	She died before August 28, 1842.

Tillotson, Freelove, widow of Jacob	Columbus, Chenango	Not a widow at the date of the act.
Tyler, Freelove, widow of Simeon	Harrison, West Chester	Not a widow at the date of the act.
Van Horn, Anna (dec'd), widow of Abraham	Mohawk, Montgomery	Not a widow at the date of the act.
Vanderbilt, Catharine, widow of Cornelius	Clarkson, Rockland	Married after service.
Van Tassel, Rachel, widow of Gilbert Potter	New York city	Married after January 1, 1794.
Vroman, Angelica, widow of Peter	Glenn, Montgomery	Married after service.
Walter, Phebe, widow of Martin	Manlins, Onondaga	Married in 1802.
Way, Mary, widow of John	Angelica, Alleghany	Not a widow at the date of the act.
Whitman, Esther, widow of Benoni	Stephentown, Rensselaer	Not a widow at the date of the act.
Whitney, Sally, widow of Ezra	Burns, Alleghany	He did not serve six months.
Weed, Delight, widow of Ithamar	South East, Putnam	He did not serve six months.
Wolcott, Sarah, widow of Samuel	Lexington, Greene	Was not a widow when the act passed.
Young, Margaret, widow of Samuel	New York city	Married in 1795.

A list of persons residing in New York who have applied for pensions under the act of June 7, 1838, whose claims have been suspended; prepared in conformity with the resolution of the Senate of the United States of September 16, 1850.

Names.	Residence.	Reasons for suspension.
Alexander, Elizabeth, widow of Benjamin, heirs of	Verona, Oneida	Not a widow at the date of the act—died before August 23, 1842.
Allen, Rebecca, widow of Reuben	Murray, Orleans	Suspended for proof of service from the Hartford comptroller.
Aikin, Chloe, widow of Ebenezer	Schenectady, Schenectady	Suspended for proof of service from the State records Boston.
Ames, Ruth, widow of Levi	Chatham, Columbia	Suspended for proof of identity with the namesake in Captain Baldwin's company.
Amerman, Charity, widow of Powel	Owasco, Cayuga	Under age—rejected.
Andrews, Hester, widow of Daniel, formerly widow of David Welch		Suspended for proof from the Secretary of Vermont.
Anderson, Isabella, widow of William	Nunda, Allegheny	For further proof and specification.
Anderson, Lydia, widow of John	Mamakating, Sullivan	For proof of identity with the matros of artillery in Lamb's regiment.
Angel, Tryphena, widow of Augustus	Orid, Seneca	Not a widow at the date of the act.
Avery, Lydia, widow of Samuel	Ticonderoga, Essex	Suspended for further proof.
Ashton, Sarah (deceased), widow of Robert	Lowville, Lewis	For proof of identity with the soldier of Captain Walkin's dragoons bearing his name.
	Ridgway, Orleans	
Bachelder, Anna, widow of Samuel	Hartland, Niagara	For proof of service from the Massachusetts records.
Baker, Rhoda, widow of Nahum	Plattsburg, Clinton	Service not fully proved.
Baker, Mary, widow of Peter	Hempstead, Queens	Proof of service deficient—died before the act of July 1, 1848.
Ballard, Mary, widow of John	Sparta, Livingston	For further proof and specification.
Banker, Catharine, widow of Nicholas	Greensburgh, West Chester	Six months' service not fully established.
Bartlett, Lydia, widow of Philip	Saranac, Clinton	No evidence of identity with either of the soldiers of the same name in the service of 1775.
Baremore, Elizabeth, widow of Henry	Clarkstown, Rockland	No action appears to have been taken on this claim.
Bartley, Agnes, widow of Samuel	Goshen, Orange	For further proof and specification.
Bates, Abigail, widow of Theodore	Niagara, Niagara	For further proof.
Bates, Abigail, widow of John	Palermo, Oswego	For proof of identity with the soldier of the same name on the Massachusetts rolls.
Beach, Abigail, widow of Dan	Middlebury, Genesee	No proof of his commission as captain in Colonel Eno's regiment.
Bearup, Caty, widow of John	Schenectady, Schenectady	Names of officers and proof from the Albany records required.
Bell, Jemima, widow of Isaac	Cornwall, Orange	Service as an artificer in the quartermaster's department.
Bell, Esther (deceased), widow of Matthew	Ephratah, Fulton	For proof of her decease and surviving children's names.

Name	Place	Remarks
Bill, Hannah, widow of Jonathan	Wayne, Steuben	For further proof of marriage.
Bellinger, Lena G., widow of Adam	Shelby, Orleans	For a new declaration under act February 2, 1848—nine months' service admitted.
Barnet, Mehitable, widow of Henry	Newport, Herkimer	For further proof from the Rhode Island records.
Barnard, Huldah, widow of Phares	Westmoreland, Oneida	For further proof and specification.
Berry, Anna, widow of Seth	Randolph, Cattaraugus	Not a widow at the date of the act.
Berry, Polly, widow of Ephraim	Danby, Tompkins	For proof of identity with the soldier of the same name on the Massachusetts rolls.
Betts, Mary, formerly widow of William Livingston	Flatbush, Kings	For further proof.
Betts, Elizabeth, widow of Preserved		Service lacks five days of six months—papers returned to Hon. Francis Brengle, January 8, 1846.
Betts, Bathsheba, widow of Peter	Brunswick, Rensselaer	For proof of service from the records at Hartford.
Bird, Hannah, widow of Nathaniel	Westfield, Chautauque	For proof of service from the records at Boston.
Bogardus, Rachel, widow of Henry	Fishkill, Dutchess	For further proof of service.
Bond, Amy, widow of Seth	Beekmantown, Clinton	For further proof of service.
Bonny, Anatji, widow of John	Schenectady, Schenectady	She died before the passage of the act.
Boughton, Mary (deceased), widow of William	Stephentown, Rensselaer	Eight months' service admitted—marriage not proved.
Brainard, Anna, widow of Seba	Batavia, Genesee	For further proof and specification.
Brace, Persis, widow of Charles	Winfield, Herkimer	For further proof.
Bunnell, Statira, widow of Ichiel	Lima, Livingston	Team service in 1781—further proof required.
Bullard, Elizabeth, widow of David	Gaines, Orleans	For further proof and specification.
Brundage, Martha, widow of Jesse	———, Orange	For further proof of service.
Brundage, Rebecca, widow of Nathaniel	Fishkill, Dutchess	For further proof of service.
Brown, Lydia, widow of Stephen	Centreville, Allegheny	Inadequate proof of service.
Brown, Miriam, widow of William	Hoosick, Rensselaer	For further proof.
Bradt, Sarah, widow of G. T. Bradt		Pensioned before the discovery of the rolls—act of July 1, 1848, removes the objections to the service.
Burleson, Rachel, widow of Dan	Almond, Allegheny	For further proof of identity with a soldier of the same name.
Burtis, Elizabeth, formerly widow of Robert	Eldridge, Saratoga	For further proof.
Canfield, Mary P., widow of Philo	New York city	Not six months' service.
Caleb, Susan, widow of Henry	Ovid, Seneca	For further proof and specification.
Campbell, Elizabeth (dec'd), widow of John	Slaterville, Tompkins	For further proof and specification.
Carpenter, Phebe, widow of Barnard	Booneville, Oneida	For proof of service.
Carner, Anna, widow of Philip	Greenbush, Rensselaer	Not six months' service.
Cash, Lois, formerly widow of Zenas Goodrich	Naples, Ontario	Not six months' service.
Casselman, Catharine, widow of John	Manlius, Onondaga	For proof of identity with the soldier of the New York records.
Catlin, Roxana, widow of Elisha	Linklaen, Chenango	For further proof of service and marriage.
Champlin, Sally, widow of James	Bath, Steuben	For further proof and specification.

STATEMENT—Continued.

Names.	Residence.	Reasons for suspension.
Chatterton, Mary, widow of Nathaniel	Champlain, Clinton	For proof of marriage—ten months' service admitted.
Church, Lydia, widow of Samuel	Trenton, Oneida	For further proof.
Cleaveland, Martha, widow of Solomon	Wilna, Jefferson	Marriage not proved—service admitted.
Clough, Dolly, widow of John	Rochester, Monroe	For further proof and specification.
Cole, Celia, widow of Seth	Pomfret, Chautauque	For further proof.
Cole, Sarah, widow of Tobias	Watertown, Jefferson	For proof of identity with the soldier of Wessenfelt's regiment and the date of the marriage.
Colegrove, Theodosia, widow of William	Newfield, Tompkins	Pensioned for nine months as a teamster—without adequate proof—the act of July 1, 1818, obviates the difficulty of the service.
Conklin, Rachel, widow of John	Oswego, Tioga	For further proof.
Clark, Lucy, widow of Etham	Rome, Oneida	Not six months' service.
Conderman, Catharine (deceased), wdow of John		
Conklin, Susannah, widow of John	Howard, Steuben	For further proof.
Conklin, Charlotte (deceased), widow of Elias	Chenango, Broome	For proof by comptroller's certificate of Albany.
	Conklin, Broome	For proof from the Secretary of State of New Jersey, and from the New York comptroller.
Costin, Sally, widow of Ebenezer	Sherburne, Chenango	For further proof.
Cotton, Ruth (deceased), widow of William	Louisville, St. Lawrence	For further proof.
Couch, Prudence, widow of John	Amsterdam, Montgomery	For further proof.
Covert, Catharine, widow of John	New York city	Names of officers required and further proof.
Crandall, Sarah, formerly widow of Jas. Coon	Brookfield, Madison	For proof of service and marriage.
Crippin, Mary, widow of Elisha	Oxford, St. Lawrence	For absence without leave or explanation.
Crist, Catharine, widow of David	Montgomery, Orange	For a report from the Albany comptroller and further proof and specification.
Cromwell, Magdalen, widow of Philip	Glen, Montgomery	For further proof of service.
Culver, Phebe (deceased), widow of Aaron	Horicon, Warren	Not a widow at the date of the act—died before August 23, 1842.
Culver, Phebe, widow of Samuel	Seneca Falls, Seneca	For description and proof of service and marriage.
Cuming, Rachel, formerly widow of Emanuel Waggaman	Lyme, Jefferson	For proof of identity with the bounty land soldier of his name on the new rolls of the line.
Davis, Elizabeth, widow of Allen	Champlain, Clinton	For further proof.
Davis, Deborah, widow of George	—— Fulton	Papers at present not complete.
Davenport, Patience (dec'd), widow of David	Lyons, Wayne	For proof and details of service and the report of the Hartford records.

Name	Place	Remarks
Day, Anna, widow of Russell	Whitestown, Oneida	Six months' service in doubt.
Dean, Zilpha, widow of Abraham	New Hudson, Allegheny	Suspended for proof of marriage.
Dean, Mary, widow of Gilbert	New York city	Six months' service not apparent.
Delavan, Martha, widow of John	Fishkill, Dutchess	For further proof.
Denton, Thankful (deceased), formerly widow of John Winn	Vienna, Oneida	Not a widow at the date of the act—died in 1839.
De Forrest, Hannah, widow of Gideon	Edmeston, Otsego	Suspended for proof of marriage.
De Noyells, Ann, formerly widow of David Burrus	Haverstraw, Rockland	Awaiting additional evidence.
Derby, Constant, widow of Benjamin	Troy, Rensselaer	For further details and proof of service.
Devoe, Harriet, widow of William	, Essex	For further proof of service.
Dils, Abigail, widow of Peter	New York city	For further proof and specification.
Dobbs, Elizabeth, widow of Jarvis	Canaan, Columbia	Not six months' service.
Doty, Rhoda, widow of Joseph	Plattsville, Ulster	For further proof.
Drake, Ruth, widow of Uriah	Austerlitz, Columbia	For further proof.
Drake, Anna, widow of Abial		For proof of identity with the soldier of his name on the Connecticut records.
Dutcher, Mary, widow of Cornelius	, Otsego	Suspended for proof of service from the books of the N. Y. comptroller.
Duval, Jemima, widow of Caleb Hazle	New York city	For further proof.
Dunham, Mary, widow of Samuel	Volney, Oswego	For further proof.
Ellsworth, Jemima, widow of Eliphalet	Macomb, St. Lawrence	Service admitted—marriage in suspense.
Ellwell, Abigail (deceased), widow of John	Rochester, Monroe	For a certificate of the day she died and her children's names.
Enos, Anna, widow of Erasmus	, Cattaraugus	For further proof of service.
Everitt, Persis (dec'd), widow of Richard C.	Saratoga Springs, Saratoga	For further proof.
Eaton, Polly, widow of Ebenezer	Sweden, Monroe	Service admitted—marriage in suspense.
Edmonds, Lydia, widow of Samuel	Hudson, Columbia	For further proof.
Edmonds, Elizabeth, widow of Andrew	Cornesville, Schoharie	He was a deserter.
Emerick, Elizabeth, widow of John Shulter	Utica, Oneida	For further proof.
Fillmore, Jemima (deceased), widow of Cyrus Flagg, Christiana, formerly widow of Joseph Akins	Collins, Erie	For a certificate of the day she died and her children's names.
Fort, Angelica, widow of Jacob	Rushford, Allegheny	For further proof and specification.
Fowler, Hanna, widow of Lewis	Fort Edwards, Washington	Not six months' service.
Fox, Ruth, widow of Lemuel	Berne, Albany	For further proof.
France, Maria, widow of Jacob	, Onondaga	For proof of identity as the widow of the soldier of Pawling's regiment.
Frisbies, Esther, widow of Israel	Fulton, Schoharie	For proof of identity with the soldier of the certificate from Albany
Fuller, Diadema, formerly widow of John Stewart	Otisco, Onondaga	For further proof of marriage.
	Eagle, Allegheny	For proof of identity with the soldier, and service credited upon the certificate of the Vermont Secretary of State.

STATEMENT—Continued.

Names.	Residence.	Reasons for suspension.
Gage, Judith, widow of Thaddeus	Rochester, Monroe	For proof of marriage, and of service, from the comptroller at Hartford.
Gardiner, Rachel (dec'd), widow of Nicholas	Rochester, Monroe	For proof of identity with the soldier and service of Willett's regiment, as shown by the New York comptroller.
Gates, Alice, widow of Zebulon W.	Lenox, Madison	For want of proof of service.
Galley, Elizabeth, widow of Daniel	——, Orange	Marriage admitted—service requires proof from the comptroller of New York.
Gearcey, Nancy, widow of Gilbert	Sharon, Schoharie	For proof of her husband's decease.
Gigart, Mary, widow of Louis Nicholas, M.D.	Groton, Tompkins	Service as surgeon in the Massachusetts line should be verified by the records at Boston.
Gillett, Abigail, widow of Asa	Italy, Yates	Suspended for further proof.
Gilman, Clarinda, widow of Philip	Sparta, Livingston	For further proof.
Gilman, Sarah, widow of Joseph	Cameron, Steuben	Service admitted—marriage in suspense.
Glann, Jane, widow of John	Seneca, Ontario	For further proof.
Glass, Jemima, widow of Alexander	Rome, Oneida	For further proof from the Hartford comptroller.
Goodale, Elizabeth, widow of Elijah	Plattsburgh, Clinton	Officers' names required in order to inspect the Massachusetts rolls.
Goutches, Rachel, widow of Abraham	Clarkstown, Rockland	Papers incomplete.
Granger, Esther (deceased), widow of Jacob	Manchester, Ontario	Marriage and service admitted—proof of the day of her decease required.
Gregory, Sarah, widow of Joseph	Bolton, Warren	Supposed attempt at fraud.
Green Patience, widow of Russell	Clarence, Erie	For proof of marriage.
Grinnell, Catharine, widow of Jethro	Sheffield, Essex co., L. Canada, taken in Owego co., N. York	No specification, and no proof of service.
Hammond, Sarah, widow of Gideon	Davenport, Delaware	Marriage admitted—proof of service not complete.
Hammond, Mary, widow of Paul	Penfield, Monroe	For further proof and specification.
Hatch, Elizabeth (deceased), widow of Samuel	Randolph, Cattaraugus	For further proof.
Harvey, Asenath, widow of Robert	Utica, Oneida	Not a widow at the date of the act.
Hathaway, Rebecca, widow of Alfred	Porter, Niagara	For further proof.
Hawkins, Elizabeth, widow of Isaac	Silauket, Brookhaven	No proof of service.
Hays, Olive, widow of John	Cairo, Greene	Service for nine months allowed—marriage in suspense.
Hedges, Hannah, widow of Christopher	Barton, Tioga	Awaiting further proof and explanation.
Henry, Esther, widow of John	Clarkson, Monroe	Pensioned for nine months before the rolls were discovered—the act of July 1, 1848, relieves this case.

Name	Place	Remarks
Hersch, Elizabeth, widow of Nehemiah	Queensbury, Warren	Marriage admitted—service as captain from Topsfield must be verified by the town records, which are in the Secretary's office at Boston.
Hicks, Phebe, widow of William	Groton, Tompkins	For further proof of service.
Hine, Mary, widow of Newton	Cortlandtville, Cortlandt	For further proof.
Hitchcock, Elizabeth, widow of Joel	Yorktown, West Chester	For reference to the comptroller at Albany.
Hobart, Dolly, widow of Rev. William	Yatesville, Yates	For proof of service—marriage admitted.
Hodgeman, Lydia, widow of Nathan	Macedon, Wayne	Not a widow at the date of the act.
Hodge, Abigail (deceased), widow of James	Annsville, Oneida	Not a widow at the date of the act—died before August 23, 1842.
Hodge, Miriam, widow of Asa	Lysne, Steuben	Not a widow at the date of the act.
Holbrook, Betsey, widow of Silas	Cocksackie, Greene	Marriage admitted—proof of identity with the Silas Holbrook of the comptroller's certificate required.
Holley, Dorothy, widow of Joseph	Spencertown, Columbia	For further proof.
Holly, Lucinda, widow of Joseph	Loraine, Jefferson	Not properly presented—papers not complete.
Holmes, Lucretia, widow of Joshua	Springville, Erie	For further proof of commission and service.
Houghton, Hannah, widow of Silas, formerly widow of Jacob Houghton	Athol, Warren	For proof of identity with the late pensioner, Jacob Houghton, and of this decease.
Hope (or Houpt), Margaret, widow of Philip	Ovid, Seneca	For further proof from the auditor's office at Harrisburg.
Hormer, Polly, widow of Ashbel	Wheatland, Monroe	Not six months' service.
Hubbard, Sillence, widow of Thomas	Russia, Herkimer	For proof of marriage.
Huggins, Sarah, widow of Zenas	Bethany, Genesee	Not six months' service.
Hungerford, Ann, widow of Levi	Milford, Otsego	For proof of marriage and of service from the Albany records.
Hurd, Lucinda (deceased), widow of Daniel	Hume, Allegheny	For proof of identity with the sergeant's service named on the secretary's books.
Husted, Mary (deceased), widow of Jonathan	Cairo, Greene	For proof of identity with the soldier in Captain Livingston's company Colonel Wessenfeldt's regiment.
Ingersoll, Lovina, widow of Moses	Owego, Tioga	For period, length and grade of service, and names of company and field officers.
Ishaim, Faith (deceased) widow of Isaac	Warsaw, Wyoming	Not six months' service.
Jackson, Eleanor, widow of John	Goshen, Orange	For proof of identity with the soldier of Captain McKinsty's company, Col. Malcomb's regiment.
Jenkins, Abigail, widow of John	New York city	For further proof of service.
Johnson, Agnes, widow of Isaac	New York city	Not a widow at the date of the act.
Jones, Elizabeth, widow of Samuel L.	New York city	For proof from the records at Hartford.
Judson, Hepsey, widow of John B.	Sherburne, Chenango	For proof of service.
Knapp, Hannah, formerly widow of Zebulon Moses	Lima, Livingston	For further proof.
Kenyon, Mary, widow of Clark	Greenville, Washington	No proof of service.

STATEMENT—Continued.

Names.	Residence.	Reasons for suspension.
Ketchum, Jemimah, widow of Ephraim	Virgil, Cortlandt	For further proof.
Ketchum, Sally, widow of Joseph	Mount Morris, Livingston	Not six months' service.
Keys, Eleanor (deceased), widow of Joseph.	Evans Centre, Erie	No proof of service or marriage.
Laman, Diadama, widow of John	Catskill, Greene	For further proof from the records at Boston.
Lanckton, Margaret, widow of Matthias	—, Madison	For proof of service and marriage.
Lane, Elizabeth, formerly widow of Jonathan Johnston		
Lane, Martha, widow of Nathan	New Paltz, Ulster	Married after January 1, 1794.
Leonardson, Sarah, widow of John T.	Yorktown, West Chester	For proof of service from New York comptroller.
	Root, Montgomery	She died before the joint resolution of July 1, 1848, and the objections to the service are continued.
Lewis, Abigail, widow of Nathaniel	Augusta, Oneida	For a new declaration under the joint resolution of July 1, 1848.
Lewis, Phebe, formerly widow of James Lyons	Gosham, Ontario	For proof of identity with the soldier in the comptroller's certificate.
Linn, Abigail, widow of James	Oswegatchie, St. Lawrence	For further proof.
Linsley, Anna, widow of Abiel	Prattsburgh, Steuben	He was a deserter.
Lindsey, Sarah, widow of Daniel	Cold Spring, Cattaraugus	Suspended for a declaration according to the printed form.
Liscomb, Bethany, widow of Samuel	Niagara, Niagara	For further proof.
Livermore, Abigail (deceased), widow of Silas	Fort Edward, Washington	For proof of her decease and her children's names.
Loaar, Catharine (deceased) widow of Jacob.	Groveland, Livingston	For further proof.
Lord, Amey, formerly widow of Edward Mead	New York city	For further proof.
Lozier (or Lorier) Christiana, widow of Jacob.	Middleport, Niagara	For further proof and specification.
Lowell, Anna, widow of Isaac	Amherst, Niagara	For proof of marriage.
Lorejoy, Anna, widow of John	—, Monroe	For further proof and specification.
Lutts, Elizabeth, widow of John	New York city	For proof of identity with the soldier in Col. Klock's and Col. Wagoner's regiments in 1779 and 1780, and Col. Wesselfelt's in 1782 as private and lieutenant.
Luli, Ann, widow of Abner	Triangle, Broome	For further proof and specification.
Mall, Seneth, widow of John	Schenectada, Schenectada	Remanded for a new declaration before a court of record.
Mapes, Experience, widow of George E.	Dix, Chenango	For further proof.
Marsh, Jane, widow of Simon	Warsaw, Genessee	Not on the New Jersey records for the period designated.
Martin, Susannah, widow of Anthony	New Windsor, Orange	Remanded for authentication and not replaced.

181   [37]

Name	Place	Remarks
Martin, Mary, widow of Joseph	Rouse's Point, Clinton	No proof of identity with any soldier or pensioner.
Marinus, Mary, widow of Thomas	Oneonta, Otsego	No evidence of service or of marriage.
Martling, Fanny, widow of Abraham	Haverstraw, Rockland	For proof of marriage.
Marvin, Mary, widow of Abraham	Homer, Cortlandt	For proof of service—marriage admitted.
McCarty, Mabel, widow of Clark	Clarkson, Monroe	For proof of service as forage master.
McCreery, Esther, widow of Robert	———, Orange	For proof of service from the comptroller's books.
McFerrin, Elizabeth, widow of William	Whitehall, Washington	For proof from the Albany or Montpelier records.
McGown, Margaret, widow of Stephen	Cherry Valley, Otsego	Barred by act April 30, 1844.
McKey, Elizabeth, widow of Alexander	Veteran, Chemung	For proof of identity with the Alexander McKey of the first New York regiment.
McMurphy, Rachel, formerly widow of Benjamin Cole	Humphrey, Cattaraugus	Her second husband was living in September, 1848.
McName, Abigail, widow of William	Poughkeepsie, Dutchess	For proof of identity with the soldiers of Pawling's regiment.
Merrinan, Chloe, widow of Elisha	Otisca, Onondaga	For further proof.
Miles, Martha, widow of Isaac	Addison, Steuben	Not a widow at the date of the act.
Miller, Rhoda (deceased), widow of Eliakim	Amerville, Oneida	Not a widow at the date of the act—died before August 28, 1842.
Moore, Esther, widow of John	Ithaca, Tompkins	For further proof from the records of New Hampshire.
Moore, Mehitable, widow of Sewell	Albany, Albany	Pensioned before the rolls were discovered. Service allowed, however, under the joint resolution of July 1, 1848.
Morenus, Margaret, widow of William	Oneonta, Otsego	Not six months' service.
Myers, Anna, widow of Henry	Kingston, Ulster	For proof of identity with some one of the soldiers in Graham's, Rawling's and Weissenfelt's regiments of the same name.
Myer, Gertrude, widow of Frederick	Kingston, Ulster	Barred by act April 30, 1844.
Neison, Dolly, widow of Moses	Rome, Oneida	For further proof.
Nellis, Mary, widow of William	Palatine, Montgomery	For proof of identity with the service credited to the same name on the comptroller's certificate.
Northrup, Rhoda, widow of Stephen	Sullivan, Madison	Not a widow at the date of the act.
Norton, Martha (deceased), widow of Oliver	Sangerfield, Oneida	Not a widow at the date of the act or application—died before August 28, 1842.
Norton, Martha, formerly widow of Caleb Cornwall	Peru, Clinton	Not a widow under the act.
Oakes, Thankful, widow of John	Wheatland, Monroe	For proof from the New Hampshire records.
Ogden, Sibal, widow of Edmond	Unadilla, Otsego	For proof of marriage—service allowed.
Orlop, Elizabeth, widow of William	Watervliet, Albany	Not six months' service.
Olmstead, Jerusha, widow of Stephen	Byron, Genessee	Further proof of service.
Ostrander, Jane, widow of Andrew	Guilderland, Albany	Not six months service.
Overbagh, Catharine, widow of Peter	Catskill, Greene	For proof of identity with the soldier named in the certificate of the comptroller at Albany.

STATEMENT—Continued.

Names.	Residence.	Reasons for suspension.
Page, Sarah, widow of Edmund	Chatham, Columbia	For proof from the comptroller at Hartford.
Page, Abigail, widow of Benoni	Unadilla, Otsego	Barred by act April 30, 1844.
Parker, Lydia, widow of Reuben	Granville, Washington	Not six months' service.
Parks, Ruth, widow of Robert	Benton, Yates	The service credited on Walbridge's rolls in 1775 is to Robert Parker not Parks.
Park, Anna, widow of Ezra	Stuyvesant, Columbia	For proof of identity with the service and soldier described in the certificate of the Connecticut comptroller.
Parsons, Hannah, widow of Joseph	Canadia, Livingston	No proof of service—not on the Connecticut rolls.
Peck, Huldah, widow of Elisha	Howard, Steuben	Not six months' service.
Peck, Mary, widow of William	Norwich, Chenango	For further proof.
Perkins, Elizabeth, widow of Jencks	Whitestown, Oneida	For further proof and specification.
Peck, Elizabeth, widow of William	Bethel, Sullivan	For further proof and information.
Perrin, Betsey, widow of Daniel	Sweden, Monroe	For further proof of marriage.
Phillips, Hannah, widow of John	Machias, Cattaraugus	For proof of identity, as there are two soldiers of the same name on Col. Willett's rolls.
Phillips, Catharine, widow of John	Cicero, Onondaga	For further proof of identity with the soldier of the New York line.
Pier, Lucy, widow of Abner	Otego, Otsego	Not six months' service.
Pool, Elizabeth, widow of John	Pike, Allegheny	For further proof and explanation.
Pomeroy, Experience, widow of Ira	Otisco, Onondaga	Not six months' service.
Poppins, Eunice, widow of Daniel	—— Orange	For proof of marriage.
Porter, Zerriah, widow of Alexander	Freedom, Cattaraugus	For proof that she is still living—marriage and service allowed.
Powell, Eveline, widow of Jonathan	Pittstown, Rensselaer	Not six months' service.
Powell, Eunice, widow of Peter	Ogdensburgh, St. Lawrence	For further proof and specification.
Pryne, Maria, widow of Peter	Ephratah, Fulton	Not six months' service.
Prevost, Eve, widow of John	Bushwick, Kings	For further proof of service.
Rathbone, Olive, widow of Moses	Greene, Chenango	For proof of marriage—service allowed.
Randall, Selah, widow of Joshua	Petersburgh, Rensselaer	Not a widow at the date of the act—died before August 16, 1842.
Rathbone, Catharine, widow of Josiah	Denmark, Lewis	Not a widow at the date of the act—died before August 16, 1842.
Rawls, Hannah B., widow of Aaron	Redfield, Oswego	For proof of identity that he was the warsman of the Connecticut line.
Reed, Elizabeth, formerly widow of Jacob Wilber	Schenectady	For testimony to be authenticated before a court of record.
Relyea, Deborah, widow of Simon	Albany, Albany	For further proof and specification, and reference to the Albany records.

Name	Place	Remarks
Reynolds, Phebe, widow of James	Willsborough, Essex	For further proof of marriage and service allowed—the decease of claimant and children's names also required.
Roberson, Judah, formerly widow of Henry Miller	Yorktown, West Chester	For further proof of marriage and service.
Roberts, Deborah, widow of Warren	Warsaw, Genesee	He was a deserter.
Rogers, Lydia, widow of Samuel	Little Falls, Herkimer	Pensioned for fifteen months without proof, since discredited by the rolls—the joint resolution of July 1, 1848, removes this objection.
Rockwell, Sarah	Somers, West Chester	Not six months' service.
Roundy, Lucretia, widow of Uriah	Scott, Cortlandt	No proof of service—not on any rolls of the Connecticut line.
Rowley, Hannah, widow of Joseph	Victor, Ontario	Not six months' service.
Royce, Abigail, widow of Isaac	———, Cortlandt	The Connecticut comptroller's certificate offered in proof, would not cover six months if admitted.
Rundle, Elizabeth, widow of Moses	Waterford, Saratoga	Not six months' service.
Ryckman, Tamar, widow of Abraham	Williamsburgh, Kings	Service not fully proved.
Ryfenburgh, Christina, widow of Adam	Germantown, Columbia	Pensioned without proof—died before the joint resolution of July 1, 1848.
Sawyer, Prudence, widow of Nathaniel	Salem, Washington	For further proof and specification.
Sawyer, Comfort, formerly widow of Isaac Eagleton	Potts, Yates	For further proof from the Rhode Island records.
Samborn, Sarah, widow of James	Attica, Wyoming	Proof of her identity and of her husband's decease—seven months twenty-one days' service allowed.
Scott, Abigail, widow of Jonathan	New Haven, Oswego	For proof of marriage.
Schoonmaker, Magdalena, widow of John	Broadalbin, Fulton	No claim—barred by act April 30, 1844—both parties died before July 1, 1848.
Schutt, Annatie (dec'd), widow of Solomon	Kingston, Ulster	Not a widow at the date of the act—died before August 16, 1842.
Shannon, Christina, widow of George	Scholarie, Scholarie	Service admitted—marriage in suspense.
Sholes, Polly (deceased), widow of Cyrus	Avoca, Steuben	For further proof and specification.
Sinsabaugh, Margaret, widow of Henry	Crawford, Orange	For further proof of service—marriage admitted.
Skeel, Phebe (deceased), formerly widow of Robert Hubbard	Booneville, Oneida	For further proof.
Skinner, Judith, widow of Jonathan	Wethersfield, Wyoming	For proof of identity with the soldier and service designated in the comptroller's certificate for 1775.
Skinner, Abigail, widow of Adonijah	Hopewell, Ontario	Further proof of service.
Smith, Sally, widow of Nathan	Lyons, Wayne	Not a widow at the date of the act.
Smith, Molly, widow of Jonathan	Edinburg, Saratoga	Not six months' service.
Smith, Susan, widow of Richard	New York city	Deficient proof of his service as wagon conductor.
Smith, Abigail, widow of David	Brutus, Cayuga	For the date of the marriage and length of the service.
Smith, Anna, widow of Wilhelmus	Canaan, Columbia	For proof from the Albany records.
Smith, Gertrude, widow of Robert	Glenville, Schenectady	For proof from the Albany records.

STATEMENT—Continued.

Names.	Residence.	Reasons for suspension.
Smith, Elizabeth, widow of Stephen	Mayfield, Fulton	For a new declaration under act July 1, 1848.
Smith, Sarah, widow of John	North Castle, West Chester	Suspended for proof of identity with the soldier of the same name in the certificate of the New York comptroller.
Smith, Deborah, widow of Ephraim	Le Ray, Jefferson	Six months' service not in proof.
Snyder, Rachel (deceased), widow of Golleil	Stark, Herkimer	For further proof from the Albany records.
Stannard, Ruth, widow of Daniel	Hoosick, Rensselaer	For proof that the soldier of company 8, sixth regiment continental line, named Daniel Stannard, was claimant's husband.
Stevens, Hannah, widow of Peter	New York city	For proof of identity that the soldier of the same name in Colonel Malcolm's regiment was husband of claimant.
Stevens, Nancy, widow of Oliver	———, Onondaga	For further proof of service.
Steinburgh, Anna M., widow of John	Milton, Saratoga	Not six months' service.
Stewart, Rebecca, widow of Lemuel	Grafton, Rensselaer	For further proof and specification.
St. John, Abigail, widow of Ezra	Salina, Onondaga	For further proof.
Stiles, Olive, widow of Asa	Chazy, Clinton	Pensioned incautiously—widow died before July 1, 1848.
Stone, Mary, widow of Olney	New York city	Married after January 1, 1794.
Swartwout, Elizabeth, widow of Anthony	Wayne, Steuben	Marriage and ten months' service allowed, if alive, January 22, 1845.
Stout, Jane, widow of James	Morristown, St. Lawrence	Marriage in suspense—husband's residence wanted when made a pensioner.
Streeter, Naomi (deceased), widow of Nathan	Brutus, Cayuga	Marriage admitted—service in suspense.
Sutton, Mary, widow of William	New York city	For proof of marriage and identity of widow with Wm. Sutton, pensioner, under act March 18, 1818.
Towler, Elizabeth (deceased), widow of Isaac Sargent.	Bristol, Ontario	For further proof of marriage and service.
Taylor, Elizabeth, formerly widow of Isaac	Salina, Onondaga	For period, length and grade of service, and names of officers, field and company.
Taylor, Ruth, widow of Samuel	Guilford, Chenango	For proof of marriage.
Tibben, Mary, widow of Henry	Potter, Yates	For proof of marriage.
Tice, Jemimah, widow of Joseph	———, Steuben	For proof of marriage and widow's identity—eight months' service admitted.
Todd, Deborah, widow of Abraham	South Salem, West Chester	For proof of identity with the soldier of the New York records.
Town, Hannah (deceased), widow of Joseph	———, Canandaigua	For proof of identity with the six months and nine months' soldier of the Massachusetts line.

Tracey, Mary, widow of Solomon	Angelica, Allegheny	For proof of identity with the soldier of the £22 certificate in the settlements of the war.
Treat, Betsey, formerly widow of Joel Boles	Aurora, Erie	For proof of service from the eight months' rolls of 1775.
Turner, Sarah, widow of Samuel	Virgil, Cortlandt	He was a deserter.
Utter, Mary, widow of Josiah	Angelica, Allegheny	For proof of service from the New York comptroller.
Upham, Tamar, widow of Ebenezer	Shelby, Orleans	For proof of marriage.
Vail, Ruth, widow of William	Hamptonburgh, Orange	Not a widow at the date of the act.
Van Pelt, Sarah, widow of John	————, Ontario	For proof of identity with the John Van Pelt of Pawling's regiment.
Vanvie, Nancy, widow of Cornelius	Albany city	For further proof and specification.
Vischer, Annatje, widow of John	Palatine, Montgomery	For further proof and specification.
Van Driesen, Anna, widow of Peter	Martinsburgh, Lewis	For further proof.
Van Gorden, Agnes, widow of John	————, Chemung	For further proof.
Watkins, Anna, formerly widow of Levi Cole	————, Otsego	For proof of widows' identity with the Levi Cole, formerly pensioner on the Maryland roll, act March 18, 1818.
Walton, Mary, widow of John	Sharon, Schoharie	Service not fully proved.
Wallenback, Joanna, widow of John	Enfield, Tompkins	Service must be proved by reference to the New York records.
Waldron, Mary, widow of William	Romulus, Seneca	For further proof.
Walter, Elizabeth, widow of Adam	————, Onondaga	Not six months' service.
Ward, Hannah (deceased), widow of Artimas	Milford, Otsego	Marriage and six months' service admitted—surviving children's names wanted.
Watkins, Abigail, widow of Jedediah	Lima, Livingston	No proof of service—claim rejected.
Weaver, Catharine, widow of David	Poughkeepsie, Dutchess	For further proof.
Werner, Maria, widow of Christopher	Blenheim, Schoharie	Not six months' service.
Weaver, Catharine, widow of George M	Deerfield, Oneida	For proof of service from the Albany records.
Webster, Sarah, widow of Timothy	Sullivan, Madison	For proof of service from the Hartford records.
Wells, Angelica, widow of Abraham	Mayfield, Fulton	Not six months' service.
Wolloben, Dorothy, widow of Abraham	Truxton, Cortlandt	Service for nine months admitted—marriage in suspense.
Wolcott, Lydia, widow of John	Richland, Oswego	For further proof of service.
West, Phebe, widow of William	Rome, Oneida	For further proof of marriage and service.
Westervelt, Jane, widow of Casparus	New York city	For proof of marriage.
Waight, Sally, widow of Thaddeus	Richland, Oswego	For further proof.
Wallis, Rebecca, widow of Hammond	Plattsburgh, Clinton	For further proof.
Westervelt, Mary W., widow of Albert	Warwick, Orange	For proof and specification and her husband's decease.
Young, Mary, widow of Henry	Troy, Rensselaer	For further proof and specification.

A list of the names of persons residing in New Jersey who have applied for pensions under the act of July 7, 1882, whose claims have been rejected; prepared in conformity with the resolution of the Senate of the United States, September 16, 1850.

Names.	Residence.	Reasons for rejection.
Applegate, Daniel	South Amboy, Middlesex	He was a deserter.
Asay, Samuel	Budd Town, Burlington	He did not serve six months.
Bloom, Peter	Alexandria, Hunterdon	Not military service.
Bunnell, Joseph	Essex	He did not serve six months.
Bryant, Benjamin	——, Hunterdon	He was not the Benjamin Bryant of the rolls.
Chamberlain, David (deceased)	——, Warren	Died before the passage of the act.
Cherdoroyne, Anthony	——, Sussex	Not in actual service.
Carpenter, Thomas	Morristown, Morris	Not military service. [Papers withdrawn.]
Cook, James	Hunterdon county	He did not serve six months.
Cole, John	Moscow, Clermont	Not military service.
Cameron, John		Service after the war.
Drew, Ezra	——, Bergen	Served as a blacksmith.
Fawrot, James	Sandiston, Sussex	He was a wagon driver.
Fuller, Matthias	Bridgeton, Cumberland	Privateer service.
Harris, Abraham	Upper Alloway's Creek, Salem	He did not serve six months.
Hambleton, William (deceased)	Mount Holly, Burlington	He did not serve six months.
Hinds, Isaac	Pequanack, Morris	Team service.
Howel, William E.	——, Brown	Not military service.
Lanning, James	Lamberton, Burlington	Not military service.
Lippincott, Eneas	Springfield, Burlington	He did not claim six months.
Lefoy, John	——, Morris	He did not serve six months.
Melick, Henry	Greenwich, Warren	He was a blacksmith.
Morris, Zechaniah	Shrewsbury, Monmouth	Not six months' military service.

Name	Location	Remarks
McCarty, Francis	Pequanack, Morris	Not six months' military service.
Morgan, Jonathan	Pequanack, Morris	Team service.
Oliver, Samuel	Independence, Warren	Not under military organization.
Oughettree, Daniel	Caldwell, Essex	He did not serve six months.
Onsterhoudt, John	Wantage, Sussex	He did not serve six months.
Parker, George	Vernon, Sussex	He did not serve six months.
Price, Teareel	Elizabethtown, Essex	Not military service.
Petley, Ebenezer	Alexandria, Hunterdon	Team service.
Rude, Noah	—, Sussex	Fraudulent.
Rush, Jacob	—, Warren	No proof of service.
Russell, Jacob	Alexandria, Hunterdon	No proof of service.
Riley, Daniel	Deerfield, Cumberland	Privateer service.
Roleson, Isaiah	Wantage, Sussex	He did not serve six months.
Strope, Christopher	Bethlehem, Hunterdon	Not military service.
Smith, Richard	Hanover, Morris	Served in the French army.
Servis, John	Amwell, Hunterdon	Teamster in the quartermaster's department.
Sutphen, Samuel	Bernards, Somerset	No proof of service.
Wright, Daniel	Vernon, Sussex	Not military service.
Whitehead, David	Woodbridge, Middlesex	Not military service.
Wood, Jacob	Newark, Essex	Under age—no proof of service.
Westbrook, Josephus	Montague, Sussex	He did not serve six months.

A list of the names of persons residing in New Jersey who have applied for pensions under the act of June 7, 1832, whose claims have been suspended; prepared in conformity with the resolution of the Senate of the United States of September 16, 1850.

Names.	Residence.	Reasons for suspension.
Abeel, David (deceased), widow of	New Brunswick, Middle	Petition for increase; already pensioned under act March 18, 1818, for more than she would under this act.
Allen, Peter	Saddle River, Bergen	Not military service.
Anthony, Philip	Lebanon, Hunterdon	For specification and proof of service.
Anthony, George	Morristown, Morris	No proof of service.
Armstrong, George	——, Somerset	Team service.
Barber, Jesse	Greenwich, Warren	For specification and proof of service.
Baldwin, Ichabod	Bloomfield, Essex	For further details of service in the New Jersey militia.
Bartholf, Jacobus	——, Bergen	Privateer service.
Booth, William	Frankfort tp., Sussex	No proof of service.
Brown, Thomas	Imlaytown, Monmouth	Not under proper military organization.
Breeze, Stephen (deceased)		For proof and specification, and claim withdrawn by L. Condict, November 10, 1836.
Brooks, Thomas		For proof and specification, and claim withdrawn by Hon. T. Lee, February 8, 1837.
Boughner, Sebastian	Flemington, Hunterdon	Claim withdrawn and abandoned by agent.
Casler, Benjamin		For proof and specification, and claim withdrawn by Hon. T. Lee, November 8, 1837.
Clayton, Jehu	East Windsor, Middlesex	For further proof.
Carkoff, Henry	Readington tp., Hunterdon	No proof of his commission as lieutenant and service under it.
Crane, Aaron (deceased), heirs of	Bloomfield, Essex	No satisfactory proof of service—alleges twenty-seven tours in the New Jersey militia.
Crane, Zadock	Bloomfield, Morris	A waiter in the body-guard of the commander-in-chief, but his name does not appear on the rolls of the staff in any grade.
Dalrymple, Jesse	Alexandria, Hunterdon	For further proof.
Davis, Conrad	Mansfield, Warren	Team service—not proved by the army returns.
Dewitt, Moses	Newton, Sussex	For further proof and specification.

Name	Location	Notes
Dodd, Isaac	Bloomfield, Essex	For further proof.
Dodd, Abijah	Bloomfield, Essex	For further proof.
Ellmore, Nathan		For proof of service, and claim withdrawn by Hon. L. Condict, November 10, 1836.
Feaster, Henry		For further proof of service, and claim withdrawn by Hon. T. Lee, February 3, 1887.
Ford, Stephen	Washington, Burlington	Whether the Mifflin, on board which it is alleged he served, was a privateer or a public armed vessel.
Giberson, Joseph	Shrewsbury, Monmouth	For further proof of service.
Giberson, James	Woodbury, Gloucester	For further proof from the State records.
Gulick, Cornelius (deceased)	——, Middlesex	His claim was unintelligible before claimant's decease, and his death has made it more doubtful and difficult to adjust.
Hand, Jeremiah	——, Cape May	The quality and duration of the service of these cases require proof. (See letter of Joseph Butler, June 14, 1839, Philadelphia.)
Hand, Recompence	——, Cape May	Proof of service required, and the date of the deceased, and if any widow living, if not, the children's names.
Hayward, Simeon (deceased)	Newton, Sussex	
Hazlett, Robert	Lebanon, Hunterdon	For more perfect details and a reponse from the records at Trenton.
Henry, Joseph	Knowlton, Warren	No satisfactory proof of service.
Hurt, Shawgar	——, Cape May	For further proof and specification.
Hickman, Thomas		For proof of service and papers withdrawn.
Hoagland, John	Amwell township, Hunterdon	Two sets of papers—original papers withdrawn, September 24, 1833. See if the applicants are one and the same.
Holmes, Nathaniel	Middle township, Cape May	For further proof of the character of the vessels Halcyon and Swan.
Heaton, Elias	——, Sussex	Not on the rolls—no proof of service.
Johnson, Lewis	——, Middlesex	Papers withdrawn—claim abandoned.
June, Joel	——, Sussex	For proof of service.
Johnson, Josiah	New Barbadoes, Bergen	Not on the rolls—no proof of service.
Keyser, Nicholas	——, Warren	Proof of service required in a regularly organised corps.
Kelly, Joseph	——, Mercer	For period, length and grade of service and names of company and field officers.
Kelly, John	——, Hudson	For period, length and grade of service and names of company and field officers.
Lane, Jacob	Dover, Monmouth	Claims as lieutenant. Further proof required of commission and service

STATEMENT—Continued.

Names.	Residence.	Reasons for suspension.
Lyon, Gideon	Princeton, Mercer	Claims as lieutenant under Connecticut authority, and service as a private in New Jersey. Proof is required from the records of both States.
Martin, Gershom	——, Middlesex	For further proof of service.
Maple, Benjamin (deceased)	——, Middlesex	This claim was impracticable before he died, and his death has interposed more serious obstacles to attaining a description of his service.
Meecher, Michael	Elizabethtown, Essex	For proof from the New Jersey records.
Mead, Eli	Newtown, Sussex	He did not perform military service.
Messler, Cornelius	——, Hunterdon	He stated more service than he was able to specify. [Claim withdrawn.]
McCollum, John		The depreciation certificate $293, discredits the grade and the term of the alleged service.
Northall, William	——, Middlesex	Team service.
Nevins, John		For further proof of service, and claim withdrawn November 24, 1886—Hon. James Parker.
Olp, John (deceased)	Mansfield, Warren	For further proof.
Onsted, George (deceased)	Newton, Sussex	For further proof.
Page, Abner	Columbus, Burlington	For further proof.
Pease, John	Freehold, Monmouth	For further proof.
Peters, John	——, Cape May	For further details and proof of service.
Pecke, Joseph	Orange, Essex	For more perfect description and proof of service.
Philhower, Christopher	Bethlehem, Hunterdon	For further proof and specification.
Pidock, Charles	Amwell, Hunterdon	For further proof and specification.
Post, Abraham	West Milford, Bergen	For further proof of service.
Price, Levi		Claim withdrawn May 23, 1886, by Hon. S. L. Southard—for further proof.
Price, Benjamin	Hopewell, Hunterdon	Team service.
Patterson, Peter (deceased)	Freehold, Monmouth	For further proof—claim withdrawn May 19, 1888, by J. T. Randolph.

Name	Location	Notes
Quick, Samuel	Oxford, Warren	He was a deserter.
Quicksall, Jonathan	Evasham, Burlington	Team service.
Reynolds, Samuel	—, Somerset	For proof of service.
Rockafellow, John (deceased)	—, Hunterdon	For further proof.
Roe, Lieut. Henry (deceased)	Woodbury, Gloucester	Evidence of six months' service not sufficient.
Ross, James	Lambertsville, Hunterdon	Discrepancies between claimant and witnesses—no satisfactory proof.
Rittenhouse, Abner	Oxford, Warren	Name not on the rolls—no proof of service.
Robbins, Samuel	—, Morris	Awaiting the return of the original declaration.
Reesh, Jacob	Greenwich, Warren	Not on the rolls—no proof of service.
Roome, Samuel	Pequanack, Morris	For further proof and explanation.
Schenck, John	Independence, Warren	For further proof and specification.
Seager, Philip	Greenwich, Warren	No proof of service or specification.
Seaman, Michael	Greenwich, Warren	No proof or specification.
Shearman, Thomas	Freehold, Monmouth	Six months' service admitted—awaiting acceptance.
Sisco, Jacob	Morristown, Morris	Papers sent November 10, 1836, to I. Condict for emendation, proof, and specification.
Smick, William	Salem, Cape May	For further and more perfect details of service.
Smoch, George	Middletown, Monmouth	Discrepancies to be explained between his original declaration and his additional testimony.
Spadder, Benjamin	—, Somerset	For a more precise statement of each militia tour.
Stone, Matthias	Belvidere, Warren	No proof of service.
Stuts, Henry	South Amboy, Middlesex	No proof of service.
Stoothoff, Elbert	—, Middlesex	For further proof.
Sanford, Peregrine	Newark, Essex	No adequate service proved amounting to six months.
Sutherland, William	North Bergen, Hudson	Not on the rolls—no proof of service.
Taylor, George	Fairton, Cumberland	For want of proof—claim withdrawn.
Thomas, John	Woodbury, Gloucester	For further proof.
Tilton, John	Woodbury, Gloucester	An invalid pensioner upon whose account the department has never been informed of his details of actual service.
Townley, George	Somerville, Somerset	For want of proof—claim withdrawn.
Vanzile, Harmonius (deceased)	Hardyston, Sussex	Awaiting proof and specification of service.
Van Gilder, Evert	Pequanack, Morris	Awaiting the return of the original papers.
Van Vleet, Samuel	Wantage, Sussex	Not on the rolls—no proof of service.
Van Campen, Abraham	Walpack, Sussex	For further proof and explanation.
Van Houton, Peter	Morristown, Morris	For further proof and explanation.
Vansickle, Elias (deceased), widow of	Elizabethtown, Essex	Made no claim during his life, and there is now no evidence of service.

STATEMENT—Continued.

Names.	Residence.	Reasons for suspension.
Vliet, William	Independence, Warren	For period, length and grade of service, and names of company and field officers.
Walter, Foster	Hopewell, Hunterdon	For further proof of service.
Westbrook, John J.	Sandyston, Sussex	For further proof and explanation.
Williams, Joel	Orange, Essex	For proof and specification.
Williams, Joshua	Dennis, Cape May	Militia service in New Jersey requires each monthly tour to be distinctly set forth.
Wooley, Samuel	Lamberton, Burlington	Wagon service.
Wilsey, William	Roxbury, Morris	Eight months two days' service admitted, but nothing for services as a minute man.
Yard, George	———, Middlesex	Not six months' service established in this case.

A list of the names of persons residing in New Jersey who have applied for pensions under the act of July 4, 1836, whose claims have been rejected; prepared in conformity with the resolution of the Senate of the United States, September 16, 1850.

Names.	Residence.	Reasons for rejection.
Brown, Phebe, widow of William	Elizabeth township, Essex	He was not entitled—her husband died in 1803, and was no soldier—the Wm. Brown who performed the service was not this claimant's husband.
Fennimore, Elizabeth, widow of Samuel	Burlington county	Case not provided for—her husband was a soldier in the regular army.
Lee, Esther, widow of John	Morris township, Morris county	She was married subsequent to her husband's service, and she died in April, 1842, and left no claim.
Scudder, Hannah, widow of Philip	Morristown, Morris	She was married subsequent to her husband's service.
Sanborn, Rachel, widow of John	Cape May county	She was married subsequent to her husband's service.

Ex.—13

A list of persons residing in New Jersey who have applied for pensions under the act of July 4, 1836, whose claims have been suspended; prepared in conformity with the resolution of the Senate of the United States, September 16, 1850.

Names.	Residence.	Reasons for suspension.
Alvard, Sarah, widow of Benjamin	Somerville, Somerset	For period, length and grade of service, and names of company and field officers.
Belleville, Ann (dec'd), widow of Nicholas	Trenton city	Not on the rolls—no proof of service.
Bellis, Noffy, widow of John	Banton t'p, Hunterdon	Suspended for return of the first declaration and proof of marriage.
Bloom, Mary, widow of Abraham	Alexandria, Hunterdon	Suspended for proof and specification.
Boylan, Eleanor, widow of John	Pluckemin, Somerset	Not six months' service established.
Britten, Elizabeth, widow of Jeremiah	Elizabethtown, Essex	Suspended for further proof and explanation.
Corrington, Mary, widow of Archibald	Somerville, Somerset	Suspended for further proof and specification.
Case, Sarah, widow of Daniel	Newton, Sussex	For period, length and grade of service, and names of company and field officers.
Coon, Margaret, widow of Isael	Somerville, Somerset	Not any proof of service except for five months' tour in 1776.
Clendenin, Mary, widow of Isaac	Somerville, Somerset	Suspended for proof and details of service and marriage.
Crawford, Sarah, widow of Richard	Cape May Court House	Suspended for further proof and papers withdrawn.
Dillentagh, Dinah, widow of Henry	Spotswood, Middlesex	Suspended for further proof and specification.
Dow, Keziah (deceased), widow of Henry	Somerville, Somerset	Suspended for proof of marriage, and identity with the warsman of Spencer's regiment.
Gard, Hannah, widow of Daniel	Roxbury t'p, Morris	Service admitted—marriage in suspense.
Green, Phebe, widow of William	Ewing t'p, Hunterdon	Suspended for details of service and proof by State records.
Hart, Susan, widow of Absalom	Lawrence t'p, Hunterdon	Suspended for proof of marriage and service.
Hart, Pamelia, widow of Ebenezer	Freehold, Monmouth	Suspended for proof from the marginal records at Trenton.
Henderson, Ann, widow of Samuel	Upper Freehold, Monmouth	Suspended for proof from the marginal records at Trenton.
Horton, Mary, widow of Jason	Somerville, Somerset	Suspended for further proof.
Middagh, Mary, formerly widow of Mortimer Decker	Newton, Sussex	Suspended for proof from the Albany records.
Miller, Elizabeth, widow of Paul	———, Middlesex	Suspended for proof of service and marriage concurrent.
Mount, Ann, formerly widow of Peter Job	Upper Freehold, Monmouth	Suspended for proof from the records at Trenton.

Niverson, Sarah, widow of John	Freehold, Monmouth	Suspended for proof and specification.
Pettit, Hannah, widow of William	Middletown, Monmouth	Suspended for proof and specification
Pedrick, Mary (deceased), formerly widow of Isaac Mallack	Woodbury, Gloucester	Suspended for further proof of marriage and service.
Post, Elizabeth, widow of John H.	Aquackanock t'p, Passaic	Service for twenty-two months admitted—marriage in suspense.
Renton, Elizabeth, formerly widow of John Richmond	New Brunswick city	Not six months' military service established.
Reeves, Ruth, widow of Thomas	Hopewell t'p, Cumberland	Suspended for further proof.
Sayre, Hannah, widow of Ephraim	Morristown, Morris	Suspended for further proof.
Sillcocks, Sarah, widow of Gabriel	South Amboy, Middlesex	Name not on the rolls—no proof of service.
Stiles, Mary, widow of John	Pequanick t'p, Morris	Claim for service as commissary—proof required.
Story, Mary, widow of Joseph	South Amboy, Middlesex	Suspended for further proof.
Sutphen, Alkche, widow of Derrick	Middletown t'p, Monmouth	Suspended for officers' names and original pay and muster rolls.
Suydam, Ann, widow of Cornelius	Redminster t'p, Somerset	Suspended for further proof.
Tunison, Maria, widow of Richard	Somerville, Somerset	Suspended for further proof.
Tindall, Hannah, widow of William	—, Burlington	For period, length and grade of service, and names of company and field officers.
Vroeland, Jane, widow of Jacob	Elizabethtown, Essex	For period, length and grade of service, and names of company and field officers.
Wood, Joanna, widow of Joseph	Newark, Essex	He was a deserter.
Walling, Mary, widow of John	Middletown t'p, Monmouth	Suspended for further proof.

A list of persons residing in New Jersey who have applied for pensions under the act of July 7, 1838, whose claims have been rejected; prepared in conformity with the resolution of the Senate of the United States, September 16, 1850.

Names.	Residence.	Reasons for rejection.
Compton, Catharine, widow of Job	Middletown tp., Monmouth	She was not a widow at the date of the act.
Johnson, Sarah, widow of Henry	Middletown tp., Monmouth	She was not a widow at the date of the act.
Myer, Anna, widow of Albertson	Delaware tp., Hunterdon	She was not a widow at the date of the act.
Zeluff, Catharine, widow of Daniel	Manchester, Passaic	Team service, not entitled; and other service not six months.

A list of the names of persons residing in New Jersey who have applied for pensions under the act of July 7, 1838, whose claims have been suspended; prepared in conformity with the resolution of the Senate of the United States of September 16, 1850.

Names.	Residence.	Reasons for suspension.
Adams, Hannah, widow of Mark	——, Atlantic	Nine months' service admitted—marriage in suspense.
Ayres, Eleanor, widow of Ezekiel	Independence, Warren	Service admitted—marriage in suspense.
Beatty, Catharine, widow of John	Trenton, Mercer	Married after the limit of the act, viz: after 1798.
Clayton, Mary, widow of Zebulon	Freehold, Monmouth	Suspended for further proof.
Colfax, Esther, widow of William	Pompton, Passaic	Not a widow at the date of the act—died before August 16, 1842.
Cortewright, Elizabeth, widow of William	Newburgh, Sussex	Suspended for proof of service and of marriage.
De Camp, Elizabeth, widow of Enoch	Rahway, Essex	If the widow deceased, leaving no children, there is no claim.
Dye, Elizabeth, widow of John	Hamilton, Mercer	Suspended for further proof.
Everhart, Margaret, widow of John	Spottswood, Middlesex	Barred by act of April 30, 1844—no claim.
Hargill, Elizabeth, widow of William	Closter, Bergen	Suspended for further proof.
Hendrickson, Phobe, widow of Benjamin	Ewing, Mercer	Period, length and grade of service, and names of company and field officers.
Higgins, Rebecca, widow of James	Westfield, Essex	Suspended for proof of service.
Houder or Heisler, Isabel, widow of David	Mount Holly, Burlington	Service admitted—marriage in suspense.
Howell, Leah, widow of Arthur	West Windsor, Mercer	Not military service.
Hudnut, Grace, widow of Richard	Princeton, Mercer	No proof and specification—not on the rolls.
Jones, Hannah, widow of Hezekiah	Alexandria, Hunterton	Suspended for proof of service.
King, Harriet, widow of Aaron	Newark, Essex	Not on the rolls—no proof of service.
Kinnard, Mary, widow of Joseph	Newton, Sussex	Not sustained by adequate proof.
Lane, Rebecca, widow of Gilbert	Branchburg, Somerset	Six months' pension offered September 1, 1845, to Jesse Dow.
Lisk, Mary (deceased), widow of John	——, Middlesex	Proof of identity with the warsman of the N. J. line is not convincing.
Ogden, Ruth, widow of James	Fairfield, Cumberland	No evidence of service.

STATEMENT—Continued.

Names.	Residence.	Reasons for suspension.
Perrine, Mary, widow Andrew	Howell, Monmouth	Suspended for proof of service.
Phinnah, Hannah, late widow of Lewis Woodruff	Elizabethtown, Essex	Claimant died leaving no children.
Smith, Sarah, widow of Joseph	Jackson, Monmouth	Proof of marriage and identity with the Joseph Smith of the records of New Jersey.
Stout, Anna, widow of Daniel	Freehold, Monmouth	Not a widow at the date of the act.
Vanhouten, Hannah, widow of John P.	Bergen, Hudson	Proof of marriage and service deficient.
Voorhees, Maria, widow of John	Freehold, Monmouth	No captain's name given—no proof of service.
Vreeland, Betsey, widow of Daniel	New Providence, Essex	Service for the war admitted—declaration withdrawn for amendment.
Vandever, Aulicke, widow of Cornelius	Middletown, Monmouth	Suspended for proof and specification.

A list of the names of persons residing in Pennsylvania who have applied for pensions under the act of June 7, 1832, whose claims have been rejected; prepared in conformity with the resolution of the Senate of the United States, September 16, 1850.

Names.	Residence.	Reasons for rejection.
Armstrong, Joseph	Upper Merion tp., Montgomery	He did not serve six months.
Abel, John	Northern Liberties, Phila.	He did not serve six months.
Allison, Guian	St. Clair tp., Allegheny	He did not serve six months.
Austin, Samuel	Toby tp., Armstrong	He did not serve six months.
Beltz, Ludwick, son of Henry	Licking Creek, Bedford	He did not serve in a military capacity.
Brown, Humphrey	Wyalusing tp., Bradford	He did not serve in a military capacity.
Bostwick, Medad	Toby tp., Armstrong	He did not serve six months.
Baker, John	Clifford tp., Susquehanna	He did not serve six months.
Boggs, William	Strasburg, Franklin	He did not serve six months.
Baker, John	New Berlin, Union	He did not serve in a military capacity.
Blanchard, Jeremiah	Preston, Luzerne	No such service was performed, as is alleged, after December, 1782.
Burkart, Jacob	Pine tp., Allegheny	Service after the revolution.
Barnhart, Philip	Boggs tp., Centre	He did not serve six months.
Beaver, John	Muncy Creek tp., Lycoming	He did not serve six months.
Barr, Samuel	——, Perry	No proof of service.
Bond, Samuel	Liberty tp., Columbia	He did not serve six months in a military capacity.
Boston, Christopher	——, Luzerne	He did not serve six months.
Boyle, Charles	——, Crawford	He was a deserter.
Brookins, William	——, Cumberland	He did not serve six months.
Brougher, Christian	Hartley tp., Union	He did not serve six months.
Burnheater, John	——, Philadelphia	Service not in a military capacity.
Byers, Ebenezer	——, Mercer	He did not serve in any regularly organized corps.
Buttermore, Jacob	Greensburg, Westmoreland	Died before the passage of the act.
Campbell, Joseph	Springfield tp., Mercer	He did not serve in any regularly organized corps.
Crowl William	——, York	He did not serve six months.
Clows, John	Brighton tp., Brown	He did not serve in the reveolutionary war.
Christ, Henry	Lancaster city	He did not serve six months.
Christ, Lorentz	——, Columbia	He did not serve six months.

STATEMENT—Continued.

Names.	Residence.	Reasons for rejection.
Clark, George (deceased), heirs of.	Chestnut Hill, Phila.	Application not in proper form—wanting in all the particulars and evidences required by law.
Cooley, Richard	George tp., Fayette	He did not serve six months.
Clark, Noah	Stoney Creek tp., Somerset	He did not serve six months.
Clapp, John	Philadelphia	He did not serve six months.
Coder, Henry	Doylestown, Bucks	He did not serve six months.
Cever, Samuel	Derry tp., Mifflin	He did not serve six months.
Culver, Reuben	Wilkesbarre, Luzerne	He was a deserter.
Dobson, George	Slippery Rock tp., Butler	He did not serve six months.
Devitt, William M.	Donagal tp., Butler	Service after revolution.
Drake, Joshua	—, Pike	He did not serve in a military capacity.
Dearwart, Martin	Lancaster city	He did not serve in a military capacity.
Dale, Henry	Ferguson tp., Centre	He did not serve six months.
Eisenhart, George	West Manchester tp., York	No proof of service.
Ellis, Richard	Genesee tp., Potter	He was a deserter.
Foulke, John P.	Philadelphia	He did not serve six months in a military capacity.
Fink, George	Hemlock tp., York	He did not serve six months.
Foust, John	—, Columbia	He did not serve six months.
Flue, William	Germantown, Philadelphia	He did not serve six months.
Faulkr, George	—, Beaver	Indian war—service in 1791.
George, John	Hempfield tp., Westmoreland	He did not serve in a military capacity.
Guin, William	Indiana tp., Allegheny	He did not serve six months.
Genther, John H.	Easton, Northampton	He belonged to the French army.
Gaw, Chambers	Philadelphia city	He did not serve six months.
Geissinger, John	Walker tp., Huntingdon	He did not serve six months.
Gore, Avery	Sheshequin tp., Bradford	He did not serve six months.
Graver, John	Wilkesbarre, Luzerne	He did not serve by order of competent authority.
Graves, Asahel	Choconut tp., Susquehanna	He did not serve six months.
Graul, Jacob	Reading, Berks	He was a blacksmith—he did not serve in a military capacity. Service after the revolution.

		Service after the revolution.
Grabe, Philip	Indiana tp., Allegheny	
Hahn, Henry	Reading, Berks	He did not serve in a military capacity.
Hall, Moses B.	Charleston tp., Tioga	He did not serve six months.
Hain, Frederick	Adamstown, Berks	He did not serve under military authority.
Hefner, Valentine	Walker tp., Huntingdon	He did not serve six months.
Hagey, Adam	Walker tp., Huntingdon	He did not serve six months.
Hays, Moses	Smith tp., Washington	He did not serve in a military capacity.
Harten, Jonathan	Slippery Rock tp., Mercer	He did not serve in a military capacity.
Honeywell, William	Dallas tp., Luzerne	He did not serve six months.
Huey, Robert	Lawrence tp., Luzerne	No proof of service.
Henderson, Thomas	Peach Bottom, York	He did not serve six months in a military capacity.
Heinish, George	Providence tp., Clearfield	He did not serve in any regularly organized corps.
Harrington, William	Bradford tp., Clearfield	He did not serve six months.
Hoof, Samuel	Muncy Creek tp., Lycoming	He did not serve six months.
Honnell, David	Allegheny tp., Westmoreland	He did not serve six months.
Itterly, Jacob	Price tp., Monroe	He did not serve six months.
Jones, Jones	Philadelphia city	He did not serve in a military capacity.
Jones, William	Scrubgrass tp., Venango	He was a deserter.
Jones, Samuel	Logan tp., Centre	He did not serve six months.
Johnston, William	Honburn Creek tp., Erie	He did not serve six months.
Keller, Jacob	——, Dauphin	He did not serve six months.
King, Robert	Mifflin tp., Lycoming	He did not serve in a military capacity.
Kerr, Andrew	——, Cumberland	Service after the revolution.
Knapp, Joseph	Pittston tp., Luzerne	Not on the rolls—no proof of service.
Knecht, Jacob	East Penn tp., Northampton	He did not serve six months.
Koehler, Michael	Bethlehem tp., Northampton	He did not serve six months.
Litzenburg, George	——, Greene	He did not serve in a military capacity.
Lowis, John	Beavertown, Beaver	Express riding.
Lemon, James	Paris tp., Northumberland	He did not serve in any regularly organized corps.
Leet, William	——, Beaver	He did not serve six months.
Leily, Matthias	West Penn tp., Schuylkill	He did not serve in a military capacity.
Lewis, William	Brooklyn tp., Susquehanna	He did not serve six months.
Mast, Jacob	Nockamixon tp., Bucks	He did not serve six months.
Mcfford, William	Connellsville, Fayette	He did not serve in a military capacity.

STATEMENT—Continued.

Names.	Residence.	Reasons for rejection.
Metcalf, Vatchall	Cross Creek tp., Washington	He did not serve six months.
Myers, Henry	Roaring Creek tp., Columbia	He was not on military duty six months.
Miller, Henry	Lebanon	He did not serve six months.
Moore, James	Newsewickly, Beaver	He did not serve in any regularly organized corps.
Maddaugh, Cornelius	Melford tp., Pike	His service was not in any regularly organized corps.
Mooney, Jacob	Hemlock tp., Columbia	Service not during the revolution.
Morris, George	Waynesburg, Greene	Did not serve in any regularly organized corps.
McFarson, William	Williamsport, Lycoming	Not on the rolls—spurious certificate.
Martin, Jacob	Chesnut Hill, Philadelphia	He did not serve six months.
Miller, Isaac	Springfield tp., Erie	He did not serve six months.
McCormick, Seth	Washington, Lycoming	Team service.
Miller, Sebastian	——, Northampton	He did not serve six months.
Miller, Conrad	——, York	He did not serve six months.
Morris, Thomas	Doylestown, Bucks	He did not serve in a military capacity.
Moyers, John	Bedminster tp., Bucks	He did not serve six months.
McIlvaine, George	Somerset tp., Washington	He did not serve six months.
McClung, Alexander	Hanover tp., Washington	He did not serve in a military capacity.
Nagle, Frederick	South Witham, Lehigh	He enlisted with the enemy whilst a prisoner.
Okeson, Nicholson	Milford tp., Juniata	Wagon service.
Oaks, John	Randolph tp., Crawford	He did not serve six months.
Ott, Jacob	Philadelphia	He did not serve six months.
Parris, Gabriel	Philadelphia	He was not a soldier—he did no military duty.
Piper, John	Chesnut Hill, Philadelphia	He was not on military duty six months.
Palmer, Daniel	North East tp., Erie	He was a deserter.
Patterson, James	Upper Chaunceford, York	He did not perform six months military service.
Price, Thompson	Wilkesbarre, Luzerne	Wagon service.
Patrick, Abel	Falls tp., Luzerne	He did not serve in a military capacity.
Pedan, Joseph	Findley tp., Washington	He did not serve in a military capacity.
Pierce, Joseph	Gibson tp., Susquehanna	He did not perform six months military service.
Pears, William	Hamilton tp., Northampton	Service subsequent to the revolution.

Pond, William	—, Crawford	He did not serve in any regularly organized corps.
Powell, Eleazar	Chippeway tp., Beaver	He did not serve in any regularly organized corps.
Peterson, Sylvanus	Abingdon, Centre	He did not serve six months.
Reed, John	Beaver	He did not serve six months in person.
Randolph, Ichabod	Deer tp., Allegheny	He did not serve six months.
Renn, Philip	Augusta tp., Northumberland	No proof of service.
Rhodes, William	Uniontown, Greene	Privateer service.
Ricker, Frederick	Hammettstown, Dauphin	He did not serve in a military capacity.
Rice, Chauncey	Easton, Northampton	No proof of service.
Rittenhouse, Garret	Philadelphia	He did not serve in a military capacity.
Rice, Christian	Milford tp., Somerset	He did not serve six months.
Roehr, Joseph	Pottsville, Schuylkill	He did not serve six months.
Runyan, Samuel	—, Mercer	His service was not military.
Russell, Thomas	French Creek tp., Venango	He did not serve six months.
Ryerson, John	Milford tp., Pike	He did not serve six months.
Sala, Peter	Beaver, Beaver	He did not serve six months.
Sayler, Michael	Somerset tp., Somerset	He did not serve six months.
Sepler, Frederick	Greensburgh, Westmoreland	He did not serve six months.
Seymour, Eli	Erie, Erie	He did not serve six months.
Sutzinger, Michael	Reading, Berks	He did not serve in a military capacity.
Smith, George	Muncy tp., Lycoming	He did not serve six months.
Schaum, Melchior	Lancaster city	He did not serve six months.
Schnell, Lewis	Franklin tp., Greene	Served in the French army.
Sill, Jabez	Wyson tp., Bradford	He did not serve in a military capacity.
Slate, Thomas	Tioga tp., Tioga	Team service.
Settler, George	Pittsburg city	No proof of service.
Shaffer, Adam	Miley tp., Centre	He did not serve six months.
Shaw, David	Greensburg, Westmoreland	He did not serve in a military capacity.
Shunk, Henry	Smithfield tp., Monroe	He did not serve in a military capacity.
Skyles, John	Carlisle, Cumberland	Wagon service.
Shields, John	—, Armstrong	He did not serve six months during the revolution.
Sigler, John	Decatur tp., Mifflin	He did not serve in any regularly organized corps.
Sleeper, Robert	—, Bradford	He did not serve six months.
Smith, Philip (2d)	—, Allegheny	He did not serve six months.
Smith, Philip (alias Seipa)	—, Beaver	He did not serve six months.
Smith, John	South Broom tp., Beaver	No proof of service.
Snell, Lewis	—, Greene	Privateer service.
Snyder, Henry	Germantown, Philadelphia	Served in the French army.

STATEMENT—Continued.

Names.	Residence.	Reasons for rejection.
Spinner, Abraham	Allentown, Lehigh	He did not serve six months.
Squire, Nathaniel	—, Mercer	Service after the revolution.
Still, John	Mahoning tp., Columbia	Wagon service.
Snares, William	Hatfield tp., Montgomery	Exclusive of team service he served but five months.
Snyder, John	Bellefonte, Centre	Wagon service.
Stewart, William	Ligonia tp., Westmoreland	He was a deserter.
Tallman, Jeremiah	Williamsport, Lycoming	He did not serve six months.
Taylor, Martin	Erie, Erie	He did not serve in a military capacity.
Truby, Michael, sen	Kittaning, Armstrong	He did not serve under military authority.
Upp, Jacob	York, York	He did not serve six months.
Vanpool, Jacob	—, Franklin	Wagon service.
Vanken, Peter	Milford tp., Pike	He did not serve in any regularly organized corps.
Wagner, Martin	Penn tp., Schuylkill	He did not serve in a military capacity.
Ward, James	Providence tp., Luzerne	Service in the commissary department.
Watson, Thomas	Buffalo tp., Butler	Left the American side and joined the British.
Weed, Frederick	—, Clearfield	No adequate proof of service.
Weighley, Isaac	—, Armstrong	Exclusive of team service, he served but four months.
Weisel, Jacob	St. Clair tp., Bedford	He did not serve six months.
Whitman, Jacob	Canal tp., Venango	He did not serve on a military footing.
Wilcox, Stephen	Franklin tp. Bradford	He did not serve in a military capacity.
William, Daniel (colored)	Philadelphia	He did not serve in a military capacity.
Williams, David	George tp., Fayette	He did not perform six months actual service.
Wirts, William (deceased)	—, Montgomery	Died before the passage of the act.
Woodcock, John	Harrison tp., Tioga	He did not serve six months.
Wood, Joseph	Formerly of Haverstraw, Rockland, N. Y., now of Tioga.	He did not serve six months.

Woodward, John	Spring tp., Crawford	He did not serve six months.
Wood, William (surgeon)	Myerstown, Lebanon	No evidence by commission or any other document.
Woolheater, Adam	Washington tp., Indiana	He served less than six months.
Winn, Henry	Sugar Loaf tp., Columbia	He was a deserter.
Zane, Samuel	New Brighton tp., Beaver	He did not serve in a military capacity.

A list of the names of persons residing in Pennsylvania who have applied for pensions under the act of June 7, 1832, whose claims have been suspended; prepared in conformity with the resolution of the Senate of the United States, September 16, 1850.

Names.	Residence.	Reasons for suspension.
Adams, John	Finley township	Not six months' service established in this case—application withdrawn.
Agnew, Robert		Suspended for want of proof of service and defects in form—awaiting the return of the original declaration.
Anderson, Samuel	Chapman tp., Lycoming	Not military service—he was a wagon driver.
Bailey, Nathaniel	——, York	For failure of proof of six months' revolutionary service.
Baldwin, Peleg	Middletown tp., Susquehanna	If he served in the coast guards, the pay tables of the Secretary of Connecticut will be the place to find the proof.
Barnhart, John Christopher (dec'd), daughter of	——, Lebanon	Suspended for further proof and specification.
Barrett, Thomas	Elk Creek tp., Erie	Alleged service in the Massachusetts militia must be proved by the Massachusetts records.
Bush, George	Smithfield tp., Monroe	Suspended for period, length and grade of service, and names of company and field officers, and the nature of the service and place of enlistment.
Banshor, Peter	Reading, Berks	Suspended for proof of service.
Bedell, Abner	Elizabeth tp., Allegheny	Suspended for proof of his captain's commission, and service in the New Jersey militia.
Betz, Solomon	Buffalo tp., Union	Period, length and grade of service, and names of company and field officers required.
Betzler, Caspar	Northern Liberties, Philadelphia	Alleged service in 1775, probably, in 1776—militia service overrated.
Bird, John	Kingston, Luzerne	Application under act 1818 rejected—no proof of service under this act.
Belknap, John	New Milford, Susquehanna	His certificate of pension is required, or he must account for its absence, and state his residence at the time he was pensioned.
Bowen, Joseph (deceased), heirs of	Northern Liberties, Philadelphia	The certificate of the New Jersey Secretary of State of the soldier from the town of Hopewell, Cumberland county, contains evidence of nine months' service in 1778, and not to the end of the war—witness's name not on the rolls.
Boren, Joseph	Sewickly tp., Beaver	Suspended for further proof of service.
Boyle, Charles	Mead tp., Crawford	Service not set forth—no officers or place of service given.

Name	Location	Remarks
Brensinger, Caspar	—, Berks	Suspended for want of proof and specification.
Breech, Thomas	Catawissa tp., Columbia	Narrative obscure and imperfect—he claims to have served eighteen months, from December 26, 1776, without stating in what troops or what term enlisted.
Brewer, Francis	Braintree, Luzerne	No proof of identity with the soldier of the same name on the rolls of the Secretary of State of Massachusetts, nor is the term of service equal to six months.
Brown, James	—, Chenango	Service for over three months established by the rolls—the wagon service must be specified as to officers and regiment to which he belonged.
Brown, John	Sterling tp., Wayne	Not on the rolls—no proof of service.
Brugler, Peter	Hemlock tp., Columbia	Suspended for want of proof.
Bruno, Peter	Pittsburgh, Allegheny	Suspended for officers of regiment, company and line, and period, length and grade of service.
Burke, John	—, York	Under age—a drummer for the guard at Lancaster barracks—aged ten years in 1781.
Carley, Simeon	—, Beaver	Regiment and colonel's name required in order to an inspection of the rolls.
Christman, Frederick	Blacklock tp., Indiana	Suspended for proof of service in the Maryland militia, flying camp, &c., by the Annapolis records.
Clark, Ichabod	Fairfield tp., Lycoming	Period, length and grade of service, and names of company and field officers required.
Clark, William	Brown tp., Lycoming	The Secretary of State of Pennsylvania will be able probably to furnish some evidence of the nature of the service in this case.
Clutter, William	Jefferson tp., Allegheny	No proof of service on the records—surviving comrades who served with him must fill the vacancy.
Coleman, Valentine (deceased)	—, York	Service in the Pennsylvania militia improperly stated.
Coal, Enos	Cassewago tp., Crawford	Suspended for further proof—a doubtful case.
Cook, Daniel	—, Berks	His service in a regiment of the Pennsylvania line is invalidated—his name is not on the rolls.
Creed, Solomon	Falls tp., Luzerne	He did not serve six months.
Cupples, James	Derry tp., Mifflin	Suspended for further proof March 17, 1885—Hon. G. Burd.
Cypher, Daniel	Hopewell tp., Bedford	
Davidson, Francis (deceased)		Suspended for want of proof February 6, 1845—H. D. Foster. [Claim withdrawn.]
Davis, Nicholas	Newport tp., Luzerne	Not on the New Jersey rolls—no proof of service February 8, 1887—John Smith.
Dawson, Peter P.	Greenwood tp., Juniata	Suspended for lack of proof—set to claimant July 28, 1889.

STATEMENT—Continued.

Names.	Residence.	Reasons for suspension.
Dazey, Jesse	Philadelphia	A new declaration required—and if he belonged to the Delaware line, service should be sustained by the Dover records July 5, 1848.—P. E. Brocchus.
Dean, Samuel	——, Fayette	Period, length and grade of service, and names of company and field officers required, May 16, 1846.—A. Stewart, H. R.
Deyo, Elias	Meadville, Crawford	Proof of identity not enough to identify claimant with the soldier of Colonel Wessenfeldt's regiment.
Dickey, Jesse	——, Lycoming	Proof of identity required that he is the soldier he claims to be, whose name is borne on the rolls of service in this office.
Decker, John Jacob	Tulpehocken, Berks	Suspended for further proof of his commission as lieutenant and captain.
Donohay, James, sen.		Suspended for further proof and explanation—papers withdrawn.
Dougherty, Mordecai C	Kittaning, Armstrong	Suspended for further proof of service.
Earl, Joseph	Clearfield, Clearfield	Not on the rolls of Wessenfeldt's regiment—two witnesses required.
Ellston, Spencer	Athens, Bradford	Suspended for more perfect details of his militia service.
Emberson, James	Union, Fayette	Suspended for further proof—not on the rolls at Annapolis.
Essick, Jacob	Liverpool, Juniata	Suspended for an exhibit of the papers upon which he was allowed a pension by the State of Pennsylvania.
Ewing, James (deceased)	Village Green, Delaware	Not on the rolls—no proof of service—claim rejected.
Fish, John (deceased), by his son Michael	——, Monroe	Service as lieutenant proved by the rolls of the seven months' men in the Pennsylvania troops—identity of relationship wanted, which does not appear.
Founder, John	Philadelphia	Not on the rolls—no proof of service.
Frazer, William	Napier, Bedford	Suspended for proof that he served in a regularly organized corps.
First, John Adam	Rapho, Lancaster	Suspended for proof of service.
Fress, John	——, Columbia	The service is apparent, but the length requires measurement.
Featherhoof, Matthias	——, Adams	Except in driving a team, his service did not amount to six months.
Gibson, Gideon	Penn tp., Armstrong	Frontier service in Indian wars of 1779, '80, '81—if this was militia service, the records at Harrisburg should account for it.
Gill, Samuel	Leo Bœuff tp., Erie	Service requires proof from the Connecticut records, which has been called for without effect.

Name	Location	Remarks
Griet, Jacob	Greenburgh, Westmoreland	Suspended for further proof and specification—claim withdrawn.
Grove, George	Warnermark tp., Huntingdon	Not admitted for want of positive testimony.
Gross, John	—, Adams	Suspended for proof and specification, and the history of the service in detail.
Gross, Nicholas	—, Berks	Suspended for proof and specification, and the history of the service in detail.
Gary, Richard	Buffalo tp., Armstrong	He is marked on the rolls of his regiment as "dead, or deserted."
Hall, William	—, Mercer	Suspended for lack of proof of service—papers withdrawn.
Hammon, William	—, Beaver	Service in 1793—no claim—not provided for.
Harrier, William	Bradford tp., Clearfield	Suspended for proof of service.
Hays, Pliny	Bedford, Bedford	Suspended for further proof of service.
Henry, Samuel	Barre, Huntingdon	Period, length and grade of service, and names of company and field officers required.
Herrick, Daniel	Mead, Crawford	Age and neighborhood reputation required. The certificate of the New York Comptroller exhibits two payments to a soldier of the same name, but this certificate was evidently the basis of the application already unreasonably long delayed. April 23, 1849, to Hon. J. W. Farrelly, Meadville.
Hickman, Isaac	Canaan, Wayne	Suspended for more perfect details. The New Jersey militia were out in alternate monthly tours, and never adopted four-month tours.
Hidler, Joshua	Hamiltonban, Adams	No satisfactory proof of service.
Hill, Frederick	—, Bedford	Suspended for want of positive proof of service—claim withdrawn.
Hillman, John	Pine tp., Allegheny	Papers defective—form was sent to Hon. A. Stewart December 16, 1845, and no action has since been had.
Hite, James	Henderson, Huntingdon	Suspended for proof of service.
Holmes, John G	Shrewsbury, Lycoming	Six months service not fully proved.
Huber, Henry	Philadelphia	Service not six months.
Hulsizer, Valentine	Hanover, Luzerne	Suspended for further proof and specification.
Hutchins, Amos	Conneaut tp., Crawford	Not on the rolls. No proof of service.
Ickes, Nicholas	Ickesburg, Perry	He did not serve six months.
Irely, John	Mifflin tp., Columbia	No proof of service. Not on the rolls—rejected.
James, Nicholas	York, York	Under age—no proof of service. Claim rejected.
Jones, Thomas	Canuwago tp., York	Name not on the rolls. No proof of service.
Johnson, Jacob	Fishing Creek tp., Columbia	No such officer known to the service. Further proof and explanation required.
Jordan, Henry	—, Mercer	Not on the rolls—no proof of service.

STATEMENT—Continued.

Names.	Residence.	Reasons for suspension.
Katzmeyer, Ludwig	——, Berks	Period, length and grade of service, and names of company and field officers required.
Keely, Joseph	Woodberry tp., Huntingdon	Not on the rolls—no proof of service.
Keiser, Jacob (deceased)	Shippensburg, Cumberland	Suspended for further proof.
Kerr, Joseph	Uniontown, Fayette	Suspended for further proof and specification.
King, Jacob	Reading, Berks	He did not serve six months.
Kemble, Peter	Fairfield tp., Lycoming	Period, length and grade of service, and names of company and field officers required, and a response from the State records at Trenton for or against the service.
King, David	Towanda, Bradford	Period, length and grade of service, and names of company and field officers required.
Kingsley, Wareham	Wilkesbarre, Luzerne	Not military service—a waiter boy to his father.
Kirkpatrick, James	Wayne, Armstrong	Four months' service admitted—further proof of further service required.
Kolb, Abraham C	Lycoming tp., Lycoming	Suspended for further proof and specification.
Kuhns, Daniel	Greensburgh, Westmoreland	No proof of service. No proof of such service as four-month tours of the militia of Pennsylvania.
Landon, Thomas	Meadville, Crawford	No proof of service—his own affidavit not sufficient.
Lane, Jacob	Indiana, Allegheny	Period, length and grade of service, and names of company and field officers required.
Lewis, John S	——, Berks	No proof of service.—under age.
Levering, John (deceased)	Philadelphia	No correct account of service attainable.
Lindsey, John	Middletown, Delaware	Not on the rolls. No proof of service.
Luckanback, Adam	Allegheny tp., Armstrong	Direct proof of service required, and a more intelligible statement thereof.
Lambright, John	——, Beaver	Name not on the rolls. No proof of service.
Lynch, David	Kiskiminitas tp., Armstrong	No proof of service. He alleges a tour which was never performed.
Lower, George (or John George)	Northern Liberties, Phila.	Rolls silent. No proof of service.
Loshe, Andrew	Bloomfield, Crawford	Suspended for proof of service—claim withdrawn.
Logue, Adam	Williamsport, Lycoming	Not military service—served in a corps of artificers.
Matthew, Frederick (deceased)	Orwigsburg, Schuylkill	Not six months service established.

Name	Location	Remarks
Mathay, Frederick	Newmanstown, Berks	Not on the Pennsylvania rolls of the flying camp. No proof of service.
Marsh, William	Cattawissa tp., Columbia	New Jersey militia service overrated in duration of tours.
Martinus, Cornelius	Franklin, Venango	New Jersey militia overrated.
Mattocks, Peter	Fallowfield tp...Crawford	He did not serve in any regularly organized corps.
Moir, Isaac	West Dougal tp., Lancaster	No proof of service on the records in the department.
Miles, Jesse	Brooklyn tp., Susquehanna	There were no Pennsylvania troops at the battle of Bunker's Hill.
Miller, John	East Brunswig tp., Schuylkill	Name not on the rolls. No proof of service. Only 13 years and 5 months old in 1776.
Mitchell, Abel	Philadelphia	Proof of service required beside his own declaration.
Moore, William, deceased, heirs of	——, Lancaster	He died in 1844, and made no claim in his lifetime; and the records of Harrisburg must verify the service upon a proper description of it. The gratuity and pension from Pennsylvania, and the bounty land and its location may show some proof of service and identity in this case.
Morris, John	Nottingham tp., Washington	Suspended for further proof and specification.
Myers, John	Bedminster tp., Bucks	Suspended for further proof—under age.
Myers, John	York, York	Name not on the rolls. As he subsequently served as a waiter, he probably did not enlist.
McArthur, Daniel	——, Fayette	Not credible service without material facts. Doubtful.
McCaskey, Daniel	——, Beaver	Not upon the rolls. No sufficient proof of service.
McElhose, Samuel	——, Mifflin	Suspended for proof from the comptroller's books, Harrisburg.
McEwen, James, deceased, heirs of	Lancaster city	Not identical with James McKown, a war's-man and recipient of bounty land, and who received the highest reward of the service. If the claimant were identical with him his proof of service would abound. The claim is asserted many years after the death of the alleged soldier.
McFarland, John M.	——, Fayette	Not on the rolls of the New Jersey line. No proof of service.
McShane, Robert	——, Fayette	Not on the rolls. No other proof offered.
Nonemacher, James	East Penn tp., Northampton	Served in the French army. Not provided for.
Nearman, James	German tp., Fayette	Service in 1791. Not under the act.
Northaumor, Jacob	Caernarvon tp., Lancaster	No proof of service.
O'Neill, Walter	——, Fayette	Not on the rolls. No proof of service.
Ott, Emanuel	Southampton tp., Cumberland	Claim admitted at the rate of a private's pay, excepting the tour in which he was wholly engaged in building a fortification.
Patterson, Peter	——, Fayette	Name not on the rolls of service. If he served every alternate month in the New Jersey militia, and cannot, from old age, specify each tour, he can only be allowed at the lowest rate provided for by the act, viz: six months.

STATEMENT—Continued.

Names.	Residence.	Reasons for suspension.
Pearce, Israel	Columbia, Bradford	Suspended for further proof.
Pedon, Joseph	——, Washington	The service was not of a military capacity.
Pierson, George, deceased, heirs of	Upper Paxton, Dauphin	Suspended for proof and specification.
Poland, Peter	Richhill tp., Greene	Suspended for a more full and circumstantial statement of each tour of militia service.
Potts, George	Pittsburg, Allegheny	Not on the rolls of Pennsylvania or Virginia—no such officer—no proof of service.
Power, James	Indiana tp., Allegheny	Suspended for proof of service. He is referred to the Land Office records at Annapolis—sixteen years delay in making his application does not improve his chances of proof.
Powell, William, deceased, heirs of	Wilkins tp., Allegheny	Further evidence of service requisite.
Riffle, Melchoir	——, York	Suspended for a more correct specification of service—militia service in Pennsylvania were not six-month tours.
Rupert, Leonard	Monteen tp., Columbia	Suspended for proof of service on board the Hyder Ally in 1782.
Rundle, Hardy	Pike tp., Allegheny	Service in 1776 lacks details, places and circumstances—certificate of service by the comptroller—states payments for various periods.
Rogers, Jonah	Huntingdon tp., Luzerne	Under age—not on the rolls—no claim.
Rogers, Michael	——, Berks	Suspended for further proof.
Robinson, Peter	Holmesburgh, Philadelphia	Suspended for want of proof of service—papers withdrawn.
Reincer, Martin	Chambersburgh, Franklin	Proof of service required from the comptroller general of Penn'a.
Riall, Nathan	——, Chester	No proof of service—seventeen years delay makes it very doubtful, even if it were not inconsistent in its statements with the whole course of the service.
Reed, James	Walker tp., Huntingdon	Proof of service deficient.
Ream, George	Walker tp., Juniata	Records afford no proof—service does not agree with the facts relative to the service of the flying camp or Sullivan's expedition.
Rankin, James	Smith tp., Washington	Claim adverse with the known facts of history.
Santee, John	——, Greene	Suspended for further proof and specification.
Schnell, George	Reading, Berks	He did not serve six months in a military capacity.
Sheetz, Philip	Pottsgrove tp., Montgomery	No proof of service from the Pennsylvania rolls of the line in which he alleges he enlisted.

Sell, John	Washington tp., Indiana	Suspended for proof of further service—five months admitted.
Shafer, Henry	—, Allegheny	Suspended for further proof of service.
Shope, Nicholas	—, Cumberland	Name not on the rolls—no proof of service.
Shull, John	—, Fayette	Suspended for further proof and specification—papers withdrawn.
Sickles, Daniel (alias Ackerly)		Not on the complete rolls of New Jersey line—no proof of service—no claim.
Simpkins, John	Clarion	No proof of service.
Spatz, Michael	Reading, Berks	No declaration filed.
Spalding, Joseph, deceased	Athens tp., Bradford	Suspended for further proof.
Stager, Peter	—, Lebanon	Only two months service established.
Stall, John	Jackson tp., Greene	No proof of service. He was a Hessian who deserted from the enemy, and he gives so imperfect an account that it is impossible to adjudicate his claim.
Stevens, Timothy	Blakely tp., Luzerne	Suspended for further details and proofs.
Stoneriug, Jacob	—, Greene	Under age—intended as a fifer—was servant to an officer.
Stourman, Charles	Conowango tp., Warren	Not military service.
Stout, John	Northern Liberties, Phila.	No proof of service—statement adverse to the facts of the history.
Swick, John	Sewickly tp., Beaver	No proof of service.
Tipton, William, sr.	Uniontown, Fayette	For a more full specification and details of service.
Tracey, Jeromiah	Dyberry tp., Wayne	Suspended for proof and specification.
Tresler, Frederick	Chambersburg, Franklin	Suspended for want of proof.
Taylor, William	Aaronsburg, Centre	No proof of service.
Trunsell, Philip	Price tp., Pike	Colonel's name wanted in order to an inspection of the rolls of the service.
Tubs, Thomas	Flemington tp., Luzerne	Suspended for particulars of service and a response from the Connecticut comptroller.
Warren, Joseph	Philadelphia city	No specification of service and no proof.
Warner, Peter	—, Schuylkill	No proof of service—discredited by the rolls—not military service.
Washburn, Isaiah	Windham tp., Bradford	Not on the rolls, no proof of service—claim disallowed.
Walters, Michael	Philadelphia city	The Pennsylvania rolls establish the service in the line so far as a soldier of the same name is evidence.
Watters, William	Tell tp., Huntingdon	Service in the flying camp alleged. The proof by at least one credible witness is required.
Walters, Ephraim, sr	German tp., Fayette	Suspended for a more perfect account of his service.
Wedeman, Daniel	Providence tp., Luzerne	Name not on the rolls of the New York line—no proof of service.
Webster, Amos	Montrose, Susquehanna	The records at Hartford must be appealed to for proof in this case.
Weidner, Michael	—, York	Suspended for details and proof of service.
Wertz, George	Napier tp., Bedford	Period, length and grade of service, and names of company and field officers required.

STATEMENT—Continued.

Names.	Residence.	Reasons for suspension.
White, William	Stroud tp., Monroe	No proof of service.
White, John	—, Perry	Suspended for proof of service.
Wilbor, Jacob	Columbia, Bradford	Suspended for proof of service.
Williams, Nathan, deceased, heirs of	—, Wyoming	No proof of service.
Wilhelm, Frederick, deceased, heirs of	Easton, Northampton	Name is on the rolls of Captain McArndt in the flying camp of Pennsylvania, but the details of service are not sufficient to identify the deceased with that soldier.
Wright, Aaron	—, Luzerne	Suspended for a more full and particular statement.
Wilt, Jacob, sr	Salisbury tp., Lehigh	Suspended for further proof and specification.
Wilt, Jacob	Northampton, Lehigh	Not on the rolls—no proof of service.—claim disallowed.
Wimer, Adam, deceased, heirs of	Slippery Rock tp., Lawrence	Officers' names and distinct tours omitted.
Winkler, John, (alias Johannes Ardulpi)	—, Beaver	Officers' names and distinct tours required.
Wither, Joduthan	Canton tp., Bradford	Under age—no proof of service.
Woods, Azariah	Greene tp., Beaver	No specifications sufficiently consecutive, and no proof of service.
Wunkler, John	Moon tp., Beaver	No records of service and no proof of any kind.
Yeager, Henry	Southwark, Philadelphia	No specification of the tours of service either by claimant or his witnesses.

A list of persons residing in Pennsylvania who have applied for pensions under the act of July 4, 1836, whose claims have been rejected; prepared in conformity with the resolution of the Senate of the United States, September 16, 1850.

Names.	Residence.	Reasons for rejection.
Beck, Agnes, widow of George	——, York	He did not serve six months.
Boss, Margaret, widow of Daniel	Allegheny	Married after the war.
Boyers, Elizabeth, widow of Asamus	Allegheny tp., Armstrong	Married after the war, to wit: in June, 1794.
Brigg, Dorothea (dec'd), widow of John	Philadelphia	Died before the passage of the act.
Brobit, Catharine, widow of John	——, Union	Married after service.
Clark, Eleanor (dec'd), widow of Seth	Richmond tp., Tioga	Died before the passage of the act.
Conrad, Catharine, widow of Philip	Germantown, Philadelphia	He did not serve six months.
Darbee, Dorothea, widow of Moses	Kingston, Luzerne	He did not serve six months in person.
Drummond, Mary, widow of Peter	Philadelphia	Married after service.
Fiscus, Catharine, widow of Abraham	Plumb Creek, Armstrong	Married after service, viz: in 1784.
Franklin, Mary, widow of Joseph	Philadelphia	A soldier of the regular army.
Gamble, Elizabeth, widow of William	Wheatfield, Indiana	Service in 1793, after the revolution.
Gales, Jemima, widow of Oliver	Springfield, Bradford	Married after service.
Geyer, Maria B., widow of Andrew	Philadelphia	He did not serve six months.
Garis, Charlotte, widow of Valentine	Williams tp., Northampton	He did not serve six months.
Howard, Catharine, formerly widow of Philip Clumberg	Philadelphia	She was married after the war.
Haugewaut, Hannah, widow of Lefford	——, Juniata	He did not serve six months.
Hoffman, Elizabeth, widow of Isaac	Southwark, Philadelphia	A soldier of the regular army.
Kann, Elizabeth, widow of Peter	——, Lancaster	Married after the service.
Keizer, Elizabeth, formerly widow of John	Philadelphia	Married after service.—not a widow 7th July, 1888.
Laham, Rosin, widow of Christiana	——, York	He did not serve six months.
Marsh, Eliza, widow of John	East Hempfield tp., Lancaster	He was a deserter.
Myers, Mary, widow of John	Philadelphia	He did not perform revolutionary service.

STATEMENT—Continued.

Names.	Residence.	Reasons for rejection.
McCracken, Mary (dec'd), widow of Philip	Southwark, Philadelphia	Married after service—died before the passage of act of July 7, 1888.
Pancoast, Ann, formerly widow of Alexander Plunket	Philadelphia city	A soldier of the regular army.
Schrader, Catharine, widow of Philip	Kensington, Philadelphia	Married after service.
Shock, Hannah, formerly widow of John Sherman	Philadelphia city	Service not under military authority.
Sigman, Henry and others, children of Jacob	Easton, Northampton	No claim—parents died before the date of the act.
Singlewood, Nancy, widow of Stephen	Philadelphia	Married after service.
Sperry, Sarah, widow of Truman	Philadelphia	Service not under military authority.
Smiley, Alice, formerly widow of Andrew	Southwark, Philadelphia	Married in 1805—not within the limits of the act.
Steiner, Mary, daughter of William Pritchard	Philadelphia	Service not under military authority.
Stevenson, Susannah, widow of Alexander	Pittsburg city	Married in 1811—not within the limits of the act.
Stover, Elizabeth, widow of Philip	Saucon tp., Northampton	He did not serve six months.
Uber, Elizabeth, widow of John	Northern Liberties, Philadelphia	A soldier of the war of 1812.
Wallace, Jane, widow of John	Philadelphia	Service not under military authority.
Woodman, Sarah (dec'd), widow of William	Westmoreland	Married after the war—died before 7th July, 1888.
White, Mary, widow of Potter	—, Crawford	Not a widow at the date of the act.

A list of the names of persons residing in Pennsylvania who have applied for pensions under the act of July 4, 1836, whose claims have been suspended; prepared in conformity with the resolution of the Senate of the United States, September 16, 1850.

Names.	Residence.	Reasons for suspension.
Allen, Elizabeth, widow of Jesse	Wysox tp., Bradford	Suspended for proof of marriage and identity with the service of the soldier named in the certificate of the New York comptroller.
Baughman, Paul (dec'd), children of	84 Plum street, Philadelphia	For proof that widow was living at the date of the act.
Bauman, Magdalena, widow of Philip	Ephrata tp., Lancaster	The evidence is not passable.
Bickerston, Elizabeth, widow of Alexander	Philadelphia	The claim is unsupported by any available evidence.
Bones, Rachel, formerly widow of Andrew Unler	Northern Liberties, Philadelphia	Suspended for further proof.
Bemensderfer, Elizabeth, widow of John	—, Lebanon	Proof of service and of marriage required.
Boyd, Mary, widow of John	Lancaster city	Proof of identity required with soldier of the line and an officer in the quartermaster's department.
Brookhouser, Mary, widow of Adam	Hayfield tp., Crawford	Evidence of commission and service not complete.
Campbell, Mary, widow of John	Philadelphia	Suspended for proof of service. [Papers withdrawn.]
Causten, Hannah (dec'd), widow of Samuel, heirs of	Philadelphia	No satisfactory proof of service.
Chase, Rhoda, widow of William	Washington tp., Erie	No proof of service, and description of it too vague.
Colvin, Sarah, widow of Philip	Abington tp., Luzerne	No specification of service.—no proof accessible.
Cooper, Mary, widow of John Martin	Pittsburg city	Proof of service defective, and also of marriage.
Crans, Elizabeth, widow of Philip	Towanda, Bradford	No tours specified or officers' names given.
Dawson, Mary, widow of Anthony	Philadelphia city	Married after service, and died before the act of July 7, 1838.
Doty, Jane, widow of Nathaniel	Derry tp., Westmoreland	Married after service—may claim under act of February 29, 1848.
Dunlap, Sarah, formerly widow of J. McLaughlin	Philadelphia	Suspended for proof of service.
Delavan, Barbary, widow of John	Philadelphia	Suspended for proof of service.

STATEMENT—Continued.

Names.	Residence.	Reasons for suspension.
Edmiston, Margaret, widow of Bugh	Southwark, Philadelphia	Suspended for proof and specification.
Ellmoro, Anna M., widow of Frederick	York borough, York	Suspended for further proof of service and marriage.
Ewing, Jane, widow of Alexander	Philadelphia city	Suspended for further proof of service and marriage.
Fricker, Eve, formerly widow of John Z. Weier	Reading, Berks	Proof of service and marriage required.
Fritzinger, Catharine, widow of John	Philadelphia city	Suspended for further proof of service.
Gehret, Christina, widow of Henry	Reading, Berks	No additional evidence since September 18, 1844.
Gehrel, Elizabeth, widow of Henry	Maiden Creek tp., Berks	No proof or specification of service.
Goforth, Rebecca, widow of William	Philadelphia city	He did not serve six months.
Gossler, Mary, widow of Philip	York, York	Married in 1775—first birth in 1783—further proof wanting.
Graeff, Margaret, widow of Frederick	Reading, Berks	Proof of marriage not satisfactory.
Griswold, Elizabeth, widow of John	Clinton tp., Wayne	Married after service and after the peace.
Groaves, Catharine, widow of Michael	Lancaster city	No proof of service.
Groscup, Sybilla, widow of Paul	District tp., Berks	Suspended for proof and specification.
Haas, Ann, widow of Jacob	Philadelphia city	Suspended for proof and specification.
Hantzell, Margaret, widow of Charles F.	Philadelphia city	No proof of service.
Horn, Christiana, widow of Henry	Harrisburg, Dauphin	Neither marriage nor service established.
Howard, Catharine, formerly widow of Philip Clumberg	Philadelphia	Married after service—papers withdrawn.
John, Isabella, widow of William	Horse Valley tp., Franklin	Suspended for further proof.
Lent, Catharine, widow of Henry	Rome, Bradford	Suspended for proof of identity—two of the same name on the New York rolls.
Lott, Eliza (deceased), widow of Zephaniah	—, Wyoming	No evidence presented of either service or marriage.
Macomber, Hannah, widow of Zenas	—, York	No claim—married in 1829.
Maze, Mary, widow of Thomas	—, Jefferson	Proof of service insufficient.

Name	Location	Remarks
McVaugh, Mary, widow of John	Oxford tp., Philadelphia	Married after the service admitted; claim under act July 7, 1888, may be allowed.
McNeill, Sarah, widow of Daniel	—, Crawford	Suspended for further proof.
Nash, Sarah, widow of William	Philadelphia	Name not on the New Jersey rolls—no proof of service.
Nicholas, Mary Magdalene, widow of Henry	Philadelphia	Proof of marriage and of service concurring not produced.
Nunglesser, Catharine, widow of John George	Mifflin tp., Columbia	Proof and specification required.
Oxer, Catharine, widow of Christopher	Lancaster city	Suspended for proof of service and marriage concurrent.
Parrish, Elizabeth, widow of Silas	—, Crawford	Suspended for proof of service.
Peciffer, Mary Magdalena, widow of George	Woodcock tp., Crawford	Not six months' service established.
Posteins, Ann, widow of Jacob	Stroud tp., Monroe	No proof of service—name not on the Pennsylvania rolls either as private or wagon master.
Reed, Martha, widow of John	—, Butler	Suspended for further proof of his commission as Lieutenant and service under it.
Robinson, Jane (deceased), widow of John	Waynesburg, Green	Marriage and six months' service not proved.
Rodes, Anna, widow of Frederick Eisenhaur	—, Crawford	Suspended for further proof.
Roper, Naomi (deceased) widow of Nathaniel	—, Bradford	Proof of identity with the soldier on the Massachusetts rolls required.
Rowan, Jane, widow of James	Philadelphia	Proof of duration of service as an issuing commissary under Gen. Lucy.
Schoonover, Margaret, widow of Thomas	Texas tp., Wayne	Specification of tours required, and the original family record.
Shimfeasell, Margaret (deceased) widow of Andrew	Reading, Berks	For further proof and specification.
Shilling, Biddy (deceased), widow of George	Mercer, Mercer	Service not set forth—no proof offered.
Shroyer, Mary, widow of Matthias	—, Butler	Service not detailed—no proof of service.
Shuman, Margaret, widow of John	Lancaster city	A soldier of the regular army.
Storry, Elizabeth (deceased) widow of Tobias	—, York	Admitted under act July 7, 1888, for six months as ensign.
Steel, Margaret, widow of Francis	Bellefonte, Centre	Suspended for proof and specification.
Thorn, Christina, widow of George	Penn Township, Philadelphia	Not on the rolls—no proof of service.
Trees, Barbara, widow of John	Franklin, Huntington	Suspended for further proof.
Walker, Hepzibah, widow of Samuel		Suspended for the duration of the service to be ascertained. [Papers withdrawn.]
Wittum, Sarah, widow of Malachi	Elk Creek tp., Erie	Proof of marriage deficient, and service too vaguely set forth.
Witman, Anna Maria, widow of John	Reading, Berks	Proof of six months' service not established.
Wolf, Mary, (deceased) widow of John	Philadelphia city	Proof of identity not satisfactory that these applicants are the children of the warsman of the Pennsylvania line, named John Wolf.

STATEMENT—Continued.

Names.	Residence.	Reasons for rejection.
Wightman, Mary, widow of William	Lower St. Clair tp., Allegheny	Proof of marriage defective.
Wunder, Ann, widow of George	West Kensington, Philadelphia	Pensioned under special act—no proof of service.
Wyrm, Catharine, widow of Henry	Franklin tp., Lycoming	Name not on the New Jersey rolls—no proof of service or of marriage.
Yentzer, Mary, widow of John	Conestoga tp., Lancaster	Suspended for proof of the marriage.
Yett, Elisabeth, widow of William	Gettysburg, Adams	Suspended for further proof of marriage and service.

A list of the names of persons residing in Pennsylvania who have applied for pensions under the act of July 7, 1838, whose claims have been rejected; prepared in conformity with the resolution of the Senate of the United States, September 16, 1850.

Names.	Residence.	Reasons for rejection.
Burch, Catharine, widow of Lewis.	Northern Liberties, Philadelphia	Served in the French army.
Brooks, Melinda, widow of Charles.	Ohio tp., Allegheny	Not a widow at the date of the act.
Brognard, Mary, widow of John.	Philadelphia city	A physician in the French army.
Conly, Mary, widow of Nicholas.	———, Allegheny	Married after January 1, 1794.
Canfield, Eunice, widow of Andrew	———, Susquehanna	Not a widow at the date of the act.
Carman, Elizabeth, widow of James.	Philadelphia city	Married after service.
Cochran, Sarah (deceased), widow of John.	Mill Creek tp., Erie.	Died before August 16, 1842.
Eakly, Maria S., widow of Abraham.	Philadelphia city	Did not serve six months.
Finch, Polly, widow of Samuel.	Lawrenceville, Tioga.	Died before August 16, 1842.
Fulmer, Mary, widow of John.	———, Philadelphia.	Husband did not serve six months.
Goode, Catharine, widow of Jacob.	Danville, Columbia.	Husband did not serve six months.
Herring, Anna Maria, widow of Lewis or Ludwig.	———, Venango.	Married after service.
Hess, Mary, widow of Peter M.	Philadelphia city.	Married after service.
Himrod, Isabella, widow of Aaron.	Waterford tp., Erie	Did not serve six months by order of competent authority.
Jennings, Nancy, widow of Nathan	Philadelphia city.	Not a widow at the date of the act.
Kochenour, Eve, widow of Jacob.	York, York.	Did not serve six months.
Kepler, Susannah, widow of Samuel.	Chapman tp., Clinton.	Not a widow at the date of the act.
Leidy, Barbara, widow of Simon.	Peters tp., Franklin.	Did not serve six months.
Muschert, Catharine, widow of John Christian	Chesnut Hill, Philadelph.	Husband served in the French army.
May, Mary, widow of Charles.	———, Fayette.	Did not serve six months.
McCann, Jane, widow of James.	———, Greene.	Not a widow at the date of the act.

STATEMENT—Continued.

Names.	Residence.	Reasons for rejection.
Moore, Amy, widow of James	——, Franklin	Married in 1808.
Moyer, Catharine, widow of John		Desertion.
Smith, Agnes, widow of John	Crawford, York	Did not serve six months.
Stuck, Elizabeth, widow of John	——, Fayette	Did not serve six months.
Thurber, Miriah, widow of Amos	——, Allegheny	Married in 1827.

A list of the names of persons residing in Pennsylvania who have applied for pensions under the act of July 7, 1838, whose claims have been suspended; prepared in conformity with the resolution of the Senate of the United States, September 16, 1850.

Names.	Residence.	Reasons for suspension.
Anderson, Esther, widow of James	Hopewell tp., York	Neither service nor marriage satisfactorily proved.
Albrecht, Sophia, widow of Martin	Shaefferstown, Lebanon	Six months' service not proved fully.
Baer, Catharine, widow of Jacob	Mount Morris, Greene	No proof of service.
Baer, Mary, widow of John	——, Columbia	Suspended for proof of service and marriage.
Butler, Mary (deceased), widow of James	Muncy, Lycoming	A soldier of the same name is on the rolls of the line, and identity and marriage requires proof.
Becker, Catharine, widow of Henry	Jackson tp., Monroe	No evidence of his service as a soldier of the Pennsylvania troops.
Bell, Mary, widow of James	Buxton tp., Dauphin	A soldier of the same name is on the rolls of the Pennsylvania line, and she must identify her husband as that soldier.
Boyer, Julia, widow of Christian	Weisenberg tp., Lehigh	Not a widow at the date of the act.
Cochran, Hannah, widow of Samuel	Lower Windsor tp., York	Suspended for proof of service and marriage.
Catlin, Mary, widow of Putnam	Great Bend tp., Susquehanna	Proof of service as a fifer for two years good—the day of marriage in suspense.
Chapman, Lydia, formerly widow of William Coahran	Montrose, Susquehanna	Marriage admitted—service needs proof.
Cummings, Mary, widow of Jacob	Rutland, Tioga	Proof of service and marriage not complete.
Evans, Elizabeth, widow of Barnabas	Springfield, Erie	Admitted to children upon proof of the mother's decease, March 15, 1850—A. C. Dodge.
Erdman, Barbara, widow of Yost	Franconia tp., Montgomery co.	Suspended for further proof of service.
Elder, Mary, widow of John	——, Centre	Not under military organization.
Franck, Juliana, widow of Johann	Northern Liberties, Philadelphia	No proof of service—referred to the New York comptroller.
Fulton, Catharine, widow of Samuel	——, Washington	Deficient in proof of six months' service.
Gee, Polly (or Polly Jay), widow of David	Middleburg tp., Tioga	Date of marriage in suspense.
Gilmore, Elizabeth, widow of Thomas	Woodcock tp., Crawford	Specification of company, regiment and officers called for.
Greenwault, Catharine, widow of Philip	——, Lebanon	Suspended for proof of service and marriage.
Grace, Maria, widow of Joseph	Springfield tp., Bradford	Proof of service and marriage both fall short.

STATEMENT—Continued.

Names.	Residence.	Reasons for suspension.
Hedrick, Susannah, widow of John	East Hanover tp., Lebanon	Not a widow at the date of the act—husband not pensioned under act of 1832.
Heston, Hannah, widow of Thomas	Philadelphia	The character, locality and facts of the service are not apparent.
Holgate, Mary, widow of Cornelius	Chesnut Hill, Philadelphia	Suspended for want of proof.
Hutchins, Irene, widow of John C.	Greenfield, Luzerne	Only five months' service established in this case.
Ireland, Elizabeth, widow of John	—, Columbia	Suspended for proof of service.
Jaqua, Ruth, widow of Simon	East Fallowfield tp., Crawford	Proof of service and of marriage not perfect.
Jones, Catharine, widow of William	Franklin tp., Allegheny	Widow's identity required with the late pensioner William Jones, on the Pittsburgh rolls, and marriage prior to January 1, 1794.
Jones, Margaret, widow of Abel	George tp., Fayette	Service not properly stated or proved.
Johnston, Margaret, widow of William	—, Perry	Proof of identity required for claimant's husband with soldier of the same name on the rolls of the Pennsylvania line at Harrisburg.
Kinsley, Catharine, widow of William	Bristol, Bucks	Suspended for further proof.
Keatley, Esther, widow of Christopher	Stratonsville, Clarion	Proof of service and marriage not satisfactory.
Kepler, Susan, widow of Samuel	Chapman tp., Clinton	Suspended for proof of service.
Kinney, Elizabeth, widow of Daniel	Waynesburg, Greene	Proof of service not sufficient.
Kinter, Isabella, widow of John	Rayno tp., Indiana	Service admitted. Marriage in suspense.
Koons, Mary, widow of Lawrence	—, Juniata	Suspended for proof of service and marriage.
Lawrence, Margaret, widow of Daniel	Pittsburg, Allegheny	Suspicion of fraud relating to her marriage.
Langhrey, Margaret, widow of William	Buffalo tp., Armstrong	No proof of service.
Lesley, Sarah, widow of Samuel	—, Lancaster	Not admitted for want of proof.
Leyman, Elizabeth, widow of Samuel	Philadelphia	No proof of service.
Long, Chri-tina, widow of Joseph	White Deer tp., Union	Service admitted—marriage in suspense.
Longwell, Rachel, widow of William	Armagh tp., Mifflin	Slain in battle on Long Island in 1776. No claim.
Madeira, Ann Elizabeth, widow of Michael	Reading, Berks	Married after service—died before July 7, 1888.
Martin, Mary, widow of Thomas	Jersey Shore, Lycoming	Not under proper military organization.
Marsden, Elizabeth, widow of John	Bellefonte, Centre	Service admitted—marriage in suspense.
Miller, Leah, widow of John	—, Mercer	Married after the limitation of the act.

Name	Location	Remarks
Moart, Elizabeth, widow of John	Mill Creek tp., Lebanon	Marriage within the act not sufficiently proved.
Moyer, Elizabeth, widow of Jacob	Antis tp., Blair	Suspended for further proof.
Munka, Rachel, widow of William	Limestone tp., Clarion	Service admitted—marriage in suspense.
McAfee, Jane, widow of Benjamin	——, Bradford	Service admitted—marriage in suspense.
McClure, Sarah, widow of William	Saltsburgh, Indiana	Proof of her husband's rank and service required from Harrisburg.
NcNeill, Sarah, widow of Daniel	——, Crawford	For proof of service and marriage.
McGune, Eleanor, widow of Richard	North Chenango tp., Crawford	For further proof.
Nai, Anna Maria, widow of Peter	Kensington, Philadelphia	For further proof and explanation.
Price, Hannah, formerly widow of E. Smith	Montrose, Susquehanna	The soldier of the Connecticut line could not have been her husband.
Phillippe, Susanna, widow of Abraham	Reading, Berks	Service requires description and proof of its material facts.
Ross, Hanna (deceased), widow of James	Dallas tp., Luzerne	The dragoon of Captain Muker's company of the New Jersey militia is not identified with this case, nor is the length of his service known—marriage and decease requires further proof.
Satterlee, Desire, widow of James	Smithfield tp., Bradford	Witnesses not certified to be credible—date of the marriage not established.
Schaum, Elizabeth, widow of Melchoir	Washington tp., Cambria	Six months' service not claimed or proved.
Schlatter, Elizabeth (dec'd), widow of Gotleib	Philadelphia	Regiment, company and line not stated—both parties deceased.
Scott, Elizabeth, widow of Thomas	Whitestown, Butler	Service of Thomas Scott for two years in Captain Swearingen's company, Colonel Morgan's regiment admitted—proof of identity not complete—marriage not fully proved.
Shaffer, Margaret, widow of Frederick	Dunstable, Clinton	Service admitted—marriage and decease requires proof.
Shinkle, Catharine (dec'd), widow of Philip	Philadelphia	Service not set forth nor her identity proved.
Shover, Catharine, widow of Francis	——, Franklin	Service admitted—marriage in suspense.
Sisler, Rachel, widow of Michael	——, Bedford	Papers informal—no proof presented.
Smith, Rebecca, widow of Alexander	——, Lycoming	The act July 1, 1848, removed the objections to this claim, except the date of the marriage, which requires proof.
Smith, Abba, widow of Benjamin	Exeter, Luzerne	A wartman of the New York line—entitled to bounty land—proof o the identity of the widow as the wife of said soldier.
Snellaker, Mary, widow of Daniel	Philadelphia	For want of proof of service.
Snyder, Catharine, widow of Henry	East Cocalico tp., Lancaster	Must identify herself as the widow of the soldier of the German regiment, whose service is credited in the certificate of the Auditor General of Pennsylvania.
South, Elizabeth (dec'd), widow of Benjamin	——, Greene	Nine months' service of her husband admitted (in the militia, for which he was pensioned) in the adjustment of her claim.
Spangenburg, Maria B., widow of Conrad	Philadelphia	Not on the rolls of Pulaski's legion—no proof of service.
Starr, Elizabeth, widow of John	Philadelphia	For further proof of service and marriage.

STATEMENT—Continued.

Names.	Residence.	Reasons for suspension.
Steel, Polly, widow of John	—, York	For further proof of service and marriage.
Stone, Betsey, formerly widow of Andrew Dewy	Erie, Erie	For further proof of service and marriage.
Stoner, Ann, widow of John	Lower Paxton tp., Dauphin	No proof of service or of marriage.
Verguson, Phebe, widow of Daniel	Lycoming tp., Lycoming	Service admitted—marriage in suspenso.
Warner, Susannah, widow of William Reed	—, Chester co.	Not a single tour specified—proof and specification requested.
Wertz, Catharine, widow of Daniel	—, York	Further proof of service required.
Whitman, Elizabeth, widow of John	Philadelphia	No proof of his alleged service as a private in the eighth regiment Pennsylvania line.
Wilcox, Mary, formerly widow of Elijah Day	—, Potter co.	Evidence of identity that she was the widow of Lieutenant Elijah Day of the Massachusetts line not good, nor of the marriage prior to January 1, 1794.
Wilson, Mary, widow of Archibald	Philadelphia	For proof and specification of service.
Young, Catharine, widow of George	Charleston tp., Tioga	Proof of service and marriage incomplete.

A list of the names of persons residing in Delaware who have applied for pensions under the act of June 7, 1832, whose claims have been rejected; prepared in conformity with the resolution of the Senate of the United States of 16th of September, 1850.

Names.	Residence.	Reasons for rejection.
Pierce, Amos	Wilmington, Newcastle	He did not serve six months.
Woodcock, William	Wilmington, Newcastle	He did not serve six months.

A list of the names of persons residing in Delaware who have applied for pensions under the act of July 7, 1838, whose claims have been suspended; prepared in conformity with the resolution of the Senate of the United States of 16th of September, 1850.

Names.	Residence.	Reasons for suspension.
Ake, Esther, widow of William	Baltimore Hundred, Sussex	For further proof of marriage.
Allen, Elizabeth, widow of Jacob	——, Newcastle.	For further proof of marriage—papers withdrawn.

A list of the names of persons residing in Maryland who have applied for pensions under the act of June 7, 1832, whose claims have been rejected; prepared in conformity with the resolution of the Senate of the United States, September 16, 1850.

Names.	Residence.	Reasons for rejection.
Bean, Henry H., sen.	———, Charles.	He did not serve six months.
Biscoe, Josiah.	———, St. Mary's.	Privateer service.
Caullifflower, Michael	———, Frederick.	He did not serve six months.
Erp, Erasmus.	———, Montgomery.	He did not serve six months.
Fowler, Sadoc.	———, Frederick.	He did not serve six months.
Gordon, Daniel.	———, Frederick.	He did not serve six months.
Hoffman, Phillip.	———, Montgomery.	He did not serve six months.
Jones, William.	———, Caroline.	He did not serve six months.
Jones, Jones.	Benjamin, Somerset.	He did not serve six months.
Krick, Jacob.	———, Washington.	He did not serve six months.
Lembert, Christopher.	Baltimore city.	Pensioned under act March 18, 1818.
McComas, Aaron.	———, Harford.	He did not serve six months.
McCracken, William.	Baltimore city.	He did not serve six months.
Mead, Samuel.	———, Anne Arundell.	Under age.
Outterbridge, Stephen.	———, Dorchester.	He was a deserter.
Oram, Spedden.	———, Talbot.	He did not serve six months.
Palmer, Michael.	———, Frederick.	He was a deserter.
Ray, Benjamin (deceased).	Annapolis, Anne Arundell.	He did not serve six months.

STATEMENT—Continued.

Names.	Residence.	Reasons for rejection.
Rohr, John	——, Montgomery	Not under military authority.
Rightmyer, Conrad	——, Frederick	He did not serve six months in person.
Rohr, Philip	——, Frederick	He did not serve six months.
Ringer, Matthias	——, Washington	He did not serve six months.
Smith, Charles	St. Michael's, Talbot	He did not serve six months.
Stottlemeyers, George	——, Frederick	Desertion.
Turner, Andrew		Not military service.
Watkins, John	Baltimore county	He did not serve six months.
White, Abraham	Baltimore city	He served in the French army.
Woolford, Thomas	——, Dorchester	Not under military organization.
White, William	——, Alleghany	Desertion.
Wiley, Matthew	Belle Air, Harford	He did not serve six months.

A list of the names of persons residing in Maryland who have applied for pensions under the act of June 7, 1832, whose claims have been suspended; prepared in conformity with the resolution of the Senate of the United States of 16th of September, 1850.

Names.	Residence.	Reasons for suspension.
Albright, John	Baltimore city	No proof of service.
Bean, Henry H	Bryantown, Charles	For proof and specification.
Benson, Joseph	Baltimore city	For further proof and specification.
Boon, John	——, Charles	For a new declaration according to the printed instructions.
Branaman, Benjamin	Baltimore city	He did not serve six months.
Blanford, Joseph (deceased)	——, Prince Georges	For further proof and specification.
Caple, Samuel	——, Carroll	For further proof and specification.
Cully, Armistead	Frostburgh, Allegheny	The original papers were mailed to an agent in 1836, and have never been replaced.
Coddington, Benjamin	——, Allegheny	For further proof and specification.
Dennis, Henry	Salisbury, Somerset	For further proof and specification.
Derr, John	——, Carroll	Desertion.
Friend, Gabriel	——, Allegheny	For further proof and specification.
Grider, Michael	——, Frederick	For proof from the archives at Harrisburg.
Harrington, Peter	——, Dorchester	No proof or specification. Minute-man's service overrated.
Hutchinson, William (deceased)	Baltimore city	Service in the Maryland militia not proved by evidence—applicable only to a soldier of the line.
Johnson, Richard (deceased)	——, Montgomery	For proof of identity with soldier of the same name of the 3d regiment Maryland line, mentioned in the certificate of the register of the land office.
Jones, John	——, Dorchester	Service in the flying camp was only five months—other militia service requires further proof and specification.
Lowe, Nehemiah	——, Montgomery	Proof required from the Register of the Land Office at Annapolis.

STATEMENT—Continued.

Names.	Residence.	Reasons for suspension.
Meek, Abner	——, Frederick	For further proof and specification.
Martin, Samuel	——, St. Mary's	He did not serve six months.
Oldham, James	Baltimore city	He did not serve six months.
Schrader, Jacob	——, Frederick	Further action awaited for the completion of the papers.
Smith, John	Baltimore city	For further proof.
Stevens, Levi	Near Salisbury, Worcester	Papers imperfect, and if better ones have ever been on file it does not appear.
Taylor, Christopher	Baltimore city	Already pensioned under 1818, his petition for increase is unfounded.
Warfield, Joseph	——, Montgomery	Not noticed on the rolls of his captain's company, and his service as lieutenant was less than six months.
Watkins, John	Fort Meeting House, Baltimore	He did not serve six months.
Whiting, Isaac	Frederick city	Not on the rolls of the Maryland ————, nor was his colonel's (Sands) who was not a continental officer.

A list of the names of persons residing in Maryland who have applied for pensions under the act of July 4, 1836, whose claims have been rejected; prepared in conformity with the resolution of the Senate of the United States, September 16, 1850.

Names.	Residence.	Reasons for rejection.
Butler, Mary, widow of Nace	——, Anne Arundell	No proof that they were ever married.
Caldwell, Mary, widow of Benjamin	Baltimore city	A soldier of the regular army.
Clemm, Catharine (deceased), widow of William	Baltimore city	Died before the passage of the act.
Conner, Mary, widow of Patrick	——, Allegheny	A soldier of the regular army.
Didderow, Catharine, widow of John	——, Frederick	Married after service.
Kelly, Martha, widow of William	——, Carroll	He did not serve six months.
Manly, Martha (deceased), widow of John, heirs of	Baltimore	Case not properly presented—papers incomplete.
Poe, Elizabeth (deceased) widow of David, heirs of	Baltimore	Died before the passage of the act.

A list of the names of persons residing in Maryland who have applied for pensions under the act of July 4, 1836, whose claims have been suspended; prepared in conformity with the resolution of the Senate of the United States of September 16, 1850.

Names.	Residence.	Reasons for suspension.
Day, Margaret, widow of Daniel	——, Baltimore	For proof of marriage and the date of her decease.
Hoffman, Elizabeth (deceased), widow of Henry	——, Frederick	No claim—married after service—died before August 16, 1842.
Howard, Mary, widow of John	Baltimore city	For further proof.
Merriman, Elizabeth, widow of Luke	Baltimore city	For further proof and specification.
Shenck, Magdalena, widow of Jacob	——, Carroll	Each tour to be specified as to period, length, grade, localities and commanding officers.
Shane, Elizabeth, widow of Daniel	Baltimore city	Died of a wound received in the war of 1812—not authenticated.

A list of the names of persons residing in Maryland, who have applied for pensions under the act of July 7, 1838, whose claims have been rejected; prepared in conformity with the resolution of the Senate of the United States of September 16, 1850.

Names.	Residence.	Reasons for rejection.
Burrough, Esther T., widow of Normand	Baltimore city	Did not serve six months.
Harvey, Elizabeth, widow of Archibald	——, Harford	Did not serve six months.
Hohn, Mary, widow of Christopher	Annapolis, Anne Arundell	Not military service.
Jones, Elizabeth, widow of Jason	Annapolis, Anne Arundell	Two husbands, but last marriage after January 1, 1794.
Lanham, Susannah (deceased), heirs of	Baltimore city	Both parties died before the passage of the act.
McCoun, Rosanna, widow of William	——, Baltimore	A soldier of the war of 1812—no claim.

A list of the names of persons residing in Maryland who have applied for pensions under the act of July 7, 1838, whose claims have been suspended; prepared in conformity with the resolution of the Senate of the United States of September 16, 1850.

Names.	Residence.	Reasons for suspension.
Barrett, Martha, widow of James	——, Harford	Suspended for further proof of marriage and service.
Burris, Margaret P., widow of Elijah	——, St. Mary's	Suspended for further proof.
Chew, Margaret, widow of Nathaniel	——, Harford	Suspended for further proof—alleges service as a lieutenant in the navy of the United States of the Revolution.
Cole, Cecil, widow of Abraham	——, Baltimore	No claim. Her husband's father was the soldier—not her husband.
Faux, Rebecca, widow of Patrick	——, Cecil	Service admitted—marriage in suspense.
Foy, Jane, formerly widow of Henry Jamar	Baltimore city	Suspended for further proof of service and marriage.
Hall, Ann, widow of Thomas	Baltimore city	Suspended for further proof—claims as sergeant.
Hamrickhouse, Mary, widow of Peter	——, Washington	The day of her decease and the names of her children must be certified by the court.
Harper, Bethula, widow of William	——, Dorchester	Suspended for proof of the date of the marriage.
Hill, Hester, widow of Captain Henry	Washington, D. C.	Suspended for want of proof of service, and papers withdrawn by Silas Wright, jr., December 26, 1888.
Hohne, Mary, widow of Christopher	Annapolis, Anne Arundel	The Annapolis records show his service, but not its length—marriage admitted.
Hook, Sarah, widow of Frederick	Baltimore city	To lie until called for—see letter on file from John Munroe, October 17, 1848.
Jeffers, Ann, widow of Jacob	——, Kent	Service admitted—marriage requires proof.
Jones, Elizabeth, (deceased,) widow of William 1st	Baltimore city	For proof of identity that he was the William Jones named in the certificate of the land office at Annapolis.
Markland, Alice, widow of Edward Darlington	Darlington, Harford	Claims for service as lieutenant on board the Dolphin—but the period and length of his service is not given.
Marsh, Temperance, widow of Joshua	Baltimore city	Suspended for further proof of marriage and service.
Moore, Magdalena, widow of Benjamin	Baltimore city	Suspended for further proof of marriage and service.

Moore, Sarah, widow of Nicholas Burton Moore.	Baltimore city	Lieutenant in 1776—promoted to a captain in 1780, company mounted militia. The Land Office Register certifies to the grade and to two tours service, but the length thereof is not given.
Morrison, Anne, widow of Daniel.	—, Frederick	Not a widow at the date of the act—not pensioned under act 1832.
Price, Hannah, widow of William. Prigg, Susan, widow of William.	Baltimore city —, Harford	Company and regiment and duration of service must be set forth. Claims an ensign in the Maryland militia. The Register of the Land Office at Annapolis must be referred to for proof.
Bewark, Susan, widow of James.	—, Anne Arundel.	Service admitted—proof of identity and marriage required.
Stewart, Elizabeth, widow of John Thomas.	Wye, Talbot.	He was a captain in the militia, as certified by the Register of the Land Office at Annapolis, but the duration of his service is not established. If she was married before the termination of her husband's service, she should apply under the act of July 4, 1836.
Stinchcomb, Catharine, (deceased,) widow of Aquilla.	Baltimore city	Suspended for further proof.
Wistel, Catharine, formerly widow of Robert Purdie.	Baltimore city	No claim—married in 1796. She can apply under act July 29, 1848, by proving herself the widow of the soldier Robert Purdie, whose service is certified by the Register of the Land Office at Annapolis, and proving that she was married prior to 1800.

[37]

A list of the names of persons residing in Virginia who have applied for pensions under the act of June 7, 1832, whose claims have been rejected; prepared in conformity with the resolution of the Senate of the United States of September 16, 1850.

Names.	Residence.	Reasons for rejection.
Anglins, Phillip	——, Henry	Domestic police in pursuit of tories.
Ashcrafts, Uriah	——, Harrison	Fraudulent.
Athy James and Spencer Sharp	——, Wood	Fraudulent.
Angles, William	——, Charlotte	Did not serve six months.
Anderson, Peter	Wheeling, Ohio	Did not serve in any regularly organized corps.
Allen, Thomas	——, Amherst	Did not serve six months.
Brickey, Peter	——, Botetourt	Did not serve six months.
Burt, Edward	——, Sussex	Did not serve six months.
Broaddus, John	Sparta, Caroline	Collecting and driving beeves for the army—civil service, not military.
Burton, Hutchins	Boydton, Mecklensburg	Did not serve six months.
Butcher, Samuel	——, Wood	Fraudulent.
Beesley, Isaac	——, Lewis	No proof of service.
Brickle, George	——, Lewis	Contemporary evidence of his age precludes his claim.
Boggs, Francis	——, Nicholas	Independent contemporary evidence adverse to his claim.
Baker, Solomon	——, Nicholas	Contemporary evidence of his age precludes his claim.
Brandon, Francis	——, Halifax	Did not serve six months.
Brown, Edward	——, Lewis	Did not serve six months.
Bonnafield, Samuel	——, Harrison	Did not serve six months.
Burns, George	——, Randolph	Contemporary evidence of his age precludes his claim.
Brake, Abraham	——, Harrison	No proof of service.
Barnett, Isaac	——, Nicholas	Contemporary evidence of his age precludes his claim.
Broaddus, Reuben	——, Caroline	Did not serve six months.
Buchnall, James	——, Lewis	Confessed to fraud.
Breadle, Edward	——, Caroline	Claims twelve months service as an artificer—not military service.
Cobb, Fleming	——, Kenawha	Did not serve six months.
Conly, John	Giles Court House, Giles	Did not serve six months.
Curtis, Jesse	——, Lewis	By evidence of his age.
Carrance, William		Did not serve six months.

Name	County	Remark
Cole, John	Harrison	Did not serve six months.
Carney, Thomas	Lewis	By evidence of his age.
Cookman, William	Lewis	Did not serve six months.
Carpenter, David	Lewis	By evidence of his age.
Cheer, Richard	Monongalia	Fraudulent.
Caul, Hugh	Lewisburgh, Greenbriar	Did not serve six months.
Conway, John	Harrison	Not provided for—services were against Indians.
Cuddy, James	Abingdon, Washington	Did not serve in a military capacity.
Cox, James	Grayson	Did not serve in any regularly organized corps.
Camp, John	Halifax	Did not serve six months.
Cato, Henry	Rockbridge	Claims for service as a waiter to General Washington. His narrative is not believed.
Collins, John	Halifax	Did not serve six months.
Croushour, Nicholas	Harrison	If he served at all, it was in 1794.
Craig, Robert	Washington	Did not serve six months.
Chapman, Isaac	Giles	Did not serve in any regularly organized corps.
Cotton, William	Chesterfield	Was a deserter.
Dew, Thomas	King and Queen's	Did not serve six months.
Dixon, William	Wood	Childish—imposed upon by a rogue.
Deveese, Abraham	Wood	Fraudulently drawn up. Applicant subsequently denied the service.
Darley, Samuel	Preston	Fraudulent.
Depue, Henry	Lewis	By evidence of his age.
Deem, Jacob	Wood	Indian wars on the frontiers.
Dulancy, Zachariah (dec'd), heirs of	Culpepper	Died before the passage of the act, and before the acts of July, 1886, and 1888.
Dellenger, Christian	Shenandoah	Did not serve six months.
Dodson, Caleb	Halifax	Did not serve six months.
Davis, Joseph	Harrison	Services as a waiter.
Dequise, Charles	Nelson	Served in the French army.
Deagles, Absalom	Middlesex	Did not serve six months.
Donally, Patrick	Louisa	Did not serve six months.
Davidson, William	Tazewell	Did not serve six months.
Dowell, Major	Albemarle	Was a blacksmith.
Dicken, Joseph	Bowling Green, Caroline	Did not serve six months.
Dance, Thomas	Whitehouse, Mecklenburg	Did not serve six months.
Drew, Carey	Lynchburg, Campbell	Was an assistant storekeeper.
Dunlop, Joseph	Morgantown, Monongalia	Did not serve six months.
Ethell, Henry	Lewisburg, Greenbriar	Did not serve six months.

STATEMENT—Continued.

Names.	Residence.	Reasons for rejection.
England, John	Richmond, Henrico	Service in a forge—not military service.
Elliott, Benjamin	—, Jefferson	No trace of service on the rolls.
Farris, Charles	—, Henry	Did not serve six months.
Fink, Mark (dec'd), heirs of	—, Madison	Did not serve six months.
Flanagan, Ebenezer	—, Randolph	Fraudulent.
Fisher, Peter	—, Nicholas	Did not serve six months.
Farrar, Matthew	—, Louisa	Did not serve in a military capacity.
Griffin, Elisha	—, Harrison	Did not serve six months.
Gallions, Gilbert	—, Harrison	No proof of service.
Gillelan, James	—, Greenbriar	A frontier's-man, not drafted, enlisted, officered or paid.
Godfrey, John	—, Lewis	His declaration was surreptitiously obtained, and he subsequently disavowed it.
Groom, Jonathan	—, Bedford	Did not serve six months.
Holman, John	—, Cumberland	Did not serve six months.
Hughes, Robert	—, Fayette	Was a deserter.
Hogg, John	—, Albemarle	Did not serve six months.
Johnson, William (dec'd)	—, Albemarle	Died before the passage of the act.
Lock, John	—, Shenandoah	Served in the French army.
Peer, John	—, Shenandoah	Did not serve six months.
Redley, George	—, Warren	Did not serve six months.
Smith, Robert	—, Lunenberg	Did not serve six months.
Smith, William	—, Louisa	Did not serve in a military capacity.
Thompson, Roger	—, Albemarle	Did not serve six months.
Watson, William	—, Buckingham	Did not serve six months.

Goodwin, Francis	—, Harrison	A frontier's-man—never enlisted or officered—claim subsequently disavowed by him.
Gandy, Uriah	—, Jackson	By evidence of his age.
Gray, Thomas	—, Scott	Service in Indian wars after the revolution.
Griffin, Elijah	—, Mecklenburg	Did not serve six months.
Green, Samuel	—, Lewis	By evidence of his age.
Green, Sampson	—, Bedford	A soldier of the French army.
Holt, John	—, Cumberland	Did not serve six months.
Howell, Thomas	Richmond, Henrico	Did not serve six months.
Harvey, Thomas	Butterwood Creek, Charlotte	Service not military—was a wagon driver.
Harris, James	St. Luke's Parish, Southampton	Did not serve in a military capacity.
Hanger, George	—, Greenbriar	Was a wagon driver.
Hannah, David	—, Greenbriar	Did not serve in any regularly organized corps.
Harbert, John	—, Harrison	By evidence of his age.
Hendrich, Henry	—, Greenbriar	A frontier's-man—not officered, enlisted, drafted or paid.
Hill, Richard	—, Pocahontas	Services at a neighborhood fort—not enlisted, drafted, officered or paid.
Hughes, Thomas	—, Greenbriar	Neighborhood service—no pay, enlistment or draft.
Hannah, Joseph, deceased	—, Greenbriar	Services at a neighborhood fort—not regularly embodied.
Hammock, Martin	—, Kenawha	No proof of service—character not good.
Handley, Ely (deceased), widow of	—, Amelia	Died before the passage of the act, and this claim was rejected 28th December, 1835, before the widows' acts and later ones passed.
Hulderman, John	Shinn Town, Harrison	Service subsequent to the revolution.
Isner, Thomas	—, Randolph	Service subsequent to the revolution.
Isner, Henry	—, Randolph	Did no service in the revolutionary war.
Ice, Adam	Morgantown, Monongalia	Indian war—frontier service—driving pack-horses.
Jones, John	—, Dinwiddie	Did not serve six months.
Jenkins, Reuben	—, Preston	Fraudulent.
Jones, John	—, Grayson	Did not serve six months.
Johnson, James	—, Mecklenberg	Did not serve six months.
Jacobs, William	—, Fauquier	Team service—not considered military service.
Johnston, Benjamin	—, Kanawha	Collecting beeves for the army—not considered military service.
Jones, James	—, Orange	Did not serve six months.
Kidd, George	—, Amelia	Did not serve six months.
Knight, Christopher	—, Harrison	Did not serve six months.
Lane, Thomas	—, Surrey	Did not serve six months.

STATEMENT—Continued.

Names.	Residence.	Reasons for rejection.
Lynott, Thomas	——, Harrison	Privateer service.
Lane, Henry	——, Amherst	Did not serve six months.
Lee, David	——, Wood	Did not serve in the revolution.
Lang, John H.	——, Goochland	Was a soldier of the French army.
Lockheart, William	——, Hampshire	Did not serve in a military capacity.
Lybrook, John	——, Giles	Did not serve in any regular organized corps.
Lewis, Abraham	——, Randolph	No proof of service—story very improbable.
Lilly, William	——, Nicholas	By evidence of his age.
Leazen, Hyrah	——, Wood	Was a deserter.
Lucas, William	——, Logan	Did not serve six months.
Morcheson, John	——, Campbell	Three months military and three months as artificer in the militia—not military.
Mitchell, John	——, Lewis	Did not serve six months.
Murphy, John	——, Norfolk, Norfolk	Did not serve six months.
McKinney, Michael	——, Harrison	Fraudulent.
Mullins, Ambrose	——, Russell	Did not serve six months.
Martin, Samuel	——, Greenbriar	Fraudulent.
Miller, Andrew	——, Randolph	Fraudulent.
Maze, James	——, Lewis	Was not a soldier of the revolution.
Mallichan, John	——, Lewis	By evidence of his age.
Mollihon, John	——, Greenbriar	By evidence of his age.
McFerren, John	——, Greenbriar	Did not serve six months.
McCain, Hugh	——, Lewis	By evidence of his age.
Mean, Robert	——, Greenbriar	Did not serve six months.
Morrison, Andrew	——, Lewis	Did not serve six months.
McVernara, George	——, Monongalia	By evidence of his age.
McElray, Thomas	——, Sussex	Was a wagoner and did not perform military service.
McKennon, Lathlin	——, Bedford	Was engaged on both sides, but enlisted last with the enemy.
Martin, George	——, Bedford	Served as an express rider.
Miller, Jacob	——, Albemarle	Did not serve six months.
Maupin, Cornelius	——, Albemarle	Did not serve in a military capacity.
McCarrahey, John	——, Bedford	Did not serve six months.

Name	County	Remarks
March, John (deceased), heirs of	——, Nansemond	Did not serve six months.
Mahone, Archelaus	——, Patrick	Did not serve six months.
Miller, Henry	——, Rockingham	Did not serve in a military capacity.
McClintick, Joseph	——, Greenbriar	Was a frontier's-man and forced at his own option.
Murray, Reuben	——, Fauquier	Did not serve six months.
Night, John	——, Nicholas	By evidence of his age.
Naylor, James	——, Kenawha	By evidence of his age.
Nutt, Rhodam	——, Lewis	By evidence of his age.
Nickle, Isaac	——, Monroe	Services were exclusively against the Indians.
Nunally, David	——, Dinwiddie	Did not serve six months.
Osborn, Zahrah	——, Randolph	Traditionary evidence against him.
O'Bannon, Thomas	——, Fauquier	Did not serve six months.
Palmer, William	——, Westmoreland	Did not serve six months.
Patton, John	——, Greenbriar	Was a farmer and lived in a fort, but was not engaged in any branch of the public service.
Peyton, Charles	——, Stafford	Did not serve six months.
Patison, John	——, Greenbriar	Was a frontier farmer—lived in a fort—did not belong to the army.
Philips, Henry	——, Lewis	Indian wars, not revolutionary service.
Philips, Isaac	——, Lewis	Indian wars, not revolutionary service.
Parks, Andrew	——, Monongalia	Performed no service as a soldier of the revolution.
Parsons, William	——, Lewis	Rejected by evidence of his age.
Pickett, Thomas (deceased), heirs of	——, Halifax	Died before the passage of the act.
Preble, Thomas	——, Wood	Not believed by his neighbors—furnishes no proof.
Pulliam, Joseph	——, Halifax	Did not serve six months.
Pulliam, Drury	——, Henry	Did not serve six months.
Rainey, William, sen.	——, Mecklenburg	Did not serve six months.
Robinson, Isaac	Point Pleasant, Mason	Did not serve six months.
Richardson, Dick	——, Louisa	Did not serve six months.
Robertson, John	——, Greenville	Did not serve six months.
Rhodes, Zachariah	——, Jackson	Was *non compos mentis* when his declaration was fraudulently obtained.
Read, Amos	——, Nansemond	Did not serve six months.
Redgway, Noah	——, Monongalia	Rejected by evidence of his age.
Read, Andrew	——, Floyd	Did not serve six months.
Read, Amariah	——, Nansemond	Did not serve six months.
Runion, Elijah	——, Jackson	Did not serve six months.
Roby, Aquilla	——, Lewis	Rejected by evidence of his age.

STATEMENT—Continued.

Names.	Residence.	Reasons for rejection.
Roe, John	—, Harrison	Fraudulent.
Raynolds, Benjamin	—, Jackson	Was an impostor.
Rush, Samuel	—, Loudon	Did not serve six months.
Rush, John	—, Rockingham	Did not serve six months.
Snidow, Jacob	—, Giles	Did not serve in any regularly organized corps.
Shimp, John	—, Berkley	Did not serve six months.
Steel, Thomas	—, Monroe	Did not serve six months.
Seamonds, Ephraim	—, Albemarle	Did not serve six months.
Sharp, Spencer	—, Wood	Fraudulent.
Sharp, William	—, Pocahontas	Did not serve six months.
Shepherd, James	Palmyra, Fluvanna	Served as a hatter.
Sayers, Alexander	—, Tazewell	Service after the revolution.
Smith, Philip	—, Amherst	Did not serve six months.
Smith, Thomas	—, Fauquier	Did not serve six months.
Smith, Thomas	—, Kenawha	Did not serve six months.
Snider, John	—, Smyth	Team service.
Standley, Richard	—, Scott	Did not serve in a military capacity.
Stalmaker, Valentine (deceased)	—, Randolph	Service before the date of the Revolution.
Spark, Frederick (deceased)	—, Preston	Evidence extremely doubtful and unsatisfactory.
Stewart, Charles	—, Jackson	Rejected by evidence of his age.
Swick, Anthony	—, Harrison	Fraudulent.
Summers, Hezekiah	—, Monongalia	Did not serve six months.
Sams, Jonathan	—, Wood	Service against Indians after 1788.
Smith, John	Weston, Lewis	Fraudulent.
Skinner, Walter	—, Harrison	Fraud.—the claimant was imposed upon.
Smith, Jonathan	—, Randolph	Services were not in a military capacity.
Schoolcraft, Jacob	—, Lewis	Rejected by evidence of his age.
Thomas, John	—, Albemarle	Did not serve six months.
Tanner, Samuel	—, Jackson	Rejected by evidence of his age.
Townsend, Richard	—, Pittsylvania	Did not serve six months.
Taylor, Nimrod	—, Scott	Did not serve six months.

245 [37]

Taylor, William	—, Orange	Did not serve six months personally.
Van Gilder, Jacob	————	Did not serve six months. [Papers withdrawn.]
Vaughan, Ephraim	—, Dinwiddie	Rejected by evidence of his age.
Williamson, Henry	—, Bedford	Did not serve six months.
Windsor, Jonathan	—, Kenawha	Did not serve in a military capacity.
Workman, Abraham	—, Tazewell	Did not serve six months.
Wampler, John	—, Wythe	Served as a wagon driver.
Walker, David	—, Goochland	Did not serve six months.
Watts, Frederick	—, Culpepper	Did not serve six months.
Wagstaff, John	—, Mecklenburg	Did not serve six months.
Westfield, Cornelius	—, Lewis	Fraud and imposition.
Waide, Pleasant	—, Greenbriar	Fraudulent.
Williams, Roger	—, Bedford	Did not serve six months.
Whitzell, George	—, Monongalia	Rejected by evidence of his age.
Warner, Jacob	—, Bedford	Did not serve six months.
Wolff, David	—, Lewis	Did not serve six months.
Williams, David	—, Greenbriar	Did not serve in any regularly organized corps.
Wamsley, Matthew	—, Lewis	Fraud and imposition.
Wright, Bazel	—, Jackson	Did not serve six months.
Weitzel, Abraham	—, Augusta	Did not serve six months.
Wood, Jonathan	—, Isle of Wight	Did not serve six months.
Windsor, Jonathan	—, Nicholas	Did not serve in any regularly organized corps.
Wilson, Andrew	—, Lewis	Fraud and imposition.
Wyer, George	—, Harrison	Fraudulent.
Young, Charles	—, Kenawha	Service previous to 1775.

A list of the names of persons residing in Virginia who have applied for pensions under the act of June 7, 1832, whose claims have been suspended; prepared in conformity with the resolution of the Senate of the United States, September 16, 1850.

Names.	Residence.	Reasons for suspension.
Anderson, Charles (dec'd), heirs of	Lexington, Rockbridge	No proof of identity of claimant with either of the soldiers of the same name in the Virginia line.
Anderson, Peter	Parkersburg, Wood	For a more perfect setting forth of service.
Arrington, Thomas	Walnut Branch, Fauquier	For further proof and specification.
Arbuckle, William	Mason	No evidence of service furnished.
Atkins, Hezekiah	Cabell Court House, Cabell	For further proof and specification.
Atkins, John	Gauly's Bridge, Fayette	For further proof and specification.
Baswell, Welden	——, Preston	Awaiting further proof.
Bates, William	——, Louisa	Did not serve six months.
Beard, James	——, Rockingham	Did not serve six months.
Branch, Thomas	——, Prince Edward	For further proof and particulars of service.
Bostick, Absalom	Halifax Court House	For further proof.
Bonnifield, Samuel	Horse-shoe Run, Randolph	For further proof and specification.
Boswell, William	Kingwood, Preston	For proof by two credible witnesses.
Board, John	——, Fauquier	Awaiting further proof.
Bobo, Joseph	——, Prince William	Did not serve six months.
Boyles, Michael	——, Randolph	Awaiting further proof and specification.
Braxton, James	——, Caroline	For further proof.
Brown, Brightbury	——, Albemarle	For further proof.
Brumfield, Robert	——, King William	No proof of service—name not on the pay roll. Disallowed.
Bryan, Luke	——, Randolph	Fraudulent.
Bond, Benjamin	——, Tyler	No evidence of service furnished.
Bennett, William (dec'd)	——, Liberty, Bedford	For a formal application to be prepared by the widow or children.
Burnett, Richard (dec'd)	——, Hanover	For further proof and explanation. Cartridge making is not regarded as military service.
Busby, William	Goochland Court House	Period, length and grade of service, and names of company and field officers required.
Byars, Joseph	Staunton, Augusta	Claims to have been an assistant wagon-master. His authority and pay and duties must be made known, as the rank is unknown to the department.

Name	Location	Remarks
Cohoon, Charles	Glade Creek, Bottetourt	For further proof and explanation.
Campbell, Thomas	——, Princess Ann	For a further specification and proof of service.
Canterbury, John	——, Monroe	No proof of service, documentary or otherwise.
Chewning, Robert	——, Orange	For further proof of service.
Christy, Rev. James	——, Monroe	No proof of service, documentary or otherwise.
Clarke, Robert	Orange Court House	Awaiting further proof.
Clarke, Joseph (dec'd)	——, Mecklenburg	For a new declaration, with the usual details.
Cook, William	——, Wythe	The service described by him does not correspond with that of either of his three namesakes on the rolls.
Cox, John	——, Scott	For further proof and explanation.
Copsy, John	——, Hampshire	Further proof required.
Cox, Bartlett	——, Mecklenburg	Awaiting proof of service for his two years in the 10th regiment, Virginia line.
Cook, Jacob	——, Monroe	His alleged services were in Indian wars, from 1773 to 1779, but furnishes no proof, documentary or otherwise.
Childress, Robert	——, Amelia	For further proof and specification.
Day, James	——, Mecklenburg	Name not on the Virginia rolls—no other proof furnished.
Davidson, Joseph	——, Mercer	Did not serve in any regularly organized corps.
Davidson, Joseph	——, Tazewell	For a supplemental declaration, in accordance with the rules.
Dyer, Samuel	——, Albemarle	Assistant clothier under Mr. Moss. (See Virginia records.) Not military service.
Dickinson, John	——, Monroe	No proof of service, documentary or otherwise.
Drumhellen, George	——, Albemarle	Did not serve six months.
Bunn, Martin	——, Louisa	For proof of service.
Dunn, John, sen	——, Monroe	No sufficient proof of service.
Ellison, John	——, Monroe	Claims for service as an Indian spy, but fails to furnish satisfactory proof.
Eckle, Philip	——, Pendleton	For further proof and explanation.
Elliott, William	——, Accomack	Specifications and proof of service wanting.
Eanes, Edward	——, Pittsylvania	Claims for three tours of militia service, and has omitted period, length and grade, and names of company and field officers.
English, Robert	——, Wythe	No evidence of service.
Facks, Philip	——, Hampshire	For more direct proof.
Feely, John	——, Pulaski	Awaiting further proof.
Fergus, Francis	——, Montgomery	Claims four months as a militia soldier and nine months as a teamster—the latter time not allowed.
Ferguson, George	——, Franklin	For proof of further service.

STATEMENT—Continued.

Names.	Residence.	Reasons for suspension.
Fielder, John...............	——, Grayson......	Exclusive of wagon service, he did not serve six months.
Fisher, George (deceased)...	——, Shenandoah...	For further proof.
Freeman, Abery (or Dabney)..	——, Rockingham...	For further proof.
Gibbs, Churchill (deceased)...	——, Madison......	Pensioner under act 1828. Claims for increase as staff officer, under act of June 7, 1882, but furnishes no proof.
Harper, Jesse...............	——, Tazewell.....	For further proof of identity with the dragoon of the depreciation certificate of £39 18s. 8d.
Henson, Robert..............	——, Fauquier.....	For further proof of service.
Hill, Alexander..............	Wheeling, Ohio....	Two credible witnesses required in this case.
Humphrey, William...........	——, Smyth.......	For further proof of service.
Henly, Hezekiah.............	....	For want of proof. Papers withdrawn April 19, 1836, by Hon. B. Stover.
Horner, Isaac, (deceased), widow of ...	——, Monongalia...	For further proof and a return of the original papers.
Hosier, Samuel...............	——, Norfolk......	For further and more direct proof.
Hutchinson, William..........	——, Monroe......	Claims for service in Indian wars—further proof required.
Hudson, John................	——, Henrico......	For fuller proof.
Hamilton, John...............	——, Logan........	For further proof and explanation.
Hanaway, Samuel............	——, Monongalia...	For further proof.
Harmon, Thomas.............	——, Mason.......	For further proof.
Hopkins, Lawrence...........	——, Lewis........	For further proof.
Harless, Fardeman............	——, Giles........	Indian wars of 1777, '78, '79 and '80.
Hughes, Thomas.............	——, Jackson......	Indian wars of 1777, '78, '79 and '80.
Harless, Philip...............	——, Giles........	Indian wars of 1777, '78, '79 and '80.
Harless, Daniel..............	——, Giles........	Indian wars of 1777, '78, '79 and '80.
Houchins, Francis............	——, Goochland....	Period, length, grade, stations, marches and names of company and field officers, and traditionary proof required.
Hunt, Benjamin..............	——, Halifax......	For further proof.
Hylton, Nathaniel P..........	——, Patrick......	Awaiting proof and specification of his actual tours of service as a minute-man.
Ingle, Henry.................	——, Russell......	For more perfect details of service.

Name	County	Remarks
Johnson, William, 1st	—, Monroe	For further proof.
Jones, John	—, Mecklenburg	For further proof and authentication.
Jones, James	—, Tyler	For further proof.
James, Jack	—, Tyler	Not on any rolls—no proof of service.
Jameson, John	—, Washington	For further proof.
Kaufman, John	—, Augusta	For further proof and explanation.
Kelch, Leonard	—, Tyler	For further proof.
Keller, George	—, Augusta	Did not serve six months.
Kendall, George	—, Prince William	The Virginia rolls being silent, he is required to furnish traditionary proof.
Killinger, George	—, Smyth	For further proof and explanation.
Luzader, Aaron	—, Monongalia	For further proof.
Langham, Henry (deceased), heirs of	—, Bedford	Remanded for a new declaration and proof of decease of soldier, and of his children's names.
Lane, Richard	—, Spotsylvania	For further proof.
Lee, Zachariah	—, Bottetourt	For further proof and explanation.
Lap (or Sap), John	—, Preston	For further proof.
McHone, Archibald	—, Patrick	For further proof.
Mason, George	—, Caroline	For a more perfect description of his service.
Mahar, Patrick	—, Rockbridge	For further proof.
Martin, John	—, Greenbriar	For further proof.
Martin, Samuel	—, Kenawha	For further proof.
Matthews, Thomas	—, Brunswick	For further proof.
Marie, James	—, Loudon	Did not serve six months.
M'Laurine, James	—, Cumberland	For defective proof. Papers withdrawn June 30, 1886, Hon. J. W. Jones.
Moore, Asa	....	Proof of service required by two witnesses.
Miller, Valentine	—, Monroe	No proof of service—not on the rolls—papers withdrawn.
Morris, George	—, Orange	For further proof.
M'Kankey, David	—, Tyler	For further proof.
Morrison, James	—, Pocahontas	For further proof.
Murray, Mark	—, Halifax	For further proof.
Nickell, Isaac	—, Monroe	For further proof.
New, John	—, Augusta	Withdrew this claim and obtained the benefit of act of May 18, 1828.
Parrott, John (deceased)	—, Caroline	No proof of service—papers withdrawn.

STATEMENT—Continued.

Names.	Residence.	Reasons for suspension.
Phillippie, Christopher	——, Wythe	For further proof.
Phelan, Jesse		No proof of service—name not on the Pennsylvania rolls—papers withdrawn.
Prewitt, Obed	——, Mason	For further proof.
Pulliam, Joseph	——, Charlotte	For further proof.
Peters, Jesse	——, Surry	For further proof.
Rice, James B.	——, Fauquier	Did not serve six months.
Reynolds, Lewis B.	Liberty, Bedford	For further proof.
Rochold, Thomas T.	——, Morgan	Awaiting further proof.
Roseberry, John M.	Point Pleasant, Mason	For further proof.
Reynolds, Benjamin	——, Lewis	For further proof and explanation.
Ridgeway, Joseph	——, Bedford	For further proof.
Riley, Charles	——, Middlesex	For further proof.
Robinson, John	——, Monroe	For further proof.
Sheets, John	——, Nottingham	For further proof.
Smith, John	——, Logan	For want of proof, and papers withdrawn.
Swope, Michael	——, Monroe	For further proof.
Stamp, Michael	——, Tazewell	For further proof.
Slusher, John	——, Montgomery	No proof of service.
Skinner, William	——, Fairfax	Militia service overrated.
Simmons, John	Wheeling, Ohio	No proof of service.
Smithers, John	——, Henrico	Awaiting a formal application and proof of service as a war's-man from the Richmond records.
Starkey, Jonathan	——, Franklin	Proof by two witnesses required, the rolls being silent.
Stevens, Robert	——, Campbell	Did not serve six months.
Shaffer, Peter	——, Berkley	For a more perfect narrative of his services.
Spencer William	——, King and Queen's	For further proof.
Spencer, William, 2d	——, Halifax	For further proof and specification.
Steel, Thomas, deceased	Charleston, Kenawha	No evidence of service.
Stephens, David	——, Patrick	Did not serve six months.
Stanly, Richard	——, Scott	No names of officers—no regiment—no proof.

Name	County	Notes
Sutherland, George	——, Fluvanna	No proof of service—claim disallowed.
Tanner, Thomas, (deceased) widow of	——, Mecklenburg	For further proof.
Taylor, Samuel	——, Buckingham	Did not serve six months.
Thompson, John	——, Tazewell	For further proof.
Townsend, John	——, Lewis	For further proof.
Tremper, Lawrence, deceased	Staunton, Augusta	No claim—left no widow nor children.
Trout, David, deceased	——, Rockbridge	No proof of service.
Vanarsdeler, Garret	——, Hampshire	No proof of service.
Vanfossen, Jacob	——, Augusta	For proof of service.
Van Gilder, Jacob	——, Monongalia	For further proof.
Walford, John	——, Hampshire	Awaiting further proof.
Wade, Richard	——, Frederick	For further proof and specification.
Wallace, Joseph, deceased	Charles city	Proof of identity doubtful between claimant and the three years soldier of the depreciation certificate bearing same name.
Walker, Francis	——, Middlesex	For further proof and specification.
Walker, Memucan	——, Greenbriar	Awaiting more perfect details of his service.
Ware, Thomas, deceased	——, Mecklenberg	The widow, or if none, the children, upon proof of his death, will be entitled from 20th March, 1831, to the day of his death.
Warren, James	——, Halifax	Period, length and grade of service, and names of company and field officers wanted.
Webb, Benjamin	——, Botetourt	For further proof.
Wells, Thomas	——, Tyler	For further proof.
Wellburn, William	——, Accomack	More perfect details of service.
White, John	——, Louisa	Not any satisfactory proof of service.
White, Rawley, deceased	——, Pittsylvania	Claims for service as ensign and surgeon's-mate in the Virginia continental line, for which proof should be found in the auditor's rolls, Richmond.
Whitmore, John G	——, Dinwiddie	Period, length and grade of service, and names of company and field officers and stations and where marched, wanting.
Wilson, William	Portsmouth, Norfolk	No proof or specification—claim rejected.
Wilson, James S	——, Kenawha	Did not serve six months in any regularly organized corps.
Williams, Christopher	——, King and Queen's	Not any satisfactory proof of service.
Williamson, John	——, Tyler	For further proof.
Williams, Richard	——, Prince George	For further proof.
Woods, Josiah, or Jonah	——, Franklin	For further proof.
Wingfield, William	——, Hanover	For further details and proof of service.
Woods, Archibald	Wheeling, Ohio	Did not serve six months.

STATEMENT—Continued.

Names.	Residence.	Reasons for suspension.
Woodson, John Stephen	——, Powhatan	Awaiting proof of service.
Wonicuth, Richard	——, Montgomery	Awaiting proof of service.
Williams, Richard, (deceased) heirs of	——, Greenbriar	For further proof.
Windee, John	——, Shenandoah	For proof of service.
Wynn, William	——, Tazewell	For further proof.
Wright, Stephen	——, Norfolk	Alleged service as an officer requires record proof.

A list of the names of persons residing in Virginia who have applied for pensions under the act of July 4, 1836, whose claims have been rejected; prepared in conformity with the resolution of the Senate of the United States, September 16, 1850.

Names.	Residence.	Reasons for rejection.
Blake, Susannah, widow of Wm. R.	Old Point Comfort, Elizabeth city.	A soldier of the regular army.
Butler, Mary, widow of Solomon	——, Bedford	Married after service.
Biggs, Mary, widow of Joseph	——, Marshall	Married after January 1, 1794.
Baker, Francis, widow of Richard	Richmond city	Married in 1811.
Doyle, Mary, widow of Ezekiel	——, Elizabeth city	A soldier of the regular army.
Heath, Martha, widow of Elijah	——, Prince Edward	A soldier of the regular army.
Heyl, Jane (deceased), widow of Christian	Norfolk borough	A soldier of the regular army.
Lyon, Francis, widow of William	——, Nelson	Did not serve six months.
Mitchen, Isabella, widow of Benjamin	——, Bedford	Did not serve six months.
O'Roark, Jane, widow of David	——, Shenandoah	Married after service.
Robertson, Martha, daughter of Thomas Morgan (deceased)	Portsmouth, Norfolk	Was a soldier of the regular army.
Scott, Drucilla, widow of Joseph	New Store, Buckingham	Did not serve six months.

A list of the names of persons residing in Virginia who have applied for pensions under the act of July 4, 1836, whose claims have been suspended; prepared in conformity with the resolution of the Senate of the United States, September 16, 1850.

Names.	Residence.	Reasons for suspension.
Ashburn, Susan, widow of Locke	——, Lancaster	For proof of marriage.
Allen, Pamelia, widow of Samuel	——	For defective proof, and papers withdrawn by P. Allen, Oct. 11, 1887.
Beach, Mary, widow of Richard B.	——, Lunenberg	No proof of service—name not on the Richmond rolls.
Bown, Mary, widow of John	——	For defective proof, and papers returned to R. B. Gaines, March 9, 1839.
Bradshaw, Sela, widow of William	Jerusalem, Southampton	Period, length, grade and localities of service, and names of company and field officers.
Brooks, Nancy, widow of William	Jeffersonville, Tazewell	Did not serve six months in any regularly embodied corps.
Burton, Sarah (deceased), widow of May	——, Greene	For proof and explanation.
Cecil, Nancy, widow of William	Jeffersonville, Tazewell	Did not serve six months in any regularly organized corps.
Chalfant, Achsa, formerly widow of James Cotton	——, Monongalia	Rejected under this act, but advised to apply under act July 7, 1838.
Cheatwood, Susannah, widow of William	——, Franklin	Proof of marriage—six months' service allowed—letter November 15, 1839—W. L. Goggin, M. C.
Clark, Mary, widow of Field	——, Lunenburg	Service as a minute man must be specified, and the amount of actual service ascertained.
Cupp, Susannah, widow of Leonard	——, Preston	For deficient proof of marriage.
Davis, Elizabeth, widow of Samuel	——, Botetourt	For further proof of service.
Darring, Barbara (deceased) widow of Henry	——	Married after service—sent papers to Hon. R. Craig, December 19, 1839. [Papers withdrawn.]
Davenport, Ann, widow of Henry	——, Buckingham	Proof of service not satisfactory.
Dickenson, Mary, widow of William	——, Caroline	For further proof of service.
Duncan, Peggy, widow of Charles	——, Giles	No claim—married after service—not a widow July 7, 1888, and died October, 1888.

255 [37]

Name	County	Remarks
Edwards, Elizabeth, widow of Michael	—, Marshall	Did not serve six months in his first term, and his second requires proof.
Feathers, Mary, widow of Jacob	—, Preston	For further proof.
Goodall, Sarah, widow of John	—, Greene	Not on Spencer's rolls—proof otherwise not satisfactory.
Grubbs, Sarah, widow of John	—, Hanover	For further proof and specification.
Hamilton, Isabella (dec'd), widow of William	—, Greenbriar	For further proof.
Hanlin, Margaret, widow of Patrick	—, Tyler	Married after service, but previous to January 1, 1794—she, or her children can claim under act July 7, 1838.
Halsey, Rachel, widow of William	—, Grayson	For further proof—she was married after service.
Hudson, Elizabeth, widow of John	—, Lunenburg	For further proof.
Howell, Rebecca, widow of David	—, Bedford	Proof of marriage deficient—not six months' service proved.
Henderson, Nancy, widow of Henry	—, Halifax	For further proof.
Howry, Catharine, formerly widow of Peter Filler	—, Floyd	Proof of service required.
Jones, Amarilla, widow of Nicholas	—, Rockbridge	Service after marriage.
Kinder, Margaret, widow of Peter	—, Wythe	Did not serve six months.
Lane, Mary, widow of Henry	—, Marshall	For further proof.
Lawyer, Eve M., widow of John Adam Lawyer	—, Frederick	For further proof.
Lincoln, Dorcas (deceased), widow of Jacob	—, Rockingham	For further proof.
Long, Elizabeth, widow of Ware	—, Greene	For further proof.
Murray, Susannah, widow of James	—, Culpepper	For further proof.
M'Ilhany, Margaret, widow of James	—, Loudon	Married after service, and she died before July 7, 1838.
Norris, Elizabeth, widow of William	Charlottesville, Albemarle	For further proof.
Oglesby, Susan, widow of Richard	Lynchburg, Campbell	For further proof.
Parsons, Anna, formerly widow of Jno. Heath	—, Jackson	For further proof.
Ragan, Cecilia, widow of Richard	—, Rockingham	For defective proof, and claim withdrawn April, 1838, by Hon. J. P. Pennybacker.
Rose, Rebecca, widow of Charles	—, Monongalia	Period, length, grade, localities and names of company and field officers must be set forth, and service verified by the New Jersey records.

STATEMENT—Continued.

Names.	Residence.	Reasons for suspension.
Skeene, Sarah, widow of Peter............	——, Russell............	For further proof.
Sims, Jane, widow of Benjamin............	——, Louisa............	For defective proof.
Singleton, Ann, widow of John............	——, Matthews.........	For further proof.
Tally, Mildred, widow of James............	——, Halifax...........	For further proof.
Terry, Nancy, widow of John Davis........	——, Norfolk...........	A warsman of the North Carolina line—proof of identity and date of the marriage required.
Thompson, Elizabeth, widow of David.....	——, Pendleton.........	For further proof.

A list of persons residing in Virginia, who have applied for pensions under the act of July 7, 1838, whose claims have been rejected; prepared in conformity with the resolution of the Senate of the United States of September 16, 1850.

Names.	Residence.	Reasons for rejection.
Bradford, Elizabeth, widow of Claude Francois alias Jenneavel	New Town, Frederick	Was a soldier of the French army.
Brown, Henrietta, widow of Barnes	———, Albemarle	Did not serve in any regularly organized corps.
Boon, Elizabeth (deceased), widow of John	Greenbriar C. H., Greenbriar	Died before the joint resolution of Aug. 23, 1842.
Clements, Mary (deceased), widow of Thomas	———, Fluvanna	Died before the joint resolution of Aug. 23, 1842.
Drumheller, Anna, widow of Leonard	———, Albemarle	Was not a widow at the passage of the act.
George, Nancy (deceased), widow of William	———, Goochland	Died before the passage of the act.
Gregory, Eleanor, widow of James	Greenbriar C. H., Greenbriar	Was not a widow at the date of the act.
Hyslop, Susan, widow of Levin	———, Accomack	Not married before January 1, 1794.
Lively, Sarah (deceased), widow of Godrell	———, Monroe	Was not living August 23, 1842.
Martin, Elizabeth, widow of George	Lynchburgh, Campbell	An express rider—not military service.
Moore, Mary (deceased), widow of Alexander	———, Spotsylvania	Not a widow at the passage of the act, and died before Aug. 28, 1842.
O'Roark, Jane, widow of David	———, Rockingham	Service after marriage.
Oldham, Winnifred, widow of Isaac	———, Brunswick	Not a widow at the date of the act.
Watkins, Hannah (deceased) widow of Robert	———, Campbell	Not a widow at the passage of the act.
Zea, Ann, widow of Martin	———, Shenandoah	Not a widow at the date of the act.

Ex.—15

[37]

A list of the names of persons residing in Virginia who have applied for pensions under the act of July 7, 1838, whose claims have been suspended; prepared in conformity with the resolution of the Senate of the United States of September 16, 1850.

Names.	Residence.	Reasons for suspension.
Alfred, Susan, widow of Thomas, formerly widow of Jesse Kenedy	——, Amherst	Proof of service not complete.
Anderson, Mary, widow of George	——, Augusta	Proof of service not complete.
Anderson, Christinna, widow of Jacob	——, Pulaski	Proof of service not complete.
Arington, Susanna, widow of John	——, Halifax	Date of marriage not fully proved.
Barker, Elizabeth, widow of Edward	——, Washington	Two years' service admitted; widow must apply in form and establish the date of her marriage prior to January 1, 1794.
Bowen, Elizabeth, widow of John	——, Albemarle	The service alleged by claimant, and that exhibited by Mr. Heath, auditor's certificate of Virginia, for a soldier of the same name, do not agree.
Boyd, Flora, widow of James	——, Monroe	The special act to claimant's husband granting a pension for twelve months' service is not regarded as conferring widow's rights under the general laws.
Bullock, Jane, widow of David	——, Louisa	Not a widow at the date of the act.
Brigandine, Nancy, widow of Bartlett	——, Rappahannock	Was married after the date limited by the act, viz., in 1798.
Bullock, Martha, widow of Joseph	——, Spotsylvania	Marriage admitted—service not fully set forth or proved.
Casson, Sarah (deceased), widow of William, children of	——, Buckingham	Proof of the kind and length of service not fully exhibited, and the proof of identity with soldiers of the same name not acceptable.
Catlett, Ann, widow of David	——, Morgan	Suspended for proof of the alleged date of the marriage.
Cavendish, Alice, formerly widow of William McClintic	——, Bath	Proof of marriage and service not complete.
Chambers, Ann (deceased), widow of James, heirs of	——, Louisa	No claim—she died before the passage of the act.
Cheatham, Judith, widow of Bernard	——, Charlotte	Minute-men's service requires distinct specification, which is not given in this case.
Chilton, Betsey, widow of Andrew	——, Lancaster	Date of marriage not fully proved.
Clarke, Elizabeth, widow of Spencer	——, Middlesex	Married after the limitation of the act.

Name	Place	Remarks
Cook, Mary, (deceased), widow of Peter	—, Kanawha	For further proof and papers withdrawn.
Cook, Mary, widow of John	—, Greenbriar	Marriage admitted. The soldier who received the Department certificate for £12 5s. 4d. was of the same name, but other and more precise proof of identity is required.
Daily, Nancy, widow of James O'Neill Daily	—, Smyth	There was no pensioner of the name—the pensioner's name was Farrell O'Neil Dailey, and drew his pension in Tennessee.
Diggs, Dolly, widow of John	—, Louisa	Marriage admitted—service not fully set forth and proved.
Ellis, Sally, widow of Stephen	—, Brunswick	Date of marriage requires proof.
Elliott, Sarah, widow of William	—, King William	For proof of identity that he was the corporal in Col. Harrington's regiment of artillery as specified in the certificate of W. H. Richardson.
Ferguson, Elizabeth, widow of Edmond	New Store, Buckingham	For further proof of service.
Finley, Margaret, widow of Archibald	—, Frederick	Not a widow at the date of the act.
Floeds, Sarah, widow of Noah	—, Buckingham	Did not serve six months.
Futton, Elizabeth, widow of Andrew		For defective proof, and claim withdrawn by Hon. A. S. Fulton, January, 1848.
Goodman, Elizabeth, widow of Horsley	—, Albemarle	Four months' service certified to; cattle driving for the balance of service not admissible.
Glover, Mary (deceased) widow of Samuel	—, Buckingham	For further proof of service from the records at Richmond.
Garret, Martha, widow of Stephen	New Store, Buckingham	Did not serve six months. [Papers withdrawn.]
Hay, Priscilla, formerly widow of James Shepherd	—, King William	Not the widow of the soldier for whose services she claims.
Hazol, Margaret, widow of Elisha	Limestone, Culpeper	Marriage admitted—service not proved or set forth—papers enclosed for authentication before a court of record.
Hernden, Susan, widow of William	—, Orange	For further proof and specification.
Hughes, Tabitha, widow of Stephen	—, Halifax	For deficient proof.
Hurt, Margaret, widow of Francis	—, Buckingham	For further proof.
Hurt, Fanny (deceased), widow of Zachariah	—, Prince Edward	No traces that the husband was a pensioner.
Jacobs, Sarah, widow of John	—, Fauquier	Proof of the marriage not complete—nor the identity of John Jacobs, a cavalry soldier of the Virginia rolls, with her husband.
Jarrell, Elizabeth, widow of William	Richmond city	For further proof of marriage and service.
Johnson, Mary, widow of Obadiah	—, Goochland	Proof of the date of the marriage not complete.
Johnson, Susan, widow of Josiah	—, Pittsylvania	For deficient proof of service.
Jordan, Anna, widow of Thomas	—, Page	For further proof.

STATEMENT—Continued.

Names.	Residence.	Reasons for suspension.
Kelly, Elizabeth, widow of James	——, King William	Evidence of identity and specification of service not complete.
King, Nancy, formerly widow of Jesse Tucker	——, Bedford	Deficient details—proof of service and of marriage defective.
Kipps, Catharine, widow of Michael	——, Montgomery	Suspended for further proof.
Kirk, Jemima, formerly widow of Daniel McCarty	——, Rockbridge	Proof of service and of marriage not complete.
Lauk, Emily, widow of Peter	Winchester, Frederick.	Not a widow at the date of the act.
Lewis, Mary, widow of David	——, Dinwiddie	Awaiting additional evidence since Oct. 8, 1844—sent to Thos. Green.
Little, Elizabeth, widow of George	——, Hampshire	Suspended for proof of service and of marriage.
Martin, Catharine, widow of George	——, Bedford	Not military service—he was an express rider.
Michael, Catharine, widow of Jacob	——, Henry	Suspended for more direct proof of service.
Michael, Catharine, widow of Jacob	——, Franklin	Awaiting more full and explicit details, and proof of service.
Hiller, Jane, (deceased), widow of Robert	——, Monroe	Period, length, and grade of service, and names of company and field officers wanting; and proof of marriage.
Mills, Lydia, widow of George	——, Prince William	Suspended for further proof of the date of the marriage.
McLaughlin, Mary, widow of Jacob	——, Russell	Proof of service required from the records of North Carolina—proof of marriage not complete.
Norvell, Margaret, widow of Hugh	——, Mecklenburg	Hugh Norvell, a corporal of the Virginia line, received a depreciation certificate for £64 6s. 8d., but there is no evidence to identify claimant's husband as that soldier.
Nowlen, Ursula, (deceased), widow of James	——, Patrick	Proof of service deficient—papers enclosed to Hon. Wm. M. Treadway, January 10, 1846.
Orr, Elizabeth, widow of John	——, Preston	No claim—her husband was improperly pensioned—his services were after the Revolution.
Parsons, Catharine, widow of William	Horseshoe Settlement, Randolph	Period, length and grade of service, and names of company and field officers wanting; and proof of marriage.
Perry, Deborah, widow of John	——, Tazewell	Record proof of his commission required, and names of regimental and company officers; and where, and when, and how long he served.

Name	County	Notes
Perry, Keziah, widow of William	——, Albemarle	Awaiting a more perfect exhibit of the length and grade and period of service; and names of officers in field and company; and the usual proof of marriage.
Pritchard, Elizabeth, formerly wid. of Brampton Hitchcock	Richmond city	Suspended for further proof of marriage, and of identity that the warsman named Brampton Hitchcock, of the Connecticut line, was her first husband.
Rains, Nancy, widow of William	——, Spotsylvania	Suspended for further proof.
Raynes, Mary, (deceased), widow of Lawrence	——, Rockingham	Proof of marriage wanting, and the date of widow's decease, and the names of the living children.
Reagon, Lydia, widow of Daniel	——, Pittsylvania	Suspended for proof of service and marriage.
Rush, Jemima, widow of Benjamin	——, Rappahannock	No narrative of service—the proofs and petition for an invalid pension to the Virginia legislature afford none of the details necessary to a decision in this department.
Querry, Sarah, widow of Elisha	——, Roanoke	Suspended for proof of the date of the marriage.
Saunders, Elizabeth, widow of George	——, Caroline	Not a widow at the date of the act.
Sampson, Mary, widow of James	——, Westmoreland	Service not sufficiently set forth—names of officers required—a three years' man should be upon the list of depreciation certificates.
Scott, Mary, widow of John	——, Mecklenburg	Suspended for further proof.
Shannon, Ann, widow of John	——, Smyth	Marriage admitted—proof of service not complete.
Sherwood, Females, widow of Henry	Norfolk city	Marriage admitted—six months service not fully proved.
Shepherd, Eleanor, widow of John	——, Culpeper	Marriage admitted—service not set forth, nor names of officers and stations given.
Smith, Basha, widow of Joseph	——, Pittsylvania	Suspended until the date of the marriage is proved.
Sneed, Sophia, widow of Robert	——, Hanover	Suspended for proof of the date of the marriage.
Starke, Sally, widow of Richard	——, Hanover	Proof of service as lieutenant not complete.
Stewart, Seley, widow of Robert	——, Norfolk	Not a widow at the date of the act.
Story, Mildred, widow of Lewis	——, Southampton	Service admitted—so far as the rolls show, a soldier of the same name, as drummer, who served in Captain Strother Jones's company, of Colonel Gist's regiment; and the bounty land, if traced, would be the best proof of identity at hand of the widow's claim to this soldier's service.
Sutherland, Elizabeth, widow of Alexander	——, Wayne	
Tasker, Mary, widow of James	——, Hampshire	Proof of marriage not complete.
Tate, Lucy, widow of Edmond	——, Campbell	No proof of service—not set forth—service, most probably, of a civil character.
Thackston, Betty Ann, widow of Benjamin	——, Prince Edward	Suspended for further proof.

STATEMENT—Continued.

Names.	Residence.	Reasons for suspension.
Tomlinson, Winifred, widow of Harris	—, Lunenburg	Proof of service not complete.
Valentine, Mary, widow of John	—, Page	Proof of service not complete.
Vines, Mary, widow of Thomas	—, Augusta	Married in October, 1795, which was after the limit of the act.
Wade, Mary, widow of Thomas	—, Giles	Date of marriage admitted—specification of service wanted.
Watson, Margaret, widow of Larner	—, Madison	Proof of marriage attempted by a spurious family record.
White, Elizabeth, widow of Thomas	—, Hanover	Evidence of service and of identity not satisfactory.
Wilson, Elizabeth, widow of Abraham	—, Spotsylvania	Further proof of service required.
Woodbridge, Fleming, widow of John	—, Appomattox	Not a widow at the date of the act.
Wright, Peggy, widow of James	—, Franklin	Proof of marriage and service not complete.

A list of the names of persons residing in North Carolina who have applied for pensions under the act of June 7, 1832, whose claims have been rejected; prepared in conformity with the resolution of the Senate of the United States, September 16, 1850.

Names.	Residence.	Reasons for rejection.
Asher, John	——, Ashe	Did not serve six months.
Ash, Samuel (dec'd), heirs of		Petition for increase not allowed—proof of service not mature.
Amey, Christian	——, Lincoln	Manufacturing shoes not considered military service.
Benton, James	——, Anson	Did not serve in any regularly organized corps.
Brown, William	——, Hartford	Did not serve six months.
Brock, Isaac, son	——, Buncombe	Did not serve six months.
Bennett, John	Lincolnton, Lincoln	Was a deserter.
Bialock, David	——, Rutherford	Did not serve six months.
Breeton, Edward	Statesville, Iredell	Did not serve six months.
Bennett, Daniel	——, Brunswick	Did not serve six months.
Biddle, Elijah	Onslow Court House	The court does not assent to his declaration.
Barnett, Jesse	——, Granville	Did not serve six months.
Collins, Jeremiah (dec'd) heirs of	——, Stokes	Died before the passage of the act.
Caldwell, Alexander	——, Haywood	Indian service west of the Blue Ridge, and transporting corn.
Campbell, Duncan	——, Cumberland	Did not serve six months.
Clark, John	Franklin P. O., Macon	Did not serve six months.
Cooper, William	——, Pitt	Did not sorve six months.
Downey, James	——, Granville	Did not serve six months.
Dubbleday, Lacker	——, Craven	Did not serve six months.
Edens, Jacob	——, New Hanover	Did not serve in any regularly organized corps.
Eubank, Daniel	——, Onslow	Did not serve six months.
Francis, Micajah	——, Stokes	Did not serve six months.
Fry, John (dec'd)	——, Stokes	Died before the passage of the act.
Frazer, James	——, Onslow	Did not serve six months.
Fulbright, Jacob	——, Haywood	Service as a blacksmith.

STATEMENT—Continued.

Names.	Residence.	Reasons for rejection.
Forehand, James	——, Wayne	Did not serve six months.
Foshee, Elijah	——, Chatham	Did not serve six months.
Grant, John	——, Onslow	Did not serve six months.
Goodwin, James	——, Hertford	Did not serve six months.
Gibson, William	——, Montgomery	Did not serve in any regularly organized corps.
Harris, John	——, Pasquotank	Did not serve six months.
Hanks, James	——, Wilkes	Was a deserter.
Hayes, Samuel	Salisbury, Rowan	Did not serve six months.
Henderson, Andrew	——, Mecklenburg	Did not serve six months.
Holt, Francis	——, Orange	Partisan service pursuing tories.
Hammond, George	——, Anson	Did not serve six months.
Hardin, James	——, Moore	Did not serve six months.
Humphrey, Joseph	Onslow Court House	No claim for service previous to April, 1775.
Holden, James	Smithville, Brunswick	Did not serve six months.
Huggins, Robert	——, Iredell	Manufacturing cartouche boxes not military service.
Hatcher, Timothy	——, New Hanover	Did not serve in any regularly organized corps.
Hopson, Benjamin	——, Wake	Did not serve six months.
Jones, Fowler	——, Granville	Two tours of three months each—one tour in catching fish.
King, John	——, Cumberland	Driving cattle, furnishing provision, driving wagon and carrying expresses, not military service.
Kinkaid, James	——, Buncombe	Did not serve six months.
Lee, Lemuel	——, Johnson	Collecting and driving cattle and hogs, packing and salting beef and pork, and driving wagons for the transportation of provisions, clothing, &c., not military service.
Link, Michael	Brummell, Davidson	Did not serve in any regularly organized corps.
Lee, John	——, Johnson	Collecting and driving cattle and hogs, packing and salting meat, driving wagons for transportation of prisoners, clothing, &c., not military.

Longworth, ——	——, Stokes	Did not serve in any regularly organized corps.
Loy, John	——, Orange	Did not serve six months.
Meally, Charles	——, Cumberland	Did not serve six months.
McCollum, James	——, Iredell	Partisan or tory war not provided for.
McKethan, Neill	——, Cumberland	Did not serve six months.
Myrack, Francis	Carthage, Moore	Did not serve six months.
McDaniel, Archibald	——, Bladen	Collecting and driving cattle not military service.
McCloud, William	——, Macon	Did not serve six months.
Mills, Andrew	Wadesboro', Anson	Did not serve six months.
Montgomery, Robert	——, Mecklenburg	Did not serve six months.
Mundle, John	——, Northampton	Attempt at fraud.
Morris, Stephen	——, Moore	Did not serve six months.
Morris, Joseph	——, Lincoln	Did not serve six months.
Manly, George	——, Caswell	Did not serve six months.
Neale, John	——, Duplin	Did not serve six months.
Odam, Uriah	——, New Hanover	Fraudulent.
Parrish, Charles	——, Wayne	Did not serve six months.
Penland, John	——, Buncombe	Did not serve six months.
Price, William	——, Lincoln	Team service—not military service.
Pottit, George	——, Surry	Transportation of lead—not military service.
Peede, Richard	——, Person	Did not serve six months.
Pearce, Samuel	Fayetteville, Cumberland	Did not serve six months.
Pittman, Arthur	——, Halifax	Did not serve six months in a military capacity.
Phillips, Adam	Ashville, Buncombe	Did not serve six months.
Price, William	——, Martin	Did not serve six months.
Pruit, Joseph	Wilksborough, Wilkes	Did not serve six months.
Ragan, Jesse	——, Person	Did not serve in a military capacity.
Shope, John	——, Buncombe	Did not serve in a military capacity.
Smith, William	——, Chatham	Was a deserter.
Sutherland, Robert	Kenansville, Duplin	Did not serve in a military capacity.
Spraill, William	——, Tyrrell	Service not in any regularly organized corps.
Sandlin, Nicholas	Kenansville, Duplin	Did not serve six months.
Spraill, Jesse	——, Tyrrell	Did not serve in any regularly organized corps.
Setser, Adam	——, Burke	Did not serve six months.

STATEMENT—Continued.

Names.	Residence.	Reasons for rejection.
Shaw, Basil	——, Haywood	Did not serve six months.
Smith, John	——, Iredell	Privateer service.
Bledman, Nathan	——, Chatham	Privateer service.
Stallings, Isaac	——, Johnson	Did not serve six months.
Stubblefield, Richard	——, Rockingham	Did not serve six months.
Smith, George	——, Ash	Did not serve six months.
Sauls, Henry	——, Greene	Did not serve six months.
Taylor, Aaron	——, Brunswick	Partisan service in pursuit of tories, not admissible.
Terry, James, sr	——, Granville	Did not serve six months.
Valentine, Daniel, (deceased), heirs of	——, Halifax	Died before the passage of the act.
Wilkins, Thomas	——, Cleveland	Did not serve six months.
Westcoat, Jeremiah	——, Brunswick	Tory warfare, partisan, or patrol not admissible.
Walls, John, (deceased), heirs of	——, New Hanover	Did not serve six months.
Wilkins, Benjamin	Tarborough, Edgecomb	Did not serve six months.
Wagg, John	——, Ash	Was a deserter.
Whitehurst, Anthony	——, Pasquotank	Served six months as a tailor.
Walker, Andrew	——, Mecklenburg	Was a teamster.
Walker, Andrew, 2d	——, Orange	Eleven months assistant commissary, and four months wagon and team.
White, David	Hawfield, Orange	Three months military, three months as bearer of despatches.
Walsot, Frederick	——, Davidson	Partisan warfare, tory chasing.
Washburn, Moses	——, Yancey	His service was not military.
Williams, Joseph, sr	——, Hyde	Did not serve six months.
Wright, John, sr	——, Stokes	Wagon service in the Pennsylvania militia.
Whitehurst, Richard	——, Pitt	Did not serve six months.
Wright, William	——, Rockingham	Did dot serve six months.
Willey, Hillory	——, Gates	Did not serve six months.
Winningham, James	——, Randolph	Did not serve six months.

A list of the names of persons residing in North Carolina who have applied for pensions under the act of July 7, 1832, whose claims have been suspended; prepared in conformity with the resolution of the Senate of the United States, September 16, 1850.

Names.	Residence.	Reasons for suspension.
Aldred, John	——, Randolph	For proof to identify him with the soldier of £31 3s. for twelve months service.
Anderson, James	——, Cumberland	For further proof.
Armstrong, Joseph	——, Orange	For proof of the identity between the Joseph Armstrong of £71 18s. 6d. pay for military services, and Joseph Armstrong, husband of claimant.
Auton, Freeland	——, Mecklenburg	No evidence of service found on the army books of New Jersey or Pennsylvania.
Bass, Edward	——, Ashe	He is referred to the army register at Raleigh for the nine months, men, for evidence of his service.
Barnhill, Robert	——, Mecklenburg	No proof of service.
Bennett, John	——, Cleaveland	For further proof.
Beasley, Jacob	——, Currituck	For more precise details of his service.
Brewer, Edward	——, Randolph	Not a military service regularly organized.
Boyt, William	——, Duplin	For proof of service.
Bright, Simon, (deceased)	——, Chatham	This case was admitted, and he died in 1830. The doubt is, that the present claimant is not his widow.
Carson, Holton, (deceased)	——, Franklin	Six months service admitted. Marriage in suspense.
Chandler, David		For deficient proof, and papers sent to Hon. M. T. Hawkins, December 29, 1837.
Chamberlain, John	——, Caswell	For further proof and specification.
Clark, William, (deceased)	——, Randolph	For further proof of identity between the pay and the service.
Coburn, Jesse	——, Martin	No proof of service to cover six months.
Cartwright, Lemuel	——, Hyde	For further proof and explanation.
Cameron, Allen, (deceased)	——, Northumberland	Militia service overrated.
Carson, John	——, Burke	For further proof.
Cargle, John	——, Haywood	For want of proof.
Cook, Isaac	——, Yancey	Not organized military service.

STATEMENT—Continued.

Names.	Residence.	Reasons for suspension.
Coons, William	—, Iredell	Did not serve six months.
Conna, Wright	—, Bertie	For further proof.
Chatam, William	—, Orange	Suspended for further proof.
Correll, Philip	—, Rowan	For further proof and explanation.
Cummins, Asa	—, Stokes	Not set forth as to period, length and grade, and names of company and field officers.
Curtis, Richard	—, New Hanover	No proof of service—contradictory statements.
Daniels, John, sen	—, Beaufort	No vessels of the names of South Key or Herald were in the State service—probably privateers.
Davis, Mashack	—, Haywood	Three certificates from the Comptroller of North Carolina to M. Davis as proof of service in this case, which are not regarded as conclusive.
Denny, Abraham (deceased), heirs of	—, Johnson	Proof of identity required between the claimant and the service for four years, proved by the certificate of the Secretary of State of North Carolina.
Edmiston, William	—, Wilkes	He did not serve six months in any regularly organized corps.
Egner, Matthias	—, Lincoln	Suspended for further proof.
Edwards, Capt. Charles	—, Wake	Papers incomplete.
Ellis, Nathan	—, Orange	No such service as he alleges in the militia of Maryland, and his name is not on the continental rolls.
Franklin, John	—, Burke	No proof of service—not on the rolls—he joined the enemy after his alleged service.
Fairchild, Abijah	—, Wilkes	He did not serve six months in any regularly embodied corps.
Folk, William	—, Rowan	No proof of service.
Gardner, James	—, Randolph	Suspended for proof from the Secretary of State of North Carolina.
Gibson, Thomas	—, Randolph	Suspended for proof to identify the soldier and the certificate of the Comptroller of North Carolina, which credits the payments.
Gollet, John	—, Washington	Suspended for further proof from the New Jersey records.

Name	County	Remarks
Gooding, Jonathan	——, Carteret	He must rebut the impression that he was the Jonathan Gooding of Colonel Putnam's regiment of '78, who was a deserter.
Green, Samuel	——, Wilkes	Claims for three years service in the New York line, and not on the rolls.
Hall, Seaburt	——, Rockingham	Suspended for further proof from the Maryland records.
Harris, John 2d (deceased)	——, Orange	Suspended for further proof of service.
Harris, Isham	——, Rutherford	Suspended for further proof and explanation.
Haines, Jonathan	——, Surry	Suspended for further proof.
Hepp, John	——, Buncombe	Suspended for further proof and specification.
Hanks, Richard	——, Lincoln	No proof of such service—it was probably unorganized partisan or patrol service.
Hethcock, Holiday	——, Johnson	For information if persons of color were liable to military duty by the laws of North Carolina.
Hewett, John	——, Onslow	For proof of service from the Raleigh records.
Higdon, Leonard	——, Macon	Suspended for further proof and explanation.
Higgins, Annanias	——, Yancey	Suspended for further proof.
Hitchcock (alias Hedgecock), Thomas	——, Macon	A person of the same name on the South Carolina records is marked as a deserter, and claimant must exonerate himself if he can from this.
Hix, David	——, Cherokee	Did not serve six months.
Holden, Job	——, Brunswick	Service as a minute man—he has specified but one month's actual service.
Holmes, John R	——, Brunswick	Fraudulent.
Howard, Henry	——, Caswell	Suspended for proof that the pay certificate of the comptroller, covering six months service, belonged to claimant.
Holland, Thomas	——, Wake	Not six months service proved in this case.
Howell, John	——, Stokes	Not entitled—not the soldier of the same name in the certificate of the comptroller of North Carolina.
Jones, Matthew	——, Robeson	Suspended for further proof and explanation.
Johnson, Jacob	——, Cumberland	Collecting provisions, butchering cattle, and salting meat not regarded as military service.
Johnston, Lewis	——, Burke	Suspended for further proof of service.
Johnson, Hardy	——, Cumberland	Suspended for deficient proof, and papers sent, May 26, 1884, to Mr. Winslow.
Joiner, Nathan	——, Nash	Awaiting the production of his original discharge—copies not admissible.

STATEMENT—Continued.

Names.	Residence.	Reasons for suspension.
Kearsey, George	—, Cumberland	Proof not satisfactory.
Kelly, Benjamin	—, Buncombe	Suspended for further proof.
Kidd, Benjamin	—, Surry	Did not serve six months.
King, Henry	—, Rockingham	For proof of identity that the certificate of depreciation for £36, for service in the Virginia continental line, was on his account.
King, James	—, Cumberland	No claim—no service—April 10, 1850, E. C. Cabell.
Knight, Moses	—, Richmond	Claims for sixteen months service in the militia—deficient in details.
Lane, William (deceased)	—, Green	Suspended for further proof.
Law, Stephen	—, Buncombe	Suspended for further proof and explanation.
Leeper, Matthew	—, Lincoln	Period, length and grade of service, and names of company and field officers and stations required.
Long, John	—, Person	Did not serve six months.
Ledford, William	—, Cleveland	For proof from the North Carolina records, and to identify him with those records.
Levan, Isaac	—, Burke	Alleges enlistment for three years under Captain Leely, Colonel Hazen's regiment—name not on the rolls.
Long James	—, Washington	Details of period, length, grade, stations and officers, all absent.
Little, Thomas, (deceased)	—, McDowell	Did not serve six months.
Little, Jacob	—, Anson	Awaiting explanation and details of his service as a minute man.
Mason, Peter	—, Macon	No such service, and no proof of any kind.
Mabley, William S	—, Rockingham	Did not serve six months.
Martin, Joseph	—, Wayne	Claim unsupported by any evidence.
McSwain, William (deceased)	—, Cleveland	For further proof, viz: of his death, and of his widow's and children's names.
Malsinger, Daniel	—, Davidson	Suspended for further proof and specification.
Matthews, Littlesbury	—, Surry	Not on the Virginia rolls—no proof nor explanation of service.
Melsaps, Thomas	—, Macon	For further explanation and character of service.
Moore, John	—, Pitt	No proof of service—he did not serve six months.

Name	County	Remarks
Miller, Martin	Rockingham	For further proof and explanation.
Moss, Gilbert	Lincoln	Did not serve six months.
Melson, William	Yancey	Privateer service.
Moody, Edward (deceased)	Ashe	Suspended until the court shall certify his death.
Murphy, James	Iredell	Awaiting the return of his original papers, and a strict compliance of the rules for specifying his service.
McIntosh, Murdoch	Moore	Making shoes for the army not regarded as military service.
Norfleet, Nathaniel	Person	For further explanation of the nature of the service.
Nash, Griffin	Stanly	No application—blank regulations for this act enclosed June 24, 1844, to Hon. E. Deberry.
Nicholston, James	Stokes	For further proof.
O'Neal, Lamentation (deceased)	Surry	For further proof and specification.
Parham, Kennon	Granville	For proof of service.
Pearson, Sterling	Chatham	No such long tours of militia—name not on the rolls of the line.
Petty, John	Chatham	For a specification of his service.
Pope, Pool Hall	Cumberland	For further proof.
Powers, Bradley	Buncombe	For further proof of identity and more perfect details of service.
Pope, Arthur (deceased), heirs of	Waldo	Six months' service allowed—widow must apply under acts July 4, 1886, or July 7, 1888, as the date of the marriage may decide.
Powers, Charles (deceased)	Columbus	Alleges service in the Maryland line—not on the rolls.
Proctor, Joseph	Granville	For proof from the archives of North Carolina.
Queary, William	Mecklenburg	Period, length, grade, stations, battles, marches, and by whom commanded, all wanting.
Quiery, John	Mecklenburg	
Rosson, John	Buncombe	For proof and explanation.
Rhodes, Jeremiah (deceased), heirs of	Wake	Period, length, grade, stations, battles, marches, and by whom commanded are required, and an inspection of the records at Raleigh.
Rodes, Peter	Henderson	Awaiting proof from the records at Raleigh.
Richardson, John (deceased), heirs of	Johnson	Awaiting proof of identity with the soldier of the North Carolina line.
Redman, Stephen	Macon	For proof from the Raleigh records.
Sawyer, William	Wilkes	No proof of service—not on any records of the line or State troops.
Shaw, John	Orange	Did not serve six months.

STATEMENT—Continued.

Names.	Residence.	Reasons for suspension.
Sams, Edmund (deceased), heirs of	——, Buncombe	For proof of his commission and service under it.
Blechfer, Henry	——, Rowan	For proof of service.
Strickland, Sampson (deceased), heirs of	——, Nash	Awaiting proof from the records at Raleigh, and of the date of his death.
Sutton, James	——, Lincoln	There was only one of the name on the rolls of the North Carolina line, and he was a deserter.
Sellers, Hardy (deceased)	——, Anson	For further proof from the Raleigh records.
Stewart, John (deceased)	——, Davidson	Awaiting additional evidence.
Stilwell, John	——, Mecklenburg	Awaiting additional evidence.
Taylor, Benjamin	——, Robeson	For proof of service from the Raleigh records.
Tharpe, Charles	——, Brunswick	Awaiting proof from the Raleigh records, and the return of his original declaration.
Van Eaton, Samuel	——, Davie	Awaiting proof from the comptroller's books at Raleigh.
Vanhorn, Abraham	——, Tyroll	For proof of identity that he was the soldier who received settlement certificates and bounty land.
Wallace, John	——, Haywood	For proof and explanation.
Warren, John	——, Orange	Proof of service not satisfactory.
West, Henry	Shelby, Cleveland	He joined the enemy—and if the vessel called the Nancy (in which he alleges service after his return,) was a public armed ship, the proof is wanting.
Webster, John (deceased), heirs of	——, Stokes	Name not being on the Virginia rolls, he is required to produce two witnesses who served with him.
Whitlow, Nicholas	——, Mecklenburg	For further proof and specification.
Wiggins, Abraham	——, Macon	Awaiting the details of his service, and proof from the North Carolina records.
Williams, James	Haw River, Orange	Did not serve six months.

Williams, John	—, Rutherford	For further proof from the rolls of North Carolina—failing them, by surviving comrades.
Williams, John	Onslow Court House	For proof of service.
Wingate, John	—, Bladen	Service only proved in part.
Winston, —	—, Franklin	Service not fully proved.
Wood, John	—, Buncombe	Service in the line as a waggoner not sustained by the rolls.
Yearly, James	—, Mecklenburg	No evidence on the rolls at Raleigh, nor in this office.

A list of the names of persons residing in North Carolina who have applied for pensions under the act of July 4, 1836, whose claims have been rejected; prepared in conformity with the resolution of the Senate of the United States, September 16, 1850.

Names.	Residence.	Reasons for rejection.
Boggs, Eve, widow of John	—, Davidson	Married after service.
Ellington, Sarah, widow of Daniel	—, Chatham	Married after service.
Mahaley, James, widow of John W	—, Stokes	A soldier of the regular army.
Mott, Rhoda, widow of Edgerton	—, New Hanover	Married after service.
Rummage, Margaret, widow of George	—, Montgomery	Married after service.
Thomas, Nancy (deceased), widow of Philip	—, Cumberland	Died before the passage of the act.
Wood, Sarah, widow of James	—, Johnson	Married after service.

A list of the names of persons residing in North Carolina who have applied for pensions under the act of July 4, 1836, whose claims have been suspended; prepared in conformity with the resolution of the Senate of the United States of September 16, 1850.

Names.	Residence.	Reasons for suspension.
Allen, Martha, widow of William............	——, Cumberland.........	Proof of service and marriage required.
Alexander, Susan, widow of John............	——, Mecklenburg.......	For proof that claimant's husband was the identical soldier credited in the certificate of the Connecticut comptroller.
Angel, Mary, widow of John............	——, Surry.........	Proof of marriage defective.
Bachelor, Frances, formerly widow of Wm. Norten.	——, Halifax.........	Married admitted. The proof of service would be, if the certificate of Captain Mebane was confirmed by one from the secretary or comptroller of North Carolina.
Baldwin, Mary, widow of Joseph............	——, Brunswick.........	For further proof and specification. Papers withdrawn.
Brown, Lucy, widow of Arthur............	——, Sampson.........	For proof of service and marriage.
Brinckley, Sarah, widow of Aaron............	——, Edgecomb.........	For proof and specification.
Bullard, Sarah, widow of James............	——, Robeson.........	For further proof.
Burk, Sally, widow of Charles............	——, Johnson.........	For further proof of identity with the record of service and of marriage.
Buck, Judah, widow of William............	——, Surry.........	Proof required to identify the soldier credited in the comptroller's certificate, with the husband of claimant.
Campbell, Euphemia, widow of John............	——, Montgomery.........	For further proof of marriage and service.
Carpenter, Surah, widow of James............	——, Wake.........	For further proof.
Chandler, Sally, widow of William............	——, Franklin.........	Proof of 18 months' service satisfactory—proof of marriage defective.
Colbreath, Martha, widow of Noel............	——, Sampson.........	For proof to identify her husband with the soldier whose name is borne on the records of the comptroller of North Carolina and of the marriage.
Copeland, Rebecca, widow of Alexander.........	——, Rutherford.........	Proof to identify claimant's husband required, with the soldier to whom the indenty from the comptroller general applies, and of marriage.
Couch, Mary, widow of Edward............	——, Orange.........	Marriage admitted—service must be sustained by the records of the comptroller general.
Cox, Elizabeth, deceased, widow of William.....	——, Moore.........	For proof of identity between claimant's husband and the soldier of the comptroller's certificate, and proof of marriage.
Danner, Catharine, deceased, widow of Frederick.	——, Surry.........	Married after service—service requires proof should she apply under the act of July 7, 1838.

STATEMENT—Continued.

Names.	Residence.	Reasons for suspension.
Early, Rachel, widow of Jeremiah	—, Surry	For proof of identity as the widow of the late pensioner.
Ector, Susanna, widow of Samuel	—, Orange	For further proof of service.
Gambill, Nancy, widow of Martin	—, Ashe	Proof of service and of marriage required.
Glasgow, Alsey, widow of Lemuel	—, Randolph	Proof of marriage not sufficient.
Grave, Mourning, deceased, widow of Philip	Pittsboro', Chatham	For proof and specification by the records of North Carolina, and proof of marriage and decease.
Gray, Elizabeth, widow of Willis	—, Johnson	For proof of the marriage and of identity of claimant's husband with the soldier of the £40 10s. 4d. certificate of the secretary of North Carolina.
Hagood, Elizabeth, widow of Jesse	Pittsboro', Chatham	Proof and specification of service and date of the marriage required.
Harris, Polly, widow of Herbert	Warrenton, Warren	For further proof.
Harris, Tabitha, widow of Robin	Warrenton, Warren	For further proof.
Harrison, Ann, widow of Joseph	—, Surry	Not a widow at the date of the act.
Hazzard, Penelope, widow of John	—, Butler	Service admitted—proof of her husband's decease and wedding day with claimant required.
Heddrick, Margaret, widow of Francis	Lexington, Davidson	For further proof of service and marriage.
Hill Sarah, widow of Joseph	—, Johnson	Proof of marriage and of service required—eighteen months' full service should be on the records of the State of North Carolina.
Ivey, Mourning, widow of John	—, Orange	Marriage admitted—some proof required of her husband's identity with the service and soldier of the comptroller's certificate.
Jackson, Jane, deceased, widow of Captain Charles Edwards.	—, Wake	Marriage admitted—proof of identity required of the soldier credited with service to the name of Edwards as claimant's husband.
Johnson, Ann, deceased, widow of Abel	—, Johnson	For proof of service and marriage.
King, Polly, widow of John	—, Franklin	Service and identity admitted—marriage in suspense.
Lashley, Amy, deceased, widow of William	—, Wake	For proof of the wedding day.
Nancy, Keziah, widow of Martin	—, Yancey	For further proof of marriage and service.

Massey, Mary, deceased, widow of John	—, Lincoln	Proof of identity that the man of the same name on the rolls of the North Carolina line was claimant's husband.
Manuel, Milley, widow of Nicholas	—, Sampson	For proof and specification of service and marriage.
Mahone, Magdalene, widow of Archelaus	—, Stokes	For specification of the details of service and proof of marriage.
McKisick, Ann, formerly widow of John Barnes	—, Haywood	Marriage admitted—proof of service deficient.
McMasters, Sarah, widow of Andrew	—, Randolph	For defective details of service.
May, Elizabeth, widow of John	—, Rockingham	Proof of service in the negative—no claim—letter, February 17, 1847, Hon. D. S. Reid.
Mullikin, Susanna T., widow of Lewis	—, Davidson	For the original license marriage bond.
Mitchell, Mary, widow of Isham	—, Wake	For further proof.
Mitchell, Rachel, widow of William	—, Bertie	For proof of marriage and service.
Martin, Jennet, widow of Samuel	—, Davidson	For want of proof of service and marriage.
Mullens, Sarah, widow of William	—, Wilkes	For further details and proof of service and marriage.
Murdock, Agnes, widow of William	—, Iredell	Not six months' service established in this case.
Murdock, Margaret, deceased, widow of James	—, Orange	For proof of marriage, deaths, and service.
Murphy, Sarah, widow of James	—, Franklin	The original marriage license bond required.
Newton. Margaret, deceased, widow of William.	—, Cleveland	Specification of the details of service is required before claimant can be benefited by the certificate of the comptroller—marriage in suspense.
O'Neill, Mary, widow of Patrick	—, Johnson	For details of service, proof of marriage, and day of decease.
Parish, Elizabeth, widow of John	—, Warren	For proof of identity with respect to the recipient of bounty land and the marriage license bond.
Pearson, Arianna, deceased, widow of George	—, Orange	He did not serve six months.
Porter, Wincey, widow of Solomon	—, Anson	For details and proof of service and marriage.
Powell, Mary, deceased, widow of Absalom	—, Columbus	Defective proof.
Powell, Ann, widow of Robert	—, Wake	Defective proof.
Prowell, Eddy, deceased, widow of John	—, Cleveland	For proof to identify claimant's husband with the soldier of the Virginia continental line credited with a depreciation certificate for £36.
Richardson, Mary, formerly widow of Elijah Bass.	—, Halifax	For proof of identity of claimant's husband with the soldier of the 10th regiment, continental line, North Carolina.
Roach, Ruth, widow of James	—, Rockingham	Further proof of the wedding day necessary.
Rogers, Rebecca, widow of John	—, Mecklenburg	For further proof of service and marriage.
Rowan, Elizabeth, widow of John	—, Warren	A specie certificate to a soldier of this name for £181 8s., and proof of identity of this soldier is wanted as the John Rowan, husband of claimant.

STATEMENT—Continued.

Names.	Residence.	Reasons for suspension.
Saunders, Lydia, deceased, widow of Philip	——, Davidson	For further proof of marriage and service.
Searcy, Sarah, widow of William	——, Chatham	For specific details and proof of service.
Sessoms, Obedience, widow of Solomon	——, Sampson	Two certificates, one for £85 specie and one for £872 currency, were paid to a soldier of the same name, and proof of identity and marriage is required.
Simpson, Mary (deceased), widow of Samuel	——, Orange	For further proof.
Smith, Milly, widow of William	——, Moore	See certificate of the Secretary of State, that Wm. Smith was a private for three years under Captain Williams of the 2d regiment of the continental line—proof of identity required.
Smith, Elizabeth, widow of John	——, Stokes	For further proof.
Summers, Ann, widow of John	——, Iredell	Period, length and grade of service, and names of company and field officers required.
Swann, Sarah (deceased) widow of John	——, Chatham	Proof of identity required that her husband was the soldier to whom the payments were made, as exhibited by the certificate of the comptroller of North Carolina.
Thomson, Susan, widow of Drewry	——, Warren	For further proof and specification.
Tyson, Sarah (deceased), widow of Henry	——, Pitt	Proof of marriage required.
Umsted, Elizabeth, widow of David	——, Orange	Not sufficient evidence to establish six months' service.
Wall, Elizabeth, widow of John	——, Davidson	For proof of service in the Maryland line.
Webb, Lucretia, widow of Jesse	——, Franklin	Six months thirteen days admitted.
Whitfield, Milly (deceased), widow of John	——, Granville	For proof of identity that claimant's husband was the John Whitfield to whom payments for military service are exhibited by the North Carolina comptroller's certificate.
Williams, Sally, formerly widow of Jesse Steed	——, Franklin	Proof of service for two and a half years as a sergeant satisfactory, and also for two years as a lieutenant. When he is identified as this claimant's husband he will be entitled to bounty land.
Wood, Sarah, widow of James	——, Johnson	Proof of identity required that her husband was the warsman she alleges, by the records of North Carolina.

Wright, Mary, widow of Thomas	—, Surry	Service admitted to allow a pension of $30 per annum, when the marriage is properly proved.
Wilson, Elizabeth, widow of William	—, Johnson	For proof of identity that her husband was the William Wilson who served under Captain Alderson in the North Carolina line.
Yeargin, Mildred, widow of John	—, Randolph	The principal difficulty is the proof of the marriage before the service had terminated.

A list of persons residing in North Carolina who have applied for pensions under the act of July 7, 1838, whose claims have been rejected; prepared in conformity with the resolution of the Senate of the United States, September 16, 1850.

Names.	Residence.	Reasons for rejection.
Browning, Francis (dec'd), widow of Robert..	—, Caswell............	She was not a widow at the date of the act.
Clark, Margaret (dec'd), widow of John......	—, Lincoln...........	She was not a widow at the date of the act.
Coleman, Keziah, widow of Theophilus......	—, Columbus.........	She was not a widow at the date of the act.
Cruse, Anna, widow of John................	—, Wake.............	Married after January 1, 1794.
Eaton, Susan, widow of Christopher	—, Stokes	Did not serve six months.
Toots, Peggy, widow of Frederick............	—, Chatham..........	Not a widow at the date of the act.
Williams, Nancy (dec'd), widow of William ..	—, Rutherford........	He died before August 28, 1842.
Williams, Delpha, widow of George.........	—, Chatham..........	Did not serve six months.

A list of persons residing in North Carolina who have applied for pensions under the act of July 7, 1838, whose claims have been suspended; prepared in conformity with the resolution of the Senate of the United States, September 16, 1850.

Names.	Residence.	Reasons for suspension.
Allen, Lucy, widow of Champin	Greenville	Did not serve six months.
Allen, Bedith, widow of Thomas	Johnson	Want of proof of duration of service.
Alexander, Martha, widow of Joseph	Guilford	Want of proof of identity with the soldier of the North Carolina certificate.
Adams, Susanna	Surry	For further proof—no papers on file.
Anthony, Elizabeth, widow of James	Surry	For more precise proof of date of marriage.
Armstrong, Jenet (dec'd), widow of Thomas	Cumberland	For proof of identity with soldier of the comptroller's certificate; also for proof of marriage and of commission as captain.
Ashley, Eleanor, widow of John	Buncombe	No proof of service.
Askins, Constante (dec'd), formerly widow of Barnaby Barxon.	Edgecomb	For proof of marriage and of husband's service, and for want of children's names.
Atkinson, Edith, widow of Amos	Johnson	For want of proof of marriage.
Baker, Bula, widow of William	Nash	For proof of identity with the soldier on the North Carolina rolls.
Barrett, Lucy, widow of Isaac	Davidson	No such pensioner as Isaac Barrett.
Barnhard, Mary, widow of Joseph	Cabanus	Want of proof of marriage.
Bass, Priscilla, widow of Joshua	Sampson	For proof of service and of marriage.
Bean, China, widow of Richard	Davidson	For proof of husband's identity with soldier of the North Carolina line, and for proof of marriage.
Bell, Jane (dec'd), widow of Thomas	Iredell	Less than six months' service established.
Billups, Sarah, widow of Thomas	Edgecombe	Want of proof of identity with soldier of same name on the North Carolina line.
Bizzell, Amy, formerly widow of Thomas Cole.	Johnson	For proof that her husband was the soldier in the line.
Boykin, Sarah, widow of Bias	Sampson	For proof of her husband's commission as captain, and service.
Bodenhammer, Agnes, widow of Peter	Davidson	For further proof of service.
Bondy, Elizabeth, widow of John	Wake	For further proof of marriage.
Bremer, Franky, widow of Jesse	Halifax	For further proof of service.
Brown, Nancy, widow of William	Richmond	For further proof of marriage.
Brown, Elizabeth, widow of Amos	Macon	Barred by act of April 20, 1844—application may be renewed under act of March 3, 1843, by the usual proof of her marriage.
Brown, Ann, widow of Richard	Bladen	Service not proved—several of the same name.

STATEMENT—Continued.

Names.	Residence.	Reasons for suspension.
Burch, Sarah, widow of Thomas	——, Wilkes	For proof that he was the soldier named in the certificate of the Comptroller of North Carolina.
Burris, Judith, widow of Solomon	——, Albemarle	For proof of service and of marriage.
Caldwell, Elizabeth (deceased), widow of John	——, Sampson	For proof of identity with the soldier of the eighth regiment.
Cathey, Margaret, widow of Alexander	——, Mecklenburg	For proof of marriage and of service.
Certain, Susanna, widow of John	——, Chatham	For proof of identity with the soldier certified by the Comptroller of North Carolina.
Church, Nancy, widow of John	——, Wilkes	For proof of marriage.
Corbett, Elizabeth, widow of John	——, Onslow	For proof of marriage.
Crain, Elizabeth, widow of William	——, Cleaveland	For proof of marriage and of service by the records of North Carolina.
Cunningham, Agnes, widow of Nathan	——, Rockingham	For further proof of service and of marriage.
Daniels, Mary, widow of Sion	——, Nash	Claim for service as dragoon and commissary, which last must be proved by his commission or other record proof.
Davis, Jane, widow of David	——, Mecklenburg	For proof of identity with the soldier in the certificate of the Comptroller of North Carolina.
Devand, Ann Julan, widow of John	Elizabethtown, Bladen	Service as lieutenant in 1777, needs proof of his commission—service in 1781 not connected with any military operation of the United States.
Devane, Helen, widow of Thomas	——, New Hanover	For proof of rank and duration of service, and of date of marriage.
Dickey, Elizabeth, widow of John	——, Iredell	For proof of rank and service in the North Carolina militia.
Earley, Rachel, widow of Jeremiah	Sloan, Surry	For proof of service from the Virginia records, and usual proof of marriage.
Easter, Barbara, widow of Michael	——, Davidson	For proof of marriage—service admitted.
Edson, Bashoba, widow of Moses	——, Johnson	For further specification.
Eccles, Jane W., widow of John	——, Orange	For proof of service.
Edwards, Sally, widow of Simon	——, Edgecombe	For proof of identity and of marriage.
Fowler, Lucy, widow of William	——, Granville	For proof of identity of husband.
Felds, Lucy, formerly widow of Isaac Wood	——, Chatham	For further evidence.

Gooch, Milly, widow of Roland	——, Wake	For proof of service.
Gray, Nancy W., widow of Thomas	——, Mecklenburg	For proof of service and of his commission.
Griffin, Cynthia, widow of John	——, Cherokee	For further evidence.
Gulley, Ann, widow of John	——, Johnson	For further proof of identity with the soldier who received certificates of pay.
Hager, Elizabeth (deceased), widow of Simon	——, Cleaveland	Not a widow June 7, 1832, and died before August 16, 1842.
Hammond, Dicy, widow of Isaac	——, Cumberland	For proof of identity with the soldier of comptroller's certificate.
Harp, Sylvia, widow of Joseph	——, Nash	For proof of husband's identity and proof of marriage.
Harris, Mary, widow of Edward	——, Orange	For proof of husband's identity with the soldier of North Carolina, in the comptroller's office of that State.
Harville, Oney, widow of William	——, Caswell	He did not serve six months.
Harris, Mima, widow of Robin Hood	——, Granville	For proof of service from the North Carolina records.
Hatmaker, Mary, widow of Malachi	——, Orange	For proof of service from the North Carolina records, and for date of marriage.
Hays, Mary, widow of John	——, Buncombe	For proof of husband's identity with the soldier who received the certificate of pay.
Henry, Mary, widow of Joseph	——, Buncombe	For further proof of service.
Hicks, Mary W., widow of Micajah	——, Wilkes	For proof of marriage.
Hill, Esther (deceased), widow of Richard	——, Johnson	For proof of marriage and of husband's identity.
Hipp, Margaret (dec'd), widow of Valentine	——, Mecklenburg	For proof of marriage.
Holland, Mary, widow of John	——, Haywood	For proof of marriage and service.
Horn, Micha, widow of Joshua	——, Orange	For proof of husband's identity with the North Carolina soldier.
Hooper, Sarah, widow of Absalom	——, Haywood	For proof of marriage.
Howell, Mary, widow of John	——, Cleveland	For further proof and specification, and evidence of husband's identity.
Humphreys, Francis, widow of William	——, Cleveland	For evidence of commission as brigade quartermaster, and for proof of his identity.
Hunter, Elizabeth, formerly widow of Captain Charles Gerrard	——, Edgecombe	For proof of marriage and of his service.
Johnston, Rebecca, widow of Moses	——, Johnson	For proof of marriage and of his service.
Jackson, Margaret, widow of David	——, Polk	For proof of marriage and of his service.
Johnson, Rhoda, widow of Drury	——, Orange	For proof of his identity with the soldier of the North Carolina comptroller's certificate.
Kerr, Margaret, widow of Nathaniel	——, Orange	For further proof of service.
Lawrence, Mary, widow of Claiborne	——, Morgan	For further proof of service.

STATEMENT—Continued.

Names.	Residence.	Reasons for suspension.
Lee, Elizabeth, widow of Owen	——, Cleveland	For proof of husband's identity with the soldier in comptroller's certificate.
Lewis, Sarah (deceased), widow of John	——, Orange	For proof of husband's identity.
Linn, Rachel (deceased), widow of John	——, Catawba	For proof of identity with the soldier of the Georgia line.
Lloyd, Hannah, widow of William	——, Orange	For proof of marriage and of husband's identity.
Martin, Wineford, widow of Obadiah	——, Surry	For proof of his commission.
Martin, Frances (dec'd), widow of Richard	——, Carwell	Not a widow at the passage of the act, and she died before the 16th August, 1842.
Massey, Elizabeth, widow of Elias	——, Anson	For more specific statement, and for record evidence from North Carolina comptroller.
McCall, Elizabeth, widow of William	——, Mecklenburg	For proof of marriage and record evidence of service.
McNeill, Isabella, widow of Daniel	——, Cumberland	For proof of his identity.
Miller, Jane, widow of John	——, Orange	For further proof.
Mitchell, Penny, widow of George	——, Johnson	For further proof of marriage.
Mitchell, Margaret, widow of James	——, Person	For further proof of marriage and of service.
Miller, Nancy, widow of David	——, Lincoln	For further proof.
Mullins, Sarah, widow of William	——, Ashe	For further proof, and return of the original declaration.
Nall, Mary, widow of Captain Nicholas	——, Moore	For proof of his commission, &c.
Owens, Elizabeth, widow of Thomas	——, Cleveland	For proof of his identity.
Patterson, Ann, widow of John	——, Irodell	For further evidence.
Patterson, Elizabeth		For further proof.
Peoney, Malinda, widow of Overton	——, Surry	For proof of marriage.
Phillip, Elizabeth (dec'd), widow of Irby	——, Rockingham	For proof of marriage.
Phipps, Jane, widow of Aaron	——, Guilford	For further specification and proof of service, and proof of marriage.
Poston, Rebecca, widow of John	——, Buncombe	For further evidence of service.
Potts, Sarah (dec'd), widow of James	——, Iredell	For further evidence of service.
Prewitt, Peaney, widow of Micajah	——, Chambers	For proof of husband's identity, and proof of marriage.

Name	County	Remarks
Prewitt, Ellender, widow of William	——, Cleveland	For proof of identity with the Virginia soldier.
Pritchell, Zeziah (dec'd), formerly widow of David Moore	——, Halifax	For further proof of marriage and service.
Rackley, Margaret, widow of Person	——, Nash	For further proof.
Reed, Elizabeth (dec'd), widow of James	——, Mecklenburg	For proof of husband's identity with soldier of the same name.
Richardson, Sarah, widow of David	——, Moore	For further proof of marriage and service.
Richards, Ann, widow of Benjamin	——, Granville	For further proof of service.
Rigsby, Elizabeth, widow of Jesse	——, Orange	Because married after 1794.
Salmons, Lucy, widow of Jacob	——, Stokes	For further proof, &c.
Spain, Jemima, widow of Thomas	——, Pitt	Not a widow at the date of the act.
Saloman, Suzan, widow of Vincent	——, Johnson	For clerk's certificate as to date of marriage, &c.
Scull, Mourning, widow of Saunders, formerly widow of Arthur Graham	——, Cumberland	For proof of service and of marriage.
Sloan, Frances (dec'd), widow of James	——, Cabarras	For further proof of marriage, death of parties, and names of children.
Smith, Sally, widow of John	——, Surry	For further proof of service.
Soots, Mary M., widow of Christian	——, Guilford	For further proof of service.
Sterling, Comfort (dec'd), widow of Seth	——, Sampson	Not a widow at the passage of the act, and died before the 16th of August, 1842.
Stevens, Barbary, widow of Charles	——, Haywood	For evidence of service from North Carolina records.
Stevens, Mary, widow of William	——, Caswell	For further proof of service.
Steward, Sarah, widow of Thomas	——, Person	For further proof.
Sullivan, Mary, widow of James	——, Lincoln	Name not on rolls of Captain Nixon's company.
Tentle, Elizabeth, widow of William	——, Henderson	For further proof.
Tagert, Nancy, widow of James	——, Mecklenburg	For proof of his commission and identity with the officer who served.
Thompson, Lurdney, widow of Charles	——, Cleveland	For further proof of marriage and service.
Tippe, Margaret, widow of Jacob	——, Burke	For further proof of *her* identity.
Twiford, Director (dec'd), widow of George	——, Guilford	Not a widow at the passage of the act, and died before the 16th of August, 1842.
Vickers, Mary, widow of Riley	——, Orange	For proof of service.
Wade, Ann, widow of Robert	——, Person	For further proof.
Wall, Molly, widow of Jesse	——, Johnson	For proof of *her* identity.
Walden, Catharine, widow of John	——, Moore	Not a widow at the passage of the act.
Walden, Elizabeth, widow of Drury	——, Northampton	Not a widow at the passage of the act, and died before the 16th of August, 1842.
Webb, Chaity, widow of John	——, Wilkes	For further proof.

STATEMENT—Continued.

Names.	Residence.	Reasons for suspension.
Ward, Lydia, widow of William	——, Davidson	For further proof.
Williams, Bidiana, widow of Stephen	——, Duplin	For further proof.
Winningham, Sarah, widow of James	——, Randolph	For further proof as to date of marriage.
Wright, Elizabeth, widow of William	——, Rockingham	For proof of his commission as a staff officer, and of his identity.
Young, Mary, widow of William	——, Stokes	For proof of marriage previous to 1794.
Zigler, Nancy, widow of Leonard	——, Stokes	For proof of marriage.

A list of the names of persons residing in South Carolina who have applied for pensions under the act of June 7, 1832, whose claims have been suspended; prepared in conformity with the resolution of the Senate of the United States, September 16, 1850.

Names.	Residence.	Reasons for suspension.
Ayres, James............	Fall's P. O., Pickens......	Alleges eighteen months service in the Virginia continental line—period, length, grade, stations, marches and names of company and field officers required.
Ayer, Darius...........	——, Marion............	Alleges six months service in the Maryland militia. He must furnish narrative of service, and give period and grade, and names of company and field officers.
Bailey, Daniel..........	——, Greenville........	Alleges twelve months as a private, and over two years as a captain in the North Carolina militia—evidence to be found in the State Department, and Comptroller's office, Raleigh.
Bolton, James..........	——, Marlborough......	Exact tour must be set forth as to time, places, officers' names, and duration of service.
Byars, Nathan..........	——, Spartanburg......	For period, length, and grade, stations, marches, and officers (field and regimental, and company), and a test by the records at Raleigh, and surviving comrades.
Burt, Moody............	——, Edgefield........	Proof of identity required that he is the same Moody Burt, to whom certificate of pay as sergeant (for £49 3s. 8d.) of infantry in the Virginia line, was issued.
Brunson, William........	——, Sumter..........	For further proof and specification.
Bonnett, George.........	——, Spartanburg......	Awaiting the return of the original declaration and the certificate of the Comptroller General of South Carolina to verify his service.
Bird, John..............	——, Union...........	For further proof and specification.
Blackman, David........	——, Marion..........	For proof of service.
Black, James...........	——, Abbeville........	Alleges seven months continuous service in a rifle company organized in Rockbridge county in 1781. If this was a militia service, and he was out but once, the tour is overrated.
Beem, Daniel...........	——, Abbeville........	Alleges eighteen months continuous service in the years 1780 and 1781, under Captain Lewis Hogg. Lewis Hogg served as a private horseman in 1780 and 1781, eight months, and as a lieutenant as late as 1782, and never was a captain of infantry or cavalry. Claimant must amend his statement.

STATEMENT—Continued.

Names.	Residence.	Reasons for suspension.
Carter, Charles	Edgefield	For proof of service by credible witnesses.
Carlisle, James	Abbeville	Awaiting the return of his original declaration which was remanded for authentication.
Campbell, Archibald	Williamsburgh	Period, length, and grade of service, names of officers, stations, marches, battles, and proof by the legislative records of the petition and documents be presented.
Clements, Clement	Lexington	For proof from the books of the Comptroller General of South Carolina.
Cole, Solomon	Laurens	Some further explanation necessary to obviate the discrepancies between his original and amended declarations.
Coffer, Joseph	Abbeville	For further proof of service.
Cornell, Francis	Lancaster	For further proof. Alleges two tours in the Virginia militia.
Copeland, Aaron	Chesterfield	For further proof.
Couch, William	Greenville	Two years service alleged, without pay, and no proof in the case.
Davis, Jesse	Greenville	He alleges only one tour in the Virginia militia, which was limited by law to three months.
Davis, Robert, (deceased), heirs of	Williamsburg	Two to three years service as trumpeter in a cavalry corps in South Carolina, under Colonel Marins and Colonel Horey. Proof of the organization of such a corps is required.
Devone, Thomas	Anderson	Awaiting the return of the original declaration and further proof.
Dye, George	Chester	For further proof, and specification.
Ellege, Abraham	Greenville	For proof of service from the records of the Comptroller General of North Carolina.
Esterling, William	Bennettsville, Marlborough	Period, length, grade, times and places, and names of officers, and his commission as captain, must be of record proof.
Floyd, Orson	Marion	Alleges two years and three months service in the North Carolina line. Name not on the army records at Raleigh. He must furnish proof by living comrades.

Fouste, Gasper	Richland	Indent, No. 444, from the Comptroller General of South Carolina, if it could be identified as claimant's, would not cover six months service.
Fowler, Samuel	Spartanburgh	For further proof from the South Carolina records.
Gilly, Francis	Pickens	For proof of service.
Golightly, David	Spartanburgh	Alleges service: 1st, pressed to drive team; 2d, a commissary at Neal's Mills; 3d, a lieutenant at the siege of Augusta; and 4th, a private at the battle of "96," in all, two years service. Proof required from the Comptroller General of South Carolina.
Goswick, Nicholas	Union	His service in the militia of North Carolina is overrated, as his name is not on the rolls in the line. Suspended for further proof.
Green, Eliaha	Greenville	For proof of additional service, as the certificate of the Comptroller General does not cover six months.
Grice, Thomas	Marion	For proof of service from the Comptroller General of South Carolina.
Griffin, Morgan, (deceased), heirs of	Richland	For description and proof of service, its period, length, grade, stations, and names of company and field officers.
Guttrig, John	Laurens	For further proof from the South Carolina records.
Hand, Robert, (deceased)	Laurens	For further proof from the Raleigh records, backed by competent witnesses.
Hanks, Epaphroditus	Sumter	Alleges five years service. Proof must be found in the archives of North Carolina at Raleigh.
Hart, Joseph	Greenville	For further proof. The indents to a soldier of the same name must be better identified as applying to him.
Harwell, Lowden	Marlborough	
Head, James	Edgefield	For proof of service under Colonel Washington.
Hill, Joshua	Abbeville	For proof from the Auditor General of South Carolina. He did not serve six months.
Hollingsworth, Elias	Pickens	The proof from the comptroller general of South Carolina does not cover six months' service.
Hudson, James	Sumter	The proof from the comptroller of North Carolina does not cover six months service.
Hutson, James	Darlington	Alleged fifteen months service in tours of three months each, but fails to specify when or where, or whom under, or what kind of service. He must amend.
Hunter, John	Chesterfield	He did not serve six months.
Jones, Josiah	Anderson	Proof required of his enlistment and service under Captain Carill.

Ex.—16

STATEMENT—Continued.

Names.	Residence.	Reasons for suspension.
King, Robert	——, Greenville	For proof of identity that he performed any part of the service covered by the certificate of the comptroller of North Carolina.
Kimbrill, Thomas	——, Spartanburg	For further proof—name not on the rolls.
Knight, John	——, Laurens	For proof of the facts and documents on which was based the pension he received from South Carolina.
Logan, William	——, York	The records of North Carolina must be examined for proof of service.
Lewis, William	Society Hill, Darlington	For further proof and specification—tours, duration, officers and places.
Lewis, William (2d)	Winnsborough, Fairfield	For further proof of services from the South Carolina records.
Loftis, Solomon	——, Greenville	For proof from the North Carolina records.
Love, Charles	Pocotaligo, Beaufort	For further details of service, and a reference to the records of the comptroller general of South Carolina.
McCall, George	——, Darlington	For proof of service from the South Carolina records.
McClelland, Archibald		Under age—suspended for further proof. [Withdrawn.]
McGarity, William	——, Chester	For further explanation.
Matthews, John	——, Edgefield	Proof from the comptroller general of South Carolina can't be found.
Mobley, Micajah (deceased) heirs of	——, Chester	Not six months' service established.
Miles, Benjamin	——, Marlborough	For proof and explanation.
Milford, Thomas	Temple of Health, Abbeville	For the facts of his case whereby he obtained a pension from South Carolina.
Moore, Henry (deceased) heirs of	——, Fairfield	Pensioned under act May 15, 1828—petitions for increase—not entitled.
McNeese, James	——, Laurens	Six months' service admitted, May 81, 1886—S. B. McNeese.
Moore, James	——, York	For a new declaration and proof by comrades—the South Carolina records.
Neese, Peter	——, Greenville	For further proof and specification—name not on the rolls of the Pennsylvania line.
Outlaw, Bentley	——, Chesterfield	For details of service and reference therewith to the books of the comptroller general of South Carolina.

Name	County	Notes
Pardue, William	Lancaster	The rolls of Georgia being very imperfect, he must find proof from some of his surviving comrades.
Prichard, William	Anderson	For a more precise account of his service, its period, length and grade, and names of officers and stations.
Porter, Philip	Pickens	Has failed to furnish evidence from the office of the comptroller general of South Carolina, which he was required to do.
Pool, William Petty	Greenville	For period, length, grade, names of company and field officers, and the evidence of his pay from the comptroller general of North Carolina.
Rall, Thomas	Lexington	For further proof of service.
Rasor, Christian	Abbeville	For further proof by comrades and the Culpeper county clerk that the designated officers were in service.
Richardson, William	Marion	One years' service in North Carolina and two years' service in South Carolina requires proof from the records of each State.
Rice, John	Marion	The department was informed that this claimant was a tory.
Robertson, Thomas (deceased), heirs of	Pickens	The service in the continental line as provod by the Secretary of North Carolina, was not claimed by applicant during his life.
Seay, Reuben (deceased) heirs of	Spartanburg	Proof of identity required that he was the artillery man of the same name marked in the depreciation certificate of the Virginia auditor.
Shaw, William	York	For period, length, grade and names of officers and stations, and proof by witnesses.
Shelby, William	Marion	For period, length and grade, and names of officers and stations.
Shumatt, Armistead	Spartanburg	For details of service and proof by survivors, and county clerk's certificate that the designated officers were in service.
Smith, Job	Pickens	For items of service as to period, length, grade and names of officers and localities.
Smith, Arthur	Sumter	Period, length, grade and names of officers and places and proof from the Secretary of State of North Carolina.
Smith, William	Beaufort	For specification of service.
Spears, Joshua	Sumter	He did not serve six months.
Stephens, Moab	Chesterfield	For each tour, period, length, grade and names of officers and places.
Stewart, Robert	Pickens	Awaiting explanation of the discrepancies between the original and the amended declaration.
Stondemier, John	Orangeburg	For period, duration, grade, nature of the service, where performed, and by whom commanded.
Tanny, Zophar	Pickens	Not on the New Jersey rolls of the warmen. He must prove his service by at least one credible witness.
Thompson, John	Chester	Not on the Virginia rolls, nor his officers—no proof of service.

STATEMENT—Continued.

Names.	Residence.	Reasons for suspension.
Wadkins, William	—, Pickens	Beginning and ending of each tour, and names of officers, company and field, and the comptroller's certificate to sustain his service.
Williams, Roger M. (deceased), heirs of	—, Edgefield	For proof of service.
Wingo, John	—, Spartanburg	For proof of service.
Wilson, James	—, Fairfield	Alleges three years service in the sixth regiment South Carolina line—records at Columbia should furnish proof.
Weed, Reuben, sr.	—, Abbeville	For further proof and specification.
Wrenn, Bates	—, Edgefield	Not on the rolls of the line, and there were no six months tours in Virginia, and no volunteers.
Young, James	—, Barnwell	Required to specify each tour with the material facts, and ascertain how far the books of the comptroller general of South Carolina verify or repudiate his services.

A list of the names of persons residing in South Carolina who have applied for pensions under the act of June 7, 1832, whose claims have been rejected; prepared in conformity with the resolution of the Senate of the United States, September 16, 1850.

Names.	Residence.	Reasons for rejection.
Ballard, Devereaux	——, Sumter	He did not serve in any regularly organized corps.
Bobo, Absalom	——, Union	He did not serve six months.
Boulton, Spencer	——, Laurens	He did not serve six months.
Bramblet, Reuben	——, Laurens	Team service.
Blakeley, James	——, Laurens	He did not serve six months.
Cartledge, Samuel	——, Edgefield	He did not serve six months.
Clark, Matthew	——, Pickens	No proof of service.
Childers, Jacob	——, York	Desertion.
Cassity, Thomas	——, Sumter	He did not serve in any regularly organized corps.
Davis, Richard	——, Anderson	He did not serve six months in person.
Dewitt, Martin	——, Darlington	He did not serve six months.
Elmore, Matthias	——, Newbury	He was a driver of a baggage wagon.
Edwards, Joseph	——, Greenville	Wagon service in the militia.
Gates, John	——, Laurens	He did not serve six months.
Gaines, Richard	——, Laurens	He did not serve in an embodied corps.
Gean, Sherrod	——, Pickens	Desertion.
Guthrie, Frederick	——, Spartanburgh	He did not serve six months.
Hairston, James	Laurens Court House, Laurens	He did not serve in any regularly organized corps.
Harper, William	——, Anderson	He did not serve in any regularly organized corps.
Hester, Charles	——, Spartanburgh	There were no artificers in the militia. Their service was civil, not military.
Keeling, Edmund	——, Abbeville	He did not serve six months.
Lifrage, William (dec'd), heirs of	——, Williamsburgh	He did not serve six months.

STATEMENT—Continued.

Names.	Residence.	Reasons for rejection.
McClain, John (dec'd), heirs of,	—, York	Died before the passage of the act.
Matthews, Hugh	—, Sumter	Express rider and wagon service.
Mayfield, Abraham	—, Greenville	He did not serve six months.
Mitchell, John	—, Edgefield	Served as a waiter, after he was made prisoner, in the British army.
McCord, John	—, Abbeville	He did not serve six months.
McBride, Hugh	—, Spartanburgh	He served as a wagoner.
Moorman, Robert	Union Court House, Union	Wagon service and express rider.
Nelson, William	—, Spartanburgh	Desertion.
Ruple, John	—, Orangeburgh	He did not serve six months.
Rosser, John	—, Marion	He did not serve six months.
Saltonstall, G. F.	—, Darlington	He did not serve six months.
Sherrill, Lewis	—, Anderson	He did not serve in any regularly organized corps.
Smith, Drury	—, Greenville	Desertion.
Stewart, James	—, Marlborough	No proof of service—rolls of the ship's crew of the Ranger silent.
Turner, John	—, Marion	He did not serve six months.
Tankersley, George	—, Greenville	He did not serve six months.
Vandevier, Edward	—, Anderson	He did not serve six months.
Wood, Henry	—, Greenville	He did not serve six months.
Woodward, Jesse	—, Sumter	He did not serve six months.
Woodward, Thomas	—, Sumter	He did not serve six months.
Wallis, John	—, York	He did not serve six months.
White, Alexander M.	—, Colleton	He did not serve six months.

A list of the names of persons residing in South Carolina who have applied for pensions under the act of July 4, 1836, whose claims have been suspended; prepared in conformity with the resolution of the Senate of the United States, September 16, 1850.

Names.	Residence.	Reasons for suspension.
Cohen, Rebecca, widow of Gershom	Charleston city	For further proof and explanation.
Coleman, Prudence, widow of Robert	Marion C. H	For further proof of service and marriage.
Crawley, Hannah, heirs of	Charleston	No claim—she died before the passage of the act.
Dominy, Margaret, deceased, widow of Andrew	—, Richland	Proof of the termination of the service, and that the marriage preceded it, is required.
Ellis, Lucy, widow of John		Rejected—not six months' service. [Papers withdrawn December 30, 1836, Hon. J. K. Griffin.]
Farrow, Rachel, deceased, widow of Landon	—, Spartanburgh	Proof required of the period of the service and the marriage prior thereto.
Forbes, Rebecca, widow of John	—, York	Proof that the marriage occurred prior to the service ending in 1782.
Hudgens, Hannah, widow of Ambrose	Charleston	For further proof and specification.
Huggins, Nancy, deceased, widow of William	Columbia, Richland	For further proof and specification.
Ingram, Ruth, widow of John	Pickens C. H	For proof of service and of the marriage prior thereto.
Jones, Rebecca, widow of Richard	—, Edgefield	Proof of the marriage not satisfactory.
Malphus, Joel B., children of		Proof of McMalthus's decease and marriage required. [Papers withdrawn May 4, 1848, R. B. Rhett.]
Martin, Joanna, widow of Joseph	—, Richland	For further proof—should make a declaration under the act of February 2, 1848.
Martin, Aley, widow of George	—, Edgefield	To procure proof from the executive records of South Carolina.
Milligan, Lucy, widow of Moses	Horry district	She must prove her present age and the day of her marriage.
Mobly, Frances, widow of William	—, Fairfield	For proof of service and of the wedding day.
McGinney, Martha, formerly widow of James Crier.	—, Georgetown	She may be entitled to the services of either husband, but not of both—she shall select and specify, and prove the marriage and the service.

[37]   296

STATEMENT—Continued.

Names.	Residence.	Reasons for suspension.
Nichols, Martha, widow of William	—, Sumter	For proof of the marriage.
Osborne, Catharine, widow of Thomas	Charleston city	For further proof.
Palmer, Mary, widow of John	Barnwell district	Proof of marriage required, and that claimant's husband was the identical soldier who is found on the South Carolina records of the line and militia service.
Pendergrass, Susan, widow of David	Chester district	Period, length and grade of service, and names of officers required, and some proof of identity of claimant's husband with the David Pendergrass mentioned in the comptroller's certificate.
Rogers, Mary Ann, widow of Lott	—, Marion	No claim—not six months' service.
Rowland, Judith, widow of David	—, Edgefield	For further proof.
Sizemore, Winney, widow of Ephraim	—, Spartanburg	Further proof of marriage required.
Smith Elizabeth, widow of Elihu	—, Spartanburg	For proof of service and of marriage.
Temple, Rachel, widow of James	—, Edgefield	Proof of the wedding day and of the service required.
Thompson, Jane, widow of George	—, Charleston	For further proof and specification.
Therrill, Lucretia, widow of Moses	—, Chesterfield	Proof of service and of the wedding day required.
Tucker, Sarah, widow of Benjamin	—, Charleston	Service on board the Argo and Pulaski, but whether public or private armed vessels claimant must prove, and also her husband's service when on board.
Weir, Jane, widow of David	—, Fairfield	Proof of service and of marriage required.
Williams, Ann, widow of Benjamin	—, Charleston	Proof of service unsatisfactory.
Wilbanks, Abarilla, widow of William	—, Union	For proof of service and of the marriage.

A list of the names of persons residing in South Carolina who have applied for pensions under the act of July 4, 1836, whose claims have been rejected; prepared in conformity with the resolution of the Senate of the United States, September 16, 1850.

Names.	Residence.	Reasons for rejection.
Howard, Captain John, deceased, heirs of	Charleston city	Died before March 4, 1831—no claim.
Mabray, Louisa, deceased, widow of Daniel	Union district	Married after the war.
Spivey, Rebecca, deceased, widow of Moses	Edgefield district	Married after the war.

A list of persons residing in South Carolina who have applied for pensions under the act of July 7, 1838, whose claims have been rejected; prepared in conformity with the resolution of the Senate of the United States, September 16, 1850.

Names.	Residence.	Reasons for rejection.
Cox, Mary, widow of Solomon	——, Edgefield	Not a widow at the date of the act.

A list of the names of persons residing in South Carolina who have applied for pensions under the act of July 7, 1838, whose claims have been suspended; prepared in conformity with the resolution of the Senate of the United States of September 16, 1850.

Names.	Residence.	Reasons for suspension.
Austin, Polly, widow of John............	——, Union............	For proof of identity with the soldier of the same name on the Virginia rolls.
Bledsoe, Sarah, widow of John...........	——, Edgefield........	Claims for eighteen months, as a Georgia ranger. The special act authorizing such a corps is wanted.
Boan, Mary, widow of Lewis.............	——, Chesterfield......	A certificate of the comptroller general is required, showing the amount of indents issued to Lewis Boan for his services: and further proof of his marriage.
Bradley, Asparia, widow of William.......	——, Greenville........	For proof of identity that he was the William Bradley who is credited with £97 9s. 5d. on the books of the Secretary of State of North Carolina.
Burns, Mary, widow of Samuel...........	——, York............	For proof from the records of the Comptroller General of South Carolina, and the date of the marriage by the usual mode of proof.
Cato, Susan, (deceased), widow of William.	——, Fairfield.........	Indent for one hundred and thirty-four days only, which is insufficient.
Cochran, Susan, widow of Benjamin.......	——, Abbeville........	Did not serve six months.
Dean, Tabitha, widow of Joshua..........	——, Edgefield........	For proof of identity that he was the soldier of the Virginia line of the same name.
Dener, Christiana, widow of George.......	Charleston city......	Claims for eighteen months service as a lieutenant, previous to the fall of Charleston. Documentary proof of his commission is required.
Dispain, Lucy, widow of Benjamin........	——, Pickens.........	For proof of service by the books of the Comptroller of North Carolina.
Foster, Sydney, widow of John...........	——, Spartanburg.....	For proof of identity that he was the person referred to on one or other of the auditor's certificates of soldiers of the same name.

STATEMENT—Continued.

Names.	Residence.	Reasons for suspension.
Freeman, Frances, widow of John.	—, Pickens.	For proof of his commission as lieutenant, and of identity with the John Freeman who is credited on the comptroller's books.
Kennedy, Cherry, (deceased), widow of John.	—, Sumpter.	For proof of service from the records at Raleigh.
Langley, Lacy, widow of William.	—, Kershaw.	For further proof.
Legare, Mary, widow of Isaac.	—, Charleston.	For further proof and specification.
Leach, Martha, widow of Joseph.	—, York.	For further proof.
McKissick, Rachel, formerly widow of John Morris.	—, Union.	For proof of service.
Odom, Elizabeth, widow of Daniel.	—, Barnwell.	For proof of service from the books of the Comptroller General of South Carolina, and the original leaf from the family record of marriage.
Phillips, Martha, widow of Eleazar.	—, Charleston.	Suspended for further proof.
Pratt, Amelia, widow of William.	—, York.	For proof of service and of marriage.
Reid, Ann, (deceased), widow of George.	—, Charleston.	Died before the passage of the act.
Reese, Anna, widow of George.	—, Pickens.	Service admitted, and original record of marriage required.
Sadler Eliza, (deceased), widow of John.	—, York.	Proof of identity deficient that her husband was the same person by whom were issued several indents as an officer and soldier to the Comptroller General of South Carolina.
Sanders, Elizabeth, widow of John.	—, Pickens.	For proof of identity that her husband is entitled to any portion of the specie certificates which were issued to soldiers of the same name for £89 6s.
Smith, Margaret, widow of Thomas.	—, Williamsburg.	For proof of service and marriage.
Snoddy, Elizabeth, widow of Samuel.	—, Spantanburg.	For further proof and specification.

Tucker, Nancy, widow of John	——, Spartanburg	For further proof.
Vandiver, Catharine, widow of Edward	——, Anderson	Further proof of service required.
Weatherall, Elizabeth, (deceased), widow of John	——, Abbeville	For further proof.
Young, Vina, widow of James	——, Anderson	Service admitted—proof of marriage deficient.

A list of the names of persons residing in Georgia who have applied for pensions under the act of June 7, 1832, whose claims have been rejected; prepared in conformity with the resolution of the Senate of the United States, September 16, 1850.

Names.	Residence.	Reasons for rejection.
Allgood, John	——, Monroe, Walton	Did not serve six months.
Anderson, James	——, Houston	No proof of service.
Awtry, Absalom	——, Henry	Did not serve six months in person.
Beaty, Thomas	——, Henry	Did not serve six months.
Banks, Drury	——, Coweta	Did not serve six months in person.
Baker, Demsey	——, Marion	Was a deserter.
Baley, Stephen	——, Monroe	Did not serve six months.
Brown, John	——, Pike	Did not serve six months in person.
Cook, Theodosius	——, Henry	Did not serve six months.
Cash, Peter	——, Henry	Did not serve six months in person.
Cotton, George	——, Warren	Did not serve six months.
Coleman, Samuel, 2d	——, Merriwether	Did not serve six months.
Cassel, Ephraim	——, Campbell	Did not serve six months.
Carter, Silas	——, Washington	Did not serve six months in person.
Daniel, Frederick	——, Pike	Did not serve six months.
Dawson, James	——, Rabun	Did not serve six months.
Dout, John	Warren Court House	Was a deserter.
Denmand, John	Elberton, Elbert	Did not serve six months.
Davis, Joseph	——, Muscogee	Service after the war.
Davie, Joseph	——, Muscogee	Did not serve six months.
Ester, Lyddal	——, Troup	Did not serve six months.
Everett, John	——, Bullock	Did not serve six months.
Farriss, William	——, Rabun	Did not serve six months in person.
Findall, James	——, Burke	Served only three months.
Flournoy, James	——, Talbot	Did not serve six months.

Green, Drewry	—, Gwinnett	Was a deserter.
Griver, John M. (deceased)	—, Bullock	Died before the passage of the act.
Gardner, Christopher	—, Gwinnett	Was a deserter.
Garland, Henry, sen	—, Upson	Was a deserter.
Hodges, Joseph	—, Bullock	Died before the passage of the act.
Hammon, John	—, Hall	Did not serve six months.
Higgs, John	—, Montgomery	Did not serve six months.
Jenkins, Lewis	—, Washington	No proof of service.
Jones, Matthew	—, Putnam	Did not serve six months.
Jordan, William	—, Newton	Did not serve six months.
Kitchens, Zachary	—, Henry	Did not serve six months.
Lewis, George	Perry Mills, Tatnall	No proof of service.
Leavealy, Thomas	—, Coweta	Was a deserter.
Lokey, William	—, De Kalb	Privateer service.
Mize, Shepherd	—, Newton	Did not serve six months.
Newsom, John	—, Warren	Did not serve six months.
Nevis, William	—, Early	Did not serve six months.
Olive, Joseph, son of John (deceased)	—, Bullock	Died before the passage of the act.
Orr, Daniel	—, Pike	Did not serve six months, except in making pork barrels.
Parker, Daniel	—, Upson	Was a deserter.
Perry, Willis	—, Muscogee	Three months' military service and three months' blacksmith.
Pool, Henry, sen		Did not serve six months. [Papers sent to J. M. Wayne, March 25, 1834.]
Quillin, James	Clarksville, Habersham	Did not serve six months in person.
Riley, William	—, Henry	Did not serve six months.
Sandige, Claiborne	Elberton, Elbert	Did not serve six months.
Sleigh, John	St. Mary's, Camden	Did not serve six months.
Snow, Mark	—, Gwinnett	Not military service.
Spalding, Henry	—, Columbia	Not military service.

STATEMENT—Continued.

Names.	Residence.	Reasons for rejection.
Smith, Robert	——, Oglethorpe	Not military service.
Stewart, John	Jackson, Butts	Did not serve six months.
Trammell, William	——, Elbert	Did not serve six months.
Truit, Purnal	Washington, Wilkes	Was a deserter.
Teel, Lodrick	——, Harris	Did not serve six months.
Thurmond, John	——, Coweta	Did not serve six months.
Town, Henry	——, Burke	Did not serve six months.
Town, James	Danielsville, Madison	Did not serve six months.
Turner, Reuben	——, Burke	Did not serve six months.
Tally, Elisha	——, Heard	Did not serve six months.
Wright, Solomon	Clinton, Jones	Did not serve six months.
Walden, Alexander	——, Coweta	Did not serve six months.
Watson, Thomas	Lawrenceville, Gwinnett	Did not serve six months.
Whorton, John	Lawrenceville, Gwinnett	Not military service.

305   [37]

A list of the names of persons residing in Georgia who have applied for pensions under the act of June 7, 1832, whose claims have been suspended; prepared in conformity with the resolution of the Senate of the United States of September 16, 1850.

Names.	Residence.	Reasons for suspension.
Agee, Joshua	Lincolnton, Lincoln	For further proof of service.
Anderson, Francis	——, Hawkins	The North Carolina rolls being silent, his service requires the testimony of two witnesses.
Andress, David	——, Fayette	Military service four months—Driving beef cattle three months—not entitled.
Armstrong, Alexander	Sandersville, Washington	For proof of service.
Asre, Jonathan	——, Troup	For proof and explanation.
Banckston, Elijah	——, Butts	For proof and explanation.
Banckston, Thomas	——, Randolph	Narrative does not accord with the known history of the service.
Barber, John	——, Carroll	No proof of service.
Barnes, John	——, Lumpkin	Claim not acted upon—no declaration—papers incomplete.
Bird, Thomas	——, Murray	For proof from the Comptroller of North Carolina.
Bouin, John	——, Jefferson	For further proof and explanation.
Brooks, George		Papers delivered to G. D. Anderson December 22, 1836—suspended for want of proof.
Bushley, Isaac	——, Madison	For proof of service from the Comptroller General of South Carolina.
Blackburn, Nathan	——, Wilkes	For further proof and the return of the original declaration.
Brooks, William	Lagrange, Troup	For a more perfect expose of his case according to the forms of the office.
Blandford, Clark	——, Early	Not on the New Jersey rolls in this office.
Boggs, Jeremiah	——, Newton	For proof of six months service as a commissioned officer.
Boyles, Charles	——, Telfair	Not on the South Carolina rolls—he was a waiter.
Brown, Joseph	Gainesville, Hall	For further proof from the books of the comptroller general of South Carolina.
Brooks, Micajah	Van Wert, Paulding	For period, length and grade of service, and names of company and field officers, and a report from the records of the State under whose authority he served.
Burkholt, Peter	——, Wilkinson	For proof from the books of the comptroller general of South Carolina.

STATEMENT—Continued.

Names.	Residence.	Reasons for suspension.
Brown, James	—, Clarke	Alleges nineteen months service in the Georgia line, but the rolls are silent.
Camp, Edward		No papers on file—claim not acted upon—July 27, 1841, Hon. R. W. Habersham.
Carithers, Robert (deceased), heirs of	—, Madison	For proof of service from the South Carolina records.
Crabb, Asa	—, Decatur, Henry	Proof unsatisfactory.
Chapman, Israel	—, Muscogee	For further proof.
Coleman, Samuel	—, Meriwether	For further proof of service.
Cox, William	—, Habersham	More proof of identity required with the soldier of the same name on the records of North Carolina.
Collins, Solomon	—, Lincoln	For further proof and specification.
Collins, Joseph	—, Upson	If he served as a captain from 1777 in the Georgia militia, the archives of that State must afford some evidence.
Cooper, Richard	—, Bullock	For further proof and specification.
Culbreath, James	—, Pike	Eight months service admitted—service subsequent to 1780 not specified.
Culpeper, Malachi	—, Coweta	For further proof.
Davis, Surrey	—, Murray	For period, length and grade of service, and names of company and field officers, and also the Indents of pay from Comptroller General of South Carolina.
Dampler, Daniel	—, Effingham	Warrant No. 2069 bounty land claim was granted to Daniel Dampler, a sergeant in the continental line of Georgia. Claimant is required to trace the disposition of this land to identify him as once owner.
Dupree, Jeremiah	—, Houston	For further proof and explanation.
Dennis, Josiah	—, Morgan	Did not serve six months.
Denton, John	—, Hancock	His name is on the rolls in this office as a private of infantry, but not in the identical corps he specifies.
Dover, Francis J	—, Habersham	Name not on either of the rolls of the Carolinas.
Dunn, Alexander	Forsyth, Monroe	Eighteen months service alleged—the rolls being silent indicate a militia service, and it requires specification into tours, and the usual proof.

Edge, John	Halcyondale, Bullock	There are rolls of the yearsmen of '81 at Raleigh, and if claimant was one his name must be there.
Etheredge, Joel	Knoxville, Crawford	For further proof—papers returned for authentication.
Ellet, Zachariah	Stowart	Alleges three years in the North Carolina line—name not on the rolls.
Edwards, Joseph	Carnesville, Franklin	For a more perfect narrative and detail of service.
Elton, Anthony	——, Jackson	No proof of service.
Evans, John	——, Jackson	For proof of service.
Ferrell, Micajah (deceased), heirs of		There is no formal application in this case.
Goff, John	——, Telfair	Fraudulent.
Green, William	——, Jasper	Militia service overrated—further explanation awaited.
George, Joseph	Lawrenceville, Gwinnett	Proof of service required by competent witnesses.
Gugal, David	Springfield, Effingham	For proof and explanation, and details of the tours of actual service.
Gurgains, David	Macon, Bibb	For proof of service by comrades, and of his pay by the Comptroller General of North Carolina.
Garrett, Robert	——, Madison	For deficient proof—original papers enclosed to Mr. Sanders April 12, 1833, and have not been since replaced.
Hackney, Robert	——, Wilkes	Alleges eighteen months service in the Virginia line—not on the rolls—other proofs required.
Handy, Nathaniel	——, Elbert	Claims for three years service in Connecticut line—rolls are silent, and he has not provided further proof.
Harper, William	——, Pike	He did not serve in any regularly organized corps.
Halsier, John	——, Fayette	For further proof, and awaiting the return of the original declaration.
Hawthorn, John	——, Twiggs	No proof from the Secretary of State's letter, and militia service was not continuous for so long a period.
Henderson, Architbald	——, Henry	Contradictory and absurd statement—a sheer fabrication.
Higgins, Henry (deceased)	Clarksville, Habersham	For deficient proof.
Hogg, Samuel (deceased), heirs of	——, Greene	Proof of identity of claimant with a soldier of the same name on the South Carolina rolls not complete.
Hicks, Henry	——, Rabun	Not on the rolls in this office—referred to the records at Richmond.
Hickman, John	Forsyth, Monroe	For further proof and explanation.
Helton, Peter		For deficient proof, and papers sent to Hon. H. A. Haralson, April 24, 1850.
Helton, Abraham (deceased), heirs of	——, Lumpkin	Not on the rolls—no proof of service.
Heard, John G.	——, Walton	For further proof and specification.
Hayman, Henry	——, Irwin	Three sets of declarations—two withdrawn—must be returned before any further action can be had.
Higdon, Daniel	——, Muscogee	For further specification, and a reference to the South Carolina records.

STATEMENT—Continued.

Names.	Residence.	Reasons for suspension.
Holman, Jacob	—, Richmond	Claims for six years service, and he is referred to the South Carolina records for proof.
Hughes, James	—, De Kalb	He has not established as much as six months' service.
Inlo, Thomas	—, Walton	Not on the rolls—no proof of service.
Jackson, Ephraim	—, Carroll	No satisfactory proof of service.
Joyner, Benjamin	Griffin, Pike	For further proof and specification.
Jordan, Charles (dec'd), widow of	Greenville, Meriwether	For further proof. [Papers enclosed to W. B. Ector, November 3, 1836.]
Jeto, Dudly	—, De Kalb	Not on the rolls—no proof of service.
Jones, David (dec'd), heirs of	Greenville, Meriwether	For the aid of witnesses who can specify the service.
Junior, Anthony	—, Jasper	Name not on the rolls—no proof of service.
Kinnard, John	—, Jasper	For proof of service from the comptroller general of South Carolina.
Kendrick, Abel	Gainesville, Hall	For further explanation.
Kemp, William (dec'd), heirs of	—, Decatur	Not properly set forth—not sustained by any proof.
Low, Lot	—, Stewart	For further proof.
Leo, Andrew	Carnesville, Franklin	He did not serve six months in any regularly embodied corps.
Loggins, John, sen	Gainesville, Hall	Narrative very imperfect. His papers afford no basis but conjecture for any computation of service.
Matthews, Philip	—, Crawford	Service proved by records of South Carolina—156 days not enough.
Martin, James	—, Franklin	He did not serve six months.
Matthews, John	—, Lincoln	Not on any rolls—no proof of service.
Meltz, Frederick	—, Washington	Not on the rolls—no proof of service.
Merryman, William	Carrollton, Carroll	He did not serve except in a local militia for neighborhood purposes.
Miles, Thomas	Milledgeville, Baldwin	All further proceedings suspended until the return of the original declaration.
Mooney, John	Gainesville, Hall	For further statements and formal papers to declare this claim.
McClure, John	—, Rabun	For proof of service for his eighteen months' each in the States of Virginia and Pennsylvania, by reference to the several State records.

McCollum, Daniel	Clarksville, Habersham	For further proof and specification.
McElheny, William	——, Jasper	Not intelligibly set forth—no precise length of service.
McKnight, Nathan (dec'd)	Lawrenceville, Gwinnett	Date of claimant's decease, and name of widow; if no widow, the childrens' names must be certified.
Moore, James	———	For further proof. [Papers returned to Lot Warren, December 21, 1842, for authentication.]
McCrosky, John	Hollingsworth, Habersham	For proof of his commission as lieutenant, and service under it.
Nelson, Thomas	Zebulon, Pike	For proof by the books of the comptroller general of South Carolina.
Nichols, Julius	——, Franklin	For proof of service. Collecting cattle under the commissary's orders not considered military service.
Oates, Richard Wyatt	Americus, Sumter	For proof of service by competent witnesses.
Odorn, Archibald	——, Pulaski	He was a deserter.
Oliver, John	Salem, Clarke	No proof of service.
Owen, John	Greensborough, Greene	For further proof.
Peacock, Archibald	Sandersville, Washington	For proof from the records at Raleigh.
Perkins, John	——, Stewart	For proof of service. Alleges twenty-three and a half months.
Pickard, Thomas	——, Talbot	For explanation and proof.
Pierce, Hugh	Clarksville, Habersham	For further proof.
Prealy, John	——, Henry	Eight months' service admitted. An answer awaited if he accepts.
Prince, John	Clarksville, Habersham	He did not serve six months.
Rogers, Zachariah	——, Washington	Not on the rolls—no proof of service.
Sapp, William	——, Randolph	Period, length and grade of service, and names of company and field officers.
Sanders, James	——, Madison	Comptroller's certificate covers four years' service. Claimant only joined the army in 1780.
Sheppard, William	——, Upson	Evidence and explanation required.
Sillery, John	——, Troupe	For further proof and specification.
Simmons, James	——, Jones	Awaiting the return of the original papers, remanded for correction 22d May, 1883.
Simmons, William J	——, Talbot	For further proof.
Smith, Lawrence	——, Muscogee	For further proof and explanation.
Smith, Joy	——, Tattnall	Awaiting better evidence and more satisfactory details.
Smith, John, 2d	——, Henry	For further proof and specification.
Smith, Hardy	——, Laurens	$20 per annum, for six months' service, offered in letter to Daniel McNeill, October 3, 1833.

STATEMENT—Continued.

Names.	Residence.	Reasons for suspension.
Snider, Christian	——, Henry	For further proof.
Spence, Nathan	Lawrenceville, Gwinnett	For specification and proof of service.
Starrett, James	——, Habersham	For further proof and specification.
Stevenson, John	——, Murray	Working at his original trade as a blacksmith, while in the army, not considered military service.
Stewart, Charles	——, Monroe	For additional evidence.
Swan, Jonathan	Lawrenceville, Gwinnett	For further proof and specification.
Taylor, Benjamin	——, Scriven	For additional evidence.
Taylor, Theophilus	——, Habersham	Alleges eighteen months' service. The proof must be procured from the records at Raleigh.
Terrell, Richmond	——, Newton	For further proof and specification.
Thomas, Absalom	——, Burke	For further proof of service.
Thornton, Samuel	Holmesville, Appling	He has failed to specify his service.
Thompson, William	——, McMinn	Claims three years' continuous service in South Carolina. Proof from the books of the comptroller general of South Carolina is required.
Thomason, William (dec'd)	——, Washington	He did not serve six months.
Thompson, Seth	——, Meriwether	No proof of service. He does not specify six months' service.
Trammell, Peter	Lincolnton, Lincoln	Not on the rolls—no proof of service.
Vanadore, Henry	——, Dooly	For proof of service from the comptroller general of South Carolina.
Vasser, Micajah	——, Laurens	For further proof and explanation.
Vickey, Hezekiah	Waynesborough, Burke	For further proof.
Wayne, George	——, Henry	He says his name was entered on the rolls as George Williams.
Watts, George	——, De Kalb	For further proof and specification.
Whately, Daniel	——, Macon	For further proof and specification.
Whitlock, James	——, De Kalb	For further proof.
White, William (deceased), heirs of	——, Walker	For proof of identity with the soldier of the South Carolina indents.
Willis (or Mills), George, (deceased) heirs of	——, Liberty	For further specification and details of actual service.
Wilson, James	Gainesville, Franklin	For further and better description of service.
Wilson, William	——, Jackson	For proof of identity that he was the soldier named in the certificate of the comptroller general of South Carolina.

Wilson, John...............	——, Warren............	No proof or favourable circumstance of service.
Williams, Samuel (deceased) heirs of........	——, Bullock...........	Service not properly set forth—lacks proof—wants authenticating.
Williams, John.............	——, Forsyth...........	No such service—not on the rolls—not under proper authority.
Williams, John.............	——, Habersham........	For further proof.
Williams, Nathan...........	——, Hall..............	For proof from the Raleigh records.
Washington, Richard........	——, Cherokee.........	For proof from the books of the comptroller general of South Carolina.
Willis, George.............	——, Dooly............	For proof of identity with the soldier of the same name on the Raleigh records.
Wright, John...............	Monticello, Jasper......	For further proof and specification.
York, William..............	....	Service not properly set forth—papers enclosed June 5, 1888, Thomas, chairman Committee on Revolutionary Pensions, U. S. Senate.

A list of the names of persons residing in Georgia who have applied for pensions under the act of July 4, 1836, whose claims have been rejected; prepared in conformity with the resolution of the Senate of the United States, September 16, 1850.

Names.	Residence.	Reasons for rejection.
Ball, Elizabeth, widow of Ambrose	——, Pike	He did not serve six months.
Epposon, Mary, widow of Thompson	——, Franklin	Married after service.
Tiller, Muscogee, formerly widow of Captain Charles M. Kiser (deceased)	——, Early	A soldier of the regular army.

A list of the names of persons residing in Georgia who have applied for pensions under the act of July 4, 1836, whose claims have been suspended; prepared in conformity with the resolution of the Senate of the United States of September 16, 1850.

Names.	Residence.	Reasons for suspension.
Boring, Phebe, widow of Isaac	——, Jackson	Further proof of service and of marriage required.
Bowen, Rachel, widow of Stephen	Jacksonville, Telfair	For proof of marriage and the genuineness of the signature of the clerk of Telfair county.
Bowers, Sally, widow of William	——, Paulding	Proof of identity with the soldier of the North Carolina rolls, and of marriage.
Bryant, Patience, widow of William	——, Gwinnet	Proof of identity as the former widow of the soldier of the North Carolina line.
Bullock, Mary, widow of Daniel	——, Bibb	Proof of service and marriage required.
Carson, Mary, widow of Walter	Athens, Clark	If her husband was a pensioner, the roll of the agency where he was paid should be given, and proof of marriage.
Cleveland, Catharine (deceased), widow of Captain John	——, Habersham	Proof of commission and marriage required.
Crawford, Rebecca, widow of John	——, Pike	Two declarations filed, and claimant avers she made but one. Papers sent to Howell Cobb, January 7, 1847, to have the facts investigated.
Edmonson, Mary, widow of William	——, Talbot	Proof of identity required with the soldier credited with £30 6s. in the certificate of the comptroller of North Carolina.
Everett, Sarah, widow of John	——, Bullock	Proof and specification of service required, and day of marriage.
Evans, Susan M., widow of George W.	——, Clark	Not six months service performed in this case.
Haygood, Mary, widow of Benjamin	——, Monroe	No evidence of six months service.
Hobbs, Margaret, widow of Jonathan	Crossville, Lumpkin	Proof of service and marriage defective.
Lane, Elizabeth, widow of Davis	Forsyth, Monroe	Supposed fraud.
Martin, Ann, widow of Benjamin	——, Hall	For proof of service.
McCrary, Mary, widow of John	——, Lowndes	For further proof and explanation.

STATEMENT—Continued.

Names.	Residence.	Reasons for suspension.
Nunnelly, Margaret, formerly widow of Miles Gibson	—, Wilkes	Proof of service and marriage defective.
Pearce, Sarah (deceased), widow of John	—, Lumpkin	Proof of identity required with the soldier of the Maryland line, and of marriage.
Philips, Sarah, widow of John	—, Ogelthorpe	Proof of identity required and service of her husband as a soldier in the North Carolina line.
Ray, Mary, widow of John	—, Wilkes	Further proof and specification of service required, and proof of marriage.
Ronton, Jane, widow of John	—, Fayette	For proof of service.
Sealy, Sarah, widow of Samuel	—, Talbot	For further proof of service.
Smith, Sally (2d) widow of Thomas	—, Morgan	For further proof of service.
Smith, Sally (1st) widow of Henry	—, Pike	Evidence of identity with the soldier to whom the several indents were issued by the State of South Carolina.
Strozier, Margaret, widow of Peter	—, Merriwether	Proof of service and of the prior marriage required.
Stroud, Hannah, widow of Sherrod	—, Cobb	For proof of service and marriage
Tate, Mary, widow of James	—, Jasper	For further proof.
Ward, Charity, widow of Henry	—, Madison	For proof and explanation.
Wolf, Mary, formerly widow of John F. Tarver	—, Jefferson	For further proof.

A list of the names of persons residing in Georgia, who have applied for pensions under the act of July 7, 1838, whose claims have been rejected; prepared in conformity with the resolution of the Senate of the United States of September 16, 1850.

Names.	Residence.	Reasons for rejection.
Carr, Elizabeth, deceased, widow of William, heirs of	Gainesville, Hall	Husband died in 1835, widow in 1839—no claim.
Fleming, Martha, widow of Robert	——, Franklin	Not a widow at the passage of the act.
Fuller, Bethany, widow of Meshac	——, Warren	Married after January 1, 1794.
Smith, Polly, deceased, widow of John	——, Clark	Was not a widow at the passage of the act, and she died before August 28, 1842.

A list of the names of persons residing in Georgia who have applied for pensions under the act of July 7, 1838, whose claims have been suspended; prepared in conformity with the resolution of the Senate of the United States, September 16, 1850.

Names.	Residence.	Reasons for suspension.
Andrew, Mary O., widow of John	——, Newton	For specification and proof of captain's commission and service.
Barron, Obediena, widow of Thomas	——, Jackson	Original family record required for proof of marriage.
Bently, Mary Scott, widow of Jesse	Monroe, Walton	For further proof and specification.
Cash, Lucy, widow of John	——, Pike	For further proof of marriage.
Cavinder, Margaret, widow of William	——, Lumpkin	For proof of identity with the soldier of the same name credited on the comptroller's books.
Cox, Elizabeth, widow of Moses	——, Washington	Service admitted under joint resolution of July 1, 1848—proof of marriage deficient.
Damaron, Polly, widow of Charles	——, Jackson	Papers withdrawn to place before Congress, and special act passed March 8, 1849.
Davidson, Sarah, widow of Joseph	——, Pike	For proof of marriage.
Dishon, Elizabeth, widow of Lewis	——, Gwinnett	For proof of service by the comptroller of North Carolina.
Edwards, Frances, widow of John	——, Jackson	For details of service, period, length and grade, and names of officers, and whether militia or continental.
Elliott, Mary, widow of Arthur	——, Habersham	No narrative of service and no proof.
Fain, Mary, deceased, widow of John	——, Gilmer	For proof by the comptroller of North Carolina.
Freeman, Catharine, widow of John	Athens, Clark	For proof of service. [Papers withdrawn January 7, 1847, H. Cobb.]
Gilbert, Nancy, widow of Benjamin	——, Putnam	For further proof of service and marriage.
Harris, Martha, widow of Edward	——, Greene	Not six months' service established.
Holbrook, Drusilla, widow of Caleb	——, Gwinnett	He did not serve six months.
Jordan, Winefred, widow of John	——, Washington	For proof of identity with the soldier of the same name of Harrison's artillery.

317 [37]

Name	County	Remarks
Kephela, Polly, widow of Christopher	—, Gwinnett	For further proof.
Keith, Jane, widow of John	—, Walton	Awaiting explanation of an attempt at fraud by altering a family register.
Kiker, Elizabeth, widow of George	Cassville, Cass	Not a widow at the date of the act.
Lavender, Lucy, widow of Charles	—, Jackson	For proof of identity with the private of infantry of the continental line who received a certificate of depreciation for £51 18. 2d.
Levert, Mary G., widow of Thomas	Monroe, Walton	For proof of service by the Georgia records.
Matthews, Sarah, widow of Jeremiah	—, Gwinnett	For further evidence of service and marriage.
Maroney, Martha, widow of Philip	—, Walker	For proof of service from the Annapolis records.
McKee, Mary, formerly widow of Abraham Alexander	—, Chatham	For proof of marriage and of service from the Raleigh records.
Murphy, Rutha, formerly widow of John Huddgins	—, Walker	Proof of his service as captain in the North Carolina militia required from the North Carolina records.
Nunnelly, Margaret, widow of Israel	—, Wilkes	Period, length and grade of service, and names of company and field officers required.
Pool, Catharine, widow of William	—, Pike	All action on this case was postponed until the agent, J. H. Kilgore, should explain the apparent fraud in Jane Keith's case. (See above.)
Queen, Disc, widow of Samuel	Blairsville, Union	For proof of service and marriage.
Rowe, Chloe, widow of John	—, Harris	For proof and explanation.
Shields, Susanna, widow of Littleberry	—, Jackson	For proof of service.
Shaw, Mary, widow of John	—, Oglethorpe	For a new declaration and the date of the marriage.
Sosebee, Elizabeth, widow of Job	—, Habersham	For proof of service and identity from the North Carolina records.
Stevenson, Jane, widow of David	—, Anderson	For further proof and specification.
Stewart, Mourning, widow of General John	Lexington, Oglethorpe	Period, length and grade of service, and names of company and field officers required.
Thompson, Sarah, widow of John	—, Walton	For further proof and specification.
Thrower, Sarah, widow of Benjamin	—, Walton	Not six months' service proved.
Walker, Sarah, widow of William	—, Oglethorpe	For further proof.
West, Nancy, widow of Benjamin	—, Hall	Barred by act of April 30, 1844.
Wilson, Phebe, widow of James	—, Clark	He did not serve six months.
Williams, Rebecca, widow of Thomas	—, Carroll	For additional evidence.
Wootten, Susanna, widow of Thomas	—, De Balf	For proof of service by the records of Georgia or by surviving comrades.

A list of the names of persons residing in Alabama who have applied for pensions under the act of June 7, 1832, whose claims have been rejected; prepared in conformity with the resolution of the Senate of the United States, September 16, 1850.

Names.	Residence.	Reasons for rejection.
Aitchley, Abraham	——, Jackson	He did not serve six months during the revolutionary war.
Austill, Malone	——, Jackson	Served after the war of the revolution.
Allen, Ananias	——, Jackson	He did not serve six months.
Albritton, Matthew	——, Wilcox	Desertion.
Busby, John	——, Jackson	He did not serve six months.
Carrall, Dennis	——, Shelby	He did not serve in any regularly organized corps.
Cavett, Richard	Huntsville, Madison	Not military service.
Campbell, Walter	Montgomery, Montgomery	He did not personally serve six months.
Cox, John	Clarkesville, Clark	He did not serve six months.
Dailey, Owen	Monroeville, Monroe	He did not serve six months.
Duncan, John	Larkin's Fort, Jackson	He did not serve six months.
Fulton, Thomas	——	He did not serve by order of competent authority. [Papers withdrawn.]
Farley, Obadiah	——, Shelby	He did not serve six months.
Gullet, Reece, sen.	——, Franklin	He did not serve six months.
Gowen, Frederick	——, Lawrence	He did not serve in a military capacity.
Gurley, Isham	——, Pickens	He did not serve six months.
Gibson, Samuel	——, Marengo	Served as a wagoner in the State service.
Grandy, Brinckley	——, Butler	He was a soldier only three months.
Hamilton, Thomas	——, Lowndes	Not six months' service.
Huff, James	——, Perry	Only three months' service.
Hill, Benjamin	——, Greene	Only three months' service.
Holmes, James	——, Perry	Only three months' service.
Jones, Reuben	Tuscaloosa	He did not serve six months as a soldier.

Name	Location	Remarks
Jones, Henry	——, Barbour	He did not serve six months.
Kenny, William	——, Morgan	Under age.
King, Parks	——, Fayette	He did not serve six months.
Kelly, Andrew	Cahaba, Dallas	Not military service.
Lawler, Jacob	——, Walker	He did not serve under military organization.
Mullens, William	Tuscumbia, Franklin	Not military service.
Massey, Alston	——, Monroe	He did not serve six months.
May, Thomas	Fayette Court House	Not military service.
Miller, Jacob	——, Lauderdale	Service after revolution.
Matthews, John	——, Sumter	Service less than six months.
Morrison, William	——, Dallas	He did not serve six months.
McCorkle, James	——, Warren	He did not serve six months.
Murray, Jack	——, Pike	Service after 1783.
McCollom, John	Blountsville, Blount	Died before the passage of the act.
McMasters, William (deceased)	——, Macon	Desertion.
Nelson, Edward	Blountsville, Blount	
Pearce, James	——, Jackson	He did not serve six months.
Pesnell, John	——, Benton	Not under military organization.
Pipkin, Stephen	——, Conecuh	He did not serve six months.
Quintin, Cornelius	——, Shelby	He did not serve six months.
Rikard, John	——, Monroe	He did not serve six months.
Biggs, James	——, Fayette	He did not serve six months.
Sanders, William	Elyton, Jefferson	He did not serve six months.
Summers, John	Bellefonte, Jackson	He did not serve six months.
Summers, John	Bellefonte, Jackson	Not military service—not revolutionary service.
Sullivan, Larkin	Huntsville, Madison	He did not serve six months.
Shepperd, Andrew	Greenville, Butler	He did not serve personally six months.
Thomas, John	Washington, Autauga	Not military service.
Tedderton, John	Clarkesville, Clark	Desertion.

STATEMENT—Continued.

Names.	Residence.	Reasons for rejection.
Thornton, Josiah (deceased)		He did not serve six months. [Papers withdrawn.]
Vaughan, Abner	——, Jackson	Wagon service and express riding.
Whedden, Noah	Greenville, Butler	He did not serve six months in person.

A list of the names of persons residing in Alabama who have applied for pensions under the act of June 7, 1832, whose claims have been suspended; prepared in conformity with the resolution of the Senate of the United States of 16th of September, 1850.

Names.	Residence.	Reasons for suspension.
Ashton, Alexander	Moulton C. H., Lawrence	For a full and complete account of each tour of actual service, and that Alexander was regularly commissioned; and direct proof must be exhibited in each case.
Ashton, James	Cortlandt, Lawrence	
Baker, Elisha, (deceased), heirs of	——, Blount	Alleged service in the North Carolina line—not verified by the records in this office.
Butts, Seth	——, Autauga	Alleged service in the Virginia line—not verified by the rolls—other proof required.
Bayley, Richard	——, Lawrence	Alleged service of eighteen months in the Virginia line—not verified by the rolls. Proof by two witnesses required.
Beasley, Cornelius	Demopolis, Marengo	Did not serve six months.
Benge, Obadiah	——, DeKalb	As militia service it is overrated. If he served in the line, the records at Raleigh should afford proof.
Blaky, William	——, Barbour	He has not given so full and particular a statement of his tours of service as the regulations require.
Blankinship, Daniel	Columbiana, Shelby	For proof of identity as the soldier of the Virginia line bearing his name.
Bonhart, Rudolph	——, Marshall	Period, length and grade of service, and names of officers, (field and company,) and the result of an inspection of the same by the North Carolina Comptroller General.
Brasher, John	Fayetteville, Fayette	For further proof and explanation.
Brewer, Isaac	——, Talladega	For more correct specification and further proof from the Raleigh records.
Buckalew, John	——, Marengo	For further proof of service.
Breckan, William	——, Dale	His case does not bear any marks of action pro or con.
Buchanan, William	Fayette C. H., Fayette	Not on the rolls of the service designated. Further proof awaited.
Capers, Jim, (colored)	——, Pike	For proof of service from the South Carolina records.

Ex.—17

STATEMENT—Continued.

Names.	Residence.	Reasons for suspension.
Colly, William	——, Tallapoosa	He enlisted for the war, but it does not appear that he fulfilled his term completely.
Craven, John	——, Dale	For proof and specification.
Connell, Thomas	Independence, Autauga	For further proof, the rolls being silent.
Day, Edward	Cahaba, Dallas	For a more full and particular statement of his service, and answers to the usual interrogatories.
Deese, Joel	Stockton, Baldwin	Name of captain, colonel and regiment wanted. Alleges four years continuous service, which could alone have occurred in the regular continental army.
Dixson, Jeremiah	Montezuma, Covington	His alleged service in the North Carolina line must be confirmed by the records at Raleigh.
Duncan, John	——, Jackson	For proof of service from the South Carolina records.
Files, Jeremiah	——, Walker	Papers sent for amendment, May 1, 1833, to P. D. Clark, Huntsville, and should be returned to the office. [David Hubbard, April 13, 1850.]
Fergason, James	Rockford, Coosa	For proof by certificate of the Secretary or Comptroller of North Carolina, or by surviving comrades.
Gilliam, Jourdan	——, Jackson	Not on the rolls of Virginia enlisted soldiers, and militia service must be set forth with more detail.
Gilly, Francis	——, Walker	For further proof and more precise specification.
Harrison, William	——, Dale	For proof of service.
Hawkins, Thomas	——, Conecuh	For proof of identity that he was the soldier who served in Brandon's regiment to whom the indent from South Carolina was issued for £65 11s. 6d. sterling.
Hollis, William	Lowndesboro', Lowndes	Militia service in South Carolina requires more precise specification.
Hawsey, John	——, Lauderdale	For further proof of service.

Hooper, Obadiah..........	—, Pickens..............	Militia service overrated. His two alleged tours for six months each in 1778 and 1781, cannot be allowed.
Ingram, Samuel...........	—, Montgomery..........	For specification for each tour and proof from the North Carolina records.
Ivey, Adam...............	—, Montgomery..........	For proof of service.
Jordon, William...........	—, Randolph............	For proof of service from the Raleigh records.
Jeffers, Samuel............	—, Morgan..............	Original declaration sent to M. M. McKenzie for correction, April 22, 1832, which has never been replaced.
Low, Ralph...............	Marion, Perry...........	Pay of a private to be allowed upon the return of the papers properly authenticated.
McDaniel, John............	—, Jefferson.............	The rolls being silent, proof of service by two witnesses required.
McFerrin, Archibald.......	—, Walker...............	Names of company and field officers, and the extent and character of the service must be set forth, and sustained by the South Carolina records.
Moody, Thomas............	Suggsville, Clark........	For proof of his commission as captain. Service in 1780 was with a wagon and team.
Meacham. Richard R.......	—, Perry................	For proof of his commission as captain, and service as one—the records at Raleigh must be consulted. He should specify more correctly each tour of actual service.
Miles, Benjamin............	Elyton, Jefferson........	Militia and minute-man's service overrated.
Murcer, James.............	—, Talledega............	The duration and details of the actual service required, and an exhibit of the same made for verification, by the Comptroller General of South Carolina.
Payne, Moses..............	Blountville, Blount......	For further proof from the Raleigh records, and a more satisfactory explanation.
Petty, Theophilus..........	—, Butler................	Examined twice, and returned for specification and proof in January, 1834, without success. The alleged service may be sustained by the books of the Auditor General of South Carolina.
Riley, John................	—, Franklin.............	For further proof from the Comptroller General of South Carolina.
Robuck, John..............	—, Marion...............	For further proof and specification and reference to the records of South Carolina.

STATEMENT—Continued.

Names.	Residence.	Reasons for suspension.
Byas, William, (deceased)	—, Morgan	The widow should apply, or if no widow, the children. Not over $20 per annum for six months service can be allowed in this case up to the death of Mr. Byas. [Feb. 8, 1886, Hon. R. Chapman.]
Rumbley, John	Centreville, Monroe	For specification of each tour of actual service, and proof according to the enclosed printed instructions.
Skipper, James (dec'd)	Williamstown, Barbour	Militia service in North Carolina overrated. Papers informal.
Smith, Bryant	—, Marshall	He has not established as much as six months' service.
Sterling, Silas C.	—, Blount	The service must be sustained by the books of the comptroller general of South Carolina.
Tarrant, James, sen., (dec'd), heirs of	Jonesborough, Jefferson	For additional evidence of actual service.
Tharp, Robert	Russellville, Franklin	For additional proof of service.
Thompson, William	—, Conecuh	For proof from the South Carolina records.
Thomas, William	Greenville, Butler	For explanation why he claimed but one year's service in his original declaration, and one year and six months' in his amended declaration.
Tipton, John	Redhill, Marshall	For further proof of service. By comptroller's certificate.
Townsend, John	—, Coosa	For further proof of service. The records at Raleigh must be inspected.
Townsend, Samuel	—, Coosa	For further proof from the Raleigh records.
Watford, Joseph	—, Dale	For proof from the records at Raleigh.
Williams, Thomas	—, De Kalb	For proof from the South Carolina records.
Wright, John	—, Montgomery	Service getting out timber for gun carriages not regarded as military service, and his other tours were under six months.
West, Thomas	—, Limestone	Proof insufficient. [Papers returned to J. L. Martin, January 6, 1837.]
Walker, Matthias	—, Wilcox	Militia service in South Carolina must be specified more strictly, and compared with the State records.

Wilson, William		Suspended for insufficient proof, and papers returned to R. Chapman, March 4, 1886.
Wilson, James	—, Sumter	Militia service from June, 1780, to October, 1782, could not have been continuous, and he must, specify each tour, however short, date, duration, officers' stations and grade.

A list of the names of persons residing in Alabama who have applied for pensions under the act of July 4, 1836, whose claims have been rejected; prepared in conformity with the resolution of the Senate of the United States, September 16, 1850.

Names.	Residence.	Reasons for rejection.
Sutton, Nancy, widow of Jacob	——, Walker	Married after the termination of the war.

A list of persons residing in Alabama who have applied for pensions under the act of July 4, 1836, whose claims have been suspended; prepared in conformity with the resolution of the Senate of the United States, September 16, 1850.

Names.	Residence.	Reasons for suspension.
Covington, Susannah, widow of John	——, Lowndes	For further proof of marriage and of service, by the books of the comptroller general of South Carolina.
Hughes, Sarah, widow of William	——, Shelby	A new declaration and proof of marriage required under act of July 7, 1838.
Pope, Mary, widow of Isaac B.	——, Clark	For additional proof of service and marriage.
Smith, Celia, widow of William	——, Tallapoosa	For additional proof of service and marriage.
Thompson, Martha, formerly widow of Francis Holly	——, Morgan	Two husbands, and married to the last after the war.
Wallace, Rebecca, widow of Thomas	——, Morgan	His grade as a commissioned officer must be proved by his commission or other documentary proof, and the service by the certificate of the comptroller of North Carolina.

A list of the names of persons residing in Alabama who have applied for pensions under the act of July 7, 1888, whose claims have been rejected; prepared in conformity with the resolution of the Senate of the United States, September 16, 1850.

Names.	Residence.	Reasons for rejection.
Hooper, Sarah, widow of Obadiah............	——, Pickens	Married after January 1, 1794.

A list of the names of persons residing in Alabama who have applied for pensions under the act of July 7, 1838, whose claims have been suspended; prepared in conformity with the resolution of the Senate of the United States, September 16, 1850.

Names.	Residence.	Reasons for suspension.
Campbell, Jane, widow of William	——, Jackson	For proof of service.
Dobson, Averilla	——	For proof of service, and a new declaration according to the printed instructions. [Papers returned for correction.]
Elmore, Patsey, widow of Thomas	——, Limestone	For proof of identity that one of the Thomas Elmore's, in the Virginia line, who served for the war, was her husband—date of the marriage requires proof.
Hart, Martha, widow of Henry	——, Greene	For proof of marriage and of service by the South Carolina records.
Merril, Elizabeth, widow of Charles	——, Marshall	For period, length, grade, stations, names of company and field officers, and a more positive proof of the date of the marriage.
Oakes, Rebecca, widow of John	——, Pike	For further proof of marriage and service.
Poe, Mary, widow of Stephen	——, Benton	For a more specific detail of the service and more perfect proof of marriage.
Ponder, Violet (deceased), widow of Amos	——, Lawrence	Some proof of identity required, that the certificate of the Comptroller General of South Carolina, covering twenty-one months twenty-seven days service, as a private, belonged to claimant's husband.
Randolph, Lydia, widow of Abraham	——, Walker	Service admitted—proof of marriage insufficient.
Turner, Nancy, widow of Lewis	——, Shelby	For proof of service by the books of the Comptroller General of South Carolina, and more perfect proof of the date of the marriage.
Thompson, Elizabeth, widow of Nicholas	——, Morgan	Service for twelve months admitted—proof of the date of marriage must be improved.

A list of the names of persons residing in Mississippi who have applied for pensions under the act of June 7, 1832, whose claims have been rejected; prepared in conformity with the resolution of the Senate of the United States of September 16, 1850.

Names.	Residence.	Reasons for rejection.
Bateman, Thomas	——, Greene	He did not serve six months.
Burney, David	——, Lawrence	Not under competent military authority and organization.
Briggs, John	Westville, Simpson	No revolutionary service.
Burrell, Cato	——, Jefferson	He did not serve six months.
Dillon, Cato	——, Jefferson	Privateer service excepting three months.
Harbinson, George	——, Perry	Not six months' service.
Harper, Lewis L.	Liberty, Amite	Only three months' service.
Knight, William	Lexington, Holmes	He did not serve six months.
Loftin, Ezekiel	Monticello, Lawrence	Only four months' service.
Mullhs, Clement	——, Copiah	He did not serve six months.
Roberts, John	Columbus, Lowndes	He did not serve six months.
Sumrall, Moses	——, Clark	No proof of service.
Vickory, Sampson	——, Yalabusha	He did not serve six months.

A list of the names of persons residing in Mississippi who have applied for pensions under the act of June 7, 1832, whose claims have been suspended; prepared in conformity with the resolution of the Senate of the United States of September 16, 1850.

Names.	Residence.	Reasons for suspension.
Allen, Arthur	——, Wayne	No proof of service—circular sent December 23, 1837.
Bozeman, John	Columbia, Marion	He has not established six months' service.
Clark, James	——, Monroe	For proof of identity with the soldier of the certificate of the Comptroller General of South Carolina.
Garter, Jacob	——, Marion	For further proof and specification.
Davis, Robert	Quitman, Clark	For further proof and specification.
Fudge, Solomon	——, Tallahatchie	For further proof from the South Carolina records.
Goff, William, sen.	——, Jackson	Required to produce his commission—service as a beef driver or guarding tories not military service.
Gray, William	Jacinto, Tishomingo	For proof from the South Carolina records.
Hawey, Joel	Westville, Simpson	For specification of each tour of militia service.
Kindrick, John	Athens, Monroe	For further details of service.
Lucas, William	——, Simpson	For further proof and specification.
M'Cain, Hance	——, Fayette	For further proof from the South Carolina records.
Miles, Hardy	——, Rankin	For further proof from the South Carolina records.
M'Williams, James	Columbus, Lowndes	For further proof and specification.
Perkins, Lewis	Liberty, Amite	For further proof from the South Carolina records.

STATEMENT—Continued.

Names.	Residence.	Reasons for suspension.
Rogers, Wilson	Jacinto, Tishemingo	For further proof from the North Carolina records.
Ross, Jesse	Ripley, Tippah	For proof from the Comptroller of North Carolina.
Shipp, Richard	—, Holmes	For further proof.
Stroud, William	—, Hinds	For further proof and specification.
Weathersby, Lewis	—, Amite	Not six months' service, except in patrolling, carrying expresses, and guarding against tories.

A list of the names of persons residing in Mississippi who have applied for pensions under the act of July 4, 1836, whose claims have been rejected; prepared in conformity with the resolution of the Senate of the United States of September 16, 1850.

Names.	Residence.	Reasons for rejection.
Null, Catharine, formerly widow of Jno. Myers	——, Leake	Service not under military authority or organization.
Whittington, Mary, widow of Richard	——, Amite	Married after the limit of the law, in 1798.

A list of the names of persons residing in Mississippi who have applied for pensions under the act of July 7, 1838, whose claims have been suspended; prepared in conformity with the resolution of the Senate of the United States, September 16, 1850.

Names.	Residence.	Reasons for suspension.
Gideon, Elizabeth, widow of Richard	——, Monroe	Not any proof of service.
Gilkee, Elizabeth, widow of Samuel	——, Winston	For proof of identity with the soldier bearing the same name in Brandon's regiment, and for proof of marriage.
Kelly, Jane, widow of Jacob	——, Jasper	For further specification of service—period, length, grade, locality and names of company and field officers.
McKee, Fanny, widow of Daniel	——, Marshall	For a more perfect form of declaration, and adequate proof of marriage and service.
Rester, Louisa, widow of Frederick	——, Harrison	Proof of marriage imperfect.
Taber, Susannah, widow of William	——, Winston	Proof of marriage imperfect.
Twiner, Judith, widow of John	——, Claiborne	For further proof of marriage.
Walker, Mary, widow of Thomas	——, Lafayette	For further proof of service and marriage.
Webb, Sophia, widow of Robert	——, Marshall	For further proof of service and marriage.

A list of the names of persons residing in Louisiana who have applied for pensions under the act of June 7, 1832, whose claims have been rejected; prepared in conformity with the resolution of the Senate of the United States of September 16, 1850.

Names.	Residence.	Reasons for rejection.
Ferguson, John	Monroe, Wachita	He did not serve six months.
Phillis, Jacob	——, St. Helena	He did not serve in any regularly organized corps.

A list of the names of persons residing in Louisiana who have applied for pensions under the act of June 7, 1832, whose claims have been suspended; prepared in conformity with the resolution of the Senate of the United States, September 16, 1850.

Names.	Residence.	Reasons for suspension.
Collins, James P.	East Feliciana, third district	Six months service only allowed—he has not specified his minute-man's service.
Dollarhide, John	Manny, Sabine	Proof of service required from the Raleigh records.
Graham, Jeremiah	Monroe, Wachita	For further proof and specification, and papers enclosed to S. W. Madox Monroe.
Iles, William	Greenwood, Caddo	For proof of service.
Lynch, Stephen	——, Rapides	For proof of his commission and service as an officer in the Pennsylvania line.
Biggs, Abraham	Franklin, St. Mary's	For further proof and specification.
Swinney, Jesse	Clinton, East Feliciana	For proof by two witnesses, who must specify date, duration, grade, locality and officers.
Thompson, Drewry	——, Claiborne	No military service performed in this case.
Yocum, Jesse	——, Natchitoches	For a specification of his several tours and further proof of service.
Zachary, William	Montpelier, St. Helena	For proof of service and grade from the South Carolina records.

A list of persons residing in Ohio who have applied for pensions under the act of June 7, 1832, whose claims have been rejected; prepared in conformity with the resolution of the Senate of the United States, September 16, 1850.

Names.	Residence.	Reasons for rejection.
Agard, John	——, Portage	He did not serve six months.
Alford, Elijah (deceased)	Windham, Portage	Died before the passage of the act.
Anderson, William	Milton, Richland	He only served two months.
Arnott, Samuel	Mansfield, Richland	His whole service was either as waiter or wagoner.
Arnold, Jacob	Wayne, Montgomery	He did not serve six months.
Bayles, David	Urbana, Champaign	He did not serve six months.
Boyer, John	——, Hamilton	Fraudulent.
Brill, Michael	——, Muskingum	He did not serve six months.
Belden, David	Farmington, Trumbull	He did not serve six months.
Bowen, George	——, Jackson	Service after the revolution.
Buffenmeyers, Henry	Perry, Wayne	Not military service.
Beebe, William	Chester, Knox	He did not serve six months.
Beard, Christopher	Porry, Franklin	Not military service.
Burnham, Jedediah	Kinsman, Trumbull	Not six months service.
Beard, William	——, Belmont	Not military service.
Bennet, Jacob	Harlem, Delaware	He did not serve in any regularly organized corps.
Buck, Charles	——, Gallia	Only four months service.
Burton, John	Cambridge, Guernsey	Not six months service.
Buckingham, Thomas	Norwalk, Huron	Not six months service.
Beem, Jacob	——, Hancock	Not six months service.
Beaty, Francis	Painesville, Geauga	Served with the French army.
Beniger, George	Green, Fayette	Only four months service.
Black, John	——, Highland	Not military service.
Blew, Frederick	——, Wayne	Not six months service.
Campbell, Samuel	——, Gallia	Not military service.
Corns, Josoph	Marlow, Washington	Alleges two years service in Bond's regiment—no such service was performed by Bond.
Crow, Elias	Youngstown, Trumbull	Desertion.
Cole, Esekiel	Salem, Jefferson	Not six months service.
Chapman, James	——, Scioto	Not six months service.

STATEMENT—Continued.

Names.	Residence.	Reasons for rejection.
Cotrell, James	——, Pike	Not under military authority.
Colson, John	Troy, Geauga	Not military service.
Corson, Robert (deceased)	Franklin, Harrison	Not six months' service.
Childs, Isaac	Waterford, Washington	Desertion.
Cowles, Noah	Geneva, Ashtabula	Not six months' service.
Canady, Meredith	Brush Creek, Scioto	Not six months' service.
Cowdery, William	Kirtland, Geauga	Not military service.
Cole, Samuel	German, Harrison	Not six months' service.
Dayhoof, George P.	Columbiana, Columbiana	Only two months' service.
Devee, Isaac	——, Hamilton	Service after the revolution.
Doud, Samuel	Howland, Trumbull	Deserter.
Davis, Nathaniel	Copley, Medina	Not six months' service.
Darst, Peter	Troy, Delaware	Not six months' service.
Denny, Walter	——, Preble	Not six months' service.
Dine, John	Madison, Butler	Desertion.
Dennis, James	Cincinnati, Hamilton	Not six months' service.
Dean, Noble	——, Columbiana	Not six months' service.
Dalrymple, John	——, Preble	Not six months' service.
Dodge, Nathaniel	Waterford, Washington	Not six months' service.
Dickson, Joseph	Newark, Licking	Service after the revolution.
Dennard, Joshua	Saline, Columbiana	Not six months' service.
Douglass, David	Greenville, Darke	Not six months' service.
Eaton, Samuel	Monroe, Ashtabula	Not six months' service.
Elliott, Samuel	Springfield, Portage	Not six months' service.
Eakin, William	——, Knox	Not military service.
Ellis, Jeremiah	——, Brown	Not under military organization.
Enochs, Enoch	——, Monroe	Not military service during the revolution.
Ellzey, Thomas	Walnut, Pickaway	Not six months' service.
Ford, Morgan	——, Clermont	Not six months' service.
Fowler, Jonathan	Painesville, Lake	Not six months' service.

Ford, John Morrison	Westfield, Delaware	Not six months' service.
Frey, John	Mount Pleasant, Jefferson	He did not serve in the revolution.
Fensternacker, John	Lower Sandusky, Sandusky	Not six months' service.
Folkner, Abraham	Steubenville, Jefferson	Privateer service.
Fouts, David	Morgan, Morgan	Service after the revolution.
Foote, John	——, Warren	Not six months' service.
Flora, Abijah	Twin Township, Ross	Not six months' service.
Francis, John	——, Ross	Not six months' service.
Fisher, Zachariah	Palmyra, Portage	Not military service.
Glasgow, Robert	——, Adams	Not six months' service.
Goodwin, Daniel T.	Auburn, Geauga	Service after the revolution.
Gregory, Samuel	——, Butler	Not six months' service.
Gates, John	Chillicothe, Ross	No adequate proof of service.
Goble, Caleb	Sydney, Shelby	No proof of service.
Gale, Jonathan	Elyria, Loraine	Not six months' service.
Gunn, Elisha	Toledo, Lucas	Not six months' service.
House, Andrew	Jefferson, Knox	Not under military organization.
Holcomb, James	Jefferson, Knox	Not six months' service.
Huntly, Daniel	New Lyme, Ashtabula	Not six months' service.
Harmon, Joseph	Painsville, Lake	Not six months' service.
Herbert, Thomas	Circleville, Pickaway	Not six months' service.
Harden, Samuel	——, Butler	Not six months' service.
House, John	——, Carroll	Not six months' service.
Hamile, Ebenezer	——, Preble	Not six months' service.
Hitchcock, Isaac	——, Perry	Privateer service.
Huston, Daniel	New Lisbon, Columbiana	Not six months' service.
Hites, John	Hardy, Logan	Belonged to the French army.
Hanks, Thomas	Belle Fontaine, Logan	Not six months' service.
Irwin, Francis	Middleburg, Somerset	Not six months' service.
Irwin, John	——, Clermont	Not six months' service.
Jackson, Charles	Chillicothe, Ross	Not military service.
Koon, Philip	——, Washington	Only three months' soldier.
Kemp, John	McKean, Licking	Not six months' service.
Kress, John	Belle Fontaine, Logan	Fabulous. Papers purporting to be discharges spurious.
Kelster, Peter	Dayton, Montgomery	Not under military authority.

STATEMENT—Continued.

Names.	Residence.	Reasons for rejection.
Kirgan, Joseph	——, Athens	Service in Indian wars after the revolution.
Kinian, Edward (deceased)	Batavia, Clermont	Not six months' service.
Loech, Thomas	——, Coshocton	Indian wars after the revolution.
Loomis, Uriah	Springfield, Clark	Not six months' service.
Lyons, Barnabas	Warren, Trumbull	Not six months' service.
Manly, Jesse	——, Fairfield	Only three months' service.
McPherson, James	Coshocton, Coshocton	Indian wars after the revolution.
Moore, James	——, Brown	Not military service.
Miller, John	Lodi, Athens	Desertion.
Morris, David	Washington, Carroll	Only four months' service.
Moe, Jacob	Troy, Miami	Under age.
McJutty, Samuel	Conneaut, Ashtabula	Served only three months.
Moore, John (deceased)	Hillsboro', Highland	Indian wars after the revolution.
Miller, Benjamin	Chillicothe, Ross	Died before the passage of the act.
Miller, George	Wooster, Wayne	Only three months service.
Miller, George	——, Monroe	Not under military organization.
Miller, Henry	Woodsfield, Monroe	Served after the revolution.
McCormick, John	——, Butler	Under age.
McDaniel, William	——, Richland	Not six months' service.
McMahon, Robert	——, Clinton	Not six months' service.
McCormick, John	——, Ross	Not military service.
McHenry, Isaac	Winchester, Adams	Not six months' service during the revolution.
McDougal Joseph	Kalida, Putnam	Indian wars on the frontiers.
Maxey, Horatio	Portsmouth, Scioto	Not six months' service.
Markham, Daniel	Xenia, Green	Not six months' service.
Manly, Jesse	Green Township, Summit	Not six months' service.
	York tp., Athens	Not six months' service.
Norris, Andrew	Cincinnati, Hamilton	Not six months' service.
Newlin, William	Buffalo, Guernsey	Not six months' service.
Norris, Richard	Georgetown, Brown	Indian wars. Frontier service not under military organization.

Orr, Thomas	Cincinnati, Hamilton	Not under military organization.
Owens, John	Coleraine, Ross	No such service—no such officers.
Oyster, John	Jefferson, Richland	Not six months' service.
Pennell, Hugh	—, Jefferson	Not six months' service.
Peck, Isaac	Parma, Cuyahoga	Not six months' service.
Pierce, James	Worthington, Richland	Not a revolutionary soldier for six months' service.
Pool, John F.	Canton, Starke	Not military service.
Philips, William	Franklin, Columbiana	Not six months' service.
Parker, Asahel	—, Ashtabula	Not six months' service of a military character.
Porter, James	Woodsfield, Monroe	Not military service.
Palmer, Daniel	Cincinnati, Hamilton	Desertion.
Puckett, William	—, Highland	Only two months' service.
Reed, Talcott	Sherman, Huron	Team service.
Read, David	Adams, Washington	Not military service.
Rhiner, alias Ryan, Rhyne, George	Springfield, Gallia	Not six months' service.
Rickels, William	Cincinnati, Hamilton	Not six months' service.
Rigg, Eleazer	Lebanon, Warren	Not six months' service.
Rowe, John	Lyme, Huron	Privateer service.
Ross, Robert	Stokes, Madison	Not six months' revolutionary service.
Radaback, Nicholas	Pleasant, Fairfield	Not six months' service.
Roddy, Ezekiel	—, Brown	Not six months' service.
Robins, John	—, Ross	Not military service in the revolution.
Rathbun, Jonathan C.	Clermont, Clermont	Privateer service.
Robbins, John	—, Ross	Not a soldier of the revolution.
Smith, Noah	Palmyra, Portage	Not six months' service.
Sharp, Spencer	—, Washington	Only three months' service.
Smith, Hazaliah	Sheffield, Ashtabula	Privateer service, excepting two months.
Swauger, Abraham	East Union, Wayne	Not six months' service.
Strader, George	—, Preble	Desertion.
Simpson, James	—, Butler	Not six months' service.
Scott, Joseph	—, Franklin	Service after the revolution.
Souther, Valentine	St. Clairsville, Jefferson	Desertion.
Smith, David E.	Steubenville, Jefferson	Not six months' service.
Stevens, Joseph	—, Adams	Not six months' service.
Stogel, James	—, Brown	Not six months' service.
Short, John	Ohio tp., Clermont	Not six months' service.
Sprague, Timothy	—, Clermont	Not six months' service.

STATEMENT—Continued.

Names.	Residence.	Reasons for rejection.
Sprott, Thomas	Clear Creek, Richland	Indian wars after the revolution.
Sayre, David	—, Preble	Desertion.
Satterly, Samuel	—, Geauga	Privateer service.
Smith, Lorentz	New Lisbon, Columbiana	A soldier of the French army.
Sheffer, Philip	Ashland, Richland	Not military service.
Snyder, Peter	—, Highland	No proof of service.
Sarfin, Joel	—, Gallia	Not under military authority.
Satterfield, John	—, Pike	Not six months' service.
Snider, John	Salem, Shelby	Not six months' service.
Shaden, Robert	—, Montgomery	He presents discharges evidently spurious.
Spencer, John	—, Warren	Not under military organization.
Stevens, Moses	—, Washington	Not six months' service.
Scott, John	Perry tp., Wayne	Not under military organization.
Starrs, Josiah	Charlestown, Portage	Not six months.
Struther, John	Cortsville, Trumbull	Service in desultory Indian wars.
Summer, William A	Westminster, Middlesex county, district London, Province of Upper Canada	
Smith, John	—, Ross	Not six months' service. Desertion.
Tignor, Thomas	Richwood, Union	Not military service for six months.
Thompson, Thomas	Centre, Columbiana	No character—no claim.
Thompson, Thomas	—, Hamilton	Fraudulent.
Terry, Julius	Townsend, Sandusky	Not six months' service.
Thompson, James	Bloomfield, Richland	Not in any embodied corps.
Thrall, Jesse	Burlington, Licking	Not military service—a waiter.
Thompson, John	—, Athens	Not six months' service.
Tufts, William	Parkman, Geauga	No adequate proof of service.
Tylee, David	Brooklyn, Cuyahoga	No adequate proof of service.
Tinker, Silas	Ashtabula, Ashtabula	Not six months' service.
Vanacker, George H	Bellefontaine, Logan	Not six months' service.
Vantilbury, Henry	—, Jefferson	Not six months' service.

Warner, Joseph	—, Madison	No adequate proof of service.
Ware, Robert	Richland, Belmont	Not six months' service.
Weager, John	Coply, Summit	Not six months' service.
Whips, Benjamin	—, Perry	Not six months' service.
Wallace, Isaac H	Brown Helm, Lorain	Not six months' service.
Worley, David	Mill Creek, Union	Desertion.
West, Clement	Chester, Wayne	Not six months' service.
White, Samuel	Hartland, Huron	Not military service.
Winegardner, Joseph	—, Darke	A soldier of the French army.
Woodruff, Cornelius	—, Union	Not six months' service.
Wooly, Asa	Atwater, Portage	Not military service.
Ware, Frederick	—, Ross	Not military service.
Wright, Simeon, (late of Pittsford, Rutland county, Vermont)	—, Licking	Not six months' service.
Wetherell, David	Kirtland, Geauga	Not six months' service.
Wallace, Aaron	—, Hamilton	Desertion.
Wise, Christian	—, Coshocton	Service after the revolution.

A list of the names of persons residing in Ohio who have applied for pensions under the act of June 7, 1832, whose claims have been suspended; prepared in conformity with the resolution of the Senate of the United States of September 16, 1850.

Names.	Residence.	Reasons for suspension.
Ackerson, Abraham	Wesley, Washington	For further proof and specification.
Andrew, James	——, Jackson	For further proof and specification.
Adams, John	Twin tp., Ross	For further proof and specification.
Applegate, Henry	Delhi, Hamilton	For further proof of service.
Allen, John	Delaware, Delaware	For further proof.
Andrews, Adam	——, Butler	Team service.
Arnott, Christian	Milan, Huron	For further proof and specification.
Auten, Thomas	——, Hamilton	For further proof of service.
Baker, Henry	Portsmouth, Scioto	For further proof and explanation.
Bailoy, Silas	Perry, Lake	For proof of service.
Barker, Phinehas	Denmark, Ashtabula	For more explicit details of service and reference to the records at Hartford.
Bebee, Thomas	——, Clermont	Wagon service in the New Jersey militia, and militia service proper, require proof.
Berry, James	Cincinnati, Hamilton	For further proof of service.
Bezzard, alias Bescard, John	Spencer, Medina	For more precise details of his tours of service in the New Jersey militia.
Bloomer, Abraham	Cincinnati city	For proof from the New York records.
Bell, Thomas	Putney, Belmont	For further proof and explanation.
Brooks, John	——, Huron	His age, as set forth in his present application, does not tally with his application when he received an invalid pension.
Brush, Eli	Monroe, Delaware	For further proof from the Hartford records.
Buck, John	——, Butler	For further proof.
Burgoon, Robert	——, Morgan	For further proof and specification.
Burt, Calvin	Rome, Athens	Team service in part, and his other service should be sustained by the New York comptroller's records.
Carter, Benjamin	Porter, Delaware	No proof of service.
Callahan, James	Adams, Guernsey	Not on the rolls—no proof of service.
Cappy, John	——, Montgomery	Not six months' service.

Name	Location	Remarks
Chamberlin, Jonathan	——, Washington	For further proof and specification.
Carmichael, John	——, Monroe	For want of proof.
Cherry, Reuben	Peru, Huron	Under age—suspended for want of proof.
Coke, Jacob	——, Trumbull	Claims as a lieutenant, but furnishes no proof of such grade—six months may be allowed as private.
Conover, John	Cincinnati city	For further proof.
Cripps, John	Liverpool, Columbiana	Neither the claimant's name nor his captain's are on the New Jersey rolls of the line.
Crouse, John	Green, Ross	For further proof.
Converse, Jeremiah	——, Madison	For further proof.
Cook, Joseph	Townsend, Huron	Not six months' service.
Crary, John	——, Hamilton	For further proof.
Crouch, Thomas	——, Fayette	For further proof and specification.
Colbert, John William	——, Clermont	For further proof and specification.
Coulter, John	Westland, Guernsey	For further proof and specification.
Crane, Caleb	Cincinnati city	Claims for several years' service in the New Jersey militia as lieutenant—must furnish details and proof of his commission.
Darling, Samuel	Medina, Medina	For further proof.
Davis, John	——, Green	No such regiment and no such colonel in the Virginia line as he names and states—service not specified correctly.
Davis, Walter	——, Jackson	For further proof and explanation.
Davis, Ichabod	Wayne, Columbiana	Proof of service required from the register of the land office, Annapolis.
Deming, Simeon, sr.	Watertown, Washington	Service not fully proved—four months and twenty-eight days admitted by the Massachusetts rolls.
Doherty, John, (deceased) heir-at-law of	——, Franklin	For proof of his commission and service under it from the auditor general of Pennsylvania.
Dyer, Edward	Painesville, Lake	For proof of service from the New Hampshire records.
Emery, George	Prairie tp., Franklin	Claims for service as quartermaster for the war—no proof of service.
Evans, Walter	——, Shelby	No proof of service—name not on the rolls—evidence by two witnesses required.
Ferry, Daniel	Granville, Licking	There is no proof that the Argo was a public armed vessel.
Fink, Michael	——, Jefferson	His name appears on the Pennsylvania rolls, but the narrative of his service does not correspond.
Farmer, Richard	——, Jefferson	For further proof and specification.
Faverty, Joseph	——, Scioto	For further proof and specification.
Finley, John	——, Delaware	A new declaration required specifying the tours of actual service.
Fisher, Peter	——, Highland	For further proof.

STATEMENT—Continued.

Names.	Residence.	Reasons for suspension.
Folsom, Thomas	Youngtown, Trumbull	Service not proved—company, regiment and officers, and residence wanted.
Fox, Matthew	Burton, Geauga	For proof from the Harrisburg records that a nine months' rifle corps was authorized in Pennsylvania in 1777.
Fox, Matthias	Burton, Geauga	For proof to the same tenor and from the same source as Matthew Fox above.
Faulkner, Thomas	——, Union	For further proof and specification.
Gwin, William	——, Clermont	For further proof.
Gay, Henry	Zanesville, Muskingum	For further proof.
Gazaway, Thomas	Chillicothe, Ross	For further proof.
Gimmings, William	Tiffin, Adams	For more full and perfect details of service.
Glass, Vincent	——, Belmont	For further proof.
Griswold, Alexander	Portage, Summit	For proof from the Hartford records.
Gunion, Hugh	——, Jefferson	Service in the line and militia of Pennsylvania, requires proof and specification.
Guey, John	Harrisville, Harrison	For want of proof and congruity in the narrative.
Harcourt, John	Pierpoint, Ashtabula	Proof required that he was detailed for a wood cutter.
Haines, Abraham	Goshen, Columbiana	Proof required from the records of New Jersey.
Hagerman, Barnet	Plain tp., Wayne	Three years' service alleged in the Pennsylvania line, for which there is no proof in the records of this office.
Heckleberger, alias Eichelberger, Hackellander, Eckelbarner, Ackelbarner, Joseph	——, Hamilton	For further proof and the return of the original declaration.
Henning, Adam	——, Starke	For further proof from the Harrisburg records.
Hempelman, George	Madison, Clark	For further proof and specification.
Henry, Enoch T.	Washington, Franklin	For further proof from the comptroller's records, New York.
Hill, Stephen	Concord, Delaware	Not under military organization.
Hillman, James	——, Trumbull	Not six months service—he was also a teamster to the French army.
Heddings, William	——, Highland	For more perfect details of service.
Hendershot, Abraham	Marlborough, Delaware	For more perfect details and proof of service.
Haines, Henry	Cambridge, Guernsey	Not six months service.

Name	Location	Remarks
Hinckley, Joshua	Royalton, Lewis	A soldier of the same name served for the war in Colonel Lamb's regiment of artillery.
Hodgkins, Samuel	Pleasant township, Brown	For proof from the records of the land office at Annapolis.
Holcomb, James	—, Warren	Not military service.
Heizer, John	—, Brown	For further proof and specification.
Hotchkiss, Thetus	Geneva, Ashtabula	Service as a teamster for eight months in 1781—not admissible.
Hyatt, William	Hartland, Huron	For want of proof.
Humphreys, Alexander	Freeport, Harrison	For proof from the records of Delaware.
Johnston, John S. (deceased)	Steubenville, Jefferson	For proof of service and decease.
Johnston, David	Newton, Trumbull	For further proof and specification.
Johnson, Henry	Franklin, Warren	Claims for eighteen months service in the Delaware line, which awaits proof from the records at Dover.
Jones, Thomas	—, Belmont	For proof from the Delaware State records at Dover.
Jones, William	—, Clermont	The colonel's name is wanted and proof by witnesses.
Kimball, Walter	Kilbuck, Holmes	Not embodied under military organization.
King, Ralph	East Union, Wayne	For proof from the records at the State department, Dover, Delaware.
Knap, Samuel	Sycamore, Crawford	Served in a company of ferrymen under Udney Hay, deputy quartermaster general.
Latimer, James	Somerset, Perry	Six months service as a wagoner and three months as a militia man—not sufficient.
Lewis, Ebenezer	—, Marion	For proof from the comptroller's books at Hartford.
Logan, John		Papers withdrawn by Hon. B. Storer, December 10, 1825—suspended for further proof and specification.
Mann, Isaiah (deceased)	Wethersfield, Trumbull	For further proof of service.
Middaugh, Adonijah	Decatur, Brown	He did not serve in any regularly organized corps.
Mitchell, Ensign	—, Madison	For further proof.
Mondy, John	Vermillion, Richland	For proof of service by living witnesses.
Moreland, Philip	Ripley, Holmes	For further proof.
McDaniel, James	—, Jackson	For period, length and grade of service, and names of company and field officers.
McCafferty, Joseph	—, Butler	For proof of service in Dayton's regiment, New Jersey line, and also of service in the New Jersey militia.
Meeker, Jonas	—, Clermont	For a specific detail of his actual service.
Marvin, Samuel	Bloomfield, Knox	For further proof and specification.
Moore, Lambeth	Colerain, Hamilton	For further proof.
Marah, John	Kirkwood, Belmont	For further proof.
McManis, Joseph	—, Stark	For further proof.

STATEMENT—Continued.

Names.	Residence.	Reasons for suspension.
Megan, John	North tp., Harrison	For proof of service.
Meloy, James		Papers withdrawn by Hon. M. H. Sibley, February 28, 1888—suspended for want of proof.
Medley, William Glover	—, Washington	A soldier of the same name enlisted in 1781, and received his depreciation certificate April 30, 1782.
Morrison, John	Solon, Cuyahoga	Not six months service.
Morrison, Samuel	—, Knox	Papers referred to Congress December 28, 1846—suspended for want of proof.
Munson, Wilmot (deceased)	Marlborough, Delaware	He did not serve six months.
McClure, Hugh	Washington, Fayette	He did not serve six months.
McCollister, James	—, Monroe	For further proof.
Mourers, Nicholas	Jeromeville, Wayne	For further proof.
Nichols, Levi		Claim not properly made out—awaiting a declaration according to the printed instructions.
Nichols, John	Burton, Geauga	For further proof.
Ogden, Sphen D.	Hillsborough, Highland	For further proof and specification.
Over, John	Perry, Wayne	For want of proof.
Parsons, John	Centre tp., Columbiana	For further proof.
Parrot, Joseph	—, Fayette	Alleges that he was appointed a commissary in 1777 by General Washington, and served as such to the end of the war.
Patch, John (deceased)	Wethersfield, Trumbull	Papers not properly prepared—defective in specifying for whom a claim is asserted.
Paynter, Nathaniel	York, Sandusky	One year's service as volunteer in 1776 and 1777, and two years as a teamster.
Piatt, Lewis	Jefferson, Adams	For further proof—the claimant set forth no service under any one of the officers mentioned in the certificate of the New York comptroller to a soldier of the same name.
Powell, Joseph	—, Marion	For further proof and specification.
Ray, George	Cross Creek, Jefferson	For proof from the Delaware records.

349 [37]

Riddle, John	Cincinnati city	He did not serve six months.
Robolus, Miller	Union tp., Lawrence	Suspended for further proof.
Roseboom, John	Dayton, Montgomery	For further proof by living witnesses.
Runyan, Adam	Portsmouth, Scioto	Suspended for further explanation.
Ricketts, Edward	Lancaster, Fairfield	For proof of his five years service as lieutenant in the militia by living witnesses, since he can furnish no commission.
Rood, Roger	Lenox tp., Ashtabula	Service not fully proved.
Rose, Jesse	Ellsworth, Trumbull	For further proof, and the return of the original papers.
Sanford, Moses	Windham, Portage	For further proof from the Connecticut rolls—service proved in part by the records of this department.
Sands, Alexander	——, Monroe	For a full and particular statement of his tours of actual service—the Maryland militia served only in short tours.
Sayres, Ephraim	——, Meigs	He did not serve in any regularly organized corps.
Scoville, Michael (deceased)	Mecca, Trumbull	He died before the passage of the act.
Scoville, Amasa	Ashtabula, Ashtabula	Not on the records of Connecticut—not on the rolls of Col. Baldwin's corps of artificers—no proof of service.
Serrine, William	Wayne, Ashtabula	For further proof and specification.
Shepherd, John	Boylton, Cuyahoga	Alleges over three years service in the Pennsylvania line—no trace of evidence on any of the records of that line appears to his credit.
Sims, Francis	——, Meigs	He did not serve in any regularly organized corps.
Skadden, Robert R	Urbana, Champlain	Claimant's name is not on the lists of those in this office who belonged to the Pennsylvania line. If he served upon that line the Auditor General at Harrisburg should bear the proof upon his records.
Sloan, Joseph	Mount Vernon, Knox	Claims as an Indian Spy after the revolution, viz., in 1790 and 1791.
Smith, Reuben	Vernon township, Scioto	For proof from the records at Montpelier, Vermont.
Smith, William	——, Butler	Service shown by the Rhode Island rolls in two places, but claimant alleges three years service in the Rhode Island line, and the details are not identified.
Smith, Andrew	Lancaster, Fairfield	For period, length and grade of service, and names of company and field officers.
Stannard, Claudius	Kirtland, Geauga	Not on the Massachusetts rolls—proof incomplete of his service also in the *Vermont* militia.
Spier, Duncan	Mount Vernon, Knox	Not on the Delaware rolls—proof by witnesses required.
St. Clair James	Lake township, Logan	For proof from the South Carolina comptroller general and traditionary reputation of revolutionary service.
Stilwell, Stephen	Shringfield, Williams	For period, length and grade of service, and names of company and field officers.
Storts, Jacob	——, Perry	For proof of service by the Maryland records.
Swaney, Timothy (deceased)	Freeport, Harrison	For proof of service from records of Dover, Delaware.

STATEMENT—Continued.

Names.	Residence.	Reasons for suspension.
Therwilleger, Clophus	Carlisle, Loraine	For further proof and specification.
Toomer, Christopher	Chillicothe, Ross	For proof of service. (Note j.)
Vanader, Peter	Cincinnati, Hamilton	For a detail of actual service and some direct proof.
Vanhissing, Henry (deceased)	——, Jefferson	For proof of commission and service under it as an officer in the New York troops.
Vanskiver, William	——, Perry	For further proof and specification.
Wade, David E.	Cincinnati, Hamilton	For more specific details and proof of service.
Westbrook, James	Mount Vernon, Knox	For proof of service and specification.
Williams, Abel	Warren, Tuscarawas	For proof of service by witnesses.
Wilson, Isaac	Newport, Washington	Service after the revolution.
Wismer, Jacob	Georgetown, Brown	For a more correct narrative, and some further and more adequate proof.
Wright, James	Hillsborough, Highland	For further proof.
Woodruff, Jonathan	Crosby township, Hamilton	Proof required that the "Gibralter" was a public armed vessel.
Wood, Jeremiah	Lancaster, Fairfield	For proof of service in the flying camp and new Jersey militia, and wagon and team.
Woolsey, Daniel	Painsville, Lake	He did not serve six months.
Wackman, Marcus	Chillicothe, Ross	For further proof and specification.
White, Samuel	Franklin, Franklin	Not on the New Jersey rolls—no proof of service—note j must be carried out.
White, George	Lancaster, Fairfield	Suspended for further proof.

A list of the names of persons residing in Ohio who have applied for pensions under the act of July 4, 1836, whose claims have been rejected; prepared in conformity with the resolution of the Senate of the United States, September 16, 1850.

Names.	Residence.	Reasons for rejection.
Adams, Elizabeth, widow of George.	Adams, Darke.	Marriage after service.
Bartholomew, Abigail, widow of Benjamin.	Harpersfield, Ashtabula.	Not military service.
Bird, Rebecca, formerly widow of David McClurg	——, Greene.	A soldier in the regular army.
Borden, Elizabeth, widow of George.	Whitecak, Highland.	A soldier of the regular army.
Curtis, Mary, widow of Daniel.	Belpre, Washington.	He was a deserter.
Corson, Huldah, widow of Thomas.	——, Franklin.	A soldier in the late war.
Haze, Honor, formerly widow of Matthew Patterson.	——, Clermont.	A soldier of the regular army.
Horton, Jaly, widow of Robert.	——, Muskingum.	Married after service.
Nessel, Lovina (deceased) widow of Conrad, children of.	Norwalk, Huron.	Died before the passage of the act.
Wiley, Rebecca, widow of Thomas.	Olive, Morgan.	Married after service.

A list of the names of persons residing in Ohio who have applied for pensions under the act of July 4, 1836, whose claims have been suspended; prepared in conformity with the resolution of the Senate of the United States, September 16, 1850.

Names.	Residence.	Reasons for suspension.
Baker, Hannah, widow of Daniel	Hamilton, Butler	For proof of service from the New Jersey State records and of the marriage.
Burnhart, Anna, formerly widow of Wm. Hunt	——, Richland	For further proof of service and marriage.
Brakeman, Eve, widow of Ledowick	Painesville, Lake	Did not serve in any regularly organized corps.
Casteel, Sarah, widow of Zadoc	Union tp., Monroe	Proof of marriage concurrent with service not complete, but good for a claim under act of July 7, 1838.
Dayton Elizabeth, widow of David	Burton, Geauga	For proof of service from the Hartford records. Marriage and identity admitted.
Fellows, Sarah, formerly widow of Benj. Fenn	Tallmadge tp., Portage	His lieutenancy requires proof both of commission and service.
Fleming, Nancy, widow of Peter	Ludlow tp., Washington	No proof of service—name not on the rolls.
Greenfield, Prudence, (deceased,) widow of William, sr.	Fairfield, Huron	For want of proof of service.
Hillman, Mary, widow of Benjamin	Porter tp., Delaware	For further proof.
Hunnason, Ann, widow of Joel	Warren, Trumbull	For period, length and grade of service, and names of company and field officers, and service, submitted to the Comptroller at Hartford for verification.
Johnson, Jane, widow of Alexander	Twinn tp., Ross	Service admitted—marriage to be proved.
McLaughlin, Elizabeth, widow of James	Wayne tp., Columbiana	For further proof and specification.
Moore, Abigail, formerly widow of Peter Riley	Fairfield tp., Tuscarawas	For further proof and specification.
Mosier, Elizabeth, widow of Daniel	Roxbury tp., Washington	Her husband was pensioned for nine months service in the Massachusetts line. The rolls discovered since discredit his service.
McGuire, Jane, widow of Thomas	Urbana, Champaign	Proof wanting of his commission and service under it.
Nation, Ireta, widow of Joseph	Eaton, Preble	For further proof.

Name	Location	Remarks
Nooney, Sarah, (deceased), widow of James..	Mantua, Portage............	Marriage admitted. Period, length and grade of service, and names of company and field officers must be adduced and submitted to the Connecticut comptroller.
Parker, Charity, widow of John.............	Washington tp., Harrison......	Married after service—no claim under this act.
Poe, Elizabeth, widow of Adam.............	Congress tp., Wayne..........	For proof of service by living witnesses.
Price, Mary, widow of John................	Woodsfield tp., Belmont.......	For further proof and specification.
Shaw, Juliana, widow of Nathan............	Augusta tp., Carroll...........	Proof of his commission required and service under it.
Smith, Elizabeth, widow of Dennis..........	Batavia, Clermont............	Suspended for further proof and specification.
Snyder, Margaret, formerly widow of Joseph Thompson.	Hillsboro', Highland..........	For proof of his commission and two years service as lieutenant under it.
Stephens, Lois, (deceased), widow of Phinehas.	——, Sandusky..............	For proof that he was a militia-man of Stow by the October returns of the eight months' men in 1775.
Swan, Anna, witow of Elias	Huron, Huron...............	For further proof of service and marriage.
Trimble, Phebe, widow of Jacob	Lebanon, Warren.............	For proof and specification.
Vanbenschoten, Margaret, widow of Aaron...	Berlin tp., Huron.............	For proof of marriage—service admitted.
Webb, Susannah, widow of John	Yok tp., Belmont.............	For proof of marriage, and of service by the records at Annapolis.
Wigton, Elizabeth, widow of Thomas.........	Kingston tp., Delaware........	Service in the Pennsylvania line must be verified by the Harrisburg records—marriage admitted.

A list of the names of persons residing in Ohio who have applied for pensions under the act of July 7, 1838, whose claims have been rejected; prepared in conformity with the resolution of the Senate of the United States of September 16, 1850.

Names.	Residence.	Reasons for rejection.
Bishop, Phebe, widow of Joel	Norwich, Huron	Not a widow at the date of the act.
Carter, Eleanor, widow of James	Batavia, Clermont	Married after the limits of the laws.
Cullens, Jane, widow of John	Zanesville, Muskingum	Not six months' service.
Dockum, Polly, widow of James	Somerford tp., Hamilton	Not six months' service.
Gardner, Lucy, widow of Benjamin	——, Brown	Not a widow at the date of the act.
Hall, Phebe, widow of Richard	Batavia, Clermont	Married after January 1, 1794.
Hall, Jane, widow of David	——, Summit	Service after the war.
Hamilton, Ann, widow of Robert	Union tp., Warren	Not a widow at the date of the act.
Heindale, Sarah, widow of Jacob	Braceville tp., Trumbull	Not a widow at the date of the act.
Lamson, Martha, widow of Ebenezer	——, Ashtabula	Married in 1818.
Orchard, Sarah, widow of Thomas	Concord tp., Ross	Not a widow at the date of the act.
Parker, Rachel, widow of James	——, Brown	No proof of service—no specification.
Phillips, Dorcas, widow of Spencer	——, Huron	Not a widow at the date of the act.
Quinn, Elizabeth, widow of John	——, Beaver	Not a widow at the date of the act.
Ridabough, Catharine, widow of Peter	——, Medina	Not a widow at the date of the act.
Sprague, Rebecca, widow of Frederick	——, Franklin	Not a widow at the date of the act.
Smith, Jane, widow of John	Batavia, Clermont	Married in 1805.
Scofield, Eunice, widow of Benjamin	Richmond, Huron	Not the widow of the soldier whose service is claimed for.
Spoon, Catharine (deceased), widow of Philip	——, Perry	Died before August 28, 1842.

South, Hannah, widow of William............	——, Clermont............	Not military service.
Waters, Anne, widow of Jacob............	——, Licking............	Not a widow at the date of the act.
Whaley, Elizabeth (dec'd), widow of Edward............	——, Franklin............	Not a widow at the date of the act—died before August 28, 1842.
White, Hannah, widow of William............	——, Brown............	Not a widow at the date of the act.

A list of the names of persons residing in Ohio who have applied for pensions under the act of July 7, 1838, whose claims have been suspended; prepared in conformity with the resolution of the Senate of the United States of September 16, 1850.

Names.	Residence.	Reasons for suspension.
Armstrong, Nancy, widow of Daniel	Columbus, Franklin	For proof of service and marriage.
Alderman, Ruth, widow of Timothy	Brookfield, Trumbull	He did not serve six months.
Bell, Elizabeth, widow of Andrew	Carrollton, Carroll	For further proof and specification.
Bender, Elizabeth, widow of Jacob	Russia tp., Loraine	Objections obviated by act of July, 1848.
Bicker, Rebecca, widow of Adam	Williamsburgh tp., Clermont	Married in 1802—no claim.
Bonnel, Rachel, widow of Aaron	Cincinnati	Service admitted—marriage in suspense.
Boyer, Sarah, widow of Daniel	——, Licking	Objections to the service obviated by the joint resolution of July 1, 1848.
Brooks, Jane, widow of David	Hampdon, Geauga	A soldier of the same name is found on the rolls of the Connecticut line.
Brown, Ann M., widow of John	South Bloomfield, Pickaway	Service admitted—marriage in suspense.
Byrne, Elizabeth (dec'd), widow of Lawrence	Batavia, Clermont	Service admitted—marriage in suspense.
Buckley, Catharine (dec'd), widow of Abraham	Springfield, Clark	A soldier of the same name received a certificate of full pay.
Call, Hannah, widow of Alexander	New Philadelphia, Tuscarawas	For further proof.
Carney, Mary E., widow of John	Delaware Court House	For period, length and grade of service, and names of company and field officers.
Clingler, Catharine (deceased), widow of John	Georgetown, Brown	John Clingler, of the third Pennsylvania regiment was discharged, according to the original document on file with these papers, but the period, length and grade of service must be ascertained at Harrisburg.
Conner, Mary (deceased), widow of Andrew	Trenton tp., Delaware	Marriage admitted—service in suspense for want of proof and specification.
Cooper, Martha, widow of John	Millersburgh, Holmes	Service admitted—marriage in suspense for an original leaf from an alleged family record.
Crafts, Sarah, widow of George	Gallipolis, Gallia	Service in the Pennsylvania line should be verified by Harrisburg records.
Croninger, Elizabeth	Bolivar, Tuscarawas	Difficulties of service obviated by the joint resolution of July 1, 1848.

Name	Location	Remarks
Crosby, Jerusha (deceased), widow of Obed	Vernon tp., Trumbull	Service for three years as corporal in Colonel Swift's regiment, by Obed Crosby, a soldier of the same name—is open to some proof of identity.
Crossley, Sarah, widow of William	——, Shelby	Difficulties of service obviated by the joint resolution of July 1, 1848.
Curtis, Eunice, widow of Thomas	Canaan tp., Wayne	For proof from the Comptroller at Hartford—he was a wagon driver.
Curry, Martha, widow of James	——, Butler	Marriage and six months' service admitted—the eight months' service as a ranger depends on the fact of Captain Miller's commission as a ranger from the records at Harrisburg.
Daines, Jane, widow of Asa	Noward, Licking	Not a widow at the date of the act.
Davis, Rachel, widow of Joseph	Washington tp., Morrow	Service admitted—marriage in suspense.
Davis, Jemima, widow of Joshua	Mill Creek tp., Hamilton	Not a widow at the date of the act.
Ditto, Eleanor, widow of Francis	——, Henry	Not a widow at the date of the act.
Dodge, Elizabeth, widow of Caleb	——, Hocking	Period, length and grade of service, and names of company and field officers, and further proof of service and marriage required.
Dond, Huldy, widow of Samuel	Middleberry tp., Knox	Service admitted—marriage in suspense.
Dudley, Anne, widow of Isaac	Tallmadge, Summit	Proof of service required from the Hartford records.
Fratt, Rebecca, widow of Henry	Clinton tp., Knox	Service admitted—marriage in suspense.
Guilder, Mary, widow of Daniel	——, Jackson	Marriage in suspense, and also the soldier's identity with the depreciation certificate of £62 10s., to a soldier of the same name—
Johnson, Sarah, widow of William	Mount Vernon, Knox	Period, length and grade of service, and names of company and field officers, and proof of service by survivors of the Morris county, New Jersey militia, and proof of marriage.
Jones, Abigail, widow of Jacob	Warren, Trumbull	Service not set forth or proved—marriage requires further proof.
Lawrence, Sarah, widow of John	Elyria, Loraine	Papers of her husband, if he was a pensioner, cannot be found.
Lacey, Elizabeth, widow of Mitchell	White tp., Hamilton	Objections to the service obviated by joint resolution of July 1, 1848.
Lewis, Mary, widow of Jacob	Wayne, Knox	Wagon master and express rider.
Lienzader, Leah, widow of Abraham	Centre tp., Guernsey	Seven months nineteen days' service admitted—marriage in suspense.
Montgomery, Rebecca, widow of Mitchell S. D.	Oxford tp., Guernsey	Not a widow at the date of the act.
Mansfield, Anna, widow of Thomas	Trimble, Athens	Declaration called for under act of July 29, 1848, and proof of marriage before 1800.
Martindale, Mary, widow of James	Gallipolis, Gallia	Objections obviated by joint resolution July 1, 1848.
Millman, Susan, widow of Briant	——, Huron	Company and regiment and locality, and date of service required in order to an inspection of the rolls.

[37]   358

STATEMENT—Continued.

Names.	Residence.	Reasons for suspension.
Morse, Mary, widow of Elijah	Williamsfield, Ashtabula	Service heretofore rejected is reinstated under July 1, 1848, joint resolution.
Miles, Mary, widow of John	Union tp., Clermont	For declaration under act February 2, 1848—proof of marriage deficient; also that she is now a widow.
Morris, Ruth, widow of John	Windsor, Ashtabula	The objections to the service heretofore are removed by the joint resolution of July 1, 1848.
Peck, Phebe, widow of William	Cincinnati city	She was not a widow at the date of the act.
Palmer, Mary, widow of Chilial	Jefferson, Ashtabula	For proof of the marriage.
Paine, Elizabeth, widow of Thomas	Huntsburgh tp., Geauga	Proof of identity required with a soldier of the same name in the certificate of the Hartford comptroller.
Philips, Mary, widow of Zachariah	McConnellsville, Morgan	For further proof of service and marriage.
Piper, Elizabeth, widow of James	Hamilton, Butler	Proof of marriage not good.
Pritchard, Comfort, widow of Nathaniel	——, Laurence	Service admitted—barred by act of April 30, 1844—may claim under act of March, 1843, from the death of her husband.
Ramsey, Catharine, formerly widow of John Leiper	Richmond, Jefferson	For further proof and specification.
Rash, Chloe, widow of Jacob	Lyme, Huron	Proof of identity with the dragoon of Sheldon's regiment.
Russell, Jane, deceased, widow of William	Amsterdam, Jefferson	For period, length and grade, and names of company and field officers, and a copy of her husband's invalid papers.
Saddler, Sophia, widow of Christopher	Dover tp., Cuyahoga	For proof of service and marriage.
Shepherd, Eleanor, deceased, widow of William	Hamilton, Butler	For proof of marriage and the names of the surviving children.
Severus, Hannah, widow of Edward	Pique, Miami	Not a widow at the date of the act.
Sexton, Jane, widow of Aaron	Carlisle, Loraine	For further proof of service.
Sheldon, Love, widow of Ebenezer	Mantua, Portage	Six months' service not fully proved.
Sinn, Margatta, widow of Christian	Bucyrus, Crawford	Service imperfectly stated.
Spaulding, Lois, formerly widow of George Moore	Jefferson tp., Franklin	For proof of identity with the soldier of the same name on the New Hampshire records.
Spyres, Rebecca, widow of Richard	Georgetown, Brown	For further proof of marriage.
Stevens, Eve, deceased, widow of John	Palmyra, Portage	For proof of identity with one of the soldiers of the Virginia line.
Sliter, Fanny, widow of James	Burton tp., Geauga	Desertion.

Thorp, Mary, widow of Augustus............	Groton, Erie..............	For proof of identity with Captain Eliphalet Thorp, of the Massachusetts rolls.
Toers, Eleanor, formerly widow of Robert Woodsides.	Xenia, Greene............	For proof of identity with the Robert Woodsides of Captain Lloyd's company, second regiment, New Jersey line.
Vrooman, Hannah, widow of Bartholomew J..	Perry tp., Lake.........	For proof of service by the New York comptroller.
Vanhorn, Mary, widow of James	Delaware, Delaware.....	Not on the rolls—no proof of service.
Wagstaff, Charity, widow of William.........	Knox tp., Geurnsey......	Difficulties of the service heretofore are now obviated by the joint resolution of July 1, 1848.
Walker, Lydia, widow of David............	——, Highland..........	For proof of his lieutenant's commission and of service by the Raleigh records.
Wallace, Mary, widow of William...........	Spencer tp., Guernsey....	Service admitted—marriage in suspense.
Weaver, Anna Maria, widow of John A.....	York tp., Darke.........	Not on the rolls in the department—must refer to the Harrisburg records.
Wheeler, Elizabeth, widow of Samuel.........	Fitchville tp., Huron	No proof of service offered—six months as an Indian spy in one tour in 1780 of doubtful duration.
White, Sarah, deceased, widow of Thomas....	——, Belmont...........	No claim—died before July 1, 1848, and left no children.

A list of the names of persons residing in Kentucky who have applied for pensions under the act of June 7, 1832, whose claims have been rejected; prepared in conformity with the resolution of the Senate of the United States, September 16, 1850.

Names.	Residence.	Reasons for rejection.
Ayers, Nathaniel	——, Laurel	Not six months service.
Arbuckle, William	——, Laurel	Service by substitute.
Boggs, Stephen	——, Green	Not six months service.
Baker, Wonsley	Mount Vernon, Rock Castle	Not six months service.
Barnett, Robert (deceased), heirs of	——, Fayette	Not six months service.
Booz, Richard		Not military service.
Blankenship, William	——, Pike	Not six months service.
Bell, Thomas	——, Bullitt	Not six months service.
Ballard, James	——, Shelby	Not military service—not under military organization.
Barker, William	——, Henry	Service after the Revolution.
Banty, Henry		Not six months service.
Bohannon, Hellen	——, Shelby	Not military service, and service by substitute.
Bagley, Richard V.	——, Christian	Only four months service.
Baldridge, Thomas	——, Barren	Not six months service.
Baugh, Jacob	Somerset, Pulaski	Indian wars before and during the Revolution.
Bennett, John	——, Whitley	Not under competent military authority.
Brown, Joseph	——, Bullitt	Team service.
Blue, David	——, Union	Not military service.
Baldrock, Richard	——, Monroe	Not six months service.
Browning, Jeremiah	——, Bracken	Not six months service.
Burton, Jarett	——, Mason	Not six months military service.
Byram, Jacob	——, Warren	Not six months service.
Banta, Samuel	——, Mercer	Not six months service.
Bennett, Jesse	——, Brown	Desertion.
Campbell, Duncan	——, Gallatin	Not military service.
Christy, James	——, Morgan	Not under competent military authority.
Chrisman, Joseph	——, Wayne	Indian wars in 1782.
Crouton, Archibald	Louisville, Jefferson	Not six months actual service.

Name	County	Remarks
Carrier, William	Scott	Service after the Revolution.
Clawson, John	Meade	Not six months service.
Cook, Matthew	Campbell	Privateer service.
Cleaver, Benjamin	Grayson	Not six months military service during the Revolution.
Crook, Jeremiah, sr.	Grant	Not military service.
Cross, William	Muhlenberg	Only three months six days service.
Cottle, Joseph	Morgan	Service after the Revolution.
Chalfant, Thomas	Gallatin	Not military service.
Dean, Samuel	Henry	Only four months service.
Dry, Jacob	Allen	Not six months service.
Denny, John	Wayne	Not six months service.
Dugan, Hugh	Campbell	Service after the Revolution.
Durrington, Walter	Simpson	Under age.
Durham, Samuel	Green	Not military service.
Dorsey, Leaven	Jefferson	Desertion.
Davis, Moses	Monroe	Not military service.
Elmore, Peter	Calloway	Not military service.
Ewbank, Joseph	Nicholas	Not six months service.
Ewing, John (deceased), widow of	Pendleton	Died before the passage of the act—rejected in December, 1884.
Fain, William	Jessamine	Only three months service.
Force, Silas	Henry	Under age.
Flanery, James	Johnson	Service after the Revolution.
Flanery, John	Johnson	Service after the Revolution.
Francis, Thomas	Johnson	Service after the Revolution.
Freeland, John	Fleming	Privateer service.
Faria, John	Laurel	Not six months service.
Figgins, William	Bracken	Not six months service.
Graham, William	Green	Desertion.
Gray, Presley	Elizabethtown, Hardin	Not six months service.
Gill, Robert	Russellville, Logan	Service not six months, except in a war against the tories.
Gray, Richard	Fayette	Not six months service.
Grigsby, Benjamin	Shelby	Not six months service.
Hacker, John	Perry	Service not in the revolution.
Hide, Jesse	Laurel	Not six months service.
Hargis, Whiteside	Paducah, McCracken	Not revolutionary service.

STATEMENT—Continued.

Names.	Residence.	Reasons for rejection.
Harrison, Zephaniah	Franklin	Not under military organization.
Hayden, James	Simpson	Service not six months before the war closed.
Horn, Nathan	Hardin	Not six months service.
Howard, Benjamin	Jessamine	Service after the revolution.
Hudson, Joshua	Kenton	Not six months service.
Hamrick, Gibson	Hardin	Not six months service.
Humphreys, William	Adair	Desertion.
Hancock, William	Morganfield, Union	Service not in any regularly organized corps.
Holt, Thomas	Garrard	Service not in any regularly organized corps.
Harmon, Jacob	Washington	Service previous to the revolution.
Higden, Joseph	Bracken	Service subsequent to the revolution.
Hathaway, John		But three months service.
Jones, John	Bath	Service subsequent to the revolution.
Jones, James	Caldwell	Not six months' service.
Johnson, John	Clark	A teamster to the French army.
Kelly, Griffin	Clark	Service after the war.
Kibby, Joseph	Union	Not six months' service.
Kryar, Frederick	Nelson	Not six months' service.
Logan, James	Lewis	He did not serve during the revolution.
Lawson, Randolph	Clinton	Not six months' service.
Larkins, Presley	Floyd	Service after the war.
Lusk, Samuel	Greenup	Service after the war.
Lush, William	Hardin	Privateer service.
Lee, Joseph	Barren	Desertion.
Lyles, Richard	Logan	Not military service.
Matthews, James	Boone	He did not serve during the revolution.
McBee, Isaac	Cumberland	Service not by order of competent authority.
Million, John	Madison	Not six months' service.
Marah, David	Wayne	His service was against the Indians.

Name	County	Remarks
Mitchell, Adam	—, Green	Not six months' service.
McBrayer, Hugh	—, Anderson	Under age.
Mills, William	Louisville, Jefferson	Not six months' service.
May, David	—, Perry	Not six months' service.
Mefford, John	—, Logan	Not six months' actual service.
McClelland, Alexander	—, Montgomery	Not six months' service.
McGuire, John	—, Morgan	Not six months' service.
Newton, Joseph	—, Muhlenburg	Not six months' service.
Norton, John	—, Woodford	Not six months' service.
Noland, Matthew	—, Fayette	Not six months' service.
Noaks, George	—, Lincoln	Not in any military capacity.
Oler, Henry, (late of Darke county, Ohio)		Service in Indian wars.
Owen, John	—, Barren	Not six months' service.
Osbourn, Ephraim	—, Perry	Not six months' service.
Power, Joseph	—, Fleming	Not six months' service.
Purvis, James	—, Pulaski	Desertion.
Paris, Robert	Shelbyville, Shelby	Not six months' service.
Pollard, Elijah	—, Henry	Not six months' service.
Phelps, Anthony	—, Hardin	Not six months' service.
Pelfrey, William		Not six months' service. [Papers withdrawn.]
Robinson, Jesse	—, Grant	Only five months' service.
Ramsey, Archibald	—, Morgan	Not in a military capacity.
Reece, John	—, Hart	Not six months' service.
Rose, John	—, Jefferson	Only three months' service during the revolution.
Roberts, John M.	—, Lincoln	Not six months' service in a military capacity.
Suddarth, John	—, Warren	Not six months' service.
Sharp, Solomon	—, Mercer	Not six months' service in a military capacity.
Smith, Thomas	—, Henry	Not six months' service.
Sanders, William	—, Mercer	Not six months' service.
Stewart, Thomas	—, Pike	He did not serve six months during the revolution.
Servgin, Robert	Paris, Bourbon	Service by substitute.
Stringer, Leonard	Lexington, Fayette	Not six months' service in a military capacity.
Smith, Jacob J.	—, Grant	Not military service.
Shoptaw, John	—, Bullitt	Not over three and a half months' service during the war.

STATEMENT—Continued.

Names.	Residence.	Reasons for rejection.
Thompson, William	—, Campbell	Service after peace, except three and a half months.
Thomas, William		Service under a contract purely civil. [Papers withdrawn 19th January, 1835. R. M. Johnson.]
Trover, J., heirs of	Hopkinsville, Christian	Died before the passage of the act.
Tolson, Thomas	West Liberty, Morgan	Name not on the rolls—no proof of service.
Tripplett, William	—, Russell	Service by substitute.
Vawter, William	Burlington, Boone	Not six months' service in a military capacity.
Watson, James	—, Lawrence	Service after the revolution.
Walston, Joseph	—, Marion	Not six months' service.
Walker, Moses	—, Jessamine	Not military service.
Williamson, Robert	—, Garrard	Not six months' service.
Westlake, Josiah	—, Greenup	Only three months' and twelve days' service.
Whooley, Peter	—, Montgomery	Service previous to the revolution.
White, Daniel	—, Henry	Desertion.
Wright, Joseph	—, Cumberland	Not six months' service.
Williams, Samuel F.	—, Henderson	Not six months' service.
Webb, Samuel	—, Spencer	Desertion.
Wright, Israel	—, Montgomery	Not six months' service.
Williams, William	—, Perry	Not six months' service.
Woodruff, Noadiah	—, Franklin	Not military service.
West, Joseph	—, Wayne	Indian wars—frontier defence.
Yocum, George	—, Montgomery	Under age.
Young, John	—, Greenup	Not military service.
Young, Christian	—, Caldwell	Service subsequent to the revolution.

A list of the names of persons residing in Kentucky who have applied for pensions under the act of June 7, 1832, whose claims have been suspended; prepared in conformity with the resolution of the Senate of the United States of September 16, 1850.

Names.	Residence.	Reasons for suspension.
Adams, William	——, Fleming	Service not specified or proved—probably antedated. Letter to claimant May 31, 1845.
Adkins, Thomas	——, Edmonson	Not sufficient proof of six months service.
Allen Richard, (deceased), by Drusilla Parker, his daughter.	——, Rockcastle	No proof of service—not on the rolls—a colonel's grade requires to be proved by his commission, or some record evidence of equal value.
Alvis, Henry H.	——, Monroe	No proof of service—not on any rolls.
Bailey, Matthias	——, Bracken	No proof of service—not on any rolls.
Bailey, Peter	Madisonville, Hopkins	A new declaration required, and to set forth his tours of actual service.
Bartley, Thomas	——, Monroe	For a more full and explicit detail of his militia service.
Barnes, Nichodemus	——, Clinton	For period, length, and grade of service, and names of company and field officers, and proof from the Maryland records.
Bartle, John	——, Campbell	Claims for service as captain in the New York line, or militia. Proof not complete.
Bridges, Benjamin	——, Jefferson	Twelve months service as commissary, and as wagon-master five months, and three months on board a commissary's vessel. Proof of service not complete.
Bowie, William	Georgetown, Scott	Not on the rolls—no proof of service.
Bowers, William	——, Nicholas	For further proof from the Richmond records.
Boyd, John	——, Christian	For proof of his commission as an officer and service under it.
Buckhart, George	——, Knot	For further proof and specification.
Beaty, Henry		For further proof and papers enclosed to Hon. B. French, February 20, 1886.
Burcham, David	——, Harden	For further proof.
Carman, John	——, Casey	For further proof.
Cam, William	——, Hart	For further proof.
Caskey, Joseph	——, Christian	For want of proof of service.
Childers, Abraham	Mount Vernon, Rock Castle	For further and more perfect details of service—name not on the rolls.
Collins, R. C.	——, Grant	For further proof of specification.

STATEMENT—Continued.

Names.	Residence.	Reasons for suspension.
Crabtree, William	——, Muhlenburg	For proof from the office of the Secretary of State of North Carolina.
Crabtree, Abraham	——, Clinton	For period, length and grade of service, and by whom commanded, and where performed.
Cassady, Thomas	——, Floyd	For further proof and specification.
Crosby, John	——, Shelby	For a further setting forth of service and the officer's names.
Crawford, James	——, Carter	No proof of service—narrative impossible—claim disallowed.
Davis, Vachal	——, Harlan	For proof from the Comptroller General of South Carolina.
Dawson, Jeremiah	——, Hart	For further proof.
Deale, Thomas	Prestonburgh, Floyd	For proof from the comptroller's books, Raleigh.
Drake, Albriton	——, Muhlenburg	For further proof from the Comptroller and Secretary of State of North Carolina.
Earthenhousen, Conrad	——, Jessamine	Period, length and grade of service, and names of company and field officers.
Eberly, Henry	——, Mercer	For further proof.
Ellington, David M	——, Crittenden	The rolls being silent, he is required to produce two witnesses.
Elmore Matson	——, Lincoln	For a more full and particular narrative of his service.
Falconer, James	——, Trimble	Not six months service.
Farris, James	——, Casey	Service after the revolution.
Fields, William, (deceased), heirs of	——, Mercer	Not more than six months service can be allowed, unless a further specification is made of the militia service.
Frayler, James	——, Floyd	For a more perfect specification of his militia service.
Gamble, Samuel	——, Fayette	Under age—enlistment requires proof—not on the rolls—served as a cook.
Galloway, John	——, Daviess	No proof of service—name not on the rolls.
Golson, William	Long Lick, Scioto	For proof of service and identity from the Richmond records.
Graham, Christopher	——, Nelson	For further proof.
Graham, William	——, Campbell	For a full and specific statement of his tours of actual service.
Grove, John	Shelbyville, Shelby	Claims for service as a wagon-master under General Hillebamner. Proof of his appointment and service required.

Name	County	Remarks
Griffin, James..........	—, Rock Castle........	Service for six months not fully proved.
Green, Benjamin........	—, Mercer.............	Service for nine months not designated whether line or militia.
Hadley, Josiah.........	....	Under age—no proof of service. [Papers withdrawn, December 29, 1835, Hon. R. French.]
Hand, Uriah...........	—, Spencer...........	Suspended for further proof and specification.
Hannon, William.......	—, Greenup...........	For proof from the Annapolis records.
Houchin, Charles.......	—, Edmonson.........	For proof by witnesses—the Virginia rolls being silent.
Hudson, Benjamin (deceased).	Lancaster, Garrard....	For further proof.
Hall, John.............	—, Perry..............	Awaiting the return of the original declaration, May 14, 1885, Hon. J. Love.
Howard, John Walker...	—, Washington........	Not on the rolls—no proof of service.
Hill, Thomas...........	—, Caldwell...........	Six months service not fully proved.
Hitch, Gillis...........	—, Pendleton.........	For want of proof of service, and papers sent to R. M. Johnson, January, 1888.
Hopkins, Dennis.......	—, Clinton............	For lack of proof of service.
Horn, Aaron...........	—, Madison...........	For further proof.
Johnson, Ebenezer.....	—, Fleming...........	For further proof and specification, and a report from the Pennsylvania Secretary of State.
Johnson, Joseph.......	—, Fleming...........	Proof refused from the Harrisburg army records.
Jewell, Jonathan.......	—, Bowen.............	Claim considered doubtful—his statement does not agree with the facts as they occurred during the course of service.
Jarvis, Solomon........	—, Scott..............	For further proof.
Jesse, Thomas.........	—, Adair..............	Six months' service not fully proved.
Kercheval, William.....	—, Logan.............	For further proof and specification.
Kilbourn, Henry........	—, Rochester.........	He did not serve in a regularly organized corps.
Lambert, Meredith.....	—, Green.............	This claim was condemned upon its own face by letter to claimant, April 22, 1845.
Lindsay, James (deceased) heirs of...	—, Gallatin...........	The children are instructed to apply, as both parents are dead, and by proving the period of their decease, they will be entitled to the amount at $20 per annum.
Logan, Joseph..........	—, Morgan............	Militia service overrated—more precise specification and further proof required.
Loven, Isaac...........	—, Laurel.............	For further proof from the Secretary of State or comptroller of North Carolina.
Majors, Thomas........	—, Madison...........	For proofs of service from the North Carolina records.

STATEMENT—Continued.

Names.	Residence.	Reasons for suspension.
Mason, Robert	——, Knox	For further proof.
Martin, David	——, Hardin	More direct proof and a more precise detail of his service is called for.
Mayner, Richard T.	——, Warren	Claims five years service—twelve months as orderly sergeant and eleven months as 2d lieutenant. He must give the names of the officers, regiment and line he served in.
Mortimer, James	——, Fleming	For further proof.
Means, John		For proof of service, and papers enclosed to Hon. R. French, June 21, 1836.
Mills, James	——, Spencer	For period, length and grade of service, and names of company and field officers.
Milner, Amos		No declaration has been filed in this case.
McAdow, John	——, Mason	More direct proof and precise specification of his four years service in the Maryland line.
McDowell, John	——, Larue	Proof required from the auditor's office at Richmond.
Nicholson, Boling	——, Spencer	For period, length and grade of service, and names of company and field officers, and where stationed or marched.
Nolen (alias Noland), William	——, Floyd	For proof of service from the books of the comptroller general of South Carolina.
McCormick, Joseph	——, Lincoln	For further proof.
Ogden, Stephen	——, Morgan	Proof of service not complete—colonel's name under whom he served in 1781.
Patrick, Ezekiel	——, Perry	For a more full and specific detail of his services as a militia man.
Phelps, Nicholas	——, Butler	Militia service overrated—three years' service alleged requires further proof and setting forth.
Phillips, Samuel	——, Jefferson	For further proof and specification.
Phillips, John	——, Graves	Proof of service required from the books of the comptroller at North Carolina.

Pigman, Leonard	—, Perry	Awaiting the return of the original declaration, April 12, 1888, W. Smith.
Pohon, William	Shepperdsville, Bullitt	For further proof.
Preble, Job		It does not appear that any formal declaration has been made in this case.
Preston, Jeremiah	—, Campbell	For further proof.
Price, Reuben W. (deceased) heirs of	—, Clinton	No definite description of act or service, or the nature of the claim, whether revolutionary or otherwise.
Rickles, William	Newport, Campbell	Not six months' service.
Rudder, Charles	—, Bath	For a more perfect detail of his service.
Roman, Isaac	Lexington, Fayette	Not six months' service.
Rogers, Ezekiel	—, Caldwell	For further proof.
Ross, Zachariah	—, Owen	For further proof and specification.
Ruggles, James, sen.	Little Sandy, Greenup	For further proof.
Sanders, John	—, Wayne	For a more precise statement of his tours of actual service.
Smith, Samuel	—, Cumberland	Local defence—neighbourhood service—no regular state military organization.
Smith, Joseph	—, Jefferson	For a more correct and particular account of his services.
Smith, Randall	—, Carter	For deficient proof of service.
Springer, Richard	—, Carroll	Claims for eighteen months' service in the Pennsylvania line or militia, in *which*, is not set forth. If under a special act it should be shown.
Stonebraker, John	—, Harden	Service not proved—proof required according to the printed resolutions.
Saunders, Thomas	—, Mercer	Not six months' service.
Stockham, John	—, Lewis	Period, length and grade of service, and names of company and field officers and stations should be given.
Sturgeon, James	—, Morgan	Six months' service not fully proved.
Taylor, Richard	—, Ohio	Service not properly set forth, or estimated or proved.
Tetterton, Thomas	—, Muhlenburg	Not properly specified—which should be done—and the result referred for proof or disproof to the comptroller of North Carolina.
Thurman, Bazo	—, Spencer	Not properly set forth—further proof and specification required.
Vice, John (deceased) heirs of		Not six months' service—papers returned to Linn Boyd, Jan. 15, 1846.
Warner, Peter (deceased)	—, Lincoln	Period, length and grade of service, where performed, and by whom commanded.

STATEMENT—Continued.

Names.	Residence.	Reasons for suspension.
Weeks, Job	——, Livingston	His militia service in New Jersey requires more correct setting forth.
Williams, Hardin	——, Cumberland	For more satisfactory proof.
Young, John (2d)	——, Bracken	A more intelligible and complete setting forth of his service is required.
Young, John	——, Greenup	The name is twice found on the Virginia rolls, but the evidence is not complete to identify claimant as any one of them.

A list of the names of persons residing in Kentucky who have applied for pensions under the act of July 4, 1836, whose claims have been rejected; prepared in conformity with the resolution of the Senate of the United States, September 16, 1850.

Names.	Residence.	Reasons for rejection.
Camper, Dinah, widow of Tilman	———, Fayette	Died before the passage of the act.
Crews, Lucy, widow of John	———, Trimble	A soldier of the regular army.
Green, Sarah Ann, widow of Gabriel	———, Henderson	Married after the war.
Hamilton, Hannah, widow of Charles	———, Wayne	Not a widow at the date of the act—died before August 22, 1842.
Kelso, Penelope, widow of Thomas	———, Wayne	Married after the war.
Langdon, Eda, widow of Charles	———, Jefferson	Married after service.
Penn, Rebecca, daughter of Benjamin	———, Franklin	Married after service.
Rasor, Mary C., widow of Paul	———, Shelby	Married after service.
Scott, Sarah, widow of Thomas	———, Henry	Married in 1802.
Shull, Anna Dorothea, widow of Peter	———, Muhlenberg	Married after service.
Vertrees, Elizabeth, widow of Isaac (dec'd), heirs of	———, Hardin	Married after service—died before the passage of the act.
Ward, Elizabeth, widow of James	———, McCracken	Not in any regularly organized corps.

A list of the names of persons residing in Kentucky, who have applied for pensions under the act of July 4, 1836, whose claims have been suspended; prepared in conformity with the resolution of the Senate of the United States of September 16, 1850.

Names.	Residence.	Reasons for suspension.
Adkins, Elizabeth, widow of James	Georgetown, Scott	Suspended for further proof and specification.
Arthur, Catharine, formerly widow of James Mackay	—, Casey	Suspended for further proof of service in 1782, and of the marriage.
Ashley, Winifred, (dec'd), widow of Peter	Madisonville, Hopkins	For proof of the date of the marriage.
Brown, Phebe, widow of Thomas	—, Estell	For proof of the date of the marriage.
Brown, Mary G., widow of William A.	—, Mercer	Married after service, which must be established if she apply under the act of July 7, 1838.
Bruce, Milly, widow of Benjamin	Long Lick, Scott	Suspended for further proof.
Cammack, Nancy, widow of John	Springfield, Washington	Proof awaited from the Richmond army records.
Clark, Charity, widow of David	—, Graves	Service admitted—proof of marriage required.
Conover, Lydia, widow of Garret	—, Adair	For further proof of marriage and service concurrent.
Delaforce, Catharine, widow of Joseph	—, Bourbon	Not any satisfactory evidence of service.
Dodd, Anna, widow of Thomas	Bedford, Trimble	Awaiting further proof and amended declaration.
Fox, Elizabeth, widow of Titus	Madisonville, Hopkins	Inadequate proof of marriage.
Fowler, Rachel, widow of Elections	Harrodsburg, Mercer	For proof of marriage and service.
Fulkerson, Margaret (dec'd), widow of John	Litchfield, Grayson	For further proof of service and marriage.
Gaines, Catharine, widow of Henry	Overton, Owen	Claim not made out in any essential respect.
Goodram, Sally, widow of Bennett	—, Warren	Awaiting proof of service and marriage.
Hagan, Rebecca (dec'd), widow of Raphael	—, Spencer	Service for more than two years as corporal in the Maryland line admitted—proof of marriage required.
Hamilton, Margaret, widow of Charles	Georgetown, Scott	Proof of service and of marriage inadequate.
Hampton, Eliza, widow of Preston	—, Grant	For further proof of service and marriage.
Harvey, Lucy, widow of Joseph	—, Monroe	Marriage admitted—proof of identity required that the soldier of the same name on the Virginia pay certificate for £16 15s. was her husband.

373 [37]

Name	Location	Notes
Hill, Rebecca, widow of Richard	Greenville, Muhlenberg	Suspended for proof of the date of the marriage.
Hale, Nancy, widow of Thomas	——, Madison	Suspended for further proof.
House, Sally, widow of Nicholas	——, Rock Castle	Suspended for proof of the date of the marriage.
Holliday, Elizabeth, widow of Moses	——, Gallatin	Suspended for further proof.
Hurst, Mary Ann, widow of Henry	——, Henry	For proof of the date of the marriage.
Horndon, Mary, widow of James	——, Christian	Claim not complete—awaiting the papers promised by the agent.
Johnson, Jane, formerly wid. of Sam'l Cooper	Georgetown, Scott	For more satisfactory proof of service.
Luttrell, Frances, widow of Rodham	Owenton, Owen	Suspended for proof of service.
Mardin, Elizabeth, widow of William	Covington city	For captain and colonel's names of the Virginia line under whom he served, and the period, length, and grade of service.
Matlock, Lucy, widow of Zachariah	Princeton, Caldwell	For further proof.
Mullins, Mary, widow of James	Harrodsburg, Mercer	Not fully proved for as much as six months' service.
Milbanks, Mary, widow of John	White Sulphur, Scott	Not any proof of the alleged service in the Virginia line.
McCaw, Margaret, formerly widow of Michael Downs	——, Gallatin	Service not set forth nor proved—no proof of marriage.
McHargue, Sarah, widow of William	——, Laurel	Further proof of service and marriage awaited.
Neal, Milly (dec'd), widow of Micajah	Shelbyville, Shelby	Not a widow at the date of the act, and died before August 28, 1842. The regiment and officers' names must be given, and further proof of service and marriage.
New, Lucinda, widow of John	——, Wayne	Service not set forth or proved—marriage admitted.
Nutter, Sarah, widow of Robert	——, Fayette	No adequate proof of his captain's commission, or of service, or of marriage.
Nutter, Elizabeth, widow of David	——, Scott	
Polly, Mary, widow of Edward	——, Letcher	Proof of marriage defective.
Ray, Henrietta, widow of Andrew	——, Edmonson	For further proof and specification.
Richardson, Mary, widow of Jonathan	——, Harrison	No definite account of marriage or service.
Roberts, Sarah (dec'd), widow of William	——, Rock Castle	For proof of identity that claimant is widow of one of the soldiers of the same name on the comptroller's certificate.
Byley, Jalilah, widow of John	Harrodsburg, Mercer	Suspended for further proof and specification.
Shannon, Catharine, widow of Robert	——, Henry	Not six months' service.
Sharpe, Elizabeth, widow of William	——, Casey	Period, length and grade of service, and names of company and field officers and stations, and a reference thereof to the records at Annapolis.
Snell, Mary, widow of Lewis	——, Harrison	Suspended for further proof.

STATEMENT—Continued.

Names.	Residence.	Reasons for suspension.
Sparks, Lucy, widow of Henry	—, Owen	Suspended for further proof.
Sproul, Jane, widow of Alexander	—, Clinton	He did not serve six months.
Taylor, Elizabeth, widow of John T.	—, Wayne	Service not set forth nor officers' names given—the service should be specified, and tested by the Richmond records.
Vandivier, Sarah, widow of Cornelius	Harrodsburg, Mercer	Suspended for further proof from the State records at Trenton, N. J.
Warmsley, Comfort, widow of Thomas	—, Montgomery	Not on the Virginia rolls—no proof of service—no particulars of service.
Wilkins, Elizabeth, widow of James	—, Todd	For proof of identity of her husband with the member of the Charleston artillery—service under Col. Wayne, of the militia, admitted.
Winnifred, Judith, widow of David	—, Adair	The name is found on the list of depreciation certificates for £22 1s. 3d., and evidence is required that this belonged to her husband.
Wood, Martha Ann	Bartholomew, Christian	Suspended for proof from the North and South Carolina records—after specifying period, length and grade of service, and names of officers and stations, under each State and term.
Yarborough, Mary	Randolph, Bath	Suspended for further proof and specification.
Young, Ann (deceased)	Reuben, Greenup	Suspended for further proof.

A list of the names of persons residing in Kentucky who have applied for pensions under the act of July 7, 1838, whose claims have been suspended; prepared in conformity with the resolution of the Senate of the United States, September 16, 1850.

Names.	Residence.	Reasons for suspension.
Alday, Sarah, widow of Seth............	Brandenburg, Mead...	A private of cavalry, pensioned for $100 per annum, died in 1847—widow must apply under act of 1848.
Austin, Elizabeth, widow of John	—, Jefferson............	Required to apply under acts of July 17, 1844, and February 2, 1848, and adduce some further proof of marriage.
Baber or Beaver, Hannah, widow of Obadiah..	Winchester, Clark......	Not six months' service.
Baker, Catharine, widow of Charles.........	Richmond, Madison...	Not a widow at the date of the act.
Baldwin, Drusilla, widow of Edward.........	Madisonville, Hopkins.	Testimony returned to Mr. Boyle for amendment September 20, 1848—does not appear to have been replaced.
Bettlesworth, Mary, formerly widow of Robertson McKinney.	Columbia, Adair.........	Proof of identity required of the widow's former husband with the matross of the same name in the certificate of depreciation of the Virginia auditor.
Black, Milly, widow of John...............	Winchester, Clark......	For further proof and specification.
Blankenship, Fanny, widow of Abel.......	—, Russell...............	For further proof and specification.
Boyd, Nancy, widow of William...........	Owingsville, Bath......	Service after the revolution—no claim.
Brackett, Lydia, formerly widow of John Ross.	Madisonville, Hopkins.	To lie until called for.
Bradford, Mary, widow of Enoch..........	Georgetown, Scott.....	Proof of service and of marriage not complete.
Bush, Nancy, widow of Drury.............	—, Perry.................	Barred by act of April 30, 1844—may apply under act of June 17, 1844.
Campbell, Sally, widow of James..........	—, Muhlenburg........	For want of proof—papers enclosed to Hon. I. Carr, May 27, 1840.
Carpenter, Mary, widow of William.......	Columbia, Adair.......	No satisfactory proof of marriage.
Cash, Dorothea (deceased), widow of William.	—, Rock Castle.........	No claim—she was not a widow under the act, and she died before August 16, 1842.
Catlett, Susan, widow of Peter............	Burlington, Boone.....	Proof wanting of his service as a lieutenant in the Virginia line.
Courtney, Catharine, widow of Thomas Courtney, alias John Smith.	Falmouth, Pendleton ...	For proof of identity of one of the John Smith's attached to the 7th regiment, Maryland line.
Davenport, Patsey (deceased), widow of William.	Cadiz, Trigg.............	For specification of service and proof of identity with the Wm. Davenport of the depreciation certificate of service in the Virginia line.
Dean, Jane, widow of John...............	—, Carroll...............	The difficulties of the proof of service are removed by the act of July 1, 1848.

STATEMENT—Continued.

Names.	Residence.	Reasons for suspension.
Dishman, Sally, widow of William	——, Barren	For proof of the date of the marriage.
Dunn, Elizabeth, widow of Richard	Richmond, Madison	For proof and specification and proof of marriage.
Eades, Sarah, widow of Charles	——, Wayne	Proof of identity required with the soldier of the same name on the depreciation certificate for £14 6s. 4d.
Farquhar, Betsey, widow of James	——, Henry	No proof or specification of service.
Fifer, Catharine, widow of Israel	——, Nicholas	For proof of service from the records at Annapolis.
Finley, Jane (deceased), widow of Joseph	Maysville, Mason	Not a widow at the date of the act—died before August 16, 1842.
Forsee, Judith, widow of James Bledsoe	——, Carroll	For further proof and specification.
Francis, Nancy, widow of John	Monticello, Wayne	Marriage admitted—proof of service not complete.
Gaines, Ann, widow of William	Versailles, Woodford	Defects in this case respecting proof of service are removed by the act of July 1, 1848.
Garrison, Mary, widow of Samuel	Long Lick, Scott	Marriage and service not fully proved.
Gillaspie, Holly, widow of John	——, Todd	Marriage and service not proved.
Gregory, Sally (deceased), widow of Thomas	Princeton, Caldwell	For further proof and specification.
Guess, Constance, widow of Joseph	Princeton, Caldwell	Marriage not fully proved.
Hamilton, Ruth, widow of William	——, Gallatin	For further proof of marriage and service.
Hall, Margaret (deceased), widow of James	Madisonville, Monroe	Died before July 1, 1848, and her children have no claim.
Hammersly, Judith, widow of James	Falmouth, Pendleton	Marriage not fully proved.
Hayes, Elizabeth (deceased,) widow of William	Somerset, Pulaski	For proof of marriage and decease, and children's names.
Haydon, Susanna, widow of James	Frankfort, Frankfort	Claims for service as an Indian spy—no proof or specification—her husband died in 1840 and failed to apply for a pension.
Hogue, Alley, widow of Andrew	Middleburgh, Casey	One year's service admitted—marriage not proved.
Holbrook, Aggia, widow of William	——, Lawrence	Marriage admitted—service requires further proof.
Hunter, Ruth, widow of John	——, Madison	For further proof.
Hutton, Hannah, widow of Henry	——, Rock Castle	Marriage admitted—service requires proof.
Jackson, Mary, widow of John	——, Garrard	For further proof and specification.
Johnson, Nancy, widow of Dilliams	Hopkinsville, Christian	For further proof.
Johns, Mary, widow of James	Jamestown, Russell	For further proof and specification.

Jones, Mary, widow of Joshua	Williamstown, Grant	Objections removed by act of July 1, 1848—service admitted—marriage requires proof.
Kendall, Elizabeth, widow of Benjamin	——, Hardin	For further proof.
Kercheval, Elizabeth, widow of John	——, Scott	J. Kercheval is found on the list of depreciation for £19 12s.—about eighteen months' service—the names of his officers wanted under whom he served in the Virginia line.
Kinkade, Mary, widow of Robert	——, Hardin	For further proof and specification.
King, Catharine, widow of John	——, Bracken	For further proof and specification.
Kitchen, Jane, widow of James	——, Carter	For proof by the Virginia records at Richmond.
Knight, Sarah, widow of John	Hopkinsville, Christian	Defective proof, and claim withdrawn.
Law, Mary, widow of Jesse	——, Jefferson	Proof of marriage deficient.
Lanham, Catharine, widow of Greenberry	——, Casey	For further proof and specification of service.
May, Sarah, widow of John	——, Jefferson	Service and marriage not fully proved—claim withdrawn.
McLean, Sarah, widow of Samuel	——, Woodford	For proof of service by the records at Harrisburg.
Minor, Mary, widow of Joseph	——, Owen	For proof of marriage.
Moreland, Elizabeth, widow of Dudley	——, Wayne	For proof of service.
Moore, Diana, widow of William	Newcastle, Henry	For proof of identity with the soldier of the Virginia line.
Moore, Mildred (dec'd), widow of John	Princeton, Caldwell	For further proof from the North Carolina records.
Morris, Susan, widow of Thomas	——, Madison	For proof of marriage.
Parish, Martha, widow of Nathaniel	Georgetown, Scott	Marriage and service not fully proved.
Penn, Margaret, widow of Shadrach	Georgetown, Scott	Captain's service in the Maryland line not sustained by the records at Annapolis, or this department.
Perkins, Gillian, widow of Moses	Frankfort, Franklin	For proof from the records of North Carolina.
Pike, Anne, widow of Ephraim	——, Montgomery	For further specification—the rolls of the Virginia line are silent.
Polk, Rhoda, widow of Ephraim	Georgetown, Scott	Service in the Pennsylvania line requires further proof and specification, the rolls being silent.
Pumphrey, Lucy, widow of Henry	Somerset, Pulaski	The difficulties of service obviated by the joint resolution of July 1, 1848, are rendered null and void by the preceding death of the widow.
Ray, Margaret, widow of John	——, Union	Service must be proved by the records at Annapolis.
Reynolds, Nancy, widow of Richard	——, Muhlenburg	For proof of marriage.
Robard, Francis, widow of Jesse	——, Mercer	Not a widow under this act—may claim under act July, 1848.
Rogers, Lydia, widow of Kinsey	——, Harrison	For a further specifying and proof of service.
Rouse, Elizabeth, widow of Lewis	Henderson, Henderson	Service allowed—marriage not proved.

STATEMENT—Continued.

Names.	Residence.	Reasons for suspension.
Saunders, Mary, widow of Thomas.	Shepherdsville, Bullitt.	For proof of identity with the soldier of the same name in the Virginia comptroller's certificate of depreciation.
Shrewsbury, Nancy, widow of Allen.	——, Garrard.	Not six months' service.
Sleet, Rachel, widow of James.	——, Washington.	Not a widow under the act—died before August 16, 1842.
Smith, Elizabeth, widow of William.	——, Russell.	Marriage not proved.
Smith, Parnuella, widow of Matthew.	——, Warren.	No proof of service—no color of claim.
Spiers, Lucy, widow of Charles.	Owenton, Owen.	Defective proof—papers withdrawn.
Stapleton, Sarah, widow of Thomas.	Manchester, Clay.	For proof of service by the North Carolina records.
Sullivan, Caty, widow of Peter.	——, Floyd.	Service admitted under act July 1, 1848, heretofore suspended for lack of proof of service.
Sinclor, Mary, formerly wid. of Wm. McClure	Somerset, Pulaski.	For proof from the Auditor's office, Richmond.
Sullivan, Jane, widow of Patrick.	Covington, Kenton.	For proof of identity with the soldier of the same name on the books of the Auditor General of Pennsylvania.
Thompson, Annis (deceased), widow of John.	——, Shelby.	Not a widow under the act, and died before August 23, 1842.
Tinsley, Sarah, widow of William.	——, Shelby.	Application not complete.
Vanzant, Margaret, widow of Garret.	Glasgow, Barren.	Proof of commission and service required from the Raleigh records.
Wages, Mary, widow of Benjamin.	——, Morgan.	Not a widow at the date of the act.
Walker, Elizabeth, widow of James.	——, Jessamin.	For proof of marriage.
Wells, Susanna, widow of Richard.	Prestonburg, Floyd.	Married in 1797, no claim—she may renew under act July 29, 1848, if she survived its passage.
Walls, Margaret, widow of Jacob.	Harrodsburg, Mercer.	Service not specified nor proved—not on the rolls of Armand's corps.
Yoakum, Magdalen, widow of Jacob.	——, Bourbon.	Not a widow at the date of the act—died before August 16, 1842.

A list of persons residing in Kentucky who have applied for pensions under the act of July 7, 1838, whose claims have been rejected; prepared in conformity with the resolution of the Senate of the United States, September 16, 1850.

Names.	Residence.	Reasons for rejection.
Boyd, Nancy, widow of William	——, Bath	She was not a widow at the time the act was passed.
Berry, Sarah, widow of James	——, Madison	He did not serve six months in a regularly embodied corps.
Childers, Sarah, widow of Pleasant	——, Pike	Her husband was living when this act was passed.
Cain, Margaret, widow of John	——, Christian	She was not a widow at the time this act was passed.
Elston, Elizabeth, widow of Benjamin	——, Trimble	Her husband was living on July 7, 1828.
Fishback, Patsey, widow of John	——, Bracken	Her husband did not serve six months.
Gibson, Mary, widow of Jacob	——, Barren	Her husband deceased after the passage of this act.
Gratz, Lucy (deceased), widow of John	——, Trigg	Widow died before the passage of the joint resolution of August 16, 1842.
Herndon, Mary, widow of Thomas	——, Scott	Her husband did not perform six months actual service.
Hudson, Jemima, widow of Benjamin	——, Garrard	He did not serve six months.
Langdon, Eda, widow of Charles	——, Jefferson	Married after service.
McKinney, Polly, widow of John	——, Bourbon	Served before the commencement of the revolutionary war.
Martin, Nancy, widow of Benjamin	——, Barry	Husband died after the passage of the act of July 7, 1838.
Metheany, Elender, widow of Luke	——, Monroe	She was not a widow at the date this act was passed.
Morgan, Patsey (deceased), widow of Philip	——, Washington	Widow died before the passage of this act.
Minton, Jane, widow of John	——, Harrison	Husband died after the passage of this act.
Nance, Maria, widow of Frederick	——, Washington	She was not married until the year 1818.
Street, Trephine, widow of Anthony	——, Mercer	He did not serve six months.

STATEMENT—Continued.

Names.	Residence.	Reasons for rejection.
Speagle, Susan, widow of Samuel	——, Nicholas	Did not serve six months.
Thompson, Keziah (deceased), widow of Lawrence	——, Madison	She died before the passage of the act.
Williamson, Nancy, widow of James	——, Allen	Husband was living at the date of the passage of the act.

A list of the names of persons residing in Tennessee who have applied for pensions under the act of June 7, 1832, whose claims have been rejected; prepared in conformity with the resolution of the Senate of the United States, September 16, 1850.

Names.	Residence.	Reasons for rejection.
Alman, Willie	Alexandria, Cannon	Only three months' and twelve days' service.
Armistead, Thaddeus	Carthage, Smith	Not six months' service.
Arnold, William	Murfreesboro', Rutherford	Not six months' service.
Allison, Hugh	Columbia, Maury	Not military service.
Brown, Claiborne (dec'd), heirs of	Murfreesboro', Rutherford	Both parties died before the passage of the act.
Barkley, John, sen	Nashville, Davidson	Not military, but team service.
Boyte, William	Clinton, Anderson	Only four months' and eight days' service.
Braden, James	Murfreesboro', Rutherford	Not military, but team service.
Bozman, Samuel	Nashville, Davidson	He did not serve six months.
Blair, Samuel	——, Greene	Not six months' service.
Brown, William	Pulaski, Giles	Not under military authority.
Bradberry, John	Franklin, Williamson	Desertion.
Bond, James	Huntingdon, Carroll	Desertion.
Bennett, Solomon	Kingston, Roane	Privateer service.
Barnett, Carter	Franklin, Williamson	Service on board his father's schooner, which was pressed into the commissary's service.
Burch, George		
Burnett, William	Washington, Rhea	Not military service.
Byrd, Jesse	Kingston, Roane	Not six months' service.
Carter, Hugh	Clinton, Anderson	Not military service. [Papers withdrawn.]
Champman, John H	Athens, McMinn	Service after the revolution.
Coffey, Eli	Waynesboro', Wayne	Not six months' service.
Copeland, John	Jonesboro', Washington	Not six months' service.
Crouch, Jesse	Boiling Spring P. O., Fentress	Not military service.
Cahill, Elisha	——, Overton	Not six months' service.
Chapin, Paul	Jonesboro', Washington	Not six months' service.
Coffman, Jonathan	Madisonville, Monroe	Service after the revolution.
Coffman, Isaac	Rogersville, Hawkins	Not six months' service.
Collier, Aaron		

STATEMENT—Continued.

Names.	Residence.	Reasons for rejection.
Call, William	Franklin, Williamson	Privateer service.
Cruchfield, John	Tazewell, Claiborne	Not six months' service.
Casey (or Kasey), Alexander	Kingston, Roane	Service after the revolution.
Cunningham, Samuel	Columbia, Maury	Not six months' service.
Duggle, Julius	Elizabethtown, Carter	Service after the revolution.
Dunn, Siles (dec'd)	Murfreesboro', Rutherford	Died before the passage of the act.
Durham, Joseph	Perryville, Perry	Not military service.
Daffron, John	Pikeville, Bledsoe	Not under military organization.
Day, John, 2d	——, Campbell	Desertion.
Everly, John	Pulaski, Giles	Not six months' service.
Edwards, John	Dandridge, Jefferson	Desertion.
Earnhart, George	Jackson, Madison	Not six months' service.
Fulton, Thomas	Waynesboro', Wayne	Service after the revolution.
Francher (or Fancher), James	Livingston, Overton	Service after the revolution.
Foster, George	Vernon, Hickman	Not six months' service.
Gwinn, Rachel	Nashville, Davidson	Died before the passage of the act.
Garrott, Thomas	Pall Mall, Fentress	Not six months' service.
Guthrie, Henry	Nashville, Davidson	Not military service.
Gillespie, David	Franklin, Williamson	Not military service.
Gibson, James	Paris, Henry	Not six months' service.
Gregory, Jacob	Gallatin, Sumner	Not six months' service.
Grammer, Joseph	Kingston, Roane	Belonged to the army of France.
Hagar, John	Nashville, Davidson	Belonged to the army of France.
Hass, Henry	Alexandria, Cannon	Team or wagon service.
Hale, Richard	Pulaski, Giles	Only three months' and twenty-one days' service.
Hitchcock, William	Sparta, White	Service after the revolution.
Hamilton, Joseph	Lebanon, Wilson	Not six months' service.
Howe, Jacob	Rogersville, Hawkins	Not six months' service.

Hodgins, Joseph	Dandridge, Jefferson	Not six months' service.
Hazlewood, Benjamin	Knoxville, Knox	Not military service.
Hargrove, Bennett	Franklin, Williamson	Not six months' service.
Henderson, John	Fayetteville, Lincoln	Wagon or team service.
Harlow, Thomas	Jonesboro', Washington	Desertion.
Harrington, Anaworth	Lebanon, Wilson	Not six months' service.
Hickman, Benjamin	Sparta, White	Not six months' service.
Holt, Featherstone	Rogersville, Hawkins	Not six months' service.
Hodges, Jesse	Purdy, McNairy	Not six months' service.
Hollingworth, Jacob	Clinton, Anderson	Not six months' service.
Horseley, Rowland	Gallatin, Sumner	Not military service.
Harpole, Adam	Lebanon, Wilson	Service not during the revolution.
Hamble, Robert	Dandridge, Jefferson	His service was not six months during the revolution.
Jarman, Emery	Knoxville, Knox	Desertion.
Jones, Thomas	Troy, Obion	Not military service—served as a butcher.
Jones, William	Paris, Henry	Not six months service.
Johnson, Jerusha	Lexington, Henderson	Not six months service.
Kimes, Conrad	Fayetteville, Lincoln	Not six months service.
Knowles, John	Sparta, White	Forage master—not military service.
Kerr, William	Cleveland, Bradley	Not military service.
Kirk, George	Jonesborough, Washington	Service after the revolution.
King, Arthur	Fayetteville, Lincoln	Not under military organization.
Lloyd, Owen		Papers withdrawn by E. J. Shields, December 28, 1837. He did not serve twelve months by order of competent authority.
Long, Reuben	Rutledge, Granger	Only five months service.
Livingston, Henry	Livingston, Overton	Not military service—driving pack-horses.
Lyles, Thomas	Dandridge, Jefferson	Not six months military service.
Lloyd, Jarrett	Lebanon, Wilson	Not military service—a wagoner.
Ledbetter, Rowland	Lewisburg, Marshall	Not six months service.
Lovel, William	Gainesboro', Jackson	Not military service.
Luttrell, James	Knoxville, Knox	Not six months service.
Lester, James	Lebanon, Wilson	Not six months military service.
Lassiter, Hezekiah	Winchester, Franklin	Did not serve six months in person.
Lane, Owen	Nashville, Davidson	Did not serve six months in person.
Latham, Samuel	Centreville, Heickman	Not six months service.
Moore, James	Sparta, White	Not six months service.

STATEMENT—Continued.

Names.	Residence.	Reasons for rejection.
Mank, Henry	Kingsport, Sullivan	Not six months service.
Morrow, Richard	Madisonville, Monroe	Not six months service.
Martin, George		Papers withdrawn by Hon. Cave Johnson, December 20, 1836. He did not serve six months during the revolution.
McMahan, Redman	McKinnville, Warren	Desertion.
Miller, Jacob	Fayetteville, Lincoln	Did not serve six months.
McKenzie, William	Murfreesboro', Rutherford	Did not serve six months.
Marshall, Daniel (deceased)	Carthage, Smith	Died before the passage of the act.
Meadon, Jonas		Not six months service.
Owen, Peter	Paris, Henry	Not six months service.
Partee, Edmund	Murfreesboro', Rutherford	Not six months military service.
Price, Jesse	Mellyville, Bedford	Served only four months.
Pitchle, Alexander	Tazewell, Clairborne	Not under military organization or competent authority.
Poe, Henry	Blountville, Sullivan	Desertion.
Rutherford, James	Gallatin, Sumner	Service as a wagoner, except three months.
Ryal, William	Chesnut Grove, Davidson	Did not serve during the revolution.
Reeder, Benjamin	Pall Mall, Fentress	Not under military organization, or competent authority.
Reynolds, Hamilton	Purdy, McNairy	Not six months service.
Robertson, Thomas	Dover, Stewart	Under age—not on the rolls—no proof of service.
Richardson, William	Sevier C. H.	Did not serve during the revolution.
Ross, William	Greenville, Greene	Served as a volunteer with wagon and team.
Bichy, John	Lewisburg, Marshall	Not six months service.
Ramsey, James	Murfreesboro', Rutherford	Already pensioned under act May 15, 1828.
Ross, Edward	Jonesboro', Washington	Did not serve six months during the revolution.
Ryland, Sylvester	Jonesboro', Washington	Service after the revolution.
Spurlock, William	Rogersville, Hawkins	Not six months service.
Swanson, William	Madisonville, Monroe	Not six months service.
Snell, Stephen	Perryville, Perry	Not military service.
Schrimspear, John	Madisonville, Monroe	Desertion.
Simpson, James	Pikeville, Bledsoe	Died before the passage of the act.

Name	Place, County	Remarks
Stanfield, Thomas	Sparta, White	Not six months service.
Sheddin, Thomas	Madisonville, Monroe	Service after the revolution.
Smith, Benjamin	Covington, Tipton	Not six months service.
Sims, Thomas	Lebanon, Wilson	Not military service—shad fishing.
Simmons, Nathaniel	Murfreesboro', Maury	Not six months service.
Sell, Henry	Blountsville, Sullivan	Not regularly organized service under competent military authority.
Sampson, Francis	Carthage, Smith	Not six months personal service.
Smith, Nathaniel	Murfreesboro', Maury	Not six months service.
Trogden, Ezekiel	Dandridge, Jefferson	Not under competent authority.
Troxell, David		He did not serve during the revolution. Papers withdrawn February 21, 1846, by Hon. R. Johnson.
Thompson, Isaac	Maryville, Blount	Not military service—pork and beef packing.
Watkins, Richard	Murfreesboro', Rutherford	Not six months service.
Winkle, James	Jonesboro', Washington	Not six months service.
Wolfinbarger, Peter	Knoxville, Knox	Not six months personal service.
Wall, Randolph	Sevierville, Sevier	Not six months service.
Winter, Frederick	Lebanon, Wilson	Not under military organization. Indian wars for self-defence.
Williams, Francis	Sparta, White	Not full six months service.
Waller, Elisha	Tazewell, Claiborne	In wars for self-defence—not regularly embodied or paid.
Williams, Thomas	Pulaski, Giles	Not under military authority or organization.
Willington, Hall	Paris, Henry	Not six months service.
Wood, John	Rogersville, Hawkins	Desertion.
Yearwood, John	Murfreesboro', Rutherford	Not six months service.
Zollinger, Alexander	Sevierville, Sevier	Only three months service.

A list of the names of persons residing in Tennessee who have applied for pensions under the act of June 7, 1832, whose claims have been suspended; prepared in conformity with the resolution of the Senate of the United States, September 16, 1850.

Names.	Residence.	Reasons for suspension.
Anderson, William	Nashville, Davidson	For further proof and more precise specification.
Atkins, Henry	Clinton, Anderson	For further proof and more correct specification.
Allen, Benjamin	Athens, McMinn	For more reliable testimony.
Baker, John	Lebanon, Wilson	For further proof and more precise specification.
Barnes, Barnet, (deceased)	——, Morgan	For further proof. Papers sent to Hon. Cave Johnson, February 1, 1840.
Begley, Henry	Stewart	He did not serve six months.
Berdsong, William	Somerville, Fayette	Period, length and grade of service, and names of company and field officers, and service submitted for proof to the North Carolina comptroller.
Bellingsly, Walter	Athens, McMinn	For direct proof of service, and that he was made prisoner. As a scout and spy he is not allowable.
Bleakley, William	Murfreesboro', Rutherford	He did not serve six months.
Blundell, Absalom		For further proof and more precise specification. Papers withdrawn by E. J. Shields.
Braly, John	Huntingdon, Carroll	For further proof from the North Carolina records, and more correct specification.
Beech, Lodovick B	Franklin, Williamson	For amended specification of the details of service.
Bearden, Richard	Purdy, McNairy	For further proof from the South Carolina records.
Branden, Josiah, (deceased) heirs of	Winchester, Franklin	No regular papers on file.
Braden, James	Clinton, Anderson	Not on the rolls—no proof of service.
Brandon, Captain William	Carthage, Smith	For proof of identity—three persons of the same name who served, and one who did not serve.
Brown, Robert	Reynoldsburgh, Humphreys	For period, length and grade of service, and names of company and field officers, and localities.
Bull, John	——, Hardin	For proof from the South Carolina records, and more precise specification.
Burnham, Ivey	——, Dickson	For proof from the North Carolina records, and more precise specification.
Bussy, Cornelius	Fayetteville, Lincoln	For proof of service by witnesses.

Name	Location	Remarks
Caldwell, Robert	Fayetteville, Lincoln	For additional evidence.
Carver, Christopher	Madisonville, Monroe	For proof from the Harrisburg records.
Caya, Ambrose	Chesnut Grove, Davidson	Defective proof of service.
Cheasher, James	McMinnville, Warren	No proof of service.
Cole, John	Lexington, Henderson	Not on the North Carolina rolls—witnesses required for the regular service.
Conner, Derby, (deceased)	Benton, Polk	No proof of service.
Condry, William	Tazewell, Claiborne	Claims for service as an Indian spy. His authority is required to serve as such.
Cannon, William	——, Green	For a more perfect setting forth of service. Declaration not in form.
Conly, Neill	——, Lawrence	A wagon driver in the South Carolina militia.
Dafnow, John	Dandridge, Jefferson	Name not on the rolls. No proof of service. If he served in the militia he must name period, length and grade of service, and names of company and field officers, and stations, battles and marches.
Davis, Joshua	Tazewell, Claiborne	For further proof of service.
Davis, Surry	Kingston, Roane	For details of service and officers, and proof from the South Carolina records.
Day, Ransom	Tazewell, Claiborne	Name not on the rolls of the Virginia line—proof by two witnesses required.
Denham, David	Rogersville, Hawkins	For proof and specification of service.
Dickson, Thomas	Clinton, Campbell	The Pennsylvania records afford no proof of his, or of his captain's service.
Dover, Joshua	Pikeville, Bledsoe	For further proof of service.
Dunaway, Thomas	Dandridge, Jefferson	For further details and proof of service.
Drewry, Richard	Trenton, Gibson	For further proof and specification.
Duff, Hugh E.	Rutledge, Grainger	Not on Colonel Preston's rolls, fifteenth regiment Pennsylvania line—nine months continuous militia service not admissible.
Elder, Andrew, (deceased)	Rutledge, Grainger	Not on the rolls of the Virginia line. No proof of service.
Ellis, James	Jonesboro', Washington	Service in Indian wars after the revolution.
Falkner, Henry	Knoxville, Knox	No proof of service—no proof of such service—claim rejected.
Fooshell, Elijah	Lebanon, Wilson	Not military service.
Fox, Matthew	——, Cocke	For period, length and grade of service, and names of company and field officers, and proof by reference therewith to the Comptroller General of South Carolina.
Fox, Gaiter	Trenton, Gibson	Survivors in Wake county, N. C., and the records at Raleigh, must furnish evidence in this case.

[37]

STATEMENT—Continued.

Names.	Residence.	Reasons for suspension.
Green, Arthur	Sparta, White	For period, length and grade of service, and names of company and field officers.
Grimsley, George	Lexington, Henderson	For period and length of each tour—North Carolina militia did not serve six months' continuous service.
Garner, Henry	Savannah, Hardin	For a more particular detail of service.
Gentry, Meshack	Madisonville, Monroe	For proof of his commission as captain, and service in the North Carolina militia.
Gibson, Charles	Rogersville, Hawkins	For more particular details of service.
Gower, Matthew	Lawrenceburg, Lawrence	For period, length and grade of service, and names of company and field officers.
Gowan, Zephaniah	Rogersville, Hawkins	Service in the militia requires specifying of each tour—period, length and grade, and names of company and field officers.
Goodwin, David	——, Bedford	Period, length and grade of service, and names of company and field officers.
Grant, Isaac	Dandridge, Jefferson	For proof of identity with the soldier of the same name on the certificate of North Carolina.
Hackney, Thomas	Clarksville, Montgomery	For further and better proof of service.
Head, Robert	Springfield, Robertson	He has not proved six months' service.
Hitchcock, Moses	Waverly, Humphreys	For further proof and explanation.
Hembree, Drewry	Clinton, Campbell	For more perfect details and less overrating of his militia service of South Carolina.
Henderson, George Lewis	Jamestown, Fentress	For proof of service.
Hendrix, John (deceased)	Elizabethtown, Carter	Militia service overrated—no proof whatever exhibited.
Hill, John	Gallatin, Sumner	There is a discrepancy in the periods of service between claimant and the certificate of pay of Comptroller of North Carolina—he states 1776 '77—the certificate, 1781, '82.
Hiffington, Archibald	Lawrenceburg, Lawrence	For further proof.
Holmes, James	Perryville, Perry	No evidence of service.
Hopkins, Robert G	Madisonville, Monroe	For further proof.
Hollis, James	Waynesboro', Wayne	For further proof.
Hobbs, Thomas	Tazewell, Claiborne	Service must be proved by certificate of pay of the Virginia comptroller or auditor.

Name	Place	Notes
Hansard, William	Knoxville, Knox	Not military service—service as a jail guard.
Hardaway, Joseph	Springfield, Robertson	For further proof of service.
Hudson, Hall	Fayetteville, Lincoln	For further proof.
Humphries, Elisha	Elizabethtown, Carter	He did not serve six months.
Hunter, Francis	Clinton, Anderson	For further proof.
Humphreys, George	Jonesboro', Washington	Service in Indian wars in 1793 and 1795—no claim.
Hutcheson, William	Pulaski, Giles	For further proof and specification.
Isom, Elijah	Athens, McMinn	He did not serve six months.
Jones, Richard	—, Weakly	No proof of service.
Johnson, Solomon	Sevierville, Sevier	For further proof and specification.
Keaton, Zachariah J	Lebanon, Wilson	Not on the rolls—no proof of service.
Kendrick, Jacob		Not on the rolls—service as an Indian spy after the peace. [Papers withdrawn by W. B. Carter.]
Lay, William	Waynesboro', Wayne	Not on the rolls—no proof of service.
Lawson, James	Paris, Henry	For further proof.
Lawson, David	Jacksboro', Campbell	Militia service overrated.
Lawson, Drewry	Rogersville, Hawkins	He did not serve six months.
Lee, Abner	Gainesboro', Jackson	Militia service overrated.
Lucas, Joel	Madisonville, Monroe	Not on the rolls—no proof of service.
Lumpkins, Dickerson	Jacksboro', Campbell	Not on the rolls—no proof of service.
Luttrell, Nathan	—, Weakly	For further proof and specification.
Lodon, James	Pikeville, Bledsoe	For proof by witnesses.
Marberry, Leonard	Brownville, Haywood	Militia service overrated.
Martin, Nathaniel	Pulaski, Giles	A soldier of the same name on the New Hampshire rolls—needs some proof to identify his service as claimant.
Mallory, John	Rogersville, Hawkins	For proof of identity with the soldier of the Virginia line.
Mason, David	Rogersville, Hawkins	For proof of his commission and service.
Marr, John	Brownsville, Haywood	For proof of identity that claimant was the soldier of the same name marked on the Virginia auditor's certificate for £41 2s, 2d.
Morris, John	Waynesboro', Wayne	For proof of identity that he is the soldier of the Virginia line bearing his name.
Measles, Cader	Spencer, Van Buren	For further proof from the North Carolina records.
Monteith, Henry	—, Greene	Not on the Pennsylvania rolls—no proof of service—papers withdrawn.
Moore, James	Kingston, Roane	Militia service overrated.
Means, Joel	McMinnville, Warren	He did not serve six months in any regularly organized corps.

STATEMENT—Continued.

Names.	Residence.	Reasons for suspension.
Mitchell, John	——, Dickson	Militia service of Pennsylvania overrated.
McClung, William	Maryville, Blount	For further proof and specification.
McDaniel, John	Washington, Rhea	For more specific details of service.
McDonough, John (deceased)	Rogersville, Hawkins	The certificate of the Virginia auditor adduced as proof, speaks of a John McDonald, a different person evidently.
McWhirter, James	Fayetteville, Lincoln	For proof of his commission as lieutenant, and service under it.
Miles, William	Gainesboro', Jackson	For proof of his commission as lieutenant, and service in the Maryland line.
Montgomery, Josiah	Kingston, Roane	Not revolutionary service.
Murray, Mark	Lebanon, Wilson	For proof from the North Carolina records.
Nevins, James	Madisonville, Monroe	Not on the rolls of the Georgia line—no proof of service.
Nichols, John	——, Hardin	For further proof of his militia service.
Norris, John	Athens, McMinn	Minute man's service overrated—suspended for better details.
Oliver, Samuel	Jonesboro', Washington	Militia service overrated—for more correct details.
Parker, Elisha	Lawrenceburg, Lawrence	For further proof.
Paul, James	Maryville, Blount	Fraudulent.
Pearce, Philip	Woodbury, Cannon	For further proof.
Primes, Record	Kingston, Roane	For further proof from the North Carolina records.
Prichard, Thomas	Paperville, Sullivan	For proof of service—papers sent to Hon. Andrew Johnson, January 17, 1848.
Prewitt, William	Cleveland, Bradley	For proof from the South Carolina records.
Pruett, Micajah	Pikeville, Bledsoe	Militia service overrated—proof and specification of each tour required.
Rawlett, William	Shelby Corner, Shelby	The records of the Virginia line afford no proof—other evidence awaited.
Robinson, Thomas	Savannah, Hardin	The certificate of the Secretary of State of North Carolina exhibits the name of Thomas Robertson, in Captain Taylor's company.—Thomas Robinson, claimant, served in Captain Harden's company.
Rogers, William	——, Lawrence	No such enlistments in 1775 for two and a half years—no proof of service.

Name	Location	Note
Seymour, Larkin	Red Hill, Grainger	For further proof.
Sharp, Moses	Red Hill, Grainger	Scant evidence for six months' service.
Shively, John	Charleston, Bradley	Name not on the rolls—no proof of service.
Skaggs, James C	Knoxville, Knox	For further proof from the records of South Carolina.
Sledge, Jesse	Bolivar, Hardeman	For some positive proof.
Simmerly, John	Maryville, Blount	For further proof—pork packing not considered military service.
Smith, Spencer	Waynesboro', Wayne	For further proof and more correct details of service.
Story, Daniel	——, Henderson	For further proof.
Snider, Peter	Paris, Henry	For proof of service by two witnesses.
Stevenson, Robert	——, Carroll	For further proof and more precise specification.
Smith, William	Pulaski, Giles	Service as a wagoner—not provided for.
Stricklin, Samuel	Columbia, Maury	For further proof. [Papers withdrawn March 30, 1844, by Hon. A. V. Brown.]
Sneed, Allen	Jasper, Marion	For proof from the North Carolina records.
Stukesbury, Jacob	Clinton, Anderson	Evidence of service insufficient.
Tucker, James	Murfreesboro', Rutherford	He did not serve six months after he rejoined the ranks from deserting.
Taylor, William	South Harpeth, Davidson	No proof of service—no proof of such service.
Taylor, Jacob	Rockholstore, Sullivan	Not on the rolls—no proof of service.
Taylor, William, alias William Snider	Paris, Ilenry	Proof of service by two witnesses required.
Tignor, Isaac	Franklin, Williamson	He did not serve six months.
Thompson, William	Nashville, Davidson	For proof of service and that the officers he names were in command at the period of his enlistment.
Turner, Thomas	Tazewell, Claiborne	For further proof of service either by the North Carolina records or by witnesses who served with him.
Varnedoor, Matthew	Kingsport, Sullivan	Claims for three years' enlistment in the South Carolina line—proof should be produced from the State records at Columbia.
Waddell, John	Newport, Cocke	For proof of service from the records at Raleigh, North Carolina.
Watkins, John	Pulaski, Giles	For proof that he was the John Watkins named in the certificate of the Secretary of State of North Carolina as a soldier of the line of that State.
Waggoner, Christopher	Reynoldsburgh, Humphreys	He has not proved six months' service.
Ware, Rowland	McMinnville, Warren	For proof from the Raleigh records.
Wells, George	Sevier C. H., Sevier	Proof of service in the North Carolina line should be found on the rolls at Raleigh.
West, George	Rutledge C. H.	For a more full description of his service, and the dates, and officers, and places if possible.
West, John	Gallatin, Sumner	For a more specific detail of his service in all its material facts.

STATEMENT—Continued.

Names.	Residence.	Reasons for suspension.
White, William	—, Gibson	Two tours in the Virginia militia would make six months' service, provided they were served out in full, which requires proof.
White, John	Benton, Polk	For proof from the South Carolina records.
White, John	Kingston, Roane	For a more correct narrative of his service, and one more within the bounds of probability.
Willbourn, Lewis	Purdy, McNairy	For further proof.
Williams, Joseph	Clinton, Anderson	For proof from the records at Albany.
Williams, Samuel	Clinton, Anderson	For proof from the South Carolina records.
Wilson, Augustus	Clinton, Anderson	He did not serve six months.
Wood, William	Gallatin, Sumner	For further proof.
Windham, William	—, Hamilton	For proof from the South Carolina records.

A list of the names of persons residing in Tennessee who have applied for pensions under the act of July 4, 1836, whose claims have been rejected; prepared in conformity with the resolution of the Senate of the United States, September 16, 1850.

Names.	Residence.	Reasons for rejection.
Anderson, Nancy, widow of William	——, Knox	Married after the war—he did not serve six months, and no allowance was made for his impressed team-service.
Baker, Mary, widow of Peter	Sparta, White	Married after service.
Courey, Susannah, widow of James	Shelbyville, Bedford	He did not serve six months during the revolution.
Craig, Barbary, widow of John	——, Morgan	Not military service—not under military authority.
Davis, Elizabeth, widow of Jonathan	——, Anderson	He did not serve six months.
Hossler, Christian, widow of Michael	——, Roane	He did not serve six months.
Jones, Elizabeth, widow of Benjamin	Manchester, Coffee	Did not serve in a military capacity.
McCampbell, Mary, widow of Andrew	——, Knox	He did not serve six months.
Peace, Rebecca, formerly widow of Laban Haislip	——, Madison	Married after the war.
Watkins, Rebecca, widow of Isaac	——, Davidson	Not in evidence that he died in the service.
West, Kitty, widow of John T.	——, Sumner	Married after the war.

A list of the names of persons residing in Tennessee who have applied for pensions under the act of July 4, 1836, whose claims have been suspended; prepared in conformity with the resolution of the Senate of the United States of September 16, 1850.

Names.	Residence.	Reasons for suspension.
Boyle, Elizabeth, widow of Andrew	Maryville, Blount	Not six months' service established in this case.
Briggs, Mary, widow of Nathan	Carthage, Smith	For proof of service.
Carroll, Keziah, widow of William	Sparta, White	For proof of marriage and of service from the South Carolina records.
Chisam, Sarah, widow of John	Sparta, White	For proof of marriage and of service from the South Carolina records.
Clay, Milison, widow of John	Murfreesboro', Rutherford	For proof of marriage before service terminated.
Craig, Anna, formerly widow of John Cunningham	Chalk Level, Humphreys	For further proof of service.
Creamer, Sarah, widow of Daniel	Greenville, Greene	Rejected—married after service.
Daniel, Elizabeth, widow of Joab	Lawrenceburgh, Lawrence	For proof of service from the Raleigh records, and the date of marriage.
Davis, Elizabeth, widow of Joseph	Montgomery, Morgan	For proof of service from the records of North Carolina and South Carolina, if he served under both States.
Edwards, Rebecca (deceased) widow of William	Springfield, Robertson	Not a widow at the date of the act.
Emmert, Barbara, widow of Frederick	Sevier, C. H., Sevier	For further proof and specification.
Etheridge, Mary, widow of John	Nashville, Davidson	For proof of the date of the marriage.
Ford, Esther, widow of John	Dandridge, Jefferson	For proof of marriage, and of service by the Pennsylvania records.
Hambright, Mary (deceased), widow of Frederick	Knoxville, Knox	For proof of service from the South Carolina records, and the date of the marriage, and her surviving children.
Harrison, Ann, widow of Barzilla	Shelbyville, Bedford	Proof of service required.

Harp, Sarah, widow of Sampson	——, Overton	For further proof of service and marriage.
Harris, Margaret, widow of Jonathan	Sparta, White	For proof of marriage.
Hatfield, Rachel, widow of Joseph	Jacksboro', Campbell	No proof of service after marriage.
Henry, Margaret, widow of David	Gallatin, Sumner	For proof of identity of her husband with a soldier of the same name on the comptroller's certificate of New York for £60 15s. 5d.
Hutchinson, Polly, widow of Samuel	——, Jackson	For proof of service from the South Carolina rolls, and proof of marriage.
Jackson, Nancy, widow of Stephen	——, Humphreys	For proof of service, from the South Carolina rolls and proof of marriage.
Jackson, Jane, widow of Samuel	Jasper, Marion	For proof of service and marriage.
Jenkins, Hannah, widow of James	——, Sevier	For further proof.
Jones, Martha (deceased) widow of William	——, Carroll	For further proof.
Lamberson, Christina, widow of Lawrence	——, De Kalb	For further proof from the New Jersey records.
Lawson, Anny, widow of John	Montgomery, Morgan	For proof of marriage and of service.
Miller, Martha, widow of Henry	Marysville, Blount	For proof of identity with the warsman of the North Carolina line of the same name.
Millasaps, Bathsheba, widow of Thomas	——, Sevier	For period, length and grade, and names of company and field officers, and the test of the North Carolina records.
Morley, Mary, widow of Lovett	Lewisburg, Marshall	No action on this case—it was mailed from Lewisburg, Tennessee, in 1840, but it is not knowrnly whom.
Morrow, Elizabeth (deceased), widow of Robert	——, Warren	If the service and marriage can be proven, the children of the deceased will be entitled to the same amount from March 4 to death of widow.
McCallister, Elizabeth, widow of Andrew	Madisonville, Monroe	Proof of service and of marriage deficient.
McCampbell, Martha, widow of James	Knoxville, Knox	Witness should testify to the duration of each tour of actual service.
McClusky, Mary, widow of Joseph	Fayetteville, Lincoln	For proof of marriage.
McCormack, Nancy, widow of William	——, Overton	For proof and specification of service.
McKennon, Elizabeth, widow of John	Murfreesboro', Rutherford	For proof of service from the records of South Carolina, and of marriage before the termination of the service.
Owens, Sally, widow of William	Boiling Springs, Fentress	For proof of service by the North Carolina records, and of the marriage before the termination of the same.
Owsley, Charity, widow of John	——, Claiborne	He was a deserter.
Peck, Jane, widow of David	——, Overton	For proof of service and marriage.
Perry, Jane (1st), widow of James	——, Hickman	For proof and specification of service and of marriage prior to the termination thereof.

STATEMENT—Continued.

Names.	Residence.	Reasons for suspension.
Pittman, Keziah, widow of Matthew, formerly widow of Benjamin Rodder	—, Marion	Eighteen months' service admitted—proof of marriage wanting.
Price, Eleanor or Ellen, widow of John	—, Sevier	For further proof.
Reeves, Eleanor, widow of Daniel	Nashville, Davidson	For proof of marriage and service from the South Carolina records.
Roberts, Patsey, widow of Ezra	Lawrenceburg, Lawrence	For further proof of service and of marriage.
Richie, Martha, widow of James	Dresden, Weakly	For proof of marriage.
Rutherford, Rhoda, widow of Julius	Knoxville, Knox	For a new declaration and the usual proof of service and marriage.
Sailor, Mary Ann, widow of Philip	Murfreesboro', Rutherford	Period, length and grade of service, and names of company and field officers and stations should be stated by the witnesses.
Saunderson, Jemima, widow of William	Carthage, Smith	For further proof and specification, and date of marriage.
Saunders, Mary, widow of John	Jacksboro', Campbell	For further proof of marriage, and service subsequent thereto.
Smith, Margaret, widow of Jeremiah	Fayetteville, Lincoln	For proof of identity that the soldier in Secretary Hill's certificate was the husband of claimant, and proof of marriage.
Smith, Blessing, widow of Robert	Jacksboro', Campbell	Names of the officers required in order to inspect the rolls—proof of marriage also required.
Smith, Sarah, widow of Jesse	Harrison, Hamilton	No claim—the rolls do not show that he died in the service.
Smith, Jane, widow of A. G.	Jacksboro', Campbell	He did not serve in any regularly organized corps.
Spencer, Elizabeth, widow of Moses	Lawrenceburg, Lawrence	Married after service.—No claim under this act.
Stapleton, Mary, widow of William	Rogersville, Hawkins	The difficulty connected with the proof of services obviated by the joint resolution of July 1, 1848.
Stevens, Milly (deceased), widow of Meshack	Dresden, Fentress	For proof of marriage.
Stone, Elizabeth (deceased), widow of Conway	Jasper, Marion	For proof of marriage prior to or concurrent with service.
Trotty, Sarah, widow of Thomas	South Harpeth, Davidson	For further proof and specification.
Webb, Elizabeth, widow of John	—, Sevier	Certificate of Secretary of North Carolina in favor of John Webb, under two enlistments from 1777 to 1788, cannot be received as proof in this case.

White, Nelly, widow of Daniel	—, Morgan	For proof of identity with the soldier of the North Carolina line, and of the marriage.
Yancy, Elizabeth, widow of John	Gallatin, Sumner	There does not appear to have been six months' service performed in this case.

A list of the names of persons residing in Tennessee who have applied for pensions under the act of July 7, 1838, whose claims have been rejected; prepared in conformity with the resolution of the Senate of the United States, September 16, 1850.

Names.	Residence.	Reasons for rejection.
Briggs, Isabella (dec'd), widow of John	Greenville, Greene	Died before the joint resolution of August 28, 1842—not a widow at the date of the act.
Butler, Elizabeth, widow of Zachariah	Blountsville, Sullivan	Barred by act of April 30, 1844.
Carroll, Hannah, widow of Daniel	Fayetteville, Lincoln	Not a widow at the date of the act—died before August 28, 1842.
Cobb, Catharine, widow of David	Carthage, Smith	Not six months revolutionary service.
Cooper, Henrietta, widow of Dabney	Carthage, Smith	Not a widow at the date of the act.
Dougherty, Mary, (dec'd), widow of George	—, Franklin	She died before the passage of the act.
Elliott, Miriam, widow of William	Jasper, Marion	Not a widow under the act.
Ferguson, Nancy, widow of Isaac	Franklin, Williamson	Not a widow at the date of the act.
Hulme, Margaret, formerly widow of John Sharpe	Franklin, Williamson	Married after the limit of the act.
Hodges, Emilia, widow of William	Blountsville, Sullivan	No proof of service—name not on the rolls.
Holland, Lavinia, widow of William	—, Morgan	Not a widow at the date of the act.
Hunter, Catharine, widow of Dempsey	Clarksville, Montgomery	Married in 1795.
Hawk, Margaret, widow of Jacob	Blountsvile, Sullivan	Not a widow at the date of the act.
Johnson, Delilah, widow of James	—, Roane	Not a widow under the act.
Maxwell Elizabeth, widow of William	Lancaster, Smith	Not a widow at the date of the act.
Magill, Mary, widow of James	Greenville, Greene	Did not serve six months—not a widow at the date of the act.
Reynolds, Mary, widow of Samuel	Winchester, Franklin	Not a widow at the date of the act.
Reed, Nancy, widow of John	—, Morgan	Married after service—papers withdrawn—J. W. Blackwell, July 2, 1844.
Reed, Sarah, widow of John	Shelbyville, Bedford	Not a widow at the date of the act.

Sloan, Elizabeth, widow of Samuel	Carthage, Smith	Not a widow under the act—died before joint resolution of August 23, 1842.
Tate, Comfort, widow of David	Rutledge, Grainger	Not a widow at the date of the act.
White, Nancy, widow of Gordon	——, Blount	Not a widow under the act—died before August 16, 1842.

A list of the names of persons residing in Tennessee who have applied for pensions under the act of July 7, 1838, whose claims have been suspended; prepared in conformity with the resolution of the Senate of the United States, September 16, 1850.

Names.	Residence.	Reasons for suspension.
Allison, Martha, widow of Robert	Blountsville, Sullivan	No proof of service.
Adams, Mary, widow of William	Morgan Court House	For proof and specification by witnesses; also for proof of marriage.
Allen, Elizabeth, widow of John	Madisonville, Monroe	For proof from the Raleigh records.
Acre, Lucy, widow of John	Blountsville, Sullivan	For proof of marriage.
Armstrong, Nancy, widow of James	Livingston, Overton	Captain's commission requires proof from the State records.
Arnold, Elizabeth, widow of Francis	Sparta, White	For further proof of marriage.
Awalt, Eve, widow of Michael	Winchester, Franklin	The joint resolutions of July 1 and 8 removed the difficulties in this case, and if living he may apply under act of February 2, 1848.
Baggerly, Rebecca, widow of David	Fayetteville Lincoln	For further proof of service and marriage.
Bazwell, Susan, widow of David	Columbia, Maury	For proof of marriage previous to 1800, and application under act of July 29, 1848.
Beavert, Rachel, widow of John	Smithville, De Kalb	For proof of marriage.
Beard, Mary, widow of John	Franklin, Williamson	For further proof of service.
Bonnett, Mary, widow of William	Manchester, Coffee	For further proof of service.
Black, Margaret, widow of John	Livingston, Overton	For further proof and specification.
Bragg, Elizabeth, widow of David	Blountsville, Sullivan	For further proof of service.
Brummett, Mary, widow of Thomas	Robertsville, Anderson	For proof of marriage.
Brecken, Elizabeth, widow of William	Lewisburg, Marshall	For proof of marriage.
Brown, Nancy, widow of Aaron	Madisonville, Monroe	Relieved from defective proof of service by the joint resolution of July 1, 1848, and proof of marriage only is required.
Brown, Mary Ann, widow of Thomas	Jonesboro', Washington	Married after the war—did not serve six months.
Bird, Nancy, widow of Baylor	Franklin, Williamson	For further proof and specification.
Campbell, Rachel, widow of Richard	Perryville, Perry	She was not a widow at the date of the act.
Cantwell, Jane, widow of John	Rogersville, Hawkins	For further proof of marriage.
Capshan, Catharine, formerly widow of John Sennbah	Maryville, Blount	For further proof of marriage and service.
Carlisle, Nancy, widow of William	———, Jackson	Barred by act of April 30, 1844.
Carney, Elizabeth, widow of John	Galladin, Sumner	For proof of marriage.

Cartright, Susannah, widow of Robert	Franklin, Williamson	For further proof and specification, and day of marriage.
Childress, Nancy, widow of Patterson	Dandridge, Jefferson	No proof of service.
Childress, Charity, widow of William	Smithville, De Kalb	For proof of marriage.
Clayton, Hannah, widow of John	Maryville, Blount	For further proof of marriage and service.
Cooper, Jane, widow of Christopher	Greenville, Green	For period, length and grade of service, and names of company and field officers.
Cooper, Mary, widow of Alexander	Sparta, White	For proof of marriage.
Coston, Lucy, widow of Thomas	Maryville, Blount	For period, length and grade of service, and names of company and field officers.
Crenshaw, Nancy, widow of Daniel	Franklin, Williamson	Suspended for further proof of service.
Crawley, Margaret, widow of Thomas	——, Van Buren	Barred by act of April 30, 1844.
Cross, Temperance, widow of Acil	Morgan Court House	No proof of service on the records of Wm. Hill's office.
Crow, Sarah, widow of Thomas	Purdy, McNairy	For proof of marriage.
Crutcher, Elizabeth, widow of William	Franklin, Williamson	For further proof of service and marriage.
Davis, Judah, widow of Henry W	Camden Court House	To be allowed if living, or upon proof of her decease and children's names.
Davis, Mary (dec'd), widow of James	Harrison, Hamilton	To be allowed from the date the husband died to the decease of the widow upon the proof thereof, and the children's names who survive.
Divine, Jemima, widow of Thomas	Maryville, Blount	Proof defective of service and of marriage.
Dewitt, Nancy, formerly widow of Geo. Kelly	——, Cocke	For a more perfect form of declaration, for which a blank is furnished.
Ensly, Deborah, widow of John	Marysville, Blount	For further proof of marriage and service.
Eoff, Margaret (dec'd), widow of Isaac	Carrollton, Carroll	For further proof—papers withdrawn December 5, 1845—A. Cullom.
Ewbanks, Catharine, widow of John	Marysville, Blount	The regiment with the names of the company and field officers required, and proof of marriage.
Finley, Nancy, widow of William	Huntingdon, Carroll	For further proof and specification.
Flowers, Sarah, widow of John	Rogersville, Hawkins	For additional evidence.
Fugate, Eleanor		No papers in this case except a marriage license—bond filed by Wm. M. Cocke, H. R., given by claimant's husband in Virginia, November 8, 1785.
Graves, Sarah (dec'd), widow of Boston	Knoxville, Knox	For proof of marriage.
Gregg, Rachel, widow of James	Blountsville, Sullivan	He did not serve six months.
Gregory, Sarah, widow of George	Harrison, Hamilton	For proof of service and marriage.
Griffith, Susanna, widow of William	Clinton, Anderson	For further proof of marriage.
Gwynee, Hanna (deceased), widow of William	Gallatin, Sumner	Service not set forth, nor sustained by any proof.
Hall, Letitia, widow of Samuel	Morgan C. H.	For proof of service and specification by witnesses.

STATEMENT—Continued.

Names.	Residence.	Reasons for suspension.
Ham, Phebe, widow of John	Purdy, McNairy	For proof of his residence in the same military beat with the officers named in the certificate credits, although said officers were not named by him.
Hambright, Nancy, widow of John	Calhoun, McMinn	For want of proof. Papers enclosed to T. J. Campbell, June 20, 1842.
Hanks, Lucy, widow of Abraham	Fayetteville, Lincoln	For proof of marriage.
Haney, Elizabeth, widow of Robert	Benton, Polk	For proof of service.
Henderson, Elizabeth, widow of John	Purdy, McNairy	Papers sent to A. V. Brown, January 17, 1846—not replaced. Act of July 1, 1848, removed the objections to the service, and the parties interested may frame a new declaration and prove the marriage, provided she was a widow July 7, 1888.
Henry, Margaret (deceased), widow of Daniel	Gallatin, Sumner	No agent and no action upon the case.
Hickey, Elizabeth, widow of James	Sparta, White	For proof of marriage.
Holt, Martha, widow of Shadrach	Winchester, Franklin	For proof of marriage.
Houseley, Lydia Ann, widow of Robert	Harrison, Hamilton	He did not serve six months.
Hull, Mary, widow of Daniel	Dandridge, Jefferson	Not six months service proved in this case.
Jackson, Elizabeth, widow of Jesse	Brownsville, Haywood	Service not set forth nor proved—no proof of marriage.
Jones, Mary, widow of John	Jasper, Marion	Sent for correction May 27, 1844, to Hon. J. W. Blackwell, and not replaced.
Jones, Mary, widow of William	Lebanon, Wilson	Not a widow under the act—died before August 16, 1842.
King, Nancy (deceased), widow of Philip	—, Warren	Marriage requires further proof.
Latimer, Mary, widow of Charles	Gallatin, Sumner	For further proof and specification.
Lane, Agnes, widow of Aquilla	Dandridge, Jefferson	For proof from the South Carolina records, or two witnesses.
Large, Mary, widow of Joseph	Dandridge, Jefferson	Barred by act April 30, 1844.
Lewis, Catharine, widow of Solomon	Tazewell, Claiborne	This case may be re-opened under the joint resolution of July 1, 1848.
Longley, Mary, widow of William	Charleston, Bradley	She was not a widow at the date of the act.
Key, Elizabeth, widow of William	Gallatin, Sumner	For proof of marriage.
Maholland, Lucy, widow of John	Lebanon, Wilson	For proof of marriage.

Name	Location	Reason
Martin, Mary, widow of Salathiel	Speedwell, Claiborne	For want of proof—papers enclosed to Hon. J. H. Crozier, March 19, 1846.
Maxwell, Esther, 2d, widow of James	Nashville, Davidson	For want of proof—papers enclosed to E. H. Foster, February 15, 1845.
May, Charity (deceased), widow of John	Benton, Polk	For proof of the date of her marriage and decease.
McAdams, Margaret, widow of Joseph	Lewisburg, Marshall	For proof of service by the North Carolina records to be specified by survivors.
McCrary, Jane (deceased), widow of Hugh	—, Bedford	Proof of marriage required and service from the North Carolina records.
McKiddy, Catharine, widow of Thomas	Washington, Rhea	Proof of service required from the South Carolina records.
Morris, Elizabeth C., widow of Edward	Lebanon, Wilson	For further proof from the Raleigh records.
McPherson, Elizabeth, widow of Barton	Athens, McMinn	Not six months service.
Murrell, Mary, widow of Benjamin	Dresden, Weakly	For further proof of service and marriage.
Neil, Mary, widow of Andrew	Lewisburg, Marshall	For proof of service by the North Carolina records.
Nelson, Delila, widow of Hanse	Kingston, Roane	For proof of the date of the marriage.
Newman, Elizabeth, widow of Austin	Dandridge, Jefferson	Period, length and grade of service, and names of company and field officers, fortified by the South Carolina records or surviving comrades.
Nevils, Sarah, widow of George	Columbia, Maury	Names of the company and field officers and number of the regiment of the original line required.
Norton, Mary, widow of Alexander	Columbia, Maury	For further proof of marriage.
Nukum, Susanna, widow of Solomon	Cleveland, Bradley	For further proof and identity.
Ollis, Barbery, widow of Boston	Morgan C. H.	For further proof of marriage.
Parks, Nancy, widow of James	Marysville, Blount	For proof of the date of the marriage.
Phillips, Milly, widow of Gabriel	Rogersville, Hawkins	Not on Col. Morgan's regimental returns—no proof of service.
Price, Mary (deceased), widow of John	Greenville, Green	If it can be clearly established that he served in 1781, a pension may be granted the children under act of July 4, 1836.
Price, Esther (deceased), widow of James	Knoxville, Knox	Died in 1838, and not more than one month's pension can be granted the children.
Price, Margaret, widow of Thomas	Sparta, White	For proof of service by the records at Raleigh.
Purcelly, Sally, widow of William	Kingston, Roane	For additional evidence.
Ransom, Keziah, widow of Richard	Murfreesboro', Rutherford	Period, length and grade of service, and names of company and field officers, and proof from the Raleigh records.
Rankin, Jane, widow of Richard		For want of proof, November 28, 1844. Papers sent to Wm. Cocke January 21, 1846.
Richardson, Nancy, widow of James	Nashville, Davidson	For a statement of the officers he served under in the Virginia line and artillery, and papers withdrawn by Hon. John Bell.

STATEMENT—Continued.

Names.	Residence.	Reasons for suspension.
Riley, Nancy, widow of John	Pall Mall, Fentress	For further proof from the records at Richmond—February 8, 1845, J. L. Kennedy.
Roach, Frances, widow of James	Springfield, Robertson	For proof of service and marriage.
Roberts, Nancy, widow of Zacheus	Kingston, Roane	For proof from the South Carolina records.
Rutherford, Elizabeth, widow of James	Gallatin, Sumner	For further proof.
Satterfield, Unicy, widow of William	Dandridge, Jefferson	For further proof of service.
Simmons, Margaret, widow of John	Springfield, Robertson	For specification and proof of service and marriage.
Sims, Milly, widow of John	Calhoun, McMinn	Not a widow at the date of the act; but her claim is reinstated under act of July 29, 1848.
Sumpter, Lydia, widow of Thomas	Knoxville, Knox	For proof of service and marriage.
Taber, Agnes, widow of John	Morgan C. H	No action on this case by order of the commissioner—received and filed from R. A. Dabney, Morgan C. H., February 4, 1840.
Taylor, Catharine, widow of George	Jamestown, Fentress	For further proof, as Captain Beal's rolls (Colonel Gibson's regiment) are silent.
Thurman, Keziah, widow of Philip	Pikeville, Bledsoe	For further proof of marriage and service.
Thurman, Nancy, widow of John	Maryville, Blount	For the names of the officers under whom he served in the Virginia line, and proof of marriage.
Thurman, Barbara, widow of Charles	Pikeville, Bledsoe	For proof of marriage or of the children's births.
Trent, Jane, widow of Alexander	Thornhill, Grainger	For proof of service from the South Carolina records, and proof of marriage.
Vickers, Nancy, widow of John	Sparta, White	For proof of service and of marriage prior to 1800.
Vincent, Eleanor, widow of George	Blountsville, Sullivan	No tour of service specified nor proved under his alleged commission as ensign.
Waddle, Phebe, widow of John	Sparta, White	For proof of service and marriage.
Walker, Jane, widow of Edward	Tazewell, Claiborne	For proof of marriage.
Washer, Judith, widow of Elias	—, Smith	For deficient proof from the rolls of the Virginia line.
Walker, Mary, widow of Jeremiah	Thorn Hill, Grainger	Service not set forth and names of officers and regiment in the Virginia line—proof of marriage also required.

Warden, Sarah, widow of William	Rock Castle, Kentucky	Printed regulations sent July 10, 1844, to Hon. John White, Richmond, Kentucky.
Weakley, Prudence, widow of Thomas	South Haspeth, Davidson	For defective proof. [Papers withdrawn January 24, 1848, by L. B. Chase.]
Weir, Margaret, widow of James	Marysville, Blount	For further proof of service—the auditor's certificate relates to James Weir, of the Virginia line—not of the militia.
Whelan, Margaret, widow of Richard	Robertsville, Anderson	For further proof of marriage.
Wooten, Nancy, widow of Turner	Cleveland, Bradford	Under act of July 1, 1848, no objections will be made on account of the service—the proof of the marriage, however, is required.
Wright, Elizabeth, widow of John	Kingston, Roane	Married in June, 1796—no claim under this act.
Yates, Jane, widow of Samuel	——, Cocke	For proof of service from the Raleigh records, and the date of the marriage.

A list of the names of persons residing in Indiana who have applied for pensions under the act of June 7, 1832, whose claims have been rejected; prepared in conformity with the resolution of the Senate of the United States of September 16, 1850.

Names.	Residence.	Reasons for rejection.
Arnold, Richard	—, Dearborne	Not military service.
Atley, John	Brookville, Franklin	Not military service—not under competent authority.
Andrews, James	Muncietown, Delaware	He died before the passage of the pension laws.
Aughe, Harman	Frankfort, Clinton	Wagon service.
Bell, Nathaniel	Franklin, Johnson	Not under military authority or organization.
Bainbrook, Ezekiel	Mars tp., Posey	He did not serve six months in a military capacity.
Buck, John	Lafayette, Tippecanoe	Service as a pilot and express rider.
Blads, Eli	Lexington, Scott	Not six months' actual service.
Barnes, John	Muncietown, Delaware	He did not serve six months.
Belout, Daniel	Rushville, Rush	He did not serve six months.
Bennett, Archibald	Greensburg, Decatur	Not under competent authority.
Buoy, Robert	Baltimore, Warren	He did not serve six months.
Booth, John	Madison, Jefferson	Under age—born in 1775.
Bivens, William	Ripley tp., Montgomery	No proof of service.
Betts, Joseph	Union tp., Montgomery	Under age—not six months' service.
Brenton, Adam	Spencer, Owen	Only four months and five days' service during the revolution.
Burch, Daniel	Brookville, Franklin	He did not serve six months.
Burke, John	Charleston, Clark	He did not serve six months.
Boyden, Jonathan (deceased), widow of	—, Washington	Both husband and wife died before the passage of the act.
Caruthers, William	—, Sullivan	He did not serve six months.
Craig, Rodrick	New Castle, Henry	Only four months' service.
Crooks, Michael	Vincennes, Knox	He did not serve six months.
Cook, Thomas	Columbus, Bartholomew	He did not serve six months.
Cary, Saul	Indianapolis, Marion	Not under military organization or authority.
Chance, Samuel	Centreville, Wayne	Only five months' service.
Covenhoner, Thomas	Covington, Fountain	He did not serve six months.
Doblings, James	Centre tp., Marion	He did not serve six months.
Davison, Samuel	Brookville, Franklin	He did not serve six months.

Name	Location	Remarks
Dale, Campbell	Muncietown, Delaware	He did not serve six months.
Devour, Elijah	Greensburg, Decatur	Not under competent military authority.
Davis, Enoch	Salem, Washington	He did not serve six months.
Douglass, David	Logansport, Cass	Only four months' service in the militia—a wagoner otherwise.
Evans, Robert	Franklin tp., Harrison	No such service—no proof of such service.
Ensminger, Joshua	Liberty tp., Shelby	Fraudulent.
Fitzgerald, James	Princeton, Gibson	He did not serve in a military capacity.
Findley, Samuel	Rockport, Spencer	He did not serve six months in a military capacity.
Foster, Samuel	Indianapolis, Marion	Not under competent military authority or organization.
Fox, Adam	Versailles, Ripley	Service short of six months.
Fitzsimmons, Thomas	Danville, Hendricks	Already a pensioner under act May 15, 1828—no increase under this act.
Flint, John	Brookville, Franklin	Not under competent military authority or organization.
Franklin, Mordecai	Spencer, Owen	Only five months' service.
Gibson, Wilbourne	Versailles, Ripley	He did not serve six months.
Glidewell, Robert	Brookville, Franklin	He did not serve six months.
Galloway, Peter	Delhi, Carroll	He did not serve six months.
Griffis, John G	Evansville, Vanderburg	Not on the rolls—no proof of service.
Hammon, Lewis	Vevay, Switzerland	Only five months' service.
Hall, Benjamin	Vevay, Switzerland	Caveat to this claim from Wm. C. Keen, Printer's Retreat, August 28, 1882.
Harrison, William	Corydon, Harrison	Not under competent military authority or organization.
Henson, Jesse	Corydon, Harrison	He did not serve six months.
Hicks, Dempsey		He was a deserter. [Papers sent to Hon. E. A. Hannegan, February 26, 1884.]
Harrison, Zephaniah	Evansville, Vanderburg	He did not serve six months.
Heaton, Ebenezer	Newcastle, Henry	His service was performed by substitute.
Holler, John	Salem, Washington	He did not serve six months.
Hopper, William	Lexington, Scott	He did not serve six months.
Howell, William E.	Vernon, Jennings	He did not serve six months by order of competent authority.
Hunter, Andrew	Frankfort, Clinton	Service after the revolution.
Iles, Samuel	Connersville, Fayette	He was a deserter.
Jackson, Andrew	Brookville, Franklin	Service after the revolution.
Johnson, James	Bath tp., Franklin	Desertion.

STATEMENT—Continued.

Names.	Residence.	Reasons for rejection.
Kimball, Jesse	Evansville, Vanderburg	He did not serve six months.
Keysacker, George	Fredonia, Crawford	He did not serve six months.
Klingensmith, Jacob	Indianapolis, Marion	Not six months revolutionary service.
Killion, John	Paoli, Orange	Only three months' service.
Kelsinger, Andrew	Spencer, Owen	Not six months' revolutionary service.
Kitchen, Thomas	Princeton, Gibson	He did not serve six months.
Lemmon, Matthias	Covington, Fountain	Not under competent military authority or organization.
Lewis, George	Charleston, Clark	Not revolutionary service.
Linther, Jacob	Bowling Green, Clay	Team service in the militia.
Largent, Nelson	Crawfordville, Montgomery	He did not serve six months.
Lucas, William	Greencastle, Putnam	Only three months' service alleged.
Low, John	Brookville, Franklin	He was a deserter.
Lee, David	La Fayette, Tippecanoe	Not under competent military authority or organization.
Leap, John	Printer's Retreat, Switzerland	He did not serve six months.
Leftycar, Uriah	Brookville, Franklin	He was a deserter.
Layton, William	Greensburg, Decatur	He was a deserter.
Lusher, John	Delhi, Carroll	He was a deserter.
McAlister, Alexander		He did not serve six months. [Papers withdrawn by Hon. J. Rariden, June 8, 1888.]
Midcap, John	Vernon, Jennings	Service after the revolution.
Martindale, William	Richland tp., Miami	He did not serve six months.
Maness, Ambrose	Spencer, Owen	He did not perform six months' actual service.
McIntosh, Francis	Greensburg, Decatur	He did not serve six months.
McConnell, Hugh		He did not serve six months. [Papers withdrawn by Hon. Lewis Cass, April 28, 1836.]
Moss, Zeally	New York, Switzerland	He did not serve in a military capacity.
Morris, Thomas	Centreville, Wayne	He did not serve six months.
McCoy, John	Danville, Hendricks	Not six months' service during the revolution.
McCool, William	Indianapolis, Marion	Only two months' service during the revolution.
Nay, Samuel	Franklin, Johnson	He did not serve six months.

409   [37]

Name	Location	Remarks
North, John	Indianapolis, Marion	Indian wars before the revolution.
Olinger, Jacob	Delhi, Carroll	Only three months twenty days' service.
Pavey, Samuel	——, Madison	Desertion.
Pry, Jesse	Rockport, Spencer	He did not serve six months.
Powell, John	Spencer, Owen	Service after the revolution.
Pruett, Archibald	Lexington, Scott	Not under competent military authority.
Pierson, Moses (deceased since)	——, Vigo	Not six months' service.
Patterson, John (deceased)	Brownstown, Jackson	Claim for alleged service in this case already allowed.
Parnell, Stephen	Greensburg, Decatur	He was a deserter.
Raines, Richard	Covington, Fountain	He did not serve six months.
Runingh, George	Bogard tp., Daviess	He served only a little upwards of five months.
Byker, John	Madison, Jefferson	He did not serve six months.
Rector, Jesse	Bedford, Lawrence	Only three months ten days' service.
Ronah (alias Rouse), Joseph	Indianapolis, Marion	He did not serve quite six months.
Scott, Justus	——, Hamilton	He did not serve in a military capacity.
Stell, John	Corydon, Harrison	He did not serve six months.
Strother, Daniel	Vincennes, Knox	He did not serve six months in a military capacity.
Stafford, John	Shelbyville, Shelby	Service after the revolution.
Snelling, William	Greensburg, Decatur	He did not serve six months.
Stipe, Frederick	Washington, Daviess	Only three months' service.
Storm, Jacob	Lexington, Scott	He did not perform six months' service.
Skinner, Thomas, sr	Covington, Fountain	Not six months' actual service.
Thrasher, Josiah	Rushville, Rush	Not under any competent military authority or organization.
Thompson, Thomas	Muncietown, Delaware	He did not serve six months.
Tibbets, George	Rushville, Rush	Not under military organization.
Thompson, David	——, St. Joseph	He did not serve six months.
Thomas, John	——, Vigo	He did not serve six months.
Thompson, James	Brownstown, Jackson	Not under competent military authority or organization.
Turner, Robert	Printers' Retreat, Switzerland	Only three months service as a soldier.
Thompson, James	Franklin, Johnson	Not six months actual service.
Vance Samuel	Connersville, Fayette	Not military service.
Van Vian, Adam	Connersville, Fayette	He was employed principally as a cook.
Watts, Charles	Rockville, Parke	He did not serve six months.

STATEMENT—Continued.

Names.	Residence.	Reasons for rejection.
Wilson, James	Rockport, Spencer	Service after the revolution.
Wright, Isaac	——, Vermilion	Not six months' military service.
Wapshot, Graves	Rome, Perry	He did not serve six months.
Willhelm, Michael	Connersville, Fayette	Privateer service.
William, Remembrance	Madison, Jefferson	He did not serve six months.
Welch, Samuel	Madison, Jefferson	Service not during the revolution.
Wells, Peter	——, Warren	He did not serve six months.

A list of the names of persons residing in Indiana who have applied for pensions under the act of June 7, 1832, whose claims have been suspended; prepared in conformity with the resolution of the Senate of the United States, September 16, 1850.

Names.	Residence.	Reasons for suspension.
Adams, John	Rome, Perry	For further proof and specification.
Adams, Gaven	Columbus, Bartholomew	For further proof and specification.
Alisla, Coonrod	Rockville, Parke	For further proof and specification.
Alexander, Thomas	Brownstown, Jackson	Claims two years service in the Pennsylvania line as an artillery artificer—proof of identity required with the Pennsylvania records of a soldier of the same name.
Allen, John	—, Hamilton	For proof of five years alleged service in the Pennsylvania line.
Ansley, John	Lawrenceburg, Dearborne	For further proof of his three years' enlistment in 1777, in Ogden's regiment, New Jersey line.
Barr, Hugh	Washington, Davis	For further proof and specification.
Barnes, Richard	Danville, Hendricks	For further proof and specification.
Berch, William	Bloomington, Monroe	For proof from the North Carolina records.
Bell, Benjamin	Bowling Green, Clay	Claims as an Indian spy on the frontiers of Pennsylvania—no proof of service.
Blake, John	Mt. Pleasant, Martin	He did not serve six months.
Blake, George	—, Jefferson	No proof of service amounting to as much as six months.
Boles, Alexander	Danville, Hendricks	Frontier service in 1791—no claim.
Blake, Alexander	Fredonia, Crawford	For further proof and specification.
Brock, George	Salem, Washington	For further proof and specification.
Brightwell, John	Rushville, Rush	Not revolutionary service—no claim.
Brown, James	Paoli, Orange	For proof from the South Carolina records.
Burrell, Francis	Brownstown, Jackson	For further proof and explanation.
Bushman, Jacob		For proof from the Annapolis records. [Papers sent to Hon. W. Wood-ridge March 2, 1846.]
Burrell, Francis	Brownstown, Jackson	Not under military organization.
Cox, Nathaniel	La Fayette, Tippecanoe	He has not established six months' service.
Cooper, Vincent	—, Hancock	For further proof and explanation.
Cassell, Ralph	Greensburg, Decatur	For further proof and traditionary reputation.
Carter, Henry	Salem, Washington	He did not serve six months.

STATEMENT—Continued.

Names.	Residence.	Reasons for suspension.
Davis, Daniel	Lafayette, Tippecanoe	He did not serve six months in the revolution.
Davis, David	Bloomington, Monroe	For further and more direct proof.
Davis, Levi (dec'd)	Brownstown, Jackson	For proof of identity with the war's-man of the Maryland line.
Demoss, Andrew	—, Greene	For further proof.
Dunham, William		Not properly authenticated. [Papers withdrawn November 30, 1832.]
Elmer, Elijah	Lima, Lagrange	For further proof.
Evans, Edward	Bedford, Lawrence	For further proof.
Farber, Daniel	Jay Court House	For further proof.
Fleck, Christopher	Paoli, Orange	Not on the rolls—no proof of service.
Fulton, Samuel	Lawrenceburg, Dearborne	For proof of service.
Gee, Parker	New Castle, Henry	For proof of service.
Hall, John	Franklin, Johnson	Not on the rolls—no proof of service.
Henson, Jesse	Mt. Peasant, Martin	For proof of service.
Herrod, John	Princeton, Gibson	For proof of service.
Hiatt, Asa	Rockville, Parke	For further proof and explanation.
High, John	—, Warren	For proof of service by witnesses.
Hitch, Gillis	Crawfordsville, Montgomery	For further proof and specification.
Houston, Peter		For further proof. [Papers withdrawn by Hon. George G. Dunn.]
Hobbs, James	Greensburg, Decatur	For proof from the records at Annapolis.
Holbrooks, George	Princeton, Gibson	Not on the rolls—no proof of service.
House, Levi	Madison, Jefferson	For proof of service by witnesses.
Hubbell, Hezekiah B.	Logansport, Cass	For further proof.
Hunt, Israel	Danville, Hendricks	Not six months' service.
Hutchinson, Thomas	Greencastle, Putnam	For further proof.
Johnson, Jacob	—, Elkhart	For further proof.

413   [37]

Name	Location	Remarks
Johnson, Joseph	West Fork tp., Jackson	Service for six months allowed, but declined.
Kelly, William (dec'd)	Rockport, Spencer	For period, length and grade of service, and names of company and field officers.
Kew, William	Lawrenceburg, Dearborne	For further proof.
Lambert, James	Wilmington, Dearborne	Not on any rolls—no proof of service.
Lemon, Moses	Liberty, Union	Not six months' service.
Lloyd, Robin	Versailles, Ripley	For further proof of service.
Maxwell, Thomas		Not on the rolls—no proof of service. [Papers withdrawn, Hon. J. W. Davis, January 22, 1836.]
Mellen, John (dec'd)	New York, Switzerland	He died before the passage of the act.
Miles, Thomas	Hartford, Blockford	For proof from the Massachusetts rolls.
Moore, George	Rensselaer, Jasper	For proof from the Annapolis records.
Ney, Samuel, sen.	Franklin, Johnson	Not on the rolls—no proof of service.
Newkirk, Henry	Brookville tp., Franklin	Not on the rolls—no proof of service.
Newnan, Joshua	Indianapolis, Marion	For proof of actual service.
Owens, Edmund	New Harmony, Posey	North Carolina militia service overrated.
Paterson, Lemuel		Under age—privateer service, New Jersey militia. Service overrated. [Papers withdrawn. Letter, December 30, 1886, Hon. W. Henderson.]
Pigman, Jesse	Liberty, Union	For authority and grade, nature and length of service.
Pool, Samuel		For further proof. [Papers sent to Clerk of House of Representatives, February 2, 1848.]
Price, Joseph	Mount Vernon, Posey	For a more satisfactory statement of his services.
Rector, Charles	Peru, Miami	Not on the Virginia rolls—no proof of service.
Reed, George	—, Warrick	For further proof and specification.
Rutledge, Peter	Versailles, Ripley	For proof from the records at Annapolis.
Scott, Samuel (dec'd)	Lebanon, Boone	For further proof.
Smith, George		Suspended for proof of service. [Papers withdrawn December 11, 1846. Letter, Hon. J. W. Davis.]
Shattle, John	Greensburg, Decatur	For proof of service.
Stewart, Thomas	Bloomington, Monroe	For further proof and specification.
Smith, Nathan	Salem, Washington	For further proof and specification.

STATEMENT—Continued.

Names.	Residence.	Reasons for suspension.
Smith, Stafford	Bloomfield, Greene	Not on the rolls—no proof of service.
Wallace, Samuel	Columbus, Bartholomew	No proof of service.
Washburn, Nicholas	Rushville, Rush	Service after the revolution.
Weatherford, John	Columbus, Bartholomew	For proof and specification by witnesses.
White, James	Bowling Green, Clay	For further proof.
Wyatt, Jeremiah	Evansville, Vanderburgh	For further proof.

A list of the names of persons residing in Indiana who have applied for pensions under the act of July 4, 1836, whose claims have been rejected; prepared in conformity with the resolution of the Senate of the United States, September 16, 1850.

Names.	Residence.	Reasons for rejection.
Alexander, Susanna K., widow of John	Boonville, Warwick	Married after the service.
Frederick, Mary, widow of Sebastian	Madison, Pike	Not six months' service.
Richardson, Elizabeth, widow of Thomas	Boonville, Warwick	Married after service.

A list of persons residing in Indiana who have applied for pensions under the act of July 4, 1836, whose claims have been suspended; prepared in conformity with the resolution of the Senate of the United States, September 16, 1850.

Names.	Residence.	Reasons for suspension.
Burton, Ann, widow of Absalom	Greensburg, Decatur	Service principally in driving pack horses.
Beall, Christiana, widow of King	Versailles, Ripley	For proof of marriage.
Carr, Juliana (deceased) widow of James	Covington, Fountain	For proof of identity with the soldier of the same name in the Virginia line.
Davis, Loassa, formerly widow of Abraham Coost	Shawnee tp., Fountain	For proof and specification by witnesses.
Funk, Elizabeth (deceased), widow of Henry	——, Crawford	For proof of identity with the three years' soldier of Clark's regiment of the Virginia line.
Ireland, Nancy (deceased), widow of James	Wishahanka, St. Joseph	Suspended for further proof.
Mitchell, Chloe, widow of William	Martinsville, Morgan	Suspended for proof of marriage.
Porter, Rachel, widow of Josiah	Otter Creek tp., Vigo	For proof of service from the comptroller general of South Carolina.
Stone, Sarah, widow of William	——, Vermillion	For period, length and grade of service, and names of company and field officers, and proof of marriage.
Wilson, Mary, widow of Thomas	——, Sullivan	Suspended for further proof. Papers enclosed to Hon. S. Breese, February 2, 1844, and not replaced.
Winship, Hannah, widow of Jabez	Lovina Falls, Hamilton	Not on the Connecticut rolls—no proof of service.

A list of the names of persons residing in Indiana who have applied for pensions under the act of July 7, 1888, whose claims have been rejected; prepared in conformity with the resolution of the Senate of the United States of September 16, 1850.

Names.	Residence.	Reasons for rejection.
Casterline, Charlotte, widow of Loami	Hartford, Blackford	Not a widow under the act.
Goddard, Frances, widow of Joseph	Vevay, Switzerland	Not a widow at the date of the act.
Piety, Mary, widow of Thomas	Vincennes, Knox	Not revolutionary service.
Wallace, Frances, widow of John	——, Owen	Married after the limitation of the act.
Young, Anna Barbara, widow of Matthew	Frankfort, Clinton	Not a widow at the date of the act.

Ex.—20

A list of the names of persons residing in Indiana who have applied for pensions under the act of July 7, 1838, whose claims have been suspended; prepared in conformity with the resolution of the Senate of the United States, September 16, 1850.

Names.	Residence.	Reasons for suspension.
Allen, Polly, widow of John	Corydon, Harrison	He did not serve six months in person.
Berry, Hannah (deceased) widow of William	——, Scott	For proof of identity with the soldier so named of the Virginia line.
Blunk, Mary, widow of Andrew	Corydon, Harrison	For further proof.
Bowling, Sarah, widow of Thomas	Corydon, Harrison	For further proof.
Boyd, Mary, widow of John	——, Hendricks	For proof of the day of her decease.
Brachett, Sally, widow of Hawkins	——, Johnson	For further proof and specification.
Brenton, Mary, widow of James	Washington tp., Pike	No agent—no action.
Calvin, Ruth, formerly widow of George Corwin	——, Henry	Not a widow under the act—died before 28d August, 1842.
Conly, Margaret, widow of Patrick	——, Henry	For proof of marriage.
Crittenden, Sally, widow of Richard	Columbus, Bartholomew	Not a widow at the date of the act.
Davis, Polly Ann, widow of Lodowick	Boonville, Warrick	For proof of marriage.
Dixon, Elizabeth, widow of John	Rising Sun, Ohio	For proof of marriage.
Dowers, Mary, widow of Conrad	Versailles, Ripley	Barred by the act of April 30, 1814—reinstated under acts March 3, 1843, and July 1, 1848.
Dukes, Elizabeth, widow of Isaac	Frankfort, Clinton	For proof of marriage.
Ewing, Sarah, widow of Timothy	Williamsport, Warren	For further proof and specification.
Fields, Martha, widow of Ansel	Shelbyville, Shelby	For proof of service by witnesses.
Grace, Lydia, widow of William	Salem, Washington	For proof of marriage.
Greenwood, Sarah, widow of Philip	Spencer, Owen	For proof of marriage.
Hammons, Martha, widow of Joseph	Bloomington, Monroe	For proof of service.
Handy, Sarah, widow of Thomas	Covington, Fountain	For proof of service.
Hanna, Nancy, widow of Adam	Greencastle, Putnam	For period, length and grade of service, and names of company and field officers.

Name	Place	Remarks
Harris, Nancy, widow of Thomas	Indianapolis, Warren	For proof of marriage.
Hickey, Jane, formerly widow of Benjamin Rennkin	Madison, Jefferson	For proof of identity with the soldier of the £90 certificate of depreciation.
Huddleston, Ann, widow of William	——, Rush	Not on the New Jersey or Pennsylvania army records in this office.
Jackson, Jane, widow of Matthew	Noble tp., Shelby	Marriage requires further proof.
Jones, Polly, widow of Thomas	Columbus, Bartholomew	For proof of identity with the soldier of the same name on the North Carolina records.
King, Mary, widow of George	Greenburgh, Decatur	For proof of marriage.
Lee, Eleanor (deceased), widow of Joseph	Greenburgh, Decatur	For proof of service.
Lee, Margaret, widow of John	Vevay, Switzerland	Not proved so far as for six months' service.
Massy, Catharine, widow of Jacob	——, Johnson	Barred by act April 30, 1844—reinstated under acts March 8, 1848, and July 1, 1848.
Maxwell, Abigail, widow of David	Versailles, Ripley	For further proof.
McClure, Margaret, widow of William	——, Knox	For further proof.
McCullough, Sarah, widow of Joseph	Bloomington, Monroe	Not on the New Jersey records at Trenton—no proof of service.
McDonald, Catharine (dec'd), widow of Peter	Charleston, Clark	For proof of marriage, and of identity with the Peter McDonald of the Virginia line—marked on the depreciation certificate for £23 4s.
Newell, Jane (deceased), widow of Samuel	Spencer, Owen	Barred by act April 30, 1844, and widow died February 11, 1848—no claim.
Peterson, Mary, widow of Conrad	Wabash, Wabash	Not a widow at the date of the act.
Pope, Phebe, widow of Samuel	Shelbyville, Shelby	For proof of service from the North Carolina records.
Porter, Rachel, widow of Josiah	——,	For further proof and description. [Full papers not yet filed.]
Prothen, Hannah, widow of Thomas	Versailles, Ripley	For proof of service.
Razor, Francis, widow of Peter	La Fayette, Spencer	Six months' service not in proof.
Roberts, Sarah, widow of John	Greencastle, Putnam	For proof and specification of service.
Rollins, Martha, widow of Hannaniah	Rising Sun, Ohio	For proof from the Maryland and New Jersey records.
Ross, Rachel, widow of William	Bloomington, Monroe	For proof from the Raleigh records.
Shannon, Ann, widow of George	Madison, Jefferson	For further proof of service.
Swords, Mary, widow of William	——, Rush	For proof of identity with the soldier of Captain Kinsburg's company of artillery attached to the North Carolina line.

STATEMENT—Continued.

Names.	Residence.	Reasons for suspension.
Wilton, Margaret, widow of Jonathan	Vincennes, Indiana	Not six months' service established in this case.
Webb, Amy, widow of Jonathan	——, Franklin	For proof of identity with the Jonathan Webb of the Connecticut and New York troops.
Watson, Sarah, widow of William	Madison, Jefferson	For further proof and specification.
Whitfield, Nancy, widow of Willis	Terre Haute, Vigo	Declaration sent for amendment April 20, 1849, to John Whitfield, and not replaced.
Weightman, Sarah, widow of Samuel	——, Union	For proof of service.

A list of the names of persons residing in Illinois who have applied for pensions under the act of June 7, 1832, whose claims have been suspended; prepared in conformity with the resolution of the Senate of the United States of September 16, 1850.

Names.	Residence.	Reasons for suspension.
Baldwin, David	Carthage, Hancock	He did not serve six months.
Baker, Isaac	Springfield, Sangamon	For specification of each tour of service.
Borders, Peter	Mount Pulaski, Logan	For proof of service and officers' names.
Brownfield, Robert	Danville, Vermilion	Not military service—ranger's service requires proof of authority.
Barrack, Peter	Palestine, Crawford	For additional evidence.
Brown, George	Nashville, Washington	For further proof and specification.
Brockmar, Thomas	Hillsboro', Montgomery	For further proof from the Virginia records.
Boutwell, Stephen	Equality, Gallatin	For further proof and information.
Conner, Samuel	Quincy, Adams	For further proof and specification.
Crabtree, John	Hillsboro', Montgomery	For further details of service, period, length, grade, localities and officers.
Cheshire, James	Shawneetown, Gallatin	Not on the rolls—proof by witnesses.
Donowey, Charles	Shawneetown, Gallatin	Not on the rolls—no proof of service.
Edwards, Joseph	Jonesboro', Union	For further proof of service.
Ellis, John	Frankfort, Franklin	For further proof and details of service.
Evans, John	Hennepin, Putnam	For further proof and details of service.
Edward, Stokes	Jacksonville, Morgan	For further proof and specification.
French, John	Decatur, Macon	Certificate withheld until some one of respectability applies for it.
Fox, Reuben	Mount Carmel, Wabash	For further proof.
Farris, John	Frankfort, Franklin	Not on the rolls—no proof of service.
Frizzell, Earl	Oquawka, Henderson	For proof of service by the Massachusetts rolls—identified by witnesses.
Griffin, William	Lewistown, Fulton	For further proof and explanation.
Hall, Simon	Carmi, White	For specification and proof of service.
Henderson, Wilson	Equality, Gallatin	For proof of service.
Holliday, Job	Ottawa, La Salle	For proof by witnesses, as the Massachusetts rolls are silent.

STATEMENT—Continued.

Names.	Residence.	Reasons for suspension.
Hudson, Samuel	Edwardsville, Madison	For proof of service.
Johnson, John	Frankfort, Franklin	No proof of service.
Johnson, Andrew	Frankfort, Franklin	No proof of service.
Jones, William	Springfield, Sangamon	For proof of service.
Layton, Thomas	Clarke C. H.	For proof of service from the Albany records. Papers sent to J. M. Robinson, December 18, 1835.
Lathrop, Isaac	Clarke C. H.	For proof from the Albany records.
Logue, Thomas	Waterloo, Monroe	For further explanation.
Lipse, John, (deceased)	Carthage, Hancock	Claim to be made by widow or children.
McMahan, Constantine	Lawrenceville, Lawrence	For proof and specification.
McNairy, Hugh	Jacksonville, Morgan	For further proof. Papers returned, Sept. 19, 1833, to Wm. Thomas.
Merifield, John	Carlinville, Macoupin	For further proof and specification.
Moore, Andrew	Hennepin, Putnam	For further proof and specification.
Moore, Thomas L.	Clinton	For return of original papers—sent September 28, 1847, to Uriah Manly.
McClintock, Samuel	Tremont, Tazewell	For further proof.
Morrell, John	Vandalia, Fayette	For further proof and more consistent statement.
Newton, Joseph	Golconda, Pope	For proof of identity with the soldier of the North Carolina line.
Olmstead, Joseph, (deceased)	Pittsfield, Pike	Died before the passage of the act.
Peebles, John	Carlinville, Macoupin	For proof from the South Carolina records.
Penkstoff, Andrew, (deceased)	Lawrenceville, Lawrence	For further proof from the Virginia records.
Robinson, James	Lawrenceville, Lawrence	For further proof.
Ross, Reuben	Morgan C. H.	For further description of his service.
Sawine, Samuel, (deceased)	St. Charles, Kane	For proof from the Massachusetts records.
Sexton, Samuel	Oquawka, Hamilton	No proof of service—no correct statement.
Sprague, Abraham	Paris, Edgar	Under age—no proof of service.
Sights, Jacob	Hillsboro', Montgomery	Not on the rolls—no proof of service.

Shoko, Anthony D............	Frankfort, Franklin	For proof from the South Carolina records.
Tharp, Wilson, (deceased)....	Paris, Edgar...............	Names of officers and regiment of the Virginia line.
Thaxton, William............	Carrollton, Greene..........	For proof of service from the North Carolina records.
Tipsoward, Griffin...........	Charleston, Coles...........	No proof of service—statement inconsistent.
Tolday, John................	Bloomington, McLean.......	Not on the rolls—no proof of service.
Ulmas, Jacob................	Lewistown, Fulton	Not six months service.
Whitaker, Alexander..........	Kaskaskia, Randolph.........	For amended declaration.
Williams, Isaiah.............	——, Boone................	For proof from the Vermont records.
Works, Asa..................	Nauvoo, Hancock...........	Not on the rolls of Bigelow's regiment—no proof of service.
West, Robert................	Equality, Gallatin...........	For further proof and explanation.

[37]

A list of persons residing in Illinois who have applied for pensions under the act of June 7, 1832, whose claims have been rejected; prepared in conformity with the resolution of the Senate of the United States, September 16, 1850.

Name.	Residence.	Reasons for rejection.
Allen, Archibald	Hennepin, Putnam	Not six months' service.
Allen, Zachariah	Atlas, Pike	Service after the revolution.
Barker, Jacob	——, Hamilton	Not six months' service.
Bigg, Elisha	Shelbyville, Shelby	Not six months' service.
Buskirk, Lewis	Quincy, Adams	Not military service.
Blevins, William	Danville, Vermillion	Not under military authority or organization.
Brush, Nehemiah	Lewistown, Fulton	Service after the revolution.
Borden, Peter	Springfield, Sangamon	Not six months' service.
Carroll, David	Peoria, Peoria	Not military service.
Casey, Levi	Frankfort, Franklin	Service after the revolution.
Cook, Jacob	Hennepin, Putnau	Under age.
Crane, Noah	Armstrong, Wabash	Not six months' service.
Crabb, John	Carrollton, Greene	Not revolutionary service.
Crane, Edmond	Danville, Vermillion	Desertion.
Dunnivan, William	Jacksonville, Morgan	Service after the revolution.
Dickinson, Kinzer	Danville, Vermillion	Not six months' service.
Dewey, Joel	Gilead, Calhoun	Service in 1795.
Ellsworth, John	Kaskaskia, Randolph	Desertion.
Fear, Edmond	Carmi, White	Not six months' service.
Flatt, John	Carrollton, Greene	Not six months' service.
Green, John, sr	Jacksonville, Morgan	Service in 1794.
Garrison, Abraham	Atlas, Pike	Frontier service—not under military organization or authority.
Glenn, John	Lawrenceville, Lawrence	No proof of service.
Harrell, Joel	Carmi, White	Not six months' service.

Hadden, Elisha		Frontier service—not under military organization.
Hooker, John	Coles Court House	Only four months' service.
Harriss, William	Frankfort, Franklin	Not six months' service.
Haggard, David	Dan-ille, Vermillion	Not six months' service.
Hunter, John	Bloomington, McLean	Only five months' service.
Harrington, John	Mount Carmel, Wabash	Not six months' service.
Howard, John	Knoxville, Knox	Not six months' service.
	Lewistown, Fulton	
Jolley, Boling	Jacksonville, Morgan	Not six months' service.
James, William	Paris, Edgar	Scant four months' service.
Johnson, Benjamin	Frankford, Perry	Only five months' service.
Lights, Jacob	Hillsboro' Montgomery	Desertion.
Lucas, Abram	Springfield, Sangamon	Not six months' military service.
Lawson, Randolph	Vienna, Johnson	Not six months' service.
Luke, Thomas	Lawrenceville, Lawrence	Not six months' service.
Langton, William G	Springfield, Morgan	Only three months' service.
Mallory, Samuel	Lewistown, Fulton	Not six months' service.
Martin, John	Quincy, Adams	Not six months' service.
Matteson, Thomas	Naperville, Dupage	No proof of service.
Magill, Andrew	Shawneetown, Gallatin	Not military service.
McKinney, John	Edwardsville, Madison	Not under military organization.
Miller, John A	Carrollton, Greene	Not six months' service.
Myers, William	——, Clinton	Privateer service.
Mitchell, Samuel	Belleville, St. Clair	Not six months' service.
Miller, Martin	Carrollton, Greene	Not military service.
Morecraft, John	Darwin, Clarke	Indian wars after the revolution.
Mabery, Frederick	——, Hamilton	Not six months' military service.
Ogle, Benjamin	Belleville, St. Clair	Not under competent military authority.
Ooley, David	Carmi, White	Not military service.
Pennington, Charles	Coles Court House	Not military service.
Perkins, Uta	Carthage, Hancock	Not six months' service.
Rogers, William	Frankfort, Franklin	Not six months' service.
Redman, Samuel	Belleville, St. Clair	Not six months' service.
Reed, Charles	Lawrenceville, Lawrence	Not six months' service.
Ritchey, John	Fulton, Fulton	Not six months' service.

STATEMENT—Continued.

Names.	Residence.	Reasons for rejection.
Shipman, David	Tremont, Tazewell	Not six months' service.
Scroggins, Humphrey	Springfield, Sangamon	Not six months' service.
Scholl, Abraham	Atlas, Pike	Not six months' service.
Stiles, Richard	——, Brown	Not six months' service.
Swain, Cornelius	——, Brown	No proof of service.
Tanner, Samuel	Frankfort, Franklin	Not six months' service.
Vincent, William	Bloomington, McLean	Not six months' service.
Waddell, Charles	McComb, McDonough	Service after the revolution.
Wader, Obadiah	Shelbyville, Shelby	Not six months' service.
Watson, Abner	Shelbyville, Shelby	Not six months' service.
Yancey, Arthur	Lewistown, Fulton	Not six months' service.
Zoll, Jacob	Frankfort, Franklin	Not six months' service.

A list of the names of persons residing in Illinois who have applied for pensions under the act of July 4, 1836, whose claims have been rejected; prepared in conformity with the resolution of the Senate of the United States, September 16, 1850.

Names.	Residence.	Reasons for rejection.
Burt, Martha, widow of Jacob	Rushville, Schuyler	Husband died before April 20, 1820, and was a soldier of the regular army.
Parks, Melinda, widow of William	Jonesboro', Union	Husband was a regular soldier, and died before April 20, 1820.

A list of the names of persons residing in Illinois who have applied for pensions under the act of July 4, 1836, whose claims have been suspended; prepared in conformity with the resolution of the Senate of the United States of September 16, 1850.

Names.	Residence.	Reasons for suspension.
Barker, Susanna, widow of Zebediah	——, Monroe	For further proof. [Papers sent to Hon. J. Carr May 27, 1840.]
Benson, Jane, widow of Levin	Knoxville, Knox	For further proof of service and marriage.
Combs, Sarah Ann, widow of William	Paris, Edgar	Not six months' service.
Dods, Margaret, formerly widow of Thomas Kirkpatrick	Springfield, Sangamon	For further proof of service.
Forrester, Mary, widow of John D.	——, Hamilton	No proof of service.
Lorton, Tabitha (deceased), widow of Robert	Carrollton, Greene	For further proof and identity.
Mullins, Mary, widow of James	Paris, Edgar	For proof and specification.
Squire, Mary, formerly widow of Benjamin J. Byrum	Carrollton, Greene	For further proof.
Whitford, Mary, widow of William	Evington, Effingham	For proof of identity with the soldier of the certificate for £106 11s.
Woodside, Jane, widow of Samuel	Kaskaskia, Randolph	For proof of service and marriage.

A list of the names of persons residing in Illinois who have applied for pensions under the act of July 7, 1838, whose claims have been suspended; prepared in conformity with the resolution of the Senate of the United States of September 16, 1850.

Names.	Residence.	Reasons for suspension.
Ammons, Catharine, widow of Thomas	——, Clinton	For further proof.
Armstrong, Nancy, widow of Robert	Petersburgh, Menard	For further proof of service.
Barthe, Susanna, widow of George	Robinson, Crawford	Six months' service allowed—proof of marriage deficient.
Canady, Mary, widow of John	Hillsboro', Montgomery	For proof of service and marriage.
Clem, Susannah, widow of John	Williamsport, Warren	No proof of service and marriage.
Cline, Caty, widow of Jonas	Lewistown, Fulton	Not six months' service proved.
Dunlap, Nancy, widow of William	Robinson, Crawford	For further proof.
Fusby, Rhoda, widow of Philemon	Toulon, Starke	For proof from the Connecticut records.
Givens, Martha (deceased), widow of Robert	——, Monroe	Not a widow under the act—died before August 16, 1842.
Griswold, Mary, widow of Adonijah	Carrollton, Greene	No proof of service—husband improperly pensioned.
Hatch, Mittee (deceased), widow of Mason	Oregon city, Ogle	Not six months' service proved.
Hassell, Mary, widow of Benjamin	——, Jefferson	Not six months' service proved.
Hughes, Kesiah, widow of Henry	——, Lawrence	For proof of service and specification.
Hult, Martha, widow of James	Danville, Vermillion	Twelve months' service admitted—proof of marriage deficient.
Jenkins, Elizabeth, widow of Job	——, Pike	For proof of marriage.
Kerr, Ruth, widow of James	Fairfield, Wayne	For proof of identity with the wars-man of the Virginia line.
Lamb, Comfort (deceased), widow of John	Carmi, White	Not a widow at the date of the act.
Mooney, Margaret, widow of Bryant	——, Adams	For further proof of service and marriage.
McCumber, Philadelphia, widow of John	Bardstown, Cass	For a new declaration and proof of service.
Meadows, Jane, widow of James	Monmouth, Warren	For further proof of service and marriage.

STATEMENT—Continued.

Names.	Residence.	Reasons for suspension.
O'Neil, Catharine, widow of Constantine	Matamora, Woodford	Defective proof of marriage.
Powell, Elizabeth, widow of Eleven H.	Tremont, Tazewell	Married in 1807—no claim.
Relker, Mary, widow of Leonard	Carrollton, Greene	For proof of service and marriage.
Skinner, Saloma, widow of Amos	Elk Grove, Cook	Declaration informal and unaccompanied by any proof.
Skinner, Saloma, widow of Amasa	—, Cook	Awaiting more formal papers.
Simpkins, Margaret, widow of John G.	Marian, Williamson	Barred under act of April 30, 1844.
Scott, Silvey R., widow of William	Jacksonville, Morgan	Six months' service allowed—marriage in suspense.
Stufflebian, Elsie, widow of John	—, Randolph	For proof of service and marriage.
Teel, Catharine, widow of John	Rushville, Schuylkill	For proof of marriage prior to 1800.
Veach, Jane, widow of Elias	Nashville, Washington	Not on the rolls—no proof of service.
Watts, Elizabeth (deceased), widow of Benjamin	Nashville, Washington	Proof of the decease of the parents and the children's names and ages.

A list of the names of persons residing in Illinois who have applied for pensions under the act of July 7, 1838, whose claims have been rejected; prepared in conformity with the resolution of the Senate of the United States, September 16, 1850.

Names.	Residence.	Reasons for rejection.
Baynes, Susannah, widow of John	—, Perry	Not a widow at the date of the act—died before August 23, 1842.
Bivens, Hannah, widow of John	—, Fulton	Not a widow at the date of the act.
Cross, Esther (deceased), widow of Zachariah	Carmi, White	Not a widow at the date of the act—died before August 23, 1842.
Duncan, Lydia, widow of John	Marion, Williamson	Not six months' service.
Goodner, Elizabeth (deceased), widow of Conrad	Nashville, Washington	Not a widow at the date of the act—died before August 23, 1842.
Long, Frances, widow of John	—, St. Clair	Not a widow at the date of the act.
Simpson, Elizabeth (deceased), widow of William	Carmi, White	Not a widow at the date of the act—died before August 23, 1842.
Scoggin, Ann, widow of Jonah	Carrollton, Greene	Not a widow at the date of the act.
Troop, Nancy, widow of William	Mount Vernon, Jefferson	Desertion.

A list of the names of persons residing in Missouri who have applied for pensions under the act of June 7, 1832, whose claims have been rejected; prepared in conformity with the resolution of the Senate of the United States, September 16, 1850.

Names.	Residence.	Reasons for rejection.
Atkinson, Matthew	Potosi, Washington	Not six months' service.
Ashbrooks, George	Potosi, Washington	Not six months' actual service.
Burrows, Michael	Fayette, Howard	Not six months' service.
Copeland, Joel	Jonesboro', Saline	Not six months service.
Chapman, Erasmus	Fayette, Howard	Only three months' revolutionary service.
Coponhaven, Thomas	Troy, Lincoln	Not six months' service.
Deck, John	Jackson, Cape Girardeau	Only three months' service.
Dewy, Joel, (Gillead, Calhoun Co., Illinois)	——, St. Louis	Indian war service after the revolution.
Duncan, Samuel	Benton, Scott	Not six months' service.
Forrester, Peter	Troy, Lincoln	Not six months' actual service.
Fitzgerald, Thomas	St. Louis, St. Louis	Not six months' revolutionary service.
Green, Henry, sen.	Liberty, Clay	Not six months' service.
Gebhart, George	Perrysville C. H., Perry	Service was under General Wayne in 1794-5.
Henderson, Joseph	Harrisonville, Van Buren	Not six months' service.
Hughes, Samuel	Boonville, Cooper	Not six months' service in person.
House, Adam	Potosi, Washington	Not six months' service.
Hammons, John	Troy, Lincoln	Not six months' service.
Jackman, Joseph	Fulton, Callaway	Not six months' service.
Lane, Charles	Gasconado C. H.	Not military service—not revolutionary service.
Morgan, Joseph	Platte city C. H.	A soldier in the French army.
Moore, John	Benton, Scott	Not six months' service.

Name	Residence	Remarks
Marshall, James	Lexington, Lafayette	Service was after the revolution.
McMeans, James	Herculaneum, Jefferson	Not six months' military revolutionary service.
McGaugh, John	Richmond, Ray	Service after the revolution.
Petty, John	Springfield, Greene	Not six months' service.
Patterson, John	St. Louis, St. Louis	Not six months' service.
Proctor, William	Boonville, Cooper	Service after the revolution.
Rector, James	Troy, Lincoln	Not six months' service.
Ross, William	Boonville, Cooper	Only two months' service.
Smith, John	Jackson, Cape Girardeau	Not six months' service.
Scott, Obadiah	St. Genevieve, St. Genevieve	Not six months' service.
Smith, William	Columbia, Boone	Not military service.
Swaney, Jacob	St. Louis, St. Louis	Not revolutionary service.
Tolson, William	Fayette, Howard	Not military service.
Trowal, William	Columbia, Boone	Desertion.
Teeter, Samuel	Fayette, Howard	Service after the revolution.
Vanbibben, James	Fulton, Callaway	Service not prior to September, 1783.
West, Littleton	Richmond, Ray	Not six months' service in person.
Wells, Charles	Columbia, Boone	Service after the revolution.
Winders, John	Boonville, Cooper	Not six months' service.
Wolford, Frederick	St. Genevieve, St. Genevieve	Service after the revolution.

A list of the names of persons residing in Missouri who have applied for pensions under the act of June 7, 1832, whose claims have been suspended; prepared in conformity with the resolution of the Senate of the United States of September 16, 1850.

Names.	Residence.	Reasons for suspension.
Abernethie, John	Jackson, Cape Girardeau	Direct proof of service as commissary required.
Bell, Joseph	New London, Ralls	For further proof and specification.
Billings, Abraham	New London, Ralls	For proof of service.
Corlen, John	Columbia, Boone	Not six months' service proved.
Drake, Isaac	Independence, Jackson	For further proof and specification.
Donaway, William	Harrisonville, Van Buren	For deficient proof.
Duncan, Samuel	Matthew Prairie, Scott	Not six months' service.
Evell, John	—, Randolph	Not six months' service.
Frashur, Micajah	Rock Creek, Jackson	For further proof and specification.
Gum, Shepherd	Fayette, Howard	For further proof and specification.
Hardy, Arnold (dec'd)	New London, Ralls	Six months allowed. Children must apply under act of July 4, 1836, if the marriage was prior to the last of the service.
Henderson, Joseph	Harrisonville, Van Buren	Not six months' service.
Horn, William	Lexington, Lafayette	Not six months' service.
Hopkins, James	Bolivar, Polk	Not six months' service.
Hudson, Isaac	Troy, Lincoln	For proof of identity with the soldier and service of the third regiment, North Carolina line.
Henson, Richard	—, Newton	For further proof.
Johns, John	Union, Franklin	For further proof, especially of his commission, from the South Carolina records.
Johnson, Micah	Fayette, Howard	For a more full and specific statement of his services.
Keffer, Joseph	Boonville, Cooper	For authority and proof of his service as a ranger.

Leatherman, Jacob	Troy, Lincoln	For further specification and proof of service.
Latimore, Richard	Boonville, Cooper	Under age—not on the rolls of the line—no proof of service.
Mabry, Braxton	—, Taney	For further proof and specification.
Miller, William	Richmond, Ray	Period, length and grade of service, and names of company and field officers and stations required.
McH., Eleazer	Boonville, Cooper	Name not on the rolls in this office. Further reference to the South Carolina record.
Patterson, William	Bowling Green, Pike	Declaration imperfect and unsupported by proof.
Pierce, Francis (colored)	Columbia, Boone	He seems to have been pensioned already, but that some other person has drawn his pay.
Peniek, John	Bowling Green, Pike	For further proof of service.
Querry, William	Richmond, Ray	Claims service as adjutant under the authorities of North and South Carolina. Further proof required.
Shearwood, William	Bowling Green, Pike	For proof of service.
Smith, Abraham	Troy, Lincoln	Claims for five years' service in South Carolina line. Proof required.
Steele, William	Jonesboro', Saline	For period, length and grade of service, and names of company and field officers.
Smith, John	Jackson, Girardeau	No proof of service.
See, George	Palmyra, Marion	For further proof.
Tong, William	Fulton, Callaway	No formal application—no papers on file.
Tombs, William		Disallowed because of the applicant's extreme youth.
Turner, S	New London, Ralls	For proof of service.
Watson, Samuel	Bowling Green, Pike	No proof of service. [Papers withdrawn by Thomas H. Benton, February 21, 1882.]

A list of the names of persons residing in Missouri who have applied for pensions under the act of July 4, 1836, whose claims have been suspended; prepared in conformity with the resolution of the Senate of the United States, September 16, 1850.

Names.	Residence.	Reasons for suspension.
Alman, Judy, widow of Thomas	——, Dallas	For proof of service from the North Carolina records, and proof of marriage.
Eason, Nancy, widow of Samuel	——, Adair	For proof of his commission and service as captain in the Virginia militia, and of marriage.
Martin, Mary, widow of Adam	——, St. Louis	For further proof. [Papers enclosed 20th October, 1845, to Robert Green, to authenticate before a court of record, and not replaced.]
Paris, Polly, widow of James	Paris, Monroe	For further proof from the North Carolina records.
Scaggs, Mary, widow of Jacob, (formerly widow of Fletcher Edwards)	Tuscumbia, Miller	For proof of service and marriage.
Slaten, Martha, widow of James	——, Howard	Marriage after service.
Thomas, Mary, widow of John	Shelbyville, Shelby	For proof of service and marriage.
Turner, Rachel, widow of Henry	——, Pike	For proof of his service and commission as an officer in the Virginia troops.
Welchel, Nancy, widow of David	——, Bates	He did not serve six months.

A list of the names of persons residing in Missouri who have applied for pensions under the act of July 7, 1888, whose claims have been suspended; prepared in conformity with the resolution of the Senate of the United States of September 16, 1850.

Names.	Residence.	Reasons for suspension.
Best, Susan, widow of James	Independence, Jackson	For further proof of marriage.
Booth, Caty, widow of James	—, Pike	Some mistake. The James Booth for whose service this claim is asserted, appears to be alive and receiving a pension.
Demaster, Mary, widow of James	Richmond, Ray	Service admitted—proof of marriage required.
Degraffenreid, Martha, widow of Vincent	Springfield, Green	Name not on the rolls of the Virginia State troops—marriage not proved.
Glover, Mary, widow of Cheeley	—, Callaway	Service not set forth—marriage not proved.
Greening, Sarah, widow of James	Columbia, Boone	Service admitted—marriage to be proved.
Kirkpatrick, Martha, widow of Robert	—, Cooper	For further proof.
Kennedy, Sarah, widow of Thomas	—, Warren	For further proof of service and marriage and identity.
Lunsford, Eve M., widow of Elisha	—, St. Francis	Proof of marriage and three months and nine days service admitted—Nine months service in the North Carolina line must have further proof.
Laughlin, Rachel, widow of James	—, Osage	He did not serve six months.
Lackey, Mary, widow of Henry	Moniteau, Cole	Service not set forth—no proof of service. Papers remanded to be executed before a court of record.
Venable, Sarah, widow of William	Nesho, Newton	For proof of service and marriage.
Wallis, Sarah, widow of Matthew	—, Greene	For further proof of service.
Walker, Elizabeth, widow of Daniel	Boling Green, Lincoln	For further proof of service from the North Carolina records, and proof of marriage.
Westbrook, Lydia, widow of Richard	Boonville, Cooper	For further proof of service and marriage.

A list of the names of persons residing in Missouri who have applied for pensions under the act of July 7, 1838, whose claims have been rejected; prepared in conformity with the resolution of the Senate of the United States of September 16, 1850.

Names.	Residence.	Reasons for rejection.
Chenoweth, Cassandra, widow of Thomas	——, Taney	No proof of service—he did not serve six months.
Calloway, Susanna, widow of James	——; Howard	Not six months' service in a military capacity.

A list of the names of persons residing in Arkansas who have applied for pensions under the act of June 7, 1832, whose claims have been rejected; prepared in conformity with the resolution of the Senate of the United States, September 16, 1850.

Names.	Residence.	Reasons for rejection.
Crane, Edmund	——, Benton	Desertion.
Cocke, Charles	——, Clark	Not under military authority or organization.
Coughran, George	——, Sevier	Not six months' service.
Finley, Us	Fayetteville, Washington	Not six months' service.
Graves, Philip	——, Hempstead	Not six months.
Garvin, Thomas	Cane Hill, Washington	Pressed with a wagon and team—service not provided for.
Nelson, Enoch	Fort Towson, Miller	Not six months' service.
Owens, Benjamin	——, Conway	Not six months' service.
Phelan, Thomas	Fayetteville, Washington	Not six months' service.
Robbins, John, jr	Clarksville, Johnson	He did not serve six months.

A list of the names of persons residing in Arkansas who have applied for pensions under the act of June 7, 1882, whose claims have been suspended; prepared in conformity with the resolution of the Senate of the United States of September 16, 1850.

Names.	Residence.	Reasons for suspension.
Brown, William	Washington, Hempstead	For further proof and explanation.
Boyd, William	Fayetteville, Washington	For further proof and specification.
Francis, Henry	——, Johnson	For proof from the records of South Carolina.
Hudson, Edward	——, Randolph	For proof of service from the South Carolina records.
Quintin, Samuel	——, Polk	For further evidences of identity as the soldier credited with two hundred and seventy-six days' service in the South Carolina militia.
Royal, John	Little Rock, Pulaski	For further proof of service.
Reeder, Micajah	Fayetteville, Washington	For further proof and specification.
Wilson, John	——, Washington	For proof of identity and his reasons for not applying under act 1818.

A list of the names of persons residing in Arkansas who have applied for pensions under the act of July 4, 1836, whose claims have been suspended; prepared in conformity with the resolution of the Senate of the United States, September 16, 1850.

Names.	Residence.	Reasons for suspension.
McCulloch, Nancy, widow of John	—, Dallas	For further proof of service, marriage, and identity.
Scott, Hannah (dec'd), widow of William	—, Philips	For further proof of marriage and service.

A list of the names of persons residing in Arkansas who have applied for pensions under the act of July 7, 1838, whose claims have been suspended; prepared in conformity with the resolution of the Senate of the United States of September 16, 1850.

Names.	Residence.	Reasons for suspension.
Murphy, Anna, widow of Bartholomew	Greenfield, Poinsett	For further proof of service and marriage.
Smith, Agnes, widow of Aaron	——, Washington	For proof of marriage.
Peters, Catharine, widow of Henry (deceased)	Van Buren, Crawford	For further proof and specification.

A list of names of persons residing in Michigan who have applied for pensions under the act of June 7, 1832, whose claims have been suspended; prepared in conformity with the resolution of the Senate of the United States, September 16, 1850.

Names.	Residence.	Reasons for suspension.
Blackman, Nathaniel	——, Genesee	For proof of service.
Burbank, Benjamin	——, Oakland	For proof of service from the Massachusetts rolls.
Cady, Elias	——, Genesee	For further proof of service.
Champion, Salmon	——, Washtenaw	For further proof and specification.
Cotterill, Daniel	——, Berrien	For further proof.
Davis, William H.	Detroit, Wayne	Not on the New York rolls. Papers returned February 1, 1837, to Hon. J. E. Crary.
Grace, Newell	Detroit, Wayne	For further proof.
Gregory, Samuel	——, Oakland	Not six months service established.
Hatfield, Mason	——, Washtenaw	For further proof and specification.
Keyser, Michall	Tecumseh, Lenawee	Under age—rejected thrice, once by Congress, twice by this department.
Quigley, Isaac	——, Jackson	For proof from the New Jersey records.
Scrambling, George	——, Washtenaw	For further proof.
Sutton, Elisha	Detroit, Wayne	For further proof. Papers withdrawn by Hon. John Norvell, January 16, 1838.
Wall, John	——, Jackson	For further proof.
Wellman, Zadoc	——, Oakland	For proof from the Connecticut records.
Wheadon, John	Milford, Oakland	Not six months service.
White, William	——, Kent	Not six months service.
Willard, Jonathan	Adrian, Lenawee	Service at too youthful an age for military standard.

A list of the names of persons residing in Michigan who have applied for pensions under the act of June 7, 1832, whose claims have been rejected; prepared in conformity with the resolution of the Senate of the United States, September 16, 1850.

Names.	Residence.	Reasons for rejection.
Britton, Claudius	Pitt tp., Washtenaw	Not six months' service.
Blackman, Sylvanus	Napoleon, Jackson	Only three and a half months' service.
Case, Stephen	Marshall, Calhoun	Not military service.
Covert, Tunis D	Milford, Oakland	Not six months' service.
Flinn, John	St. Clair Court House	Desertion.
Garnsey, Southmayd	Marshall, Calhoun	Not six months' service.
Knowlton, Christopher	——, Oakland	Not six months' service pending the revolution.
Lucas, Daniel	Bridgewater, Washtenaw	Not six months' service.
Loomis, Benjamin	——, Oakland	Under age—no proof of service.
McGee, David	Napoleon, Jackson	Not six months' service.
Sanborn, Elijah	Sherman, St. Joseph	Only three months twenty-nine days' service.
Smith, John	Detroit, Wayne	Not six months military service.
Scholl, David	Jonesville, Hillsdale	Not six months' service.
Sybrook, Henry	Edwardsburg, Cass	Not six months' service.
Stewart, Charles	Grand Blanc, Genesee	Not six months' service.

A list of the names of persons residing in Michigan who have applied for pensions under the act of July 4, 1836, whose claims have been rejected; prepared in conformity with the resolution of the Senate of the United States of September 16, 1850.

Names.	Residence.	Reasons for rejection.
Beard, Elizabeth, widow of Henry	——, Shiawassee	Married after service.
McCloskey, Felicity, widow of William	Detroit, Wayne	Married after January 1, 1794.

A list of the names of persons residing in Michigan who have applied for pensions under the act of July 4, 1836, whose claims have been suspended; prepared in conformity with the resolution of the Senate of the United States of September 16, 1850.

Names.	Residence.	Reasons for suspension.
Alward, Catharine, widow of Samuel	——, Washington	Period, length and grade of service, and names of company and field officers required, and proof of marriage.
Richards, Cynthinia, widow of Thomas	Macomb tp., Macomb	Proof wanting of marriage prior to or concurrent with the service.
Shepherd, Rachel, formerly widow of Michael Parker	——, Berrien	For further proof of service and marriage.
Vanderworker, Ann Maria (deceased), widow of Martinus.	——, Kalamazoo	For proof of identity that claimant's husband and the soldier of the New York line of the same name were one and the same man.

A list of persons residing in Michigan who have applied for pensions under the act of July 7, 1838, whose claims have been rejected; prepared in conformity with the resolution of the Senate of the United States of September 16, 1850.

Names.	Residence.	Reasons for rejection.
Cole, Thankful, widow of William............	De Witt, Clinton	Not a widow at the date of the act.

A list of the names of persons residing in Michigan who have applied for pensions under the act of July 7, 1838, whose claims have been suspended; prepared in conformity with the resolution of the Senate of the United States of September 16, 1850.

Names.	Residence.	Reasons for suspension.
Bennett, Mary, widow of David	Lyndon, Ouachita	For further proof of service from the New Jersey records, and also proof of marriage.
Helme, Huldah, widow of Peleg	—, Lenawee	Service for two years admitted, but proof of identity and marriage required.
Horington, Hannah (dec'd), wid. of Vespasian.	Ann Arbor, Washtenaw	For further proof—claim must be renewed by the children. She died before the passage of the act.
Howe, Joanna, widow of Antipas	Niles, Berrien	
Kimmey, Margaret, widow of Isaac	Niles, Berrien	For further proof of marriage and service.
Miller, Esther, (deceased), formerly widow of Timothy Lockwood	Mount Clemens, Macomb	Further proof awaited—claim to be renewed by the children.
Root, Lucinda, widow of Eleazer	Manchester, Washtenaw	For further proof.
Royal, Elsie, widow of John	Farmington, Oakland	For further proof of marriage and service.
Smith, Susan, widow of Matthew	Port Huron, St. Clair	For further proof of marriage and service.
Terry, Eleanor, widow of William	Pontiac tp., Oakland	For proof of the marriage.
Short, Elizabeth, formerly widow of Uriah McLane	—, Genesee	For proof of the marriage.

A list of the names of persons residing in Florida who have applied for pensions under the act of June 7, 1832, whose claims have been suspended; prepared in conformity with the resolution of the Senate of the United States, September 16, 1850.

Names.	Residence.	Reasons for suspension.
Bozeman, Ralph	Tallahassee, Leon	For proof from the records at Columbia, South Carolina.
Carey, Alexander	Alaqua, Walton	For proof of service.
Gray, Morton		Six months' service allowed—proof from the North Carolina records required for his tour under Major Eaton. [Papers sent for collection to Hon. C. Downing, December 22, 1887.]
Goff, William	———, Jefferson	For further proof and specification.
Hudgins, William	Almirante, Walton	For further proof and explanation.

Ex.—21

A list of the names of persons residing in Florida who have applied for pensions under the act of June 7, 1832, whose claims have been rejected; prepared in conformity with the resolution of the Senate of the United States, September 16, 1850.

Names.	Residence.	Reasons for rejection.
Campbell, Daniel	Almirante, Walton	Not six months service.
Daniel, John, sr	——, Gadsden	Not six months service.
Hall, Hudson	Marianna, Jackson	Not six months service.
Walker, Littleberry	——, Columbia	Service after the revolution.

A list of the names of persons residing in Florida who have applied for pensions under the act of July 4, 1836, whose claims have been suspended; prepared in conformity with the resolution of the Senate of the United States, September 16, 1851.

Names.	Residence.	Reasons for suspension.
Ridgely, Elizabeth S., widow of Thomas	——, Duval	For further proof.
Anderson, Ann, widow of David	——, Leon	Proof not satisfactory.
Sauls, Samuel, (deceased,) heirs of	——, Nassau	Proof of marriage and dates of decease of parents and names of children.

A list of the names of persons residing in Florida who have applied for pensions under the act of July 4, 1836, whose claims have been rejected; prepared in conformity with the resolution of the Senate of the United States of September 16, 1850.

Names.	Residence.	Reasons for rejection.
Lowther, Esther, widow of Bourbon L.	——, Duval	A soldier of the regular army. Died after leaving service, and not of wounds.

A list of the names of persons residing in Texas who have applied for pensions under the act of June 7, 1832, whose claims have been rejected; prepared in conformity with the resolution of the Senate of the United States of Septemeer 16, 1850.

Names.	Residence.	Reasons for rejection.
De Se Baume, Joseph	Bex, or San Filip de Austin	Not six months' service.
Hickman, Theophilus	Jasper, Sabine	He did not serve six months.
Polk, Charles	——, San Augustin	He did not serve six months.
Sparks, William	Nagodoches	He did not serve six months.

A list of the names of persons residing in Iowa who have applied for pensions under the act of June 7, 1832, whose claims have been rejected; prepared in conformity with the resolution of the Senate of the United States of September 16, 1850.

Name.	Residence.	Reasons for rejection.
Figgins, Fielding	——, Washington	Service after the revolution.

A list of the names of persons residing in Iowa who have applied for pensions under act June 7, 1832, whose claims have been suspended; prepared in conformity with the resolution of the Senate of the United States of September 16, 1850.

Names.	Residence.	Reasons for suspension.
Bailey, Roger, alias David Clark	——, Clinton	No satisfactory proof of service.
Glover, Amos	Van Buren	No satisfactory proof of service.

A list of the names of persons residing in Iowa who have applied for pensions under the act of July 7, 1838, whose claims have been rejected; prepared in conformity with the resolution of the Senate of the United States of September 16, 1850.

Names.	Residence.	Reasons for rejection.
Perkins, Keziah, widow of George	Harrison tp., Lee	Not a widow at the date of the act.

A list of the names of persons residing in Wisconsin who have applied for pensions under the act of June 7, 1832, whose claims have been rejected; prepared in conformity with the resolution of the Senate of the United States of September 16, 1850.

Names.	Residence.	Reasons for rejection.
Walrath, Jacob H	Raymond, Racine	He did not serve six months.

A list of the names of persons residing in Wisconsin who have applied for pensions under the act of July 7, 1838, whose claims have been suspended; prepared in conformity with the resolution of the Senate of the United States of September 16, 1850.

Names.	Residence.	Reasons for suspension.
Harrison, Lydia, widow of Joel	Heart Prairie, Walworth	For proof of service and marriage.

A list of the names of persons residing in the District of Columbia who have applied for pensions under the act of June 7, 1832, whose claims have been rejected; prepared in conformity with the resolution of the Senate of the United States, September 16, 1850.

Names.	Residence.	Reasons for rejection.
Elliott, Richard	Washington city	Papers withdrawn to present to Congress June 10, 1836—Rev. J. L. Elliott.
Frank, George	Alexandria	Only four months' service.
Mahoney, Michael	Washington	He abandoned the service of the United States during the war.
Neal, Christopher	Alexandria	Desertion.

A list of the names of persons residing in the District of Columbia who have applied for pensions under the act of June 7, 1832, whose claims have been suspended; prepared in conformity with the resolution of the Senate of the United States, September 16, 1850.

Names.	Residence.	Reasons for suspension.
Hall, William	Washington city	No formal declaration presented to the department. His claim was addressed to Congress, but was not allowed.

A list of persons residing in the District of Columbia who have applied for pensions under the act of July 7, 1836, whose claims have been rejected; prepared in conformity with the resolution of the Senate of the United States of September 16, 1850.

Names.	Residence.	Reasons for rejection.
Mattingly, Elizabeth, widow of James	Georgetown, Washington	The agent says these papers are forged.

A list of the names of persons residing in the District of Columbia who have applied for pensions under the act of July 7, 1838, whose claims have been suspended; prepared in conformity with the resolution of the Senate of the United States of September 16, 1850.

Names.	Residence.	Reasons for suspension.
Harper, Mary, widow of William	Alexandria	For proof of identity with the soldier of the line as shown by the auditor general's certificate of Pennsylvania.

www.ingramcontent.com/pod-product-compliance
Lightning Source LLC
Chambersburg PA
CBHW071222290426
44108CB00013B/1265